WARSHIP 2004

WARSHIP 2004

Warship Editor: Antony Preston

Warship 2004 compiled by:

Martin Robson & Stephen Dent

CONWAY MARITIME PRESS

Frontispiece:
The cruiser USS Charleston. *Stern view showing her temporary all 6in armament. The ship is featured in Peter Brook's article 'Armstrongs' Contribution to the New United States Navy' in this edition*. (Library of Congress Print & Photographic Department, Detroit Publishing Co.)

First published in Great Britain in 2004 by
Conway Maritime Press

An imprint of Chrysalis Books Group plc

The Chrysalis Building,
Bramley Road,
London W10 6SP
www.conwaymaritime.com

British Library Cataloguing in Publication Data
A record of this title is available on request from the British Library.

ISBN 0 85177 948 4

Warship editor: Antony Preston
Warship 2004 compiled by Martin Robson and Stephen Dent
Printed in Spain

CONTENTS

EDITORIAL

Welcome to *Warship 2004*, the 26th issue of the prestigious annual. It has undoubtedly been noticed that the previous issue, *Warship 2002-2003*, was late. This has resulted in a decision to permanently move the publication of the annual from autumn/winter to the spring. Regular readers will already have noticed the slight change in title of the annual, removing the two-year spread from its name. This was causing some confusion among readers. We feel that renaming the title to contain just one year (thus this year's annual is *Warship 2004*) will remove any grounds for confusion as to when the annual is to be published.

Regular contributors and readers may already know that Antony Preston, the regular and esteemed Editor of *Warship*, has recently been unwell. All at Conway Maritime Press send Antony our very best wishes, and we hope to have him back at the helm next year for what will be an important issue, coming as it does in the Trafalgar bi-centennial year. In the meantime the Conway team have stepped up into the breach to do our best to try to fill Antony's admittedly considerable Editorial shoes for this issue of *Warship*. Many individuals have also rallied to the cause providing assistance and help. It is evidence indeed of the high standing in which *Warship* is held that all calls for assistance have been answered in the affirmative. Firstly, special mention must be made of Conrad Waters, who kindly submitted this year's 'Navies in Review' section in a style and with the comprehensive coverage *Warship* readers expect and demand. Help also came from D K Brown, Lawrie Phillips, Ralph Dunn of the DPA Press Office, Mike Dent, Andy Field, Wyn Davies, Monika Majlinder, John Bowen, Ian Sturton, David Evans and of course Stuart Robertson in the Conway office.

Although we were delighted at the helpful response from all areas, this was tempered a great deal by the sad news of the passing of Peter Brook. As many of you know, Peter was a regular and valued contributor not only to *Warship* but also other journals including the *Mariner's Mirror*. He was the author of *Warships for Export: Armstrong Warships, 1867-1927* (World Ship Society, Gravesend, 1999). Peter's contributions to the annual were always lucid, informative and a joy to read. He will be sadly missed. Peter's article for this year, 'Armstrongs' Contribution to the New United States Navy', can be found on p.57 with an obituary from Ian Sturton on p.75. In this article he demonstrates his unrivalled knowledge of the ships designed and built by Armstrongs. Interestingly, the company did not build any vessels directly for the USN. Of the seven Armstrong-designed ships that found their way into USN service, three were built in the US, while four were actually built by the firm but for other navies, two for Brazil and two for Spain. The design, construction and service careers of each of the seven vessels remind us that while many countries aspire to a clear programme of warship construction, in reality opportunistic procurement can be a more attractive alternative.

This year the running order commences with the second part of Iain McCallum's trilogy examining the shell problems of the Royal Navy during the First World War. Ships are designed to fight, but to do so they require suitable ammunition, and even the heaviest-armed vessels can be rendered impotent by faulty firepower. Here the emphasis is on the test of action, in particular the action off Heligoland and the controversial naval bombardment of the Dardanelles. Concerns about the effectiveness of British projectiles were raised after Heligoland and at the Falkland Islands, where shells had failed to burst sufficiently to cause maximum damage. Churchill, worried that such revelations might impact on naval morale, shouted down these concerns. The direct result (in striking similarity to Admiral Duckworth's expedition of 1807) was the navy's failure to mount an effective purely naval bombardment at the Dardanelles, due to shell shortages and design problems. This led to the controversial, costly and ultimately unsuccessful deployment of land forces, proving Corbett's dictum that naval forces are not a panacea for all ills; in order to be effective, naval force must be able to project power ashore by working closely with land forces in order to have a decisive influence.

Steve McLaughlin has continued to amaze *Warship* readers with his breadth of knowledge and his ability to pick out fascinating episodes in Russian and Soviet warship development that serve to broaden our understanding of history. This year he tackles one of the hardest of subjects: ships that were never actually completed. In 'Project 69: The *Kronshtadt* Class Battlecruisers' he examines the Soviets' ambitious plans for capital ship design during the 1930s. His understanding of the political factors influencing ship design and the bureaucracy that goes with it should be recommended reading for all those with a vested interest in warship history. Readers who feel suitably inspired to tackle the intricacies of research in modern day Russia might also like to consult his *Warship* Note on p.171, which provides invaluable advice.

After the big gun ships, two contributions from *Warship* regulars provide readers with an examination of two solutions to littoral minelaying in different decades. In chronological order, Dan Harris examines the Swedish *Clas Fleming* minelayer, built specifically for offensive minelaying in the Baltic. Meanwhile, John Jordan looks at the *Marine Nationale*'s inter-war efforts to restrict future German naval movements by extensive minelaying. The result was *Pluton*, a cruiser design which was (apart from HMS *Adventure*) quite unique. It is interesting that both of these ships had chequered histories. The pre-First World War *Clas Fleming* saw some action in both World Wars and underwent several reconstructions before being scrapped in 1960. Despite this she spent the majority of her time under dockyard control. The ill-fated *Pluton* lasted only a few days into the Second World War when on 13 September 1939 she was blown to bits by an explosion while unloading mines in Casablanca.

Another regular contributor to *Warship* is George Moore, whose work on the post-1945 Royal Navy has enlightened many readers. This year his subject is the first-class *Salisbury*, *Leopard* and *Whitby* frigates constructed against the backdrop of the hard won experience gained during the Second World War. The designs also encompassed the important technical developments that evolved in the immediate post war era when the future international situation was unclear. The *Salisburys* and *Lepoards* were complex classes of ships, dogged by engine problems. But the later *Whitbys* benefited from the experience of building the earlier ships, and provided the basic hull design for the famous *Leander* class - a clear example of lessons being learned and then implemented by naval constructors.

After encompassing the Baltic, Mediterranean and Atlantic, Colin Jones takes us to warmer climes in his article examining the histories of the four warships that have been named *Anzac*. The name is one of the most revered in the Royal Australian Navy, stemming as it does from the Gallipoli landings of 1915. The RN first used the name in 1916 for a hired ex-trawler. A subsequent *Anzac* was built as a destroyer leader. The RAN's first *Anzac* was a destroyer launched in 1948, and the current *Anzac*, a frigate, was commissioned in 1998. All of these vessels have had interesting careers, which Colin details in an engaging style.

One important factor in the continued success of *Warship* over the past 26 years has been the influx of new contributors. This issue is no different with two contributions from authors new to the annual. Kathrin Milanovich has been researching the warship construction history of the Japanese Navy for several years, and it is hoped that her article '*Naniwa* and *Takachiho*: Elswick-Built Protected Cruisers of the Imperial Japanese Navy' will be the first of many. The ships were purchased from Armstrongs in response to Chinese naval aggrandizement at the turn of the century and fitted into a wider Japanese plan to build up naval forces. Both saw action at Tsushima in 1905, but this was the highlight of their careers, *Naniwa* running aground and sinking in 1912 and *Takachiho* sunk by the German torpedo boat *S-90* off Tsingtao in late 1914. Last, but certainly not least, Enrico Cernuschi and Vincent O'Hara have managed to compress a century's worth of history into a lucid and informative examination of the Italian Navy's lengthy attempts to build a true single-engine purpose-built submarine, a dream eventually achieved in 2003 with the launch of the new U212A-type submarine, *Salvatore Todaro*.

Finally, special mention must be made of D K Brown's 'Slippery Ships', which, although a little too short to be run as a main article, has been included in the *Warship* Notes section. This contribution has kept up his amazing record of contributing to every single year of *Warship*, and will continue next year when he will be looking at Steam Torpedo boats of the Royal Navy. In a break from tradition this year *Warship* Notes is followed by a number of contributions in response to Antony Preston's recent book, *World's Worst Warships*. Readers will be delighted (and possibly enraged at the same time) at the stimulating debate Antony's controversial book has provoked. Readers who wish to follow Rowland Wylde, Andreas Lüdke, Philip Sims, Stephen Dent and D K Brown and contribute to the debate, in response to the book or the correspondence in this issue of *Warship*, can write to the Managing Editor at the Conway office.

The continued success of *Warship* is driven by the quality of the contributions, and we always welcome submissions of full length articles, shorter pieces to be included in *Warship* Notes, reviews and images for the Gallery.

Submissions can be on any subject to do with naval history from the mid-nineteenth century onwards, and should preferably be supplied as double spaced typescript on single sides of paper, accompanied by an electronic version on disk, in text only format. Ideally submissions should be accompanied by illustrations, either hard copy - photographs, print outs etc. - or digital images on disk. To assist those readers who wish to supply images in this latter form, either scans or from a digital camera, then what is required is as follows:

1. Pictures should be either at 300 dpi resolution, to give a width of approximately 16cm, or if at 72dpi resolution, then the width will have to be approximately 60cm in order to allow for a four times reduction to obtain an acceptable image for reproduction. Smaller sizes will result in images that can only be used across one column, as opposed to full page width.
2. Images should be saved either as EPS, TIFF, or JPEG format.
3. In addition, we would prefer hard copies of the images to be included, to give a fallback should the digital images not prove adequate.

Questions on this matter, and with submissions generally, should be addressed to the Managing Editor at the Conway office.

THE RIDDLE OF THE SHELLS, 1914-18

Part Two: The Test of Battle, Heligoland to the Dardanelles

In the second part of his trilogy, **Iain McCallum** reviews the nature of the heavy shell supplied to the Royal Navy's capital ships during the early phases of the First World War. With the notable exception of the attack at the Dardanelles, actions at sea were generally successful. Nevertheless in the light of experience the Fleet's gunnery officers were increasingly inclined to question the effectiveness of their projectiles.

In the years before 1914 relations between the British naval officer and his counterpart in the German High Seas fleet were cordial enough on the personal and professional level, each eyeing the other with wary respect. When in 1908 Margot Asquith travelled to Devonport to launch the dreadnought HMS *Collingwood*, she asked Admiral Fawkes in her blunt way if he or any of his sea friends were afraid of the German fleet. He said he thought the navy that was copied and did not copy was likely to remain the most powerful, and he added that they knew all about the German fleet except its record of target practice at sea. It was a significant proviso. The Germans were careful to withhold details of firing exercises, which took place in the Baltic beyond the prying eyes of foreign observers. Just the same, Sir John Jellicoe noted on his visits the excellent practice ground at Kiel Bay with every appliance for carrying out gunnery exercises, the thoroughness of the German training and their high allocation of ammunition for practice firing.

Being a young service and having to train up its crews almost from scratch, the German navy devoted much time to gunnery exercises under realistic battle conditions, while the German dockyards were organised to cope with a regular programme of re-lining the inner tubes of their lighter, high velocity guns. The British were more concerned to avoid wear to the gun barrels and the expense of re-lining, a consideration which limited the practice allowable. The inner tube of the 12in 50 calibre was reckoned to have a life of 130 firings, and a ship needed to be re-gunned whenever the remaining life of her guns reached a figure of 80 firings. Since an over-ambitious gunnery training programme could be embarrassing in the event of war, low power charges were normally used and firings on full charge were restricted to six a year, usually on the occasion of the battle practice.

As to fighting ranges, British and Germans alike believed that conditions of visibility in the North Sea, the most likely battle-ground, were such as to preclude engaging at great distances. When in 1913 Beatty's battle cruiser squadron carried out a shoot against towed targets at 16,000 yards, the exercise was generally dismissed as a waste of ammunition. On the German side a cloak of secrecy concealed what the High Seas fleet was doing until after the war broke out, when the Admiralty was able to publish details of its firing exercises.[1] These revealed that while broadly following the example of the British in firing at a mean range of about 8,000 yards, the German capital ships were also scoring eight per cent of hits on ship targets at 12,000-14,000 metres, a result which could indicate that they had the edge in terms of gunnery efficiency.

Assessing these and other strengths and weaknesses, some at the Admiralty were not without misgivings, suspecting that the Germans made up in quality for what they lacked in sheer numbers and weight of metal. Jellicoe in particular was inclined to be alarmist, having formed the impression that 'in matériel the Germans were ahead of us'. In 1909, as Controller of the Navy, he pointed out that German steel 'was and possibly is superior [to the British] owing to the crucible method of manufacture that is used', and in July 1914 he caused irritation to the first lord, Winston Churchill, by setting out at some length the supposed advantages enjoyed by the High Seas fleet. He made no specific reference to guns or shells, but suggested that the Germans had benefited from starting relatively late in the naval race, and so had been able to incorporate the most recent design features in the construction and armament of their ships.

Needless to say, such views were not shared within the Service, which had every confidence in the superiority of its firepower as in the quality of its ships. In *The Great Naval Race*, Peter Padfield describes the Grand Fleet on the eve of war as 'a great, grey-steel armada holding more power in its long guns than any fleet before it, prepared by years of intensive training to hitherto unknown precision in gunnery and fleet manoeuvre, its officers and men conditioned by three hundred years of history to believe their proud Service unbeatable'. Already the first of a new fast division of oil-fuelled battleships was nearing completion. HMS *Queen Elizabeth* was regarded as the last word in the constructor's art, mounting as she did eight 15in guns, each capable of hurling a 1,920lb projectile to a distance of 30,000 yards. The new guns had been built at Elswick and Barrow and were being installed in great secrecy and with all possible despatch. Although Churchill's brainchild, their introduction owed much to the enthusiastic advocacy of Lord Fisher, who, while nominally retired, still exerted much influence behind the scenes. 'Nothing less than the 15in gun,' he wrote, 'could be looked at for all the battleships and battle-cruisers of the new programme. To achieve the supply of this gun was the equivalent of a great victory at sea; to shrink from the endeavour was treason to the Empire. What was it that enabled Jack Johnson [world heavyweight boxing champion] to knock out his opponents? It was the big punch.'

The essential feature of the punch was the bigger and presumably more destructive explosive charge carried by the huge 15in projectiles. In September 1913 an article in *The Engineer* commented that: 'Until recently it has usually been laid down as an axiom that hard-faced armour should be attacked by a projectile whose calibre is approximately equal to the thickness of the plate...(but) experience which has been gained regarding the effect of large projectiles after perforating hard modern armour has led to the introduction of what are generally termed "super-calibre" projectiles'. The assumption was that these would not only penetrate armour plate 12 to 15in thick, but go on to burst inside an enemy's hull with devastating results. This, however, they could do only if fully functional, and unfortunately by the summer of 1914 trials of bursting charges and fuzes for the new projectiles had not been completed.

The delay was in part due to the fact that the nature of shell to be provided for the 15in guns had yet to be decided. The 12in guns of the older capital ships were equipped with HE (high explosive) common shell filled lyddite and, for the attack of armour, common pointed and armour-piercing shell with, respectively, a large and small charge of black powder. Only the projectiles for the 13.5in guns, consisting of HE common filled lyddite, common pointed capped shell (CPC) filled black powder, and armour-piercing capped shell (APC) with a small bursting charge of lyddite were of modern design. But shortly after war broke out all existing outfits were thrown into the melting pot by the declaration of the War Office that it proposed to implement the change from lyddite to TNT as the burster in service shell. To this intention added urgency was given by the destruction of the Belgian forts by German heavy howitzers, an event which caused as much alarm to the admirals as it did to the generals. The Director of Naval Ordnance (DNO), Frederick Tudor, assured the Cabinet that German naval projectiles did not carry such a large bursting charge as the British HE common shell, but he did acknowledge that, like those fired by the howitzers, the German projectiles were filled with TNT.

The decision to go over to TNT was, therefore, also approved by the Admiralty, the Ordnance Board confirming that 'all the heavy HE common shell at present afloat are filled lyddite, with No. 13 fuzes, but no difficulty would be experienced in filling with TNT and No. 45 fuze'. Changes in respect of CPC and APC being less easy to introduce, production of these projectiles was inevitably affected, especially as the navy found itself in competition with the army for limited supplies of cordite propellant and toluene for the manufacture of TNT.

The aftermost 12in guns of HMS St. Vincent, *the first British dreadnought to mount the 50 calibre version of the weapon.* (CPL)

Admiral Sturdee's battlecruisers Invincible *and* Inflexible, *pictured from the armoured cruiser HMS* Kent *during the Battle of the Falklands, 8 December 1914.* (CPL)

Under these circumstances the Department of Naval Ordnance was reluctant to embark on a precipitate conversion to the new explosive, and fortunately, as no major naval engagements took place early in the war, there was no immediate crisis. Existing stocks of shell filled with black powder and lyddite were thought sufficient to meet foreseeable needs, and trials with TNT and new fuzes were not pressed forward with any urgency.

As the months went by, however, doubts began to be raised about the performance of naval shell. Although in August Admiral Beatty's cruisers scored a success at the Heligoland Bight, sinking three light cruisers and a destroyer, the encounter pointed up a lesson 'of fateful consequence to the future, which the Germans marked, but were careful to conceal, that British shell were of such poor quality that many broke up on impact, so that instead of penetrating and dealing hard blows, they often inflicted no more than superficial wounds'.[2] In December, at the Falkland Islands, Doveton Sturdee's battle cruisers caught up with the German Far Eastern Squadron under Admiral Graf von Spee. Not only were the slower German armoured cruisers at a disadvantage in terms of firepower, but, having vanquished Cradock's weaker force at Coronel a few weeks earlier, they were short of ammunition. Outgunned, outranged and after an hour or two hardly able to defend themselves, they were nevertheless under orders not to strike their colours. The battle cruisers *Invincible* and *Inflexible* therefore stood off, keeping up a prolonged bombardment until four out of the five German ships went to the bottom.

To Fisher, now reinstalled as First Sea Lord, the battle was a striking vindication of his belief in the combination of long range gunfire and superior speed. But amid the general rejoicing, questions were raised about the effectiveness of the 12in projectiles. The battle cruisers had expended three-quarters of their supply of ammunition, yet the *Scharnhorst* had to be battered for three hours before going down, and the *Gneisenau*, despite being hit by at least 50 shells, was not sunk by gunfire, but scuttled by what remained of her gallant crew. The gunnery officer of *Inflexible*, Commander Verner, wrote that 'although our shots were obviously falling all over the *Scharnhorst*, we could not stop her firing...(and) I remember asking my rate operator: "What the devil can we do?"' Captured German officers stated that the British fuzes appeared not to be sensitive enough, so that '12in shell seemed to go right through the ship without exploding in most cases'. According to the official German history, 'the explosive effect [of the British projectiles] was less than one would expect of 12in shells', and such damage as was done was cumulative due to the sheer number of hits. It was also observed that: 'Quite a number of the lyddite did not detonate, but burst with a green or yellow smoke.'

In January 1915 the first major clash between modern

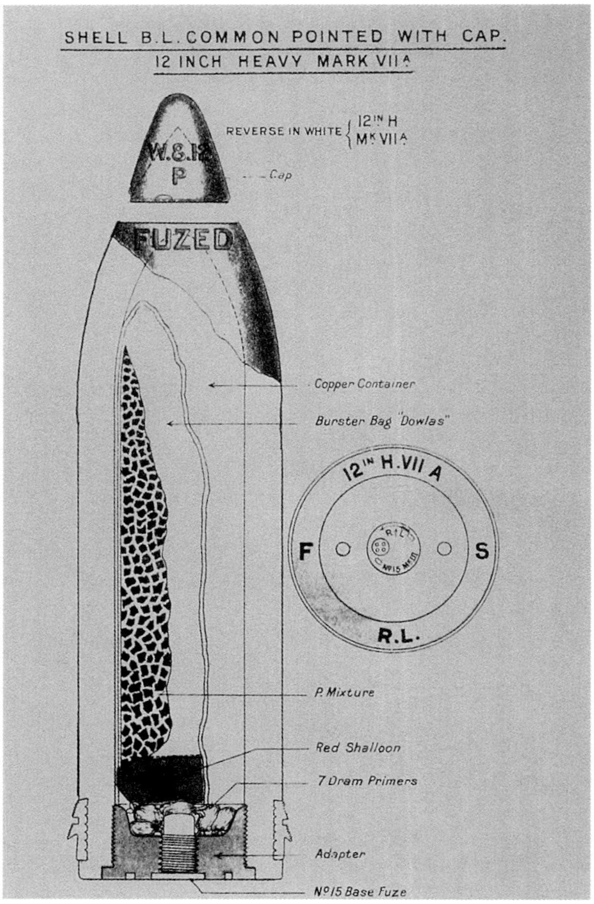

Base fuzed Common Pointed Capped (CPC) shell charged with black powder. (Admiralty Library)

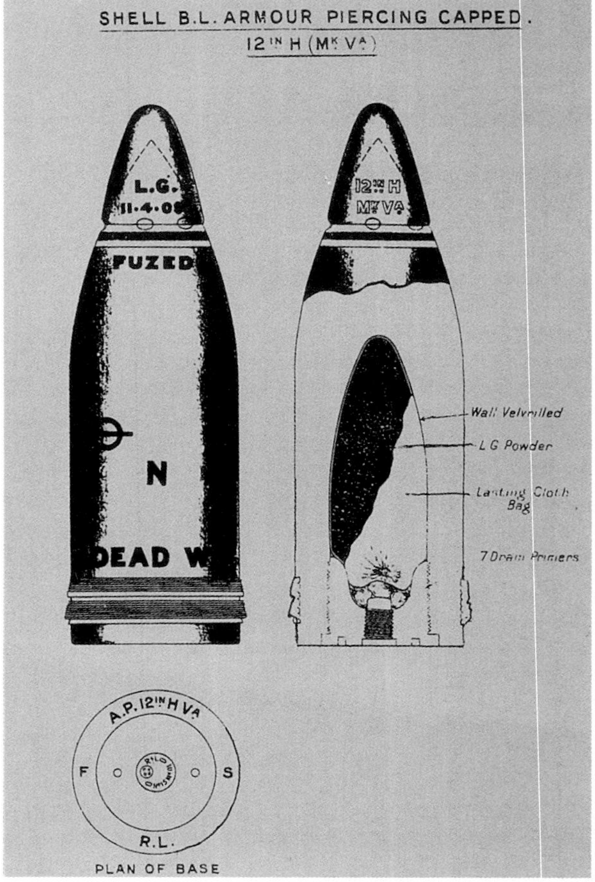

Base fuzed Armour Piercing Capped (APC) forged steel shell charged with Lyddite. (Admiralty Library)

battle\cruisers took place at the Dogger Bank, early hits being scored at a range of 17,000 yards. Confronted by Beatty's larger squadron, the Germans at once ran for the shelter of Heligoland, and the battle took the form of a pursuit. At last the navy's 13.5in guns were seen in action, and according to Churchill their 'immense power...(was) clearly decisive on the minds of the enemy'. Nevertheless the outcome was disappointing. At long range the efficiency of their Zeiss rangefinders enabled the Germans to score more hits than the British, and Beatty's flagship, the *Lion*, was heavily damaged. Only one German ship, the relatively thinly protected cruiser *Blücher*, was sunk. Apart from one shell which knocked out two of the turrets of the battle cruiser *Seidlitz* and started a dangerous fire, the British guns seemed unable to inflict serious injury on their opponents, and even at point blank range the disabled *Blücher*, after being struck by some 60 heavy projectiles, had finally to be sunk by torpedoes. 'There seemed no doubt,' recalled Beatty's flag-captain Ernle Chatfield, 'that our gunners had not succeeded in hitting the enemy sufficiently, or if they had, then why had they not been put out of action? Were our projectiles the cause? But all the experts had faith in them.'[3]

'The effectiveness of British hits with armour-piercing shells,' writes Professor Sumida, 'was once more probably reduced by their failure to burst properly. In two hours of long range firing the British were able to do no more than cripple the armoured cruiser *Blücher* and badly damage the battle cruiser *Seidlitz*, after which the bulk of the German force...escaped.' At the Admiralty Churchill firmly discouraged any criticism of ships, guns or shells which might lower the morale of the Service, and he assured the House of Commons that: 'Although the German shell is a most formidable instrument of destruction, the bursting, smashing power of the heavier British projectile is decidedly greater'. By this time the first lord was committing himself to a larger enterprise which he believed would at last enable the Royal Navy to make a decisive contribution to winning the war, and he was not to be deflected by quibbles about shortcomings in matériel. There is in any case little sign that Churchill, any more than Fisher, possessed any detailed knowledge of the technical aspects of shells and fuzes. These were matters dealt with by subordinates, who in turn relied on the advice of specialists in the Ordnance Board and the trade.

The larger enterprise, now under active consideration, was an attack on Turkey by way of the Dardanelles. This depended for its success entirely on the navy's firepower, for the original plan was that British and French warships, unsupported by land forces, would use their heavy guns to blast a way through the Straits into the Sea of Marmora and so to Constantinople. From the outset it was seen as a calculated risk, for the opinion of most naval men, confirmed by experience during the Russo-Japanese war, was that the purpose of the battle fleet was to engage the enemy's battle fleet, and that warships were not suited to the task of overcoming well-defended fortifications on land.

By January 1915, however, attitudes were changing under the pressure of events. The army in France and Belgium, pinned down for want of gun ammunition and heavy artillery, had been forced on to the defensive, and Churchill was inclined to welcome any initiative which would give the navy the chance to make its presence felt and relieve the pressure on the military. A few weeks earlier, following Turkey's entry into the war on the side of the Central Powers, an Allied squadron had briefly opened fire on the outer forts at the Dardanelles. No resistance had been encountered, and a lucky shot from the battle cruiser *Inflexible* had blown up the magazine at Sedd el Bahr, severely damaging the fort and disabling its guns. When the Grand Duke Nicholas appealed for help against the Turkish forces in the Caucasus, the first lord saw a golden opportunity to link up with the Russians, force Turkey out of the war and swing Britain's old friend Greece and other uncommitted Balkan countries to the side of the Allies. He therefore proposed to the War Council that the Admiralty should mount a naval expedition 'to bombard and take the Gallipoli Peninsula with Constantinople as its objective'. Kitchener, who thought little of the Turks' fighting capacity, was prepared to believe that the navy could do the job. Many at the Admiralty had reservations, but such were Churchill's authority and powers of persuasion that the proposal was agreed despite its vague wording.

Churchill's success in overriding the opposition was due in large part to the impression made four months earlier by the destruction of the Belgian forts, seen as 'battleships on land'. If, it was reasoned, the German projectiles had been able with such ease to shatter modern cupola forts of steel and ferro-concrete, the heavy projectiles fired by the Fleet should have little difficulty in demolishing Turkish earthworks originally constructed in 1837. Intelligence reports confirmed that these were rudimentary in design and defended by a miscellaneous collection of elderly Krupp guns not thought to present any serious threat.[4] Mines were to be expected, but these could be cleared once the guns had been silenced. In any case the British and French striking force was to consist of pre-Dreadnought battleships nearing superannuation, so that if some were lost this would be no serious matter.

At no point was Fisher altogether convinced. He had his own pet schemes, among them amphibious operations to seize the Frisian island of Borkum in the North Sea or to assist a Russian landing on the Baltic coast of Pomerania. Like others on the Admiralty staff, he was unhappy about the feasibility of a naval attack at the Dardanelles unsupported by the military. Sceptics such as Percy Scott questioned whether battleships were suited to the task of bombarding extensive fortifications, which was not after all the purpose for which the naval guns and shells had been designed. According to the Gunnery Manual of 1907, trials had revealed that 'little or no effect on (land based) guns or their crews can be produced by

HMS Queen Elizabeth, *pictured late in the war at anchor in Scapa Flow.* (CPL)

either common or lyddite shells bursting on earth parapets'. Before the war, notes an internal Admiralty paper, 'the reduction of fortified positions by men-of-war was not contemplated...because the question of bombarding was nobody's special business it remained entirely undeveloped before the requirements of war forced attention to the problems involved.'[5]

But all such objections were swept aside by Churchill's enthusiasm, which also infected Fisher, overcoming, as he was later to declare, his better judgement. They were finally stilled when Churchill and Fisher hit on the idea of sending *Queen Elizabeth* to join the expedition. By a fortunate coincidence she had just completed and was due to proceed for firing trials, and Fisher asked the experts at Elswick 'whether there was anything to prevent *QE* firing all her ammunition at the Dardanelles forts instead of uselessly into the sea at Gibraltar'. There was not, and she was ordered to sail direct to the eastern Mediterranean. Since the new battleship was thought to revolutionise all previous notions of naval warfare, Fisher was led to opine that past experience was no longer a reliable guide. Her 15in guns would easily outrange the guns in the Turkish forts, so neutralising any advantage the latter enjoyed by virtue of their fixed position. The way ahead seemed clear. The forts would be attacked and destroyed one by one, the minefields would be swept, and the Fleet would advance through the Narrows into the Sea of Marmora and so to Constantinople. There was a general perception that the Ottoman Turks, weakened by internal dissension and defeats during the Balkan wars, would collapse when confronted by the visible might of the Royal Navy.

In the words of the report of the Royal Commission later appointed to inquire into the Dardanelles operation, Churchill was now 'carried away by his sanguine temperament and his firm belief in the success of the undertaking which he advocated'. Distrusted by many of his colleagues at the Admiralty, he made little attempt to seek the advice of the junior sea lords. While concerned, he was undeterred by rumours of a shortage of ammunition due to competition with the army for supplies of cordite propellant, or by the revelation that no high explosive shell was available for the 15in guns of *Queen Elizabeth*. On 25 January the first lord informed the secretary to the Admiralty: 'The position regarding cordite is serious, and calls for prompt action....The War Office have written officially to say that...American gun-cotton cannot be used for the manufacture of cordite. Consequently there is very little chance of our obtaining for the Navy this year from Nobel's any part of the 1,800 tons...that the proposals put forward in these papers were intended to provide'. He therefore gave instructions for the building of an independent naval cordite factory, which was begun at Poole in Dorset but not opened until January 1916.

As to the projectiles for *Queen Elizabeth*, Churchill records that 'we had been discussing at the Admiralty and in connection with the Dardanelles operations, the reduced bursting power arising from the use of shell filled with powder instead of lyddite; and my discontent there-

HMS Queen Elizabeth *at the Dardanelles, showing the new 15in guns of which so much was expected.* (CPL)

with.'[6] On 15 January he minuted to the Director of Naval Ordnance: 'We cannot rest content with 15in shells being powder-filled only....The Germans are able to fill their shells with high explosives, and if the Ordnance Board are not able to solve the problem for us...changes will have to be made. Has any attempt been made to use TNT in shells of the larger guns?' There is no indication that he received a reply. The Ordnance Board was still grappling with the long-standing difficulties involved in fuzing large naval projectiles charged with TNT, which was in any case in desperately short supply. More research was needed before the manufacture of such projectiles could be put in hand, and over a year was to pass before a limited number of shells filled with TNT could be made available to the Fleet.

On 19 February, shortly before the arrival of *Queen Elizabeth*, an imposing if elderly flotilla of British and French warships approached the Dardanelles and, taking position outside the range of the Turkish shore batteries, opened a deliberate fire on the four outer forts. After ten days, despite interruptions due to poor weather, the forts had fallen silent and the Fleet began to probe inside the Straits. In London there was a brief surge of optimism until it was observed that although the defences had been extensively damaged few of the guns in the forts had been hit, so that many had to be blown up by landing parties of marines. Since the main objective was to knock out the guns, this was disturbing. None of the seaplanes launched from *Ark Royal* was in the air long enough to spot the fall of shots fired across the peninsula by *Queen Elizabeth*, while attacks so far, reported the commander-in-chief, Admiral Carden, had shown that 'the effect of long-range bombardment by direct fire on modern earthwork forts is slight'. In one case the embrasures 'appeared to be hit on many occasions by 12in common shell well placed, but when the ships closed in all four guns opened fire....Although a heavy and prolonged fire at short range was poured into the forts, 70 per cent of the heavy guns were found to be in a serviceable condition when the demolition parties landed'.

The ships now turned their attention to the defences inside the Straits, which consisted of strategically placed forts and minefields protected by mobile batteries of howitzers and field guns. Their task seemed a straightforward one, to concentrate the firepower of the combined fleet on the forts and guns: with these out of action, a lane could be cleared through the mines and the way opened for the ships to pass through the Narrows. This proved to be more difficult than anticipated. Coming under fire from the Turkish battleship *Barbarossa*, the *Queen Elizabeth* was obliged to move out to 20,000 yards, at which range her guns could make little impression on forts such as Kilid Bahr. After many days of more or less desultory bombardment it became clear that the ships were losing their duel with the land artillery, and in fact of over 100 guns in the forts only eight were hit and four destroyed. According to later evidence given to the Dardanelles Commission it needed a direct hit to knock out a gun, and the chances of such a hit being scored from a moving ship were very small. Even those shells that landed close by the guns 'though causing great alarm to the defenders did little serious damage'.

The fleet was in fact stymied. At long range its heavy guns were unable to search out their primary targets in the forts, even less howitzers and field guns behind cover or concealed in folds in the ground. As soon as the ships ventured into the Straits they came under the direct fire of the shore batteries. As long as the Turkish guns remained intact, the minefields could not be swept. On 10 March Carden reported that the operation was being 'greatly retarded by concealed batteries of howitzers', the effect of which was 'as formidable as the heavy guns of the permanent batteries' In view of the build-up of enemy strength on the peninsula it was no longer possible to land demolition parties, and at the Admiralty Sir Henry Jackson suggested that 'the time has now arrived to make use of military forces to occupy the Gallipoli Peninsula, and clear away the enemy artillery'.

In London the realisation that the navy would not be able to force the Straits without the help of the army had been dawning for some time, and the more the prospect of military action was contemplated the less attractive it appeared. Sir Ian Hamilton, appointed to take charge of the Mediterranean Expeditionary Force, was greeted on his arrival by Vice-Admiral de Robeck with discouraging news: 'The Peninsula is rapidly being fortified, and thousands of Turks work like beavers all night on trenches, redoubts and entanglements...the German officers have grappled with the situation, and have got their troops heavily entrenched. So much so that they have not much to fear from the flat-trajectory guns of the navy.' As he reviewed the scene, it was evident to Sir Ian that the army's task was going to be a formidable one.

During the coming years the reasons for the failure of the naval attack were to be the subject of much argument and recrimination. Sir Percy Scott claimed in his memoirs to have been aware from the beginning that the exercise was misguided: 'with all the advantages on the side of the shore guns...the ships alone could not defeat them, and the authorities should not have made the attempt'. During the lengthy investigation carried out by the Dardanelles Commission the evidence of witnesses runs to thousands of pages. There was much reference to direct versus indirect fire, the comparative effect of shells fired from guns and howitzers, the difficulty of shooting accurately from moving ships, and the lack of efficient minesweepers and aircraft for spotting the fall of shot. Not until after the war could all the factors involved in the operation be openly discussed and objectively assessed. The results of this exercise were summed up in a confidential Cabinet paper which has since been known after the president of the committee responsible for producing it as the Mitchell Report.[7]

The authors of the Report concluded that the failure of the navy was mainly due to the combined effect of the harassing fire of the land-based artillery, particularly the mobile howitzer batteries, and the 'lack and unsuitability of ammunition' available to the ships' guns. After November 1914 the Turks had, with the active support of their German allies, set about improving the defences at the Dardanelles. Forts and guns were renovated and some 400 contact mines laid. Field guns covered the minefields.

The vulnerability of the outer forts being recognised, it was decided to concentrate on the inner defences. Ten years earlier the Germans had noted the successful deployment of howitzers by the Japanese against the Russian battle fleet at Port Arthur. Now, despite doubts about the effectiveness of their lighter projectiles against armoured ships, 32 Krupp 5.9in (155mm) howitzers were among other weapons brought in to give cover to the forts on either side of the Straits. Their purpose was 'to attack ships by barrage fire, so as to prevent them taking up positions inside the Straits', it being known that it was difficult to fire with accuracy from a ship under way.

In *The World Crisis* Churchill asserts that the ships at the Dardanelles were needlessly held back by instructions to exercise caution in the use of ammunition. Reserves of naval shell had not, he insisted, been seriously depleted, and were fully adequate to meet all foreseeable needs. At a time when for want of propellant, explosives and fuzes the general shell shortage was at its most acute, this is not easy to accept. More likely, whatever the state of the central reserve, Lord Fisher was not prepared to put the Fleet at risk by committing an undue proportion of its heavy ammunition to the Dardanelles. It was the first manifestation of a growing divergence of opinion between the two men. Never a wholehearted supporter of the operation, Fisher was later to acknowledge that one of the reasons for his hesitation was 'the shortage of shell and cordite'. As a politician concerned with broad issues of strategy, Churchill was emotionally wedded to the Dardanelles expedition. As first sea lord, Fisher saw himself as a restraining influence, concerned with the overall security of the Fleet and especially its primary responsibilities in the North Sea. It was Fisher who decreed that only enough ammunition should be supplied to the ships in the eastern Mediterranean to enable them to do the job, and approved instructions to captains in the light of this consideration.

In any case early indications were that large quantities of ammunition would not be needed. In the light of the rapid reduction of the Belgian forts and the success of the naval bombardment in November (when the hit on the magazine at Sedd el Bahr created a wholly misleading impression), it was calculated that between five and ten 15in shells should be enough to neutralise each of the outer forts. At the Admiralty Sir Henry Jackson estimated that ten heavy calibre rounds would probably suffice to knock out each of the 200 enemy guns: 'If it requires ten rounds on board to put each gun on shore out of action, 2,000 rounds at least will be required, and this must be from heavy guns, with long range.' He decided therefore that the expedition should be allocated 3,000 rounds of ammunition for the primary armament. It was recognised that naval projectiles did not have the same destructive force as large howitzer shells, but the expectation was that this would be more than offset by their greater accuracy. The outer forts having been battered into submission by the 15in guns of *Queen Elizabeth*, the older vessels would close in to demolish the inner defences with their 12in, 7.5in and 6in guns. Had matters so turned out, no great expenditure of heavy ammunition would have been called for.

In the event neither the quantity nor the quality of the 15in and 12in projectiles available was able to achieve such a result. Notwithstanding Churchill's claims about the state of the ammunition reserve, it was clear from the outset that shells were in short supply. According to the Admiralty War Staff orders issued to the Fleet, it was important that the 15in guns of *Queen Elizabeth* 'should not be unduly worn , nor a large quantity of her valuable ammunition expended'. As to the 12in guns: 'Their ammunition is limited, though not to the same extent, and wasteful expenditure...may result in the operations having to be abandoned before a successful conclusion is arrived at.' But even with captains exhorted to strict economy (deliberate fire by single guns, salvoes not to be fired, reduced charges to be used wherever possible), it soon became apparent that the guns of the inner defences could not be knocked out *without* a high expenditure of ammunition. To obtain anything like the accuracy required the ships had to shorten the range and come to a standstill, which at once exposed them to the fire of the Turkish gunners. As the Mitchell Report confirms: 'The destruction of the forts...was prevented by the placing of howitzers on both sides of the Straits, in such positions that the Fleet could not fire at the forts except under the fire of these howitzers. This ensured that the ships must remain under way when firing...and thus an accurate fire on the forts was effectively prevented'.

During the first half of March the ships sustained many hits from the shore batteries as they attempted to close in or to clear the minefields. Of these 33, including five on *Queen Elizabeth*, were inflicted by the 5.9in howitzers, which, moved about by teams of bullocks to confuse the Allied gunners, fired a 90lb shell charged with TNT. Carden's chief of staff Commodore Roger Keyes wrote to his wife: 'the plunging shots are very destructive...(the shells) come down from Heaven very steep and do a great deal of damage'. In fact the damage was more apparent than real, being described in the Mitchell Report as 'not serious'. However, the disruption caused to the Fleet's gunfire and to its morale was of the first importance. Experience showed that even when stationary the ships could not expect to score more that two per cent of direct hits on the enemy guns; when they were kept moving and harassed by gunfire, accuracy was reduced *below the capability of the ammunition on hand*. As Vice-Admiral de Robeck pointed out to the Admiralty on 10 March: 'It has proved impossible to control the fire of howitzers....They would press the attack more vigorously, but...this was not possible without expenditure of ammunition out of all proportion to that available'. A related consideration was that since the 15in projectiles fired by *Queen Elizabeth* were not as effective as had been hoped, the burden of the day had to be carried by the 12-in guns of the older battleships. These were, therefore, subject to a degree of wear and tear which before long gave cause for anxiety.

Nevertheless on 18 March, in response to urgings from Churchill, the Allied fleet made a determined attempt to penetrate the Straits and overwhelm the Turkish gunners by intensive fire at relatively short range. This was done, according to Admiral Wemyss, despite 'a very heavy expenditure of ammunition which could ill be afforded', especially in view of anticipated further action against

Turkish and German warships in the Sea of Marmora. Carden's health having cracked under the strain, the command devolved on John de Robeck, whose expectation was that 'the ships will dominate the forts to such an extent as to make it impossible for them to interfere with the (mine) sweeping operations'. But the attack was a failure. The North Sea trawlers doing duty as minesweepers were unable even to reach the minefields, and, besides being raked by shellfire, the warships ran on to a line of undetected mines in Eren Keui bay: of the sixteen vessels engaged most were damaged, three were sunk and four put out of action. This would not have mattered if the aim of the operation, to neutralise the Turkish land defences, had been achieved. Sadly, it was all too evident that despite the spectacular cannonade, forts, guns and mobile batteries remained substantially intact.

The frustration was palpable. According to the journalist Ellis Ashmead-Bartlett, 'the expectations formed of the Fleet's guns dismally failed to be realised....Nothing has been more disappointing than the effect of these high-velocity, low-trajectory shells...a high explosive shell of this sort must have something to burst against, and if there is no parapet (they) merely burst in front, making huge holes in the ground'. Next day the American correspondent of the Associated Press Agency walked over the forts to assess their condition. He reported that: 'In all cases the damage done to the Turkish positions was repaired overnight, and today...the Turkish forts are as

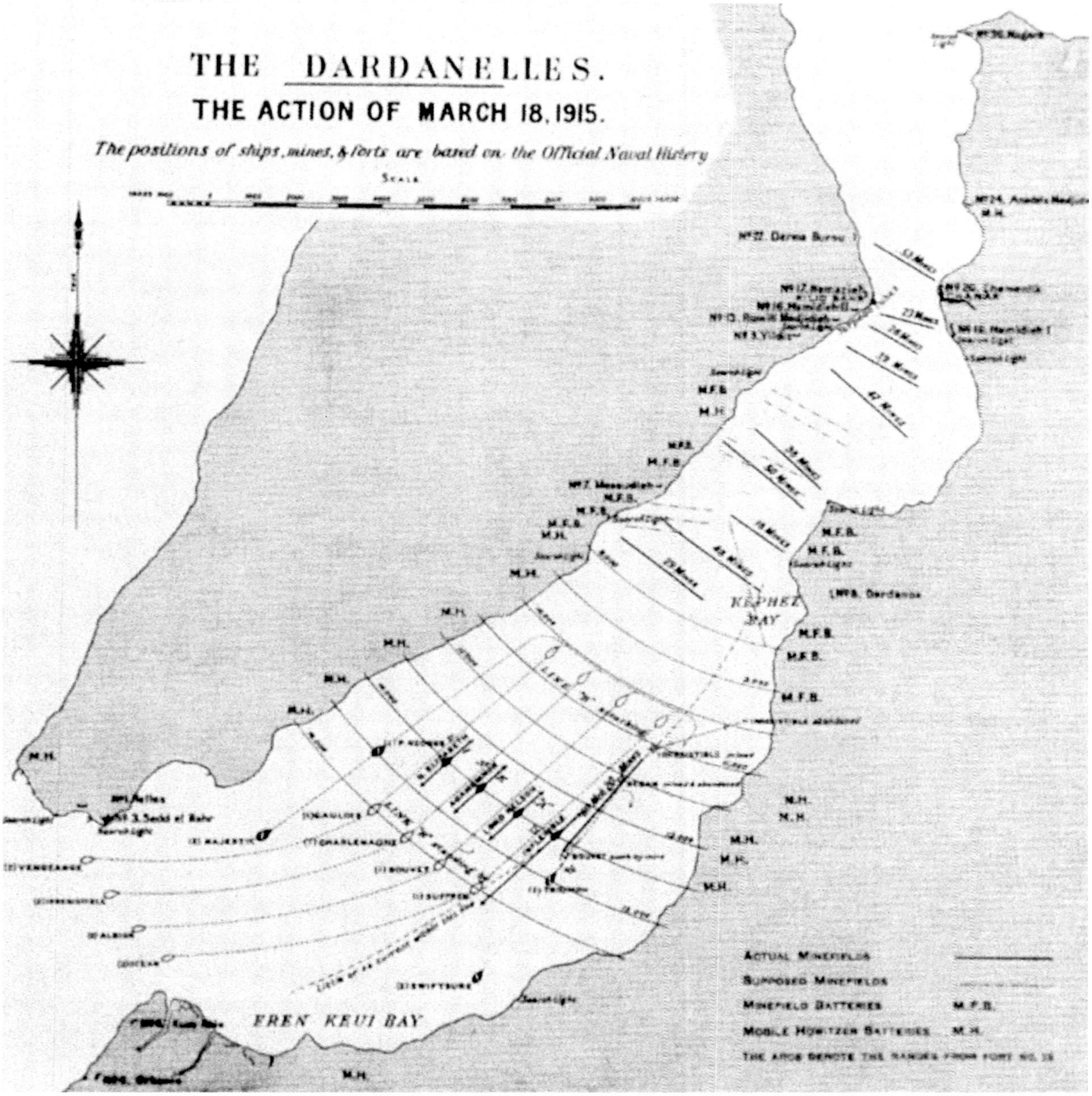

The naval attack at the Dardanelles, 18 March 1915. It is noteworthy that the furthest point reached by the advancing warships was well short of the main enemy minefields between Kephez Bay and Chanak. (Private collection)

good as ever. Against stonework the shells of the Allies had proven effective....In soft soil and sand they had been impotent. The areas under fire had been literally ploughed...everywhere [there were] craters of varying dimensions.' This is curiously reminiscent of the accounts of the 1882 attack on the forts at Alexandria, which is perhaps understandable given that many of the projectiles fired by the British ships were of a pattern little changed since the earlier action.

The repulse of the Fleet posed questions to which during the war it was difficult to come up with answers, even in evidence to the Dardanelles Commission. However, the authors of the Mitchell Report were in no doubt that the navy's inability to destroy the Turkish guns had more to do with the inadequacy of its projectiles than the quality of its shooting:

> ...the disappointing nature of the results obtained from numerous well placed hits from heavy shell on traverses, parapets, gun emplacements, expense magazines...would appear to be primarily due to the shells fired by the ships not having been of the most suitable nature for acting against earthworks....The naval shell were, of course, designed entirely for use against ship targets...and have not the outstanding features necessary for use against shore fortifications....Moreover, the proportion of HE [ie lyddite] common shell in no ship's outfit was more than 30 per cent. The attack on the forts was, therefore, largely carried out with powder common and AP shell. In particular, the *Queen Elizabeth* had no HE common and fired exclusively powder-filled shell. For attack against personnel or for obtaining the maximum destruction from a direct hit on a gun, there is no doubt that a HE shell with a graze fuze is what is required.

The result was that in addition to the shortage of ammunition and the threat of excessive wear to the 12in guns, the Fleet was handicapped by the inability of its projectiles to inflict decisive damage on the Turkish defences. Lyddite had never been satisfactory as a burster in projectiles designed to *penetrate*, and again it was noted that nose-fuzed, HE common shell filled lyddite had a mainly local effect and often failed to detonate fully, especially in sand or soft ground. Many AP shells did not burst at all because against soft targets their base fuzes failed to operate, and reports from ships refer to common shell being used because lyddite so frequently failed to explode.

As for common shell filled with black powder, these did extensive damage to masonry but were otherwise disappointing. The expectation was that the large bursting charge of the 12in and 15in projectiles would shatter forts and guns together, or at least that a gun would be destroyed by a near miss. This did not happen, partly because black powder does not have the force of high explosive, partly because neither shell was equipped with a delay action fuze which would give full value to its detonation. Under the section 'Conclusions and Lessons to be learnt', the Mitchell Report is critical of the bursting charge and fuzing of the British shells. The military members of the committee, familiar with the problem from their experience on the western front, drove the point home: 'To obtain the maximum results against guns protected by earthworks...HE shell are preferable to powder-filled shell, and to penetrate and explode main and expense magazines heavy shell should be fuzed so as to admit of adequate penetration prior to detonation'.

Consequently the forts were only superficially damaged and no magazine was blown up, as might reasonably have been expected. On this the Mitchell Report comments that: 'As regards the attack on magazines, several cases occurred when the shell exploded so close to the magazine as to blow in its wall, but in only one case (the bombardment of Sedd el Bahr in November 1914) was a main magazine put out of action'. Nor did the enemy's morale suffer, as on past occasions had been the cause of forts surrendering to attack by naval guns. According to a Turkish source: 'The first days of the naval bombardment had a certain effect on the morale of the troops, because they were not yet accustomed to the loud noise; but when they saw the slight material effect of the bombardment this disappeared...and spirits rose'. The gunners took refuge in dug-outs as the ships approached, emerging as the ships retired to clear away debris and clean the dirt and grit from the guns.

After the debacle of 18 March it became evident that the operation would have to be reconsidered. Sir Ian Hamilton telegraphed to Kitchener: 'I am being most reluctantly driven towards the conclusion that the Dardanelles are less likely to be forced by battleships than at one time seemed probable'. Admiral Robeck was worried not only by the unswept mines but by the risks involved if the Fleet did get through without the Gallipoli Peninsula being in Allied hands. For all the navy's best efforts the guns in the Turkish forts remained a threat despite reports that they were short of ammunition. 'The original approved plan,' he wrote, 'for forcing the Dardanelles by ships was drawn up on the assumption that gunfire alone was capable of destroying forts. This assumption has been conclusively proved to be wrong....Shells which hit either expended their destructive power uselessly on the parapet or destroyed some unimportant building in the background of the fort; to obtain direct hits on each gun has been found impractical even at ranges of 700 to 800 yards....The utmost that can be expected of ships is to dominate the forts to such an extent that the gun crews cannot fight the guns; any more permanent disablement could only be carried out with an excessive expenditure of ammunition at point blank range....Conclusions drawn from the attack on the cupola forts at Antwerp by heavy howitzers are quite misleading'.

It was, however, unthinkable that the Allies should simply back away with their tails between their legs. Kitchener was acutely conscious that British authority and prestige throughout the Middle East and India were at stake. The naval attack, he believed, had 'committed us to offensive action', and it was decided that 'the cooperation of the whole military force will be necessary'. The secretary of state therefore decreed that 'if the Fleet would not get through the Straits unaided, the Army ought to see the business through. The effect of a defeat in the Orient would be very serious. There could be no going back'. Thus the tactical roles were reversed, the army being

Sedd el Bahr, pictured in April 1915. The destruction of the fort is evident. In a grim portent of how the campaign was going to unfold, troops can be seen huddled on the foreshore, while the barge in the foreground contains wounded men on one side, and the bodies of the dead on the other. (CPL)

pressed into service to eliminate the Turkish artillery and open the door for the navy. As Sir Ian Hamilton put it: 'The Army's share will not be a case of landing parties for the destruction of forts etc. but rather a case of a deliberate and progressive military operation carried out in force in order to make good the passage of the Navy', and in this Kitchener concurred.

The story of the Gallipoli campaign is well known. When on 25 April the Allied troops approached their landing beaches, they were confronted by Turkish forces ably led by German officers, quickly reinforced and supported by carefully sited field artillery, howitzers and machine guns. After two weeks of fierce fighting the attackers had gained no more than precarious toeholds on the peninsula at a cost of 20,000 casualties, and the situation soon settled into the kind of stalemate already familiar on the western front. The navy played its part by bombarding the Turkish positions, but with little discernible effect. As the shells burst on the low hills, Sir Ian Hamilton observed that 'the naval guns do not seem able to knock the Turkish infantry out of their deep trenches, although they can silence their fire for a while'.

With the army held in check, the ever resourceful Roger Keyes arranged for destroyers to be adapted and equipped as more effective minesweepers before urging de Robeck to renew the naval attack. Churchill was in favour of a 'limited operation', but against any such notion Fisher reacted with the force of an explosion, writing on 11 May to the first lord: 'I have clearly expressed my opinion that I did not consider the original attempt to force the Dardanelles with the Fleet alone was a practicable operation...I have always insisted that the North Sea is the proper theatre of operations of our Fleet, and [as to this new proposal] I feel impelled to inform you definitely and formally of my conviction that such an attack...is doomed to failure and, moreover, is fraught with possibilities of disaster utterly incommensurate to any advantage that could be obtained'.

Although the ships continued to deploy their firepower in support of the hard-pressed troops on land, it was effectively the end of the Navy's ill-starred venture. 'I regret,' Kitchener informed the War Council, 'that I was led to agree in the exercise by the statements made, particularly as to the power of the *Queen Elizabeth*, of which I had no means of judging'. The military finding it hard to accept defeat, Kitchener instructed the commanders to 'push on and make such progress as is possible', and for the rest of the year the armies on the peninsula fought one another to a bloody standstill.

Could the navy have broken through at the Dardanelles if it had been provided with a sufficient supply of the right kind of heavy ammunition? Certainly it is arguable that if more Turkish guns had been knocked out the Allied commanders might have been encouraged to press home the attack with more vigour. Churchill never ceased to believe that this was what was lacking, and it is indeed possible that a more determined assault would have demoralised the Turks and obliged them to exhaust their limited stocks of ammunition. From the German side Captain D Weniger agreed, maintaining that the British could have achieved their objective if they had persisted, and if the ships had not been handicapped by the need to economise in the use of heavy shell. 'Herein,' he wrote, 'lies the main cause of the failed attack'.[8] Arthur Marder also believed that a renewed assault early in April should have been attempted. In his view the campaign was 'the one imaginative strategic idea of the war on the Allied side', and its greatest tragedy 'the lost opportunity of

April, one of the most poignant might-have-beens of the First World War'.[9]

At the Admiralty there was a natural reluctance to admit failings either in the quality or the supply of the navy's heavy projectiles. Even had these been acknowledged, there was little that could be done to put matters right. At the time the overriding priority was for shell to keep up with the demands of the artillery on the western front, and it was hardly possible to contemplate any radical change in the naval outfits. There are indications that in the light of experience at the Dardanelles attempts were made to improve the situation by speeding up the introduction of shells filled with TNT. These were, however, frustrated by the refusal or inability of the War Office and the Ministry of Munitions to release sufficient quantities of the scarce explosive to enable the Fleet to be supplied with projectiles so charged, nor was a fuze evolved which would ensure their satisfactory detonation.

For the time being, therefore, the navy had to make do with existing patterns of black powder and lyddite filled projectiles, and, this being so, it is perhaps fortunate that no major engagement with the German High Seas fleet took place during 1915 or the early months of the new year, 'a period,' in Churchill's words, 'of naval inertia and passivity from which there was a fearful awakening.' The Royal Navy continued to believe that in a ship-to-ship action its projectiles were more than a match for those of the Germans. Not until the early summer of 1916 was the performance of its heavy shell again called in question, and the need for remedial action to be forced on the attention of the Admiralty.

Notes

1 *Germany: Results of Firing Practices, 1912-13*, published by the Admiralty War Staff, Intelligence Division, December 1914.

2 G Bennett, *Naval Battles of the First World War*, (1968).

3 *The Navy and Defence: the Autobiography of Admiral of the Fleet Lord Chatfield*, (1942), pp.136-7.

4 The defences mounted some 85 heavy cannon of which only 22 were long guns using modern shells with smokeless powder; the remainder were short barrelled guns firing old-style shells with black powder bursters and propellant.

5 CB 902 dated 1918: *Progress in Naval Gunnery, 1914-18*.

6 W Churchill, *The World Crisis, 1915*, p.115.

7 CB 1550: *Report of the Committee appointed to investigate the attacks delivered on and the enemy defences at the Dardanelles Straits*, compiled 1919 and published in 1921 by the Admiralty Naval Staff (Gunnery Division).

8 Article in the *Marine-Rundschau*, 'Der Flottenangriff gegen die Dardanellen', Berlin, January 1925.

9 A Marder, *From the Dardanelles to Oran. The Dardanelles revisited: further thoughts on the Naval Prelude*, (1974), p.32.

HMS Queen Elizabeth *as flagship of the Grand Fleet, November 1918. (CPL)*

THE MINELAYING CRUISER *PLUTON*

During the First World War extensive minefields were laid in the North Sea off Belgium and the Netherlands to restrict the operations of the German High Seas Fleet. Postwar naval planning by both the French and the British continued to envisage minelaying by cruisers and submarines as an important element in their strategy for containing future German naval operations. The first purpose-built minelayer for the *Marine Nationale* in the interwar period was the cruiser *Pluton*. Here **John Jordan** examines the rationale behind the design, and the chequered career of this unique vessel.

British interest in fast minelayers after the First World War led to the design of HMS *Adventure*, a 6,740t cruiser laid down in November 1922. With a maximum speed of 28 knots and a main armament of four single 4.7in (120mm) guns, *Adventure* had a capacity of 300 mines, stowed on four tracks at main deck level and discharged from four traps in a transom stern.

In the year she was laid down the *Marine Nationale* contemplated the construction of a similar ship. The *Pluton*, as she was to become, was authorised under the 1925 *tranche* of the naval programme, but could not be laid down for a further three years because of production bottlenecks in the French naval shipyards. She was finally laid down at the Arsenal de Lorient in April 1928 and completed slightly less than four years later. In the interim it was decided to convert two ex-Russian 14-knot icebreakers during 1927-28 at Lorient as *Castor* and *Pollux*. These ships would trial the new high-speed minelaying system developed by Sautter-Harlé from the end of 1929. The trials were a complete success, and influenced the design of the system which would be installed in *Pluton*.

The general characteristics of the ship were quickly agreed but there was much discussion regarding the gun armament to be installed. It was known that the Royal Navy considered *Adventure*, which was armed only with 4.7in guns for self-defence against enemy torpedo craft, to be under-gunned. In 1925 it was being proposed that *Pluton* be armed with two single 203mm (8in) in the lightweight mounting developed postwar, with 115 rounds per gun in the magazines. The remaining armament was to comprise four single 75mm Mod.1922 AA and four single 37mm Mod.1925 AA. By the end of the year two single 138mm had been added to the main armament. However, in 1926 the single 203mm guns were rejected in favour of a uniform main armament of four single 138mm.

The ship was initially typed *mouilleur de mines de surface* but was subsequently reclassified as *croiseur mouilleur de mines* (the first *sous-marin mouilleur de mines*, the *Saphir*,

Table 1: COMPARISON WITH ADVENTURE

	Adventure	*Pluton*
Displacement	6,740tW	5,300tW
Length oa	158.5m	152.5m
Beam	18m	15.55m
Power	40,000shp	57,000shp
Trial speed	27.75kts	31kts
Armament	4 x 1 120mm	4 x 1 138mm
Mines	300	220/250
Complement	400	424
Laid down	Nov 1922	Apr 1928
In service	May 1927	Jan 1932

was laid down in the same year as *Pluton*). Besides the primary minelaying mission, it was envisaged that the ship would also be used as a fast troop transport, 1,000 troops being accommodated on the mine deck, which although at upper deck level was covered by a shelter deck amidships.

Hull and Superstructures

The hull of *Pluton* was of longitudinal construction with 15 watertight transverse bulkheads. Like that of the smaller *contre-torpilleurs* it was totally unprotected, and relied on tight subdivision for survival in the event of action damage. In order to save weight extensive use was made of duralumin alloy for the superstructures and accessories (ladders, boat booms and so on), and this was to result both in structural weaknesses and corrosion problems.

The silhouette of the ship was broadly similar to that of the contemporary Treaty cruiser *Suffren*, with twin tripod masts inclined at 5° and the characteristic widely-spaced funnels which reflected the unit arrangement of the machinery. *Pluton* could, however, be easily distinguished by the comparatively small gunhouses superimposed fore and aft, by the absence of a catapult for reconnaissance floatplanes, and by the raised platform for AA guns above the stern.

Three Byers type 4,000kg anchors were in hawsepipes forward, of which two were 'active' (*Pluton* was the first ship in the *Marine Nationale* to have a bow anchor – in this case the 'spare'). There was a single 1,400kg Byers type stern anchor on the centre-line, and two sheet anchors of 1,020kg and 760kg respectively were provided.

The single rudder was of the counter-balanced type with a surface area of 19.87m^2 powered by an electric servo-motor. The latter proved to be underpowered, as in other French ships of the period. At 27 knots with 25°of rudder the turning circle was 875m (greater than the 8,000t cruiser *Duguay-Trouin*, which was 30m longer).

Machinery

Two of the four small-tube boilers, rated at 20kg/cm^2, were, were manufactured by F C de la Gironde, the other two by the Chantiers Normand (Le Havre). They were housed in four boiler-rooms paired back-to-back, the forward pair being separated from the after pair by the forward engine room. All four main boilers were close to the centre-line, the forward pair being slightly offset to starboard and the after pair to port, with their own auxiliaries. There was also an auxiliary boiler on the 1st Deck forward of the first funnel to provide power and water when the ship was alongside.

The two shafts were powered by two groups of Bréguet single-reduction impulse turbines, the forward group powering the starboard shaft and the after group powering the port shaft. Each turbine group comprised two identical turbines working in parallel, with separate cruise turbines. The reversing turbine was in the housing for the main turbines. The propulsion machinery could operate as two completely independent units, thereby making the ship more resistant to machinery breakdown or action damage. The three-bladed propellers had a diameter of 4.08m.

The designed power of the propulsion machinery was 57,000shp for 30 knots. On trials *Pluton* largely exceeded this figure, registering 31.3 knots on 64,705shp over three hours. It subsequently proved possible to sustain 28 knots even with a full load of mines. Endurance was calculated to be 7,700nm at 14 kts and 4,900nm at 20kts. However, once the ship entered service with a full complement aboard these figures were revised downwards to 4,510nm at 14 knots, 2,235nm at 24 knots. The problem, as with all French surface ships of the period, was the heavy demands made by the auxiliary machinery which provided lighting and water for the crew, and generated electrical power for the ship's weapon systems and other electro-mechanical systems such as boat cranes, the ship's rudder and so on. When the auxiliary machinery was operating in service, the ship's fuel consumption increased by a massive 50 per cent.

Power generation when underway was provided by two 200kW (266kW max.) turbo-generators located in the forward engine room (to port of the turbines), which served a 235V 'cruiser' electrical circuit. There were also three 100kW (120kW max.) diesel generators for use in

A magnificent early view of Pluton *dated 23 January 1932, shortly after her arrival at Toulon (she would enter service two days later). Note the angled mine tracks, designed to reduce the impact when the mines hit the ship's wake, and the raised platform for 37mm/50 AA guns above the stern.* (Marius Bar)

This view is dated 2 May 1933, and shows Pluton's *configuration following the initial modifications to enable her to serve as a gunnery training ship. The strengthened tripod foremast, with its prominent 75mm HACS atop the upper platform, is particularly prominent, and a large DCT for the 138mm main armament has been located atop the bridge structure.* (Marius Bar)

emergency and when alongside, powering a 220V circuit; two of these were located in the after engine room (to starboard of the turbines) and the third in a special compartment on the 1st Deck.

Artillery

The 138mm/40 Mod.1923, disposed fore and aft in four single mountings Mod.1924, was the same weapon installed in the second group of *contre-terpilleurs*, the *Guépard/Valmy* classes. It had a traditional Welin screw breech, unlike later guns of this calibre, and the theoretical rate of fire was therefore only 8-9 rounds per minute; in practice it proved to be even less. Elevation was between -10° and +35°; at maximum elevation range was 18,200m with a muzzle velocity of 700m/sec. The mounting weighed 13 tonnes.

The 138mm/40 Mod.1923 fired the then-standard OPf Mod.1924 AP and OEA Mod.1924 HE shells, weighing approximately 40kg. A total of 150 rounds per gun was provided. 'B' and 'X' guns each had 30 starshell plus 20 exercise rounds; 'A' and 'D' each had 60 exercise rounds. Separate hoists for shells and charges served each of the four guns.

Fire control for the main artillery was provided by two OPL coincidence rangefinders each with a 3-metre base, which fed data into a mechanical computer Model 1923 located between decks. One of the rangefinders was atop the bridge, the second abaft the mainmast. There were also four 0.75m searchlight projectors for night fire: two on the upper platform of the tripod foremast, and two on the upper platform of the mainmast.

Pluton was completed without the 75mm AA she was designed for, although the deck seating was retained with a view to future installation. In their place, as a temporary measure, there were a further six 37mm/50 Mod.1925 AA, for a total of ten: two on the forecastle, six to port and starboard of the shelter deck between the funnels, and two on a raised platform above the stern (to clear the inner pair of mine tracks). 1,000 rounds per gun were provided with 144 rounds in ready-use boxes close to each gun. There was also provision for twelve elderly Hotchkiss 8mm MG Mod.1914 in six twin mountings: two atop the bridge, two atop the ventilation housing for the after boiler room, and two just forward of the tripod mainmast.

Mines

Pluton was designed for a normal deckload of 220 1,500kg Sautter-Harlé mines (250 maximum load). The base of the mines was hooked onto rails running on either side of the superstructures at 1st Deck level. There were four sets of rails (two to port, two to starboard), which terminated in ramps angled at 30° to the stern to reduce the height above water (and therefore the impact) of the mines when laid. Each mine track had a separation of 0.5m, and the mine bases were linked together by continuous 192m chains powered by electric motors located together with a minelaying control station beneath the mine deck aft. At

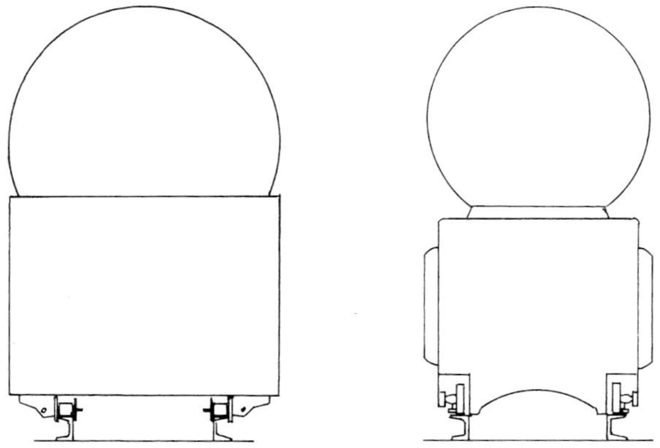

Schematic of the Sautter-Harlé (left) and Breguét B4 (right) mines

The Bréguet B4 mine, which was to be laid from the stern rails of the fast minelaying cruiser Emile Bertin *(see* Warship 1996*) and the* contre-torpilleurs *of the* Vauquelin *and* Le Fantasque *classes (see* Warship 1994 *and* Warship 2000-01 *respectively), had smaller dimensions than the Sautter-Harlé mines for which* Pluton *was designed. This meant that larger numbers could be embarked (270 versus 220), but the B4 was to prove less robust than its predecessor. Note the U-shaped mine-laying rails, on which the mine bases were moved on wheels, the continuous 92m drive chains being located between the rails. The mines were immobilised by clamps which fastened onto the upper arm of the U-rail.* (Drawn by the author)

their forward end each pair of rail tracks converged on circular turntables linked by a single athwartships set of rails. This permitted all four tracks to be used for minelaying even when mines were embarked on only one side. The mines were embarked close to the turntables using two electrically-powered cranes installed on the 2nd deck, and were laid alternately from the port and starboard tracks over the stern. The mine deck openings could be closed in by steel panels with watertight leather seals to enable the ship to be used for transporting troops (capacity 1,000). During *Pluton*'s service as a gunnery training ship the mine deck openings were progressively closed off as more trainees were embarked.

The minelaying system was designed by Sautter-Harlé, and when the later Bréguet B4 mine was embarked it proved less secure. This was to be cited as a factor in the eventual loss of the ship by the Board of Inquiry. The Bréguet B4 mine, which proved to be less robust than its predecessor, had smaller dimensions and a maximum of 270 could be accommodated.

Boats and Complement

The boat deck was located between the second funnel and the mainmast. The inboard boats were on cradles while the two outboard boats, which included the CO's 9m *vedette*, were on wheeled trolleys, which enabled them to be stowed abeam the second funnel using rails set into the deck (see plan view). All these boats were handled by a duralumin boat crane powered by electrically-driven winches with an 800kg capacity and a reach of 10.5m.

An excellent starboard quarter view dated March 1934. As yet there is no temporary accommodation on this side of the ship, as evidenced by the open mine deck. The single 75mm/50 AA guns have been installed between the two funnels on open mountings. Note the five 3/4-metre rangefinders atop the raised after superstructure. (Marius Bar)

Table 2: *Range-finder Outfit as EATM Ship 1933-1939*

	April 1933	February 1936
Bridge structure	2 OPL (S)* 3-metre 2 Zeiss (S) 3-metre 2 Barr & Stroud (C)* 2-metre 2 Zeiss (S) 1.5-metre	4 OPL (S) 3-metre (Mod.1927/32) 2 Zeiss (S) 3-metre 2 SCM (C) 3-metre (Mod.1926) 1 Barr & Stroud (C) 2-metre
Amidships	1 Barr & Stroud (C) 4.57-metre 1 OPL (S) 3-metre	none
After deckhouse	1 OPL (S) 4-metre 1 OPL (S) 3-metre	1 SOM 5-metre 2 OPL (S) 4-metre (Mod.1933) 4 OPL (S) 3-metre (Mod.1924/27) 3 SOM (S) 3-metre (Mod.1932) 1 SOM (C) 3-metre (Mod.1931)
HACS director	none	1 OPL (S) 3-metre (Mod.1926)
Searchlight command platform	none	2 OPL (S) 3-metre (Mod.1926/27)
(for light AA)	none	8 OPL (S) 1-metre Mod.J30

* (C) = coincidence; (S) = stereoscopic

This had to be replaced within two years of the ship's entry into service because of serious corrosion. The complement of boats was completed by two 8m whalers, which were mounted on davits outboard of the mainmast.

The initial complement comprised: a Rear-Admiral, 17 officers, 87 petty officers and 320 men (including 4 *agents de service*); a total of 424. The ship was designed for a wartime complement of 17 officers, 92 petty officers and 404 men; a total of 513.

Service 1932-39

Pluton entered service on 25 January 1932; on her arrival at Toulon she was attached to the Training Squadron of the *1re Escadre*. Her trials had revealed various problems, some of which would continue to plague the ship throughout her active service. In particular there were numerous machinery breakdowns: the turbo-pumps were prone to serious oil leaks even when tested in the factory prior to installation; the reduction gearing tended to overheat, and there was excessive play in both cruise and one of the main turbines.

The *Commission Permanente des Essais* (CPE), which was responsible for the initial evaluation of *Pluton*, considered her to be well-adapted to the mission intended. However, there was concern regarding the military value of the ship, and especially the relatively feeble main armament, given her size and cost.

On 27 April 1932, when *Pluton* had been in service barely four months, it was decided to convert her to a gunnery school ship (EATM: *Ecole d'Application du Tir à la Mer*) as a replacement for the elderly armoured cruiser *Gueydon*. It was stipulated that this conversion should in no way impair the ship's primary mission as a minelaying cruiser, and that the statutory annual minelaying exercises should proceed. Conversion involved the installation of:-

- a 10,000ton cruiser type transmitting station
- the 138mm director control system from *Gueydon* (the DCT was located atop the enlarged bridge structure)
- four single 75mm/50 Mod.1922 AA from *Gueydon*
- an HACS director control system for the 75mm AA
- two twin 13.2mm/76 Hotchkiss MG from *Gueydon*, plus a further four to replace the elderly 8mm Hotchkiss MG
- additional rangefinders atop the bridge, between the funnels and on the stern platform (see Table 2)

It also involved the conversion of two after crew spaces to accept eight dismountable cabins for trainee midshipmen (to be removed in four days), and temporary spaces for 40 men on the port-side mine deck (the openings were permanently closed with steel panels).

These additions resulted in some modifications to the bridge structure and mast platforms, and the strengthening of the tripod foremast to take the weight of the HACS director (the topmast was reduced to a stump). One of the forward searchlight projectors was disembarked, the other moved to a platform beneath the director. There was a slight reduction in the ship's stability because of the additional topweight.

The armament was now: four single 138mm/40, four single 75mm/50, two single 37mm/50, and six twin 13.2mm/76 Hotchkiss MG (two on the forecastle, and two on either side of the upper deck amidships).

In 1933-34 full RPC was provided for the 75mm AA, a range clock was installed on the forward superstructure, and the after gangway, which was made of duralumin and had badly corroded, was replaced. The following year the forward gangway was replaced, together with the boat crane and boat booms, which had suffered similar corrosion. Temporary spaces were provided for a further 40 men on the starboard-side mine deck, the 75mm guns were fitted with protective shields, and eight (later 16) Brest-type life floats were fitted. In 1936 the fore topmast was suppressed and a further ten range-finders fitted (the total was by now 31!). The boilers and condensers were overhauled and the turbines inspected.

During a major refit during 1937-38 the turbines and

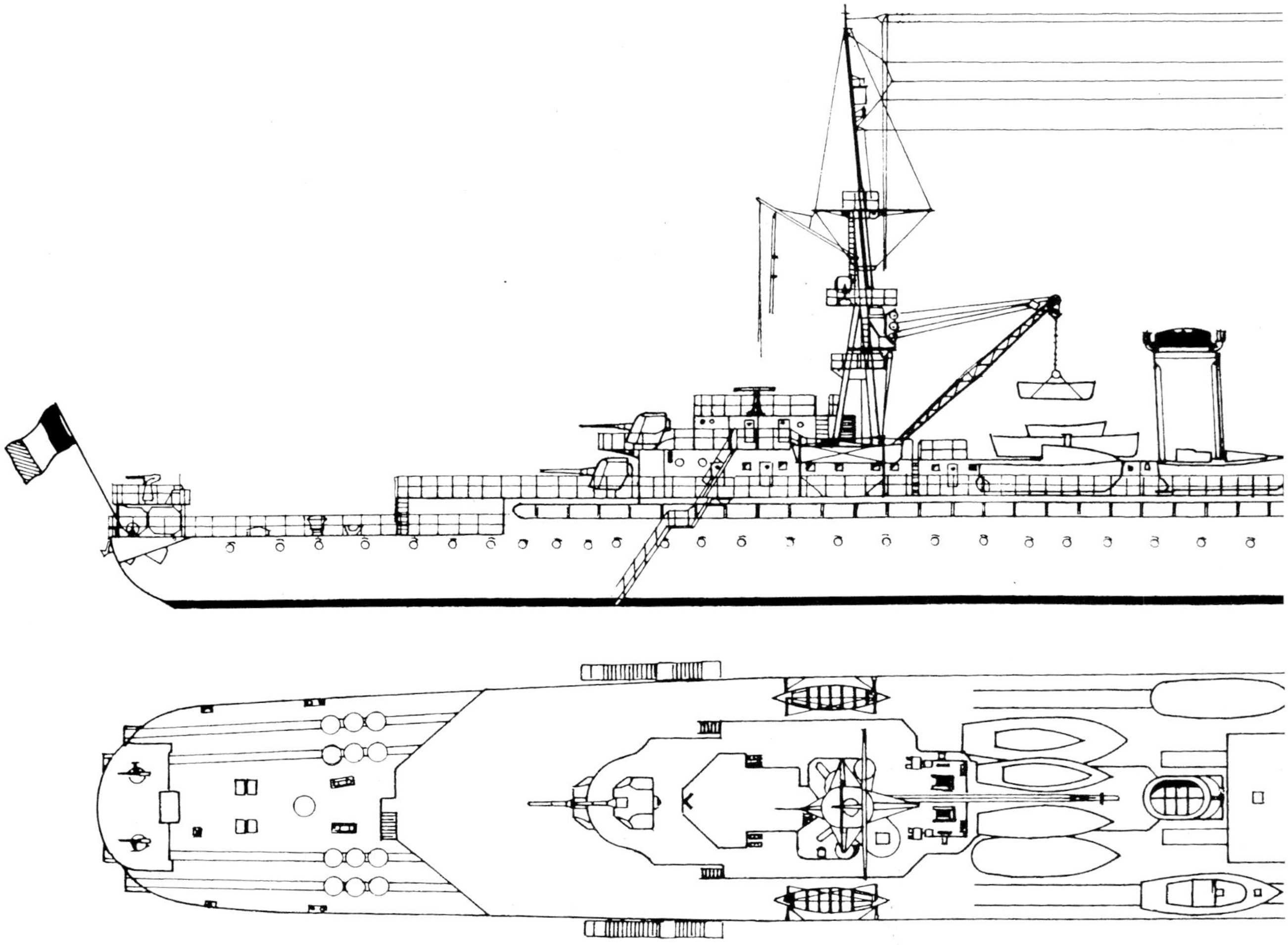

In this photograph, taken 14 October 1936, the fore topmast, previously a stump, has been completely suppressed. The 75mm/50 AA guns are now fitted with prominent shields. (Marius Bar)

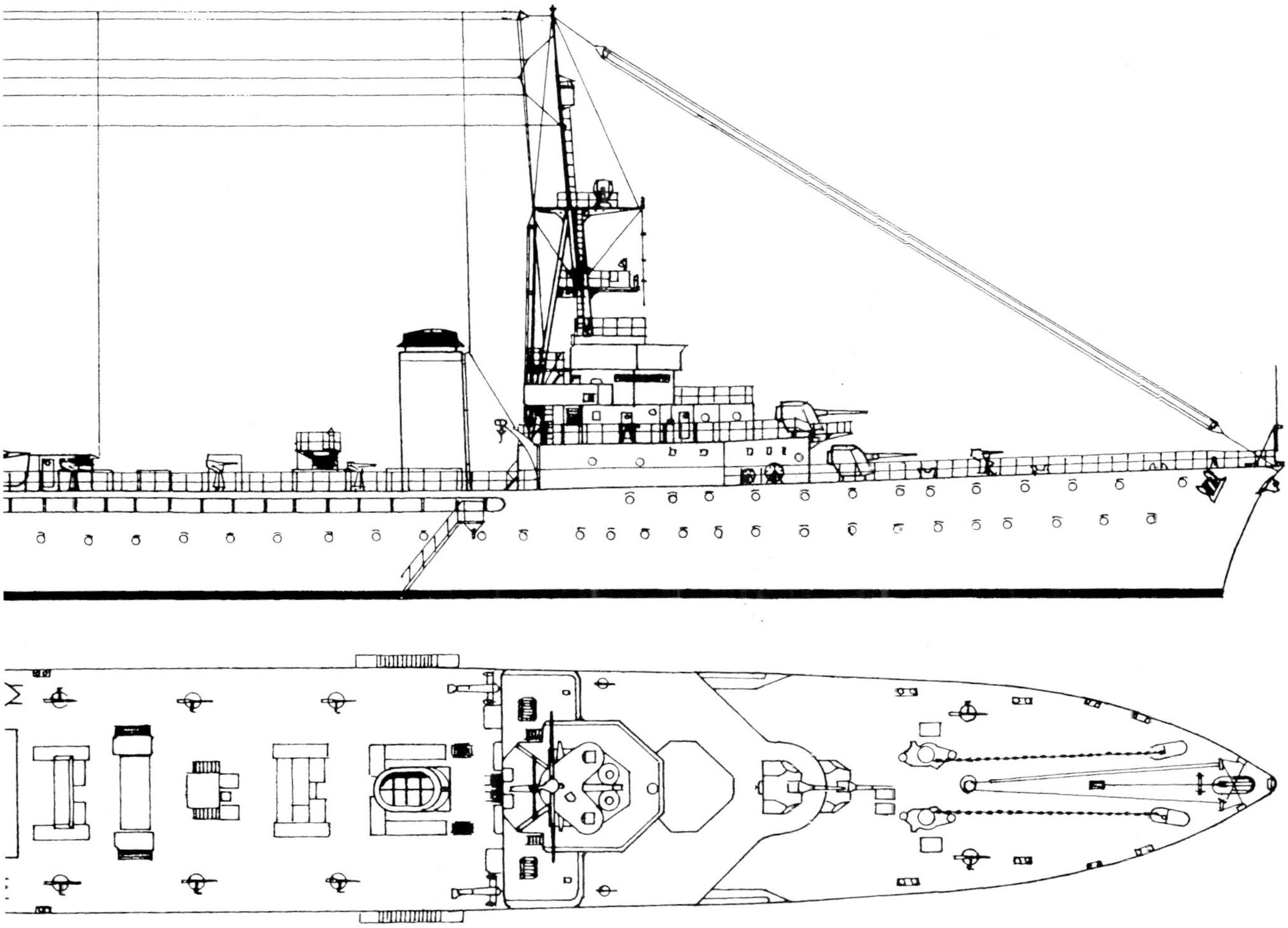

Pluton: *profile and plan views*

The profile and plan views are based on official plans dated Lorient 22 September 1932. They show Pluton *as completed, with six single 37mm/50 Mod.1925 mounted as a temporary measure amidships in place of the 75mm/50 AA of the original design. In the plan view, note the absence of a chain for the bow anchor and the 37mm AA platform above the stern straddling the inner pair of mine tracks.* (Drawn by the author)

Table 3: PLUTON

	Name	Builder	Laid down	Launched	In service
1925 Programme	*Pluton*	Arsenal de Lorient	16.04.28	10 04 29	25.01.32

Characteristics (as completed)

Displacement:	5,300 tons standard 5,321 tonnes normal 6,214 tonnes full load
Length:	144m pp, 152.5m oa
Beam:	15.5m
Draught:	5.2m max.
Machinery:	Four du Temple small-tube boilers, 20kg/cm^2; two-shaft Bréguet geared steam turbines for 57,000shp; speed 30kts (designed)
Oil fuel:	1,150 tonnes; radius 4,500nm at 14kts, 2,200nm at 24kts
Armament:	Four 138mm/40 Model 1923 in four single mountings Model 1924 (600 rounds); ten 37mm/50 Model 1925 AA in single mountings (10,000 rounds); 220/250 Sautter-Harlé H5 or 270 Bréguet B4 mines.
Protection:	none
Complement:	424 peacetime; 513 wartime

reduction gearing were refurbished, and a massive DCT *type croiseur de 8,000t* was fitted atop the bridge structure in place of the original. Remote power control (azimuth only) was provided for the main artillery, and the two forecastle 13.2mm mountings, which had proved to be too exposed to the elements, were relocated to the bridge structure.

In 1938-39 the boilers were retubed, the HACS director was completely enclosed, and the 13.2mm MG received protective shields. The original boat crane was replaced by a trellis beam with almost twice the lift capability (1,500kg); it could also now handle mines. Outriggers were fitted to the second funnel to handle a revised communications outfit.

War Service and Loss

On 10 May 1939 a new organisation of the fleet had been implemented, and *Pluton* was attached to the newly-created 5ᵉ *Escadre* under Rear-Admiral Moreau, which would be based on Lorient and would embrace all training ships. It was envisaged that in the summer of 1940 *Pluton* would be replaced as gunnery training ship by the 8,000t cruiser *Duguay-Trouin*, and would become the consort of the midshipman training ship *Jeanne d'Arc*. She would then be renamed *La Tour d'Auvergne*, the name *Pluton* being traditionally associated in the *Marine Nationale* with ships tasked either with minelaying or mine disposal. In the event the change of name never took place, and (contrary to claims in a number of standard reference books) the name *Pluton* remained with the ship up to the time of her loss.

In July 1939 the deterioration in the international situation prompted the *Marine Nationale* to re-convert the *Pluton* to her original function as a minelayer. All temporary accommodation was removed, as was most of the rangefinding and monitoring equipment associated with the gunnery training mission. On 28 August, with the outbreak of war imminent, the composition of the 5ᵉ *Escadre* was modified and the two cruiser divisions (the 6th, with *Duguay-Trouin* and *Primauguet*, and the 7th, with *Pluton* and *Jeanne d'Arc*) were relocated to the main Atlantic Fleet base at Brest.

This new organisation lasted for only three days, after which the 7th Cruiser Division was withdrawn and tasked with other duties. On 2 September *Pluton* left for Casablanca with 125 Bréguet mines embarked to accompany the *Force de Raid*. It was feared at the time that the German battlecruisers *Scharnhorst* and *Gneisenau* might operate off Morocco. *Pluton* arrived unaccompanied at Casablanca on 4 September, and following new intelligence was ordered to lay her mines in an anti-submarine barrage in the approaches to the port. This order was rescinded the following day, after the mines had been fuzed in readiness, and the ship was ordered to disembark the mines. This delicate operation began on the morning of 13 September. At 10.40 (local time) the ship was destroyed by a massive explosion, which caused no fewer than 186 deaths and 73 injuries among the crew; a further 47 casualties were experienced by shore support personnel, and other ships in the harbour were seriously damaged by flying debris. The subsequent enquiry highlighted the fragile nature of the Bréguet B4 mine, the indecisiveness displayed by the high command in countermanding its own orders, the lack of practical experience among the crew in defuzing mines (no prior exercises had taken place in the lifetime of the ship), and the failure to move the ship to an isolated berth before attempting such an inherently dangerous procedure.

Sources

Jean Guiglini and Albert Moreau, *Les croiseurs Jeanne d'Arc & Pluton*, Marines Edition (Bourg-en-Bresse, 1999).
Official plans of *Pluton*, Centre d'Archives de l'Armement.

NANIWA AND TAKACHIHO:

Elswick-built Protected Cruisers of the Imperial Japanese Navy

During the nineteenth and early twentieth centuries the River Tyne was a source of numerous warships for the world's navies. Perhaps two of the most interesting were the cruisers *Naniwa* and *Takachiho*, built for the Imperial Japanese Navy. Purchased in response to Chinese naval aggrandizement, both saw action at Tsushima in 1905. **Kathrin Milanovich** details their background, construction and careers.

At a time when the only governmental managed shipyard of the Imperial Japanese Navy (IJN), Yokosuka Naval Yard,[1] was building composite ships of 1,500 tons displacement[2] the IJN ordered two steel-made protected cruisers from the British Armstrong, Mitchell, & Co. Ltd, Elswick shipyard. The design philosophy of these ships were based on Armstrongs belief that the highest value should be set on this class of vessel a replacement for armourclads.[3] The features of the protected cruisers were:

- high speed and good manoeuvring qualities to obtain the most favourable tactical position in a clash with an armourclad
- direct protection by a transversely and longitudinally curved, strong protective deck and indirect protection by cofferdams and coal storage
- exceptional large offensive power

The combination of these three factors in comparatively small ships resulted in shorter construction periods and much reduced expenditures compared to an ironclad. The opinion prevailed that three protected cruisers could be built for the cost of one armoured battleship. Moreover, it was believed that the former would overwhelm the latter in combat by making full utilisation of the qualities mentioned above.[4]

The IJN, one of the smallest navies in the world at that time but was facing danger from the strongest armourclads in the Orient: the German-built Chinese battleships of the *Chen Yuen* class, eagerly took up the protected cruiser concept.[5] At this time the only IJN ships worth mentioning were the British-built armoured frigate *Fuso* and the waterline-belted corvettes *Kongo* and *Hiei*[6] but they were no match for the Chinese battleships. Therefore three protected cruisers were included in the Fifth Naval Expansion Program of 1883, of which two, namely the later *Naniwa* and *Takachiho*, were immediately ordered from England. The order for the third ship, the later *Unebi*, was given to the French *Société des Forges et Chantiers*, Le Havre.[7] Thus the IJN took the first step in building up a fast cruiser force against that from the Chinese Northern Fleet. In this respect, the IJN's first protected cruisers are remarkable ships, well worth being remembered as the starting point of the cruiser age of a navy which, throughout her history, emphasised this kind of warship; sometimes as substitute of the capital ship and sometimes as an indispensable assisting force.

When *Naniwa* was completed the London *Times* praised her qualities, in particular pointing out her speed, which made her the fastest ship among all the warships afloat, the enormous effect of the main guns, and the very complete protection. *The Times* predicted that if there was a war in the Japan or China Seas, the IJN could obtain great results because *Naniwa* was equipped, amongst other things, with the most modern armaments, large calibre guns, hydraulically operated carriages, torpedoes and electric lighting.

The important British technical magazine *Engineering* also evaluated *Naniwa* and *Takachiho* as embodying 'a high attainment of formidable offensive and defensive qualities'[8] and sincerely congrulated the Japanese Government on the acquisition of these fine ships' pointing out that 'it is certainly an indication of the immense development which has taken place in Japan of late years that she can now claim to be the possessor of the fastest and in some respects most formidable cruisers afloat'. The writer was also sure 'that the officers of the Japanese Navy are fully capable of appreciating their valuable properties' and agreed with his colleague of *The Times* that these men were also capable 'of making efficient use of them should an opportunity be presented'.

As predicted in the newspaper and the magazine, *Naniwa* became famous for firing the first shot in the

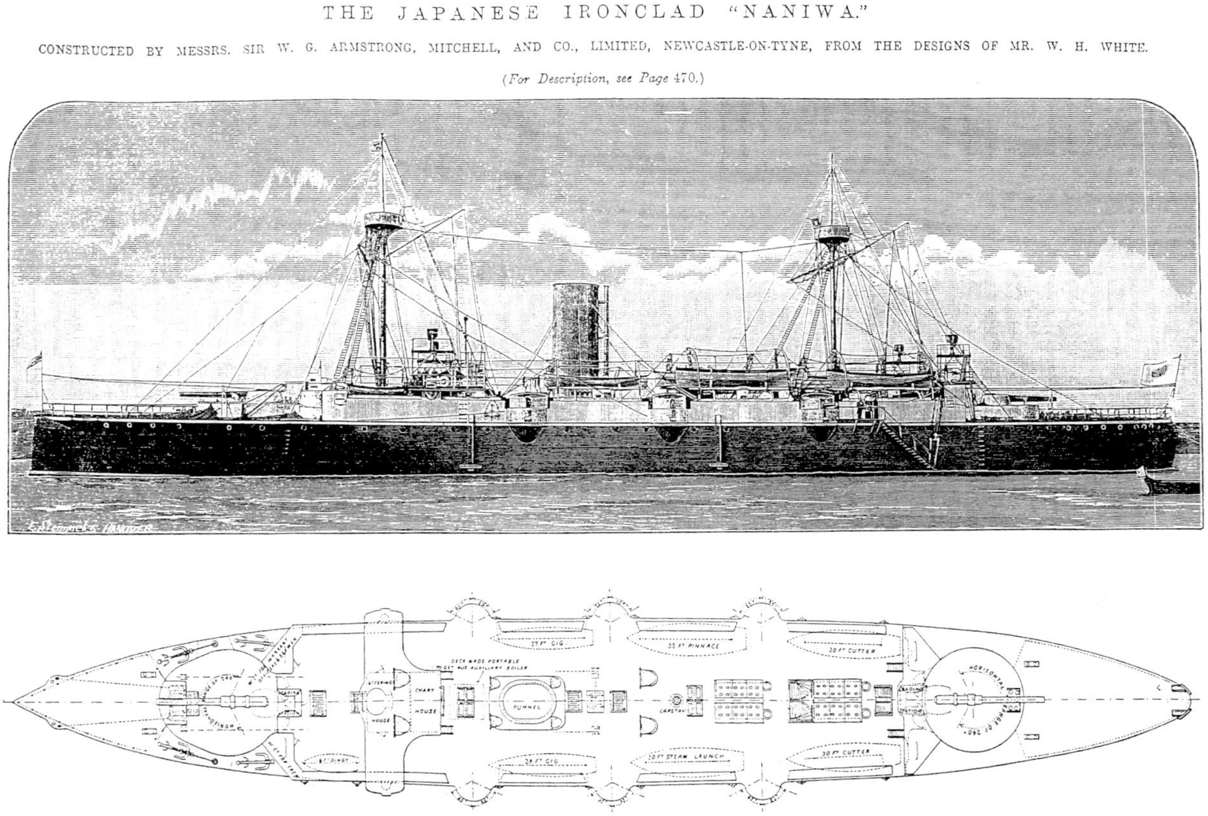

Naniwa *as pictured in* Engineering, *14 May 1886*. (Author's collection)

Sino-Japanese War (SJW) and, on the same day, sinking the Chinese-hired British steamer *Kowshing*, which was transporting Chinese soldiers to Korea. At that time *Naniwa*'s commander was Captain Togo Heihachiro who, eleven years later, would become Japan's most famous Admiral by annihilating the Russian Fleet at the Battle of Tsushima.

A Short Excursus: French Navy's La Jeune École

The utilisation of mines and spar torpedoes in the American Civil War (1861-1865) strongly influenced the efforts to produce an automobile (or locomotive) torpedo in order to overcome the most serious defect of the former: to be capable of carrying out the attack at a relatively great range from the enemy instead of closing to a few metres.[9] This problem was successfully solved in the decade following the American Civil War. With the development of the 'offensive' torpedo to a powerful practical weapon and the appearance of specially designed small and fast torpedo-carriers, torpedo warfare attained a recognised and important place in maritime war until the beginning of the 1880s. However, the importance of the new weapon was greatly exaggerated and resulted in the theories of the French *la jeune école*. The 'young school' favoured the building of numerous small craft of simple construction and specialised purposes, armed with light guns or a single large calibre gun but all possessing high speed[10] instead of the heavily armed and armoured battleship whose impotence to resist the destructive power of the submarine attack seemed to be apparent. In company with the change in strategic thinking towards attacking the enemy's commercial and financial resources by destroying his seaborne trade and bombarding his coastal commercial cities,[11] torpedo warfare greatly influenced naval construction in the 1880s.[12] The IJN's *Sankeikan* may be seen, to some degree at least, as one example of this concept. These vessels were the materialisation of the idea that if a navy desired to have capital ships armed with large calibre guns, there ought to be only one such gun in each ship so that several could be built for the same expenditure required for the construction of one large armoured battleship, whose loss would be irreplaceable. In contrast the loss of a cheaper, lighter armed, indirectly protected ship requiring a much shorter construction period, would be compensated by utilising existing similar ships or even building a replacement.[13]

Other examples may be the proposals of the Naval Technical Department to Navy Minister Kawamura Sumiyoshi on 19 May 1884 and 21 February 1885 to revise the Naval Expansion Program of 1883. In the former 25 ironclads, cruisers and gunboats were included beside 15 torpedo boats, whereas in the latter the ironclads were excluded in favour of 18 armoured and 24 2nd class torpedo boats, while five small cruisers, 14 gunboats and three torpedo deport ships were to be built. In the latter report the Naval Technical Department promoted Admiral Aube's view, although his name was not mentioned, and estimated that 25 torpedo boats could be built at the cost of one ironclad. It is unlikely that IJN officers were familiar with the theories of the 'young school' at the time when the building of *Naniwa* class was decided, but articles about Aube's views soon appeared in some issues of the *Navy Magazine* (*Kaigun Zasshi*) published by the Office of the General Staff, and his ideas must have been discussed in some circles of IJN officers, although it did not become the IJN policy. However, the February 1885 proposal was doubtless along the lines of *la jeune école* but the Naval Technical Department[14] did not conceal that this plan was not supported by many officers and found it worthy only of consideration.[15] In fact, the IJN wanted strong ocean-going ships, preferably ironclads, and the philosophy expressed in the aforementioned proposals may be considered a short-lived excursus rather than a shift in policy.[16]

Armstrongs Substitute Cruisers for Armourclads

Even if Armstrong cruisers were of much more rational design than the later *Sankeikan*, the fundamental philosophy was comparable to a large degree. In 1882[17] Armstrong advocated the building of small, fast, protected and powerfully armed cruisers in the belief that (1) to secure battleships against the penetration of shells fired from the most powerful guns afloat armour of such thickness (more than 600mm) was necessary, thus the protected area would become very small due to weight limitations, (2) owing to the large unprotected areas and the construction of the hull below the waterline armourclads have the same defects as unarmoured vessels against attack from torpedo and ram, (3) armour can be substituted by coal to a considerable degree, (sail power must be abandoned; coal supply increased and protection by coal improved), (4) the partial armoured deck of the hitherto built cruiser was to be extended throughout the entire length of the ships and placed as low as possible, preferably below the waterline. The protection was to be completed by the arrangement of several longitudinal and many transverse bulkheads and a rather minutely subdivided cellular layer comprising cork cofferdams below the waterline and coal above (and also below), (5) with the expenditure on one armoured battleship, three unarmoured ships each with an armament equal to that of the armoured battleship but higher of speed, may be built, (6) the latter will be able to destroy the former by gunfire, torpedo attacks or by ramming; therefore battleships were not needed to combat enemy battleships, instead their role and all other services may better be fulfilled by large numbers of small, fast, unarmoured but protected and powerfully armed cruisers.

The first ship built in accordance with these ideas, and regarded as the prototype of the modern protected cruiser, was the Chilean *Esmeralda*,[18] which was later sold to Japan and renamed *Izumi*. Designed by George Rendel, famous for his 'Rendel Gunboats', the first of the so-called 'Elswick Cruisers' was characterised by high speed, good manoeuvrability, powerful armament and exceptionally good protection for a ship of 2,950 tons displacement. On the other hand, such a light vessel could never be a steady platform for 25.4cm (10in) guns[19] in rough seas and seaworthiness was limited by the low freeboard, which always restricted the use of the guns, especially the bow or chasing gun, by green seas in a seaway. There were other defects, such as the absence of a double bottom and the rather small coal capacity, but they were overlooked in view of the previously listed characteristics. The *Esmeralda* was completed in 1884 before the introduction of strong explosives and quick-firing guns of effective calibre and therefore she was in a much better position in a decisive clash with an armoured vessel than if completed at the end of that decade. After the *Esmeralda*, the Italian *Giovanni Bausan* (see *Warship 2002-3*) was built followed by the Japanese *Naniwa* and *Takachiho*. These ships were designed by Sir William White who introduced many improvements to the original design.

第 13 図　　巡洋艦　浪速

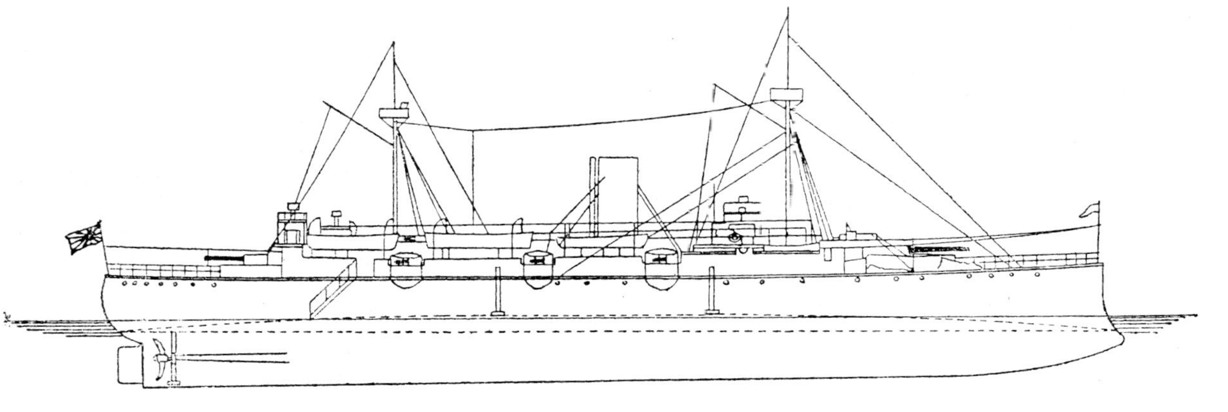

Naniwa, *note the aft gun has been incorrectly drawn.* (Author's collection)

Table 1: PLANNING AND REALISATION OF ONE PART OF THE IJN'S FIFTH EXPANSION PROGRAMME

	Prop. 24 Feb 1883		Planing to realise the Programme			Ships constr. acc. 25 May 1883	
Type	Unit	Price (Yen)	Unit	Already completed	To be built	No	Names
Large	5	7,500,000	6	*Fuso*	5	3	*Naniwa, Takachiho, Unebi*
Medium	8	7,800,000	12	*Kongo, Hiei, Kaimon, Tenryu*	8	5	*Katsuragi, Takao, Yamato, Musashi, Tsukushi*
Small	7	2,520,000	12	*Seiki, Amagi, Banjo, Hosho, Dai Ni Teibo*	7	3	*Atago, Chokai, Maya*
TGB	12	8,820,000	12	–	12	–	–
Total	32	26,640,000	42	10	32	11	

Note: TGB means Torpedo Gunboat

The IJN's Fifth Naval Expansion Program

On 20 December 1881 Navy Minister Sumiyoshi submitted a motion of a new expansion programme[20] including the construction of 60 war vessels within 20 years, by building three ships each year from 1882 onwards.[21] The expenditures during the first period[22] of the total programme was calculated as 40,140,340 Yen.[23] This planning, of course, far exceeded Japan's financial and economical capabilities, and was not permitted.[24] On 15 November the following year Kawamura proposed a variation of this programme reducing the number of ships to be built to 48 and choosing the remaining 12 vessels from the already completed ones. These 48 ships were to be built in eight years by completing six ships per year, spending 4,020,000 Yen (of silver)[25] as warship construction expenses and 694,646 Yen 40 Sen as maintenance expenses for six ships in the fiscal year (FY) 1883.

This motion formed the basis for the decision of permitting Warship Construction Expenses (*Gunkan Seizo Hi*) as a new budget item for IJN from FY 1883 onwards.

Before the new item (Warship Construction Expenses) was decided, on 15 December 1882 Premier Sanjo delivered the Imperial Prescript for Military Expansion to all Ministers.[26] This was accompanied by his order to save management expenses in the ministries. After the investigation of the budgets proposed by the military forces in the Finance Ministry on 30 December 1882 Sanjo ordered Kawamura to re-investigate the kinds of ships and the annual budgets of warship construction and maintenance and to prepare a programme according to the wishes of the Emperor and the statement from the Finance Minister Matsukata Masayoshi.[27]

On 6 February 1883 Kawamura proposed to shorten the construction period for the aforementioned 48 warships from eight to five years, but this motion was rejected. Therefore, on 24 February, he proposed the construction of 32 ships in eight years with annual expenses of 3,330,000 Yen[28] to make total expenditures of 26,640,000 Yen. This time he obtained permission.[29]

In the same year on 25 May, Kawamura proposed a clever variation of his motion, this time requesting the supplementation of the shortage of naval budgets for FY 1883 to 1885 by transferring them to the budgets for FY 1884 to 1886. Even if this meant the construction of vessels earlier than scheduled it was permitted and, until the collapse of the Fifth Naval Expansion Program in FY 1885,[30] a total of eleven ships could be laid down or pur-

Table 2: CONSTRUCTION EXPENSES AND OTHER EXPENDITURES

Budget	Warship Construction Expenses		Special Expenditures	
FY/Name	*Naniwa*	*Takachiho*	*Naniwa*	*Takachiho*
1883	443,428,320	442,603,320		
1884	827,745,655	771,637,240		
1885	362,098,069	296,709,971		
1886	101,837,031 *	188,328,073 *	32,793,060	34,105,507
1887	231,700,540 *	152,753,218 *	18,146,980	11,461,845
1888	38,353,74 *	38,348,007 *	5,546,104	1,998,947
1889			1,170,789	1,165,690
Total	2,005,163,352	1,890,379,429	57,656,933	48,731,989
Excl.*	1,633,272,044	1,510,940,531		
Distribution	97%	98%	3%	2%

Notes:

(1) * Costs taken over to the corresponding fiscal year (FY)

(2) 2,005,163,352 means 2,005,163 Yen 35 Sen 2 Rin

(3) The pure construction expenses were as follows:

Name	Hull and Engine	Armament	Total
Naniwa	1,300,112,586	314,427,486	1,614,540,072
Takachiho	1,317,708,343	255,178,990	1,561,887,333

chased in FY 1883 to 1885. This process is shown in Table 1. The construction costs and other expenditures for *Naniwa* and *Takachiho* are given in Table 2.

The Process Until the Conclusion of the Building Contract And Afterwards

When conflict erupted in Korea during 1882 and the Chinese forces took prompt action, the IJN immediately asked the British naval architect Edward Reed to mediate the purchase of ready-made warships from abroad.[31] That inquiry was officially made through the Foreign Ministry to the Japanese Minister in London where Commander Kurooka Tatewaki came in contact with Reed. At that time the purchase of warships was an easy matter. Peru and Chile were fighting each other in the Pacific and the construction of their warships ordered from shipyards in Europe countries, which had declared neutrality, had been suspended for the time being. Reed told Kurooka of three ships, two of which were Peruvian vessels detained at Howaldswerke at Kiel (*Diogenes* and *Sokrates*) and a Chilean vessel at Mitchell's Low Walker Yard (*Arturo Prat*).[32] Kurooka arrived at Berlin on 3 September 1882 and visited Schwartzkopff Co. (for torpedoes) and then saw the Peruvian cruisers at Kiel. He was not allowed to board them for inspection but reported them suitable for serving in the IJN.

By the end of 1882 the naval expansion was authorised by Prime Minister Sanjo and the fund for two cruisers was included in the FY 1883 budget in February 1883. These cruisers were to be named *Tsukushi* (*Diogenes*) and *Kasagi* (*Sokrates*). But it was found that the trial speed could not fulfil the contract conditions and that their fighting power was comparable only to a despatch vessel (*Tsuhokan*). On 3 March the IJN decided not to purchase them and cancelled the contract.

Saso Sachu, who had studied naval architecture in Britain from 1871-1878 and returned aboard the *Hiei* to Japan, examined the *Arturo Prat* and found her well suited. Then Navy Minister Kawamura ordered Rear-Admiral Ito Toshiyoshi to negotiate to reduce the price to £80,000. Chile agreed to reduce to £82,000 by April 1883, excluding a set of electric apparatus, two steam launches and other materiel. By Saso's recommendation and Ito's success in reducing the price, the Navy Ministry got the approval of the Premier to change the funds for the Peruvian cruisers to this ship on 3 May and Kawamura ordered Ito to purchase her at that price (without some accessories) the following day. Saso, however, was eager to

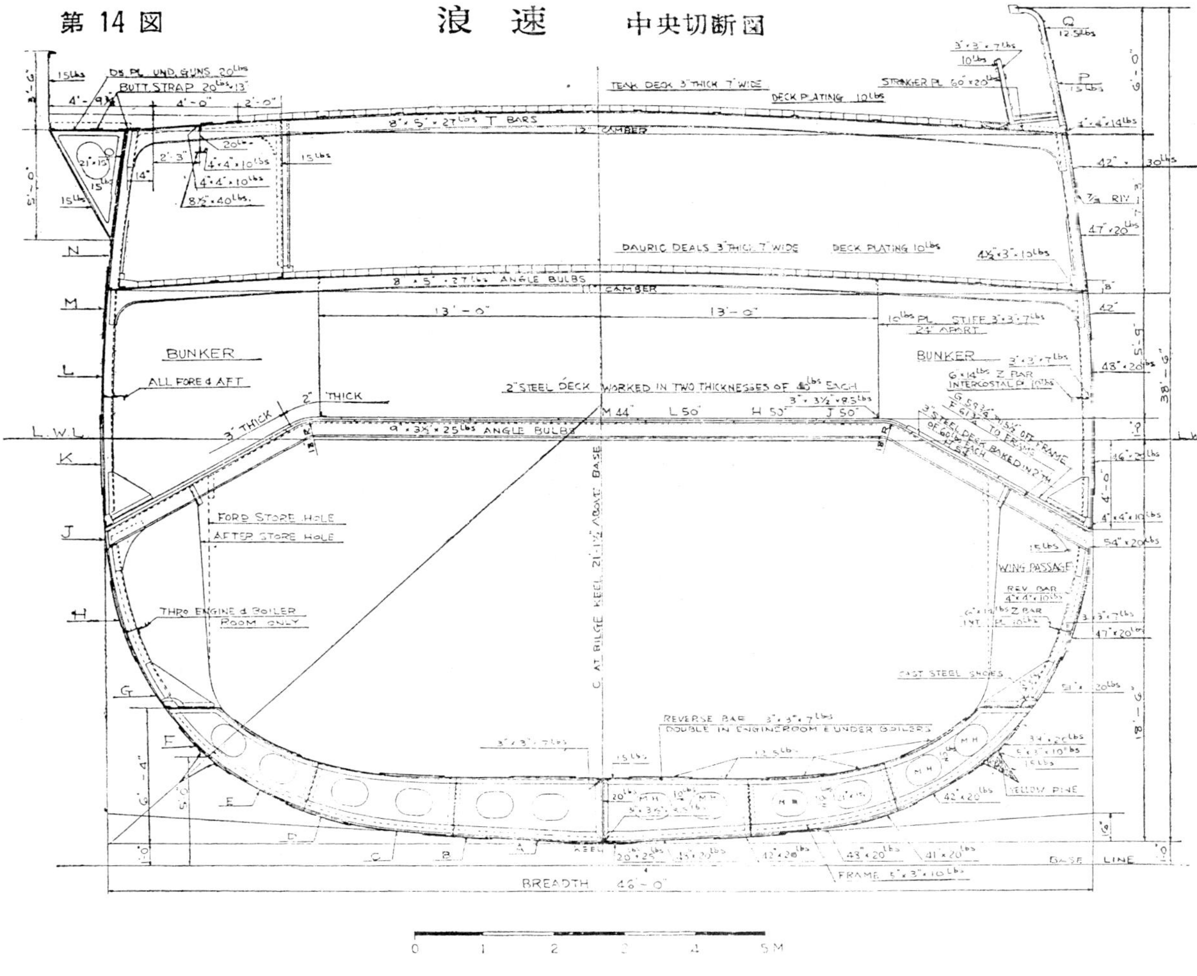

Naniwa *cross section.* (Author's collection)

buy the electric apparatus (£350) and steam launches (£960) and succeeded in gaining a reduction of £1,200. Kawamura approved the purchase on 16 June and the Navy Ministry notified her name as *Tsukushi* on the same day, diverting the name from the aforementioned cruiser (i.e. *Diogenes*).[33]

At that time, the Naval Technical Department (NTD) drew up plans for a 6,500ton ironclad and 5,500ton cruiser and proposed them on 5 May. By Kawamura's order the plans had to be revised and the NTD submitted the drawings of a 7,100ton central battery ship (the armament was the be consisted of each two 30.5cm and 24cm guns) like the Chinese *Tei Yuen* class and a 5,200ton protected cruiser on 13 July. The construction of each ship according to these plans was approved by Premier Sanjo on 19 July 1883.

There was another Chilean cruiser at Low Walker Yard under the control of Armstrong whose construction had been suspended. This was the *Esmeralda* designed by Rendel, which Chile also wanted to sell. Saso Sachu was impressed by her arrangement, clear lines and rational design in general. He recommended her purchase and the Navy Ministry decided upon her in place of building the 5,200ton protected cruiser. But, before a contract could be concluded the war between Peru and Chile wound down and Chile now refused to sell her.[34] Armstrong protested but it was in vain and the *Esmeralda* was finally delivered to Chile.

When the attempt to purchase *Esmeralda* failed, William White, then chief designer of Armstrong Co., recommended building two protected cruisers of a revised *Mersey* type. This may be regarded as clue to the origin of the *Naniwa* class.

The Navy Ministry sent the drawings of the previously mentioned ironclad designed by the Naval Technical Department to England. They arrived in London on 1 September to be examined by White.[35] He thought them 'old-fashioned'[36] and instead recommended a barbette ship like the *Collingwood*. But the cost of such a ship was too expensive.

On the other hand, Ito reported White's proposal to the Navy Ministry on about 1 September 1883 and recommended acting accordingly.[37] On 7 October Ito reported the price as £210,000. On the basis of his recommendation on 16 October the Navy Ministry requested building the revised *Mersey* in place of the 5,200ton protected cruiser. This was permitted and she became *Naniwa*. On the same day Kawamura ordered Ito to start negotiations for the purchase of one revised *Mersey* and wanted to know specifications because Ito's report had not made it

Photo 1. *The hull of the protected cruiser* Takachiho *on her builder's berth, Elswick Works, Newcastle-upon-Tyne. Photo taken by the builder on 18 March 1885, less than one month before launching. Note the shape of the underwater hull with the sharp but only mediocre projected ram, bilge keels at the middle body, propeller shafts and struts. The raised and sunken system of the outside plating indicates the use of liners and the very smooth working proves excellent British shipbuilding techniques. The hull and the shelter deck are completed and in front of the superstructure the barbette of the forward main gun is visible. The sponsons for the side guns are also completed as are the lower parts of the forward and aft bridges. Note also the Imperial Chrysanthemum on both sides of the bow surrounded by an ornament plate (the latter removed after the refitting) and the line of bull-eyes fitted directly below the upper deck and even in between the sponsons. The marking of the waterline is rather narrow.*

This photo was supplied to the late Hans Dresseler by the late Shizuo Fukui in exchange for photos of warships of the former Imperial German Navy. Mr. Dressler's collection was bought by the Library of Contemporary History when Prof. Jürgen Rohwer was the director.

Photo 2. Naniwa *after completion at Newcastle-upon-Tyne ready for her delivery cruise to Japan. This photo was taken by Armstrong & Co. a few days prior to her sortie, i.e. about 20 March 1886. Note the men sitting on the main gun hoods (fore and aft) and barrel (aft) and those handling the searchlights upon the fore and aft bridges. Also note the different colour of hull and superstructures. She sortied from Newcastle-upon-Tyne on 24 March 1886 but had to return because of engine problems. This was the first but not the last and according to some Japanese sources there were several periods in her career when she was troubled by engine disorders. After repair she sortied again on the 28th and, after passing through the Suez Canal, arrived at Shinagawa on 26 June . Being the first vessel transferred to Japan from the European builder's yard by a Japanese crew her voyage was given special attention and was the object of a detailed report. Her commander, Captain Ito Yuko, became famous as the C-in-C of the Japanese fleet in the Sino-Japanese War. The signature of the photo is a register number of the former Imperial German Navy.*

Photo 3. Takachiho *in the spring of 1886 flying the builder's flag at the stern. This photo was taken by Armstrong Co. most probably in April during one of the trials conducted in the Dover Strait. After tking on water, coal and other provisions she left Plymouth on 10 May and entered Yokosuka on 3 July. Note the remarkable time difference of the transfer cruises: roughly three months in case of* Naniwa *but less than two months for* Takachiho *by a hired crew (but bearing in mind the engine trouble experienced by the former).*

This photo was originally printed in the 1934 edition of 'Shashin Nihon Gunkan Shi' (Pictorial History of Japanese Warships - *reprinted in 1983). I thank Mr. Todaka Kazushige, who holds the copyright of the reprint for permission (letter of 5 July 2001) to use all the photos.*

clear if the price included armament and so on. Ito's reply was delayed for more than a month.

In the meantime the IJN was still trying to reduce the price of the *Collingwood* type armourclad because it vastly exceeded the assigned budget. If one ship of this type was built, the domestic construction of sloops and gunboats would have to be suspended. Because the financial problem could not be solved, Navy Minister Kawamura Sumiyoshi decided to postpone the building of the ironclad until the improvement of the budget on 6 December. On 10 December he reported to the Premier to build a revised *Mersey* type in place of the ironclad. Sanjo agreed and so, *Naniwa*'s sister, *Takachiho*, appears.[38]

Kawamura, now having Ito's reply in his hands, ordered him to prepare the contract for two revised *Merseys* at £225,000 per ship on 16 December. The contract of the two cruisers was signed by Oyama Kosuke, acting Minister at London, on 22 March 1884. The price of the two ships was £406,000 without main and secondary guns, which were ordered directly from the German Krupp Co.

According to Vol. 2 of *Kaigun Seido Enkaku* (Outline of Naval Administration System) Rear Admiral Ito was ordered to supervise the building work of *Naniwa* and this marks the beginning of the dispatch of supervisors (*Kantoku-kan*) to foreign countries.[39] Ito borrowed a room in the Japanese legation and worked there.

The *Takachiho* was brought to Japan by a British commanding officer and crew. For this purpose J.M. James was hired for the transfer, the collection of the crew and so on. In addition, a number of Japanese nationals were also aboard as observers. With her returned ten artisans[40] from Yokosuka shipyard who had been despatched to Armstrongs in 1884 in order to supervise the construction of vessels of this type. This, without doubt, must have contributed much to the subsequent building of all-steel ships in Yokosuka and was, most probably, a preparatory measure for shifting from composite and iron hulls to steel-made ones in that establishment.

In contrast to this *Naniwa* made her cruise to Japan by a purely Japanese crew and did not depend on foreign assistance.[41]

Afterwards Japanese ships built abroad were always brought to Japan by a Japanese crew which was transported to the builder's place some weeks in advance to be trained in the handling of engines, boilers, auxiliary machinery, equipment and fittings and to master the ship in general.

A Short Description

General

From their appearance these ships may be characterised by the high freeboard (3.96m above crown of the protective deck to the connection of the upper deck to the hull sides; 4.27m from the load waterline to the same position; 4.57m from the load waterline to the middle part of the upper deck (due to the camber of the latter), and 6.1m from the load waterline to the shelter deck), vertical stem, rounded stern, arrangement of the main guns in barbettes on the centreline bordering the shelter deck at the fore and aft, the equally spaced sponsons for the side (second-

Photo 4. Takachiho *anchoring in Yokosuka naval port in 1893-94. Note the reconstruction of the aft bridge. Hull and superstructures are painted uniformly in greyish tone (called warship and also wartime grey) so that the photo was probably taken in July 1894 when she returned from Honolulu. At that time the declaration of war on China had already been decided in the Cabinet.*

This photo was reproduced from 'The Russo-Japanese War Fully Illustrated', No. 9, July 1905, p.1234 (Kinkodo Shoseki Kabiushiki Kaisha, Honcho, Nihonbashiku, Tokyo, 1905). This is a series of ten lavishly illustrated volumes dealing not only with the Russo-Japanese War but also providing insight into the daily life in Japan during the late nineteenth and early twentieth centuries (besides the reproduction of the official reports, many anecdotes and various aspects of Japanese customs and manners are dealt with. Even though the intention must have been primarily propaganda the contributions about early foreign intercourse, medieval history and establishment of a Western type navy are interesting and many of the photos are seldom found in other publications).

Photo 5. Naniwa *(?) anchoring in Yokosuka naval port in 1894. She returned from Honolulu on 15 April 1894 so that this photo may have been made after that date and before July of the same year. The question mark refers to the number of bull-eyes between the second and third sponson, which is apparently identical in photos 4 and 5 so that there are doubts about the correctness of the original captions. See the caption to photo 10.*

This photo was reproduced from 'The Russo-Japanese War Fully Illustrated', No. 9, July 1905, p.1263.

ary) guns, the two military masts with fighting tops and absence of rigging, the tall funnel between the masts, the roomy forward bridge between forward mast and funnel, and the stowage of the ship boats.

With Lwl of 97.54m (Lpp 91.44m), moulded width of 14.02m, length/breadth ratio was 6.96 showing a comparatively fat ship. This form was generally favourable to obtain excellent manoeuvrability and transverse stability (besides offering sufficient room for the machinery, coal bunkers and crew accommodation) but on the other hand it was not so fat so as to negatively influence propulsion resistance. This may also be proven by the B/d ratio which was 2.486. D/d ratio was 2.026 (in case of taking the shelter deck) and 1.702 (in case of excluding shelter deck and taking the distance from load waterline to the connection of the upper deck to 0-strake) and these values show a ship with a high freeboard and rather large reserve buoyancy. As seen from the drawing of the midship section the respective coefficient was rather large and when taking into consideration the slight tumble-home the depiction of the upper deck indicates a large waterline coefficient. Judging from these coefficients it can be assumed that prismatic and block coefficients were also comparatively large corresponding to the tendency at that time.

The hull was constructed of steel throughout and the strakes, as shown in one of the photographs and the drawing of the midship section, were connected using the raised and sunken system with liner. The joints of the plates were extraordinarily flat[42] and this proves the then excellent British shipbuilding techniques. Steel, as material for the construction of warships, was introduced for the combination of economy of material with due regard to strength and enabled the construction of stronger and larger ships than possible with the use of iron or composite materials.

The keel consisted of two horizontal plates, 12.7mm and 15.9mm in thickness, connected to the A-strake of 12.7mm in thickness. This was quite contrary to the French warship design method preferring the vertical keel. The double bottom ended 1.63m above the base line. The plates of the inner bottom were 7.94mm thick in general, those of the outer bottom 12.7mm, the same as other strakes, except the sheer strake of 19mm in thickness.

The sharp ram-shaped stem was formed of a solid steel forging, and was strongly supported by the fore end of the protective deck. The stern had also the typical contemporary cruiser shape, nicely rounded but straight at the lower end to mount the non-balanced rudder. The bilge keels were rather short extending only on one part of the midship and their depth was also moderate. They were triangularly shaped, made from wood (yellow pine) but covered by a steel sheet. The struts were two rectangular shaped bars connected obliquely to the hull and the stern tubes, the latter extending rather long from the point of treading out of the hull. At that time the stream-lined arrangement of shaft brackets to reduce resistance had not yet been introduced.

Above the protective deck, described later, there were two decks throughout the entire length: the middle (berth) and upper deck, having a camber of 0.28m and 0.305m respectively, and covered by dauric and teak deals respectively having a thickness of 76mm and width of 178mm on both decks. Spaced amidships were three sponsons, the upper end (about 1.05m) being part of the shelter deck whose sides were formed by the P- and Q-strakes. The lower part of the sponsons extended to a depth of roughly 1.55m and a width of 1.14m. To take in the forces when firing the side guns 25.5mm thick deck plates, fitted in two thickness of 12.7mm each, were used. The shelter was bordered fore and aft by oblique walls connected to the barbettes of the main guns and being higher than the shelter deck that was also covered by the usual wooden deals.

Near the fore and aft ends of the shelter deck, which was arranged amidships for about 60 per cent of the Lwl, there were two military masts (pole masts) with the then usual fighting tops but no equipment for sails. In order to obtain the necessary stiffness, and also as countermeasure against vibrations, the masts were secured by a number of steel wires arranged as to provide no obstruction on the deck. To reach the fighting tops, the men had to climb up rope-ladders, the same as in rigged ships.

Behind the masts there were the forward and after bridges. In the former there was a conning tower of steel armour with a thickness of 51mm and within it were placed the hydraulic steering wheel,[43] the engine room telegraphs, the directors for simultaneous electric firing of the guns, various voice-tubes to remote control stations and so on.

The ellipse-shaped funnel was placed behind the forward bridge between the military masts. Comparatively tall in appearance, and with the usual steam tube at the aft end, its dimensions were adequately to the proportions of the hull and contributed to the distinctive appearance of these ships.

The ship boats were one 32ft (9.75m) pinnace, two 30ft (9.14m) cutters, one 30ft steam launch, two gigs – one of 28ft (8.53m) and one of 27ft (8.22m), and one 16ft (4.87m) dingy. They were carried, except the dingy, in

Photo 6. Takachiho *anchoring in Kobe port on 2 February 1897 for attendants to the funeral of the Imperial Doyen.*

Note the shift of the fighting tops to a lower position in order to reduce the height of the centre of gravity. This was the result of a lesson of the Sino-Japanese War. The top of both masts have been altered and the Krupp side guns replaced by 15.2cm Armstrong QF guns, but otherwise she seems to be still in the original configuration.

First published in the excellent album War Vessels of Japan *(1906) this photo is reprinted in numerous subsequent publications such as* Shashin Nihon Gunkan Shi, Bakumatsu Iko Rekishi to Shijitsu, *Nakamura's* Zokan Kaiso *and was also supplied to the late Hans Dresseler by the late Shizuo Fukui in exchange of photos of warships of the former Imperial German Navy.*

davits and spaced along both sides of the shelter deck.[44]

The two bow anchors were placed on flat parts beside the forward main gun barbette. Of these the forward one was jointed to the anchor chain.

At each side of the bow there was an attractive decoration centred on the Imperial Chrysanthemum. The decoration was removed in later years but the chrysanthemum remained. The arrangement of the Imperial heraldic figure on both sides of the bow was exceptional; the usual position being just on the front of the bow.

The interior of the ships must have been well arranged and also well fitted, above the then standard.

A contemporary source especially points out (1) the spacious and admirable arrangements for the accommodation of the officers and crew, (2) the excellent contrive of the fittings throughout, (3) the particularly well lighted and ventilated main state rooms amidships, (4) the liberal supply of electric incandescent lamps in the engine rooms, 'which render the rooms as light as day, even with the fighting shutters closed'.[45]

The current for the approximately 300 incandescent lamps was fed by the electric generators, which also supplied the four searchlights, placed on each wing of the two bridges. The switchboards were independent but cross-connection was possible so that each generator could supply any part of the system. The liberal supply of electric lamps is especially noteworthy because lighting inside the ship by lamps (prior to this oil lamps and candle lanterns were used) was introduced in the IJN by the purchase of *Tsukushi* (ex *Arturo Prat*) in 1883 and then followed in *Naniwa* and *Takachiho*.

Protection

The protective deck, which gave this kind of cruiser the name, was arranged throughout the entire length of the hull and covered the vital parts such as engine and boiler rooms, fore and aft magazines and steering gear. It was the result of the lesson that positioning the vitals below the waterline with coal protection only could not prevent the destruction of such 'unprotected' ships by several hits from guns mounted on comparable vessels. The flat part amidships was 7.92m in width and 0.305m above load waterline. It had a 51mm thick steel deck worked in two thickness of 25.4mm each and was supported by angle bulbs. It was jointed with a radius of 0.41m to sloped parts (angle about 30°) at both sides which extended to 1.22m below waterline to be connected to the outer plating (J-strake). These slopes were built up in the same way as the flat part but the thickness was increased to 38.1mm (making a total of 76.2mm). At that time fighting ranges were close and the trajectory of shells comparatively flat; thus making the slopes to an area much more in danger to be hit than the flat part. At a distance of 0.305m from the protective deck a second layer was arranged whose function must have been comparable to the splinter protection below armour decks (or armoured flight deck) of various Japanese warships participating in the Pacific War. When this arrangement is compared to the prototype, the Chilean *Esmeralda* (later the IJN's *Izumi*), which had an uniform thickness of 25.4mm, the remarkable improvement becomes obvious.

The fore and aft ends of the protective deck, on a length of about 16.5m, were slightly sloped down to the same depth as the transverse slopes. The reason was the same as stated for the latter slopes but this time it was, of course, to protect the vitals against raking fire.

The openings in the protective deck were provided either with armoured shutters or gratings to stop projectiles from penetrating, and, around the passages, which had to be kept open in action, cofferdams were fitted for the same purpose and to complete the protection.

Generally speaking, the protective deck was comparable with a vault to offer remarkable resistance to the penetration of the projectiles of rather low property.

At the ends of the flat part, thin longitudinal walls (reinforced by stiffeners each 0.6m apart) were fitted and jointed to the middle (berth) deck. The spaces thus formed and bound by them, the outer walls and the slopes, were narrowly subdivided cellular layers filled with coal to protect the boiler and engine rooms (i.e. used as bunkers of appreciable thickness and height). Below the slopes and roughly half of the width of the bunkers were wing passages bordered by the double bottom at the lower end which had not yet been fitted in *Esmeralda*. Further indirect protection was afforded throughout by the division of the hull into watertight compartments, numerous by the standard at that time but not compared to watertight subdivision 30 years later.

The direct protection (the protective deck was intended to secure the vital parts against artillery fire), the indirect protection (the cellular layer partly filled with coal and stores) and the watertight compartition below the waterline, was designed to maintain buoyancy and stability in the case of damage resulting from the lack of adequate side armour.[46]

As stated before, it was this low-arranged vault like protective deck and the absence of any side armour which gave this kind of ship the name 'protected cruiser' to distinguish from the unprotected and armoured cruisers then already in existence.

Due to the lack of side protection Captain Ito Yuko, who took over the *Naniwa* from the builder, feared their loss by torpedo and bought torpedo nets for both ships. Torpedo nets were invented for the protection of armoured ships below the waterline belt and since these ships had no such armour their equipment had not been considered in the design and quite naturally the storage of these heavy nets in the ship, as well as their fitting, caused problems. Therefore in March 1887 the Shipbuilding Conference (*Zosen Kaigi*) decided not to take the torpedo nets aboard of the ships.

Armament[47]

Main Guns

The main guns were two 35cal 26cm Krupp guns[48] mounted in revolving centre-pivot carriages and placed on the centreline fore and aft. Owing to the oblique walls of the shelter deck the guns had an uninterrupted arc of fire of

Photo 7. Takachiho. *Date and place are uncertain but supposed to be taken around the time of the Sino-Japanese War because she still carries her original armament and has the fighting tops, but I am puzzled by the mounting of apparently heavy 47mm Hotchkiss QF guns on the shelter deck. Note the ensign flying on the stern and the colour of the funnel.*

240°. Training was effected by means of hydraulic engines situated directly below the guns but beneath the protective deck in order to reduce the danger of damage to them. The engines were connected to a shaft which was led up to the deck and carried a pinion on its upper end which engaged in a rack fixed to the base of the revolving carriage, thus moving the gun to the position desired. There are indications that it was the first time that IJN warships were fitted with hydraulic training gears.[49] Being a new invention there were two engines per gun, each capable of performing the rotation. The duplication of parts was, of course, to greatly reduce the risk of loss.

Instead of revolving on a roller-path (as used in turrets) the barbette mountings of *Naniwa* and *Takachiho* turned on the large diameter under-wheels of the carriage, their holders being also used as clamps to prevent the carriage from bucking.

Elevation and depression of the guns (+14° to –5°) were easily carried out by a simple gearing (toothed arc and toothed wheel).

The handles for the hydraulic training gear and the gear for the vertical movement of the guns were fitted on the working platform which was at the rear of the carriage and revolved with it. This working chamber provided space for the gun crew who were protected by a steel shield at the front.

Photo 8. *An unidentified photo of* Naniwa *class but supposed to be* Naniwa*. Date and place are uncertain but it may haven been taken around the same time as photo 7 for the same reasons as stated before.*

The carriage was fitted with Vavasseur compressors (recoil presses) which ran out the gun automatically into the position of firing after having recoiled to the rearmost position (recoil distance was 0.84m and was also controlled hydraulically).

Loading was carried out at a fixed station placed on the centreline inside the shelter deck and protected by stout steel armour. Inside this station were situated the upper ends of the hoists for the projectiles and powder charges, the loading tray and the hydraulic rammer. This meant that fixed loading was possible only and for this operation the gun had to be trained to 0° and elevated to 14°, thus reducing the firing speed by the time necessary for these movements and also the return to the firing position.

This mounting was designed by Armstrong Co. (heavily depending on George Rendel's barbette[50]) but included some novel points and proved satisfactory in practice.

In 1891, when the experiments carried out by *Naniwa* were ended successfully, the manual firing (by ripping line) was also changed to the electric method in order to improve hit probability by excluding the unavoidable time gap between firing order and the ignition of the primer in the former method.[51]

Secondary Guns

These were six 35cal 15cm Krupp[52] guns mounted in Vavasseur centre-pivot carriages fitted with protective shields. This mounting was designed by J. Vavasseur early in the 1880s and its characteristic feature was the hydraulic compressor brake, which consisted of a pair of hydraulic cylinders being one part of the carriage, and pistons whose rods were attached to the slide. The special design of the piston head secured uniform recoil of definite length. Due to the considerable inclination of the slide to the rear, running out was ensured by gravity. The slide ran on a ring of live rollers on a pivot plate attached to the strongly supported deck plate.

Elevation/depression and training were effected by worm and wheel, and rack and pinion gearing.

Three guns were mounted on each broadside in equally spaced sponsons. This arrangement was chosen to obtain an uninterrupted arc of fire of 130° since the shelter deck was occupied with bridges, masts, funnel, boats and large openings. The disadvantage was that only half of the guns could be brought to action for broadside firing.

Auxiliary and Machine Guns

In order to protect the vessels from torpedo boat attack two 6pdr (57mm Nordenfelt) rapid-fire guns on *Naniwa,*[53] and two heavy 3pdr (47mm) Hotchkiss QF guns on *Takachiho*, were situated on the ends of the fore bridge, and ten 25.4mm quadruple Nordenfelt machine guns were placed on the shelter deck at every space which provided a sufficient horizontal range. In addition, two 11mm 10 barrelled Gatling MG[54] fitted with shields were mounted in each of the fighting tops of the military masts.

Saluting Guns

The mounting of copper saluting guns was common in Japan but these guns were troubled by frequent misfires and when *Naniwa* was ordered to patrol in Hawaiian waters in November 1893 the C-in-C of the Standing Fleet permitted the use of the 6pdr as saluting guns. It is said that the saluting guns were landed afterwards.

Searchlights

Four powerful searchlights of British Gramme type were placed on elevated stations at either wing of the forward and after bridges. This arrangement enabled the lighting and searching of the entire area surrounding the ship and assisted in the protection of the ship against night attack by small, fast and quickly manoeuvring torpedo boats. The current for the operation was fed by four Gramme old type electric generators (2-pole, double wound, 410rpm, 80 V, 75 A, 24kW) mounted in the engine rooms.

The fitting of searchlights and dynamos is remarkable since comparative tests with searchlights of American, French, and German types had not taken place before 1 May 1884.

In 1897, the electric generators were changed to two units of Edison 4-pole type with 400rpm, 80 V, 200 A and judging from this it seems that the searchlights were also changed (very probably to the German Siemens type then favoured by the IJN).

Torpedoes

According to the original contract the ships were not to have torpedo armament but the contract was revised in February 1885 to fit torpedo tubes (TT).[55] Therefore, when completed, four 35.6cm TT supplied by the German Schwartzkopff Co. had been fitted. These TT were situated immediately before and abaft the coal bunkers on the protective deck two on each broadside. They were of fixed type, thus the torpedoes could be discharged to the broadside only.

Schwartzkopff torpedoes, designated Type 84 Year by the IJN, were used and the number of torpedoes mounted aboard of the ships was decided to be 12. However, it was changed to Type 88 Year a later (from 1908 these torpedoes were designated Types 84 and 88 respectively).

Trial Firing of Brown Coloured Hexagonal Type Powder by Takachiho's *Main Guns*[56]

In 1892 *Takachiho* was used for tests with brown-coloured hexagonal powder and in 1893 the order was given to use this type of powder in the Krupp guns. The following section is no record but merely a note providing some background to the Japanese designation of Krupp guns in 'Pre-80-Years Type' and '80-Years Type' and the beginning of domestic production of brown powder:

> The burning speed of the powder depends on the type, but by changing the shape of the powder burning time can be controlled (i.e. burning speed altered).
>
> The powder burns on the surface and the fire proceeds from outside to inside.
>
> The larger the surface the more the burning volume in one time.

The previously mentioned rules were not generally known

for a long time, but after the utilisation of black powder in various shapes it was found that cubic-shaped powder bodies of the same size always gave the shell the same muzzle velocity.

In 1882 the brown coloured[57] hexagonal powder with one hole in the centre was invented in Germany. This was called *82 nen shiki Kayaku* (82-year type powder) in Japan and when export sale was begun in 1884, the IJN purchased it the following year and brought it to Japan with the *Naniwa* to be utilised for the Krupp guns mounted aboard her and *Takachiho*. The brown powder was much more suited than the black powder, with either one or seven holes, cureently in use for the Pre-80-Years-Type Krupp guns.

Among Krupp guns, those designed to use brown (hexaprismatic) powder from the beginning were called *80 nen shiki* (80-Years-Type), while those designed in the black powder days were called *80 nen zen shiki* (Pre-80-Years-Type) or *Kyu shiki* (Old Type).

The reason why the Krupp gun was called either old type or new type was to indicate the difference between using the past type black powder or new type nitrate powder. The new brown coloured hexagonal type powder gave the shell the same amount of kinetic energy with lower pressure inside the barrel. Thus the gun could be made lighter with a thinner barrel, which meant that with the same amount of material a longer barrel could be produced, thus greatly improving the ballistic properties.

The change from black powder to brown coloured (nitrate) powder allowed the length of the barrel to be elongated from 25 cal to more than 30 cal, the amount of the propellant could be increased to 2.08 times without changing the pressure inside of the barrel, the muzzle velocity could be increased to 1.12 times and the destructive power (kinetic energy) of the shell could be increased to 1.56 times.

The IJN decided to produce brown powder domestically in 1885. Chief engineer Otto von Farrot of the governmental powder factory at Berlin-Spandau was hired by the Bureau of Ordnance (*Heikikyoku*) for 2 years on 20 December 1885. As the Bureau of Ordnance was abolished on 20 January 1886, he signed the contract again with the chief of the successor organisation, the Powder Factory (*Kayaku Seisosho*). Beside others, Farrot advised the equipment necessary for the manufacture of brown powder but unfortunately he was killed in a traffic accident on 10 July 1886. Afterwards the chief of the Production Section, LT Rinoiye Masata, continued test production of, and experimentation with, brown powder with great effort till June 1887. Then this batch was successfully tested. The chairman of the Board of Ordnance reported to the Navy Minister on 29 September 1887 that the powder was acceptable except for the pending endurance test, which required at least a further 2 years. Based on this report the Navy Minister directed to adopt the brown hexagonal powder newly produced at *Kayaku Seisosho* for Navy use on 13 October.

The installations of the Powder Factory were designed for the production of black powder and not the brown powder, which required quite a different production processes. Therefore the previously mentioned batch was only an experimental one. Before that, and based on the advise of von Farrot, Krupps had been asked about procuring a whole manufacturing plant for brown powder early in 1887. Navy Minister Saigo Tsugumichi, who made an inspection trip through Europe,[58] met Johann Nepomuk Heidemann, the Director of the Rheinisch-Westfälische Pulverfabriken AG, at Köln. This meeting resulted in the conclusion of a contract (worth 1.5 million Marks) for the purchase of a large amount of brown powder (executed from 1889 till 1891) and included an option to establish a complete powder factory in Japan.[59] In February 1889 the German engineer Hermann Behncken (armed with a 2-year-contract) arrived in Japan, bringing the production

Photo 9. Naniwa *at Yokosuka in 1897-98 with lowered fighting tops and new type side guns.*
Reproduced from Fred T. Jane The Imperial Japanese Navy, *p.61. Reprinted in 1984 by Conway Maritime Press. I have used the original (1904) edition available in the Library of Contemporary History at Stuttgart.*

Photo 10. Naniwa *after refitting in Kobe harbour at the end of 1902 (most probably 11 or 12 December).*
All the slow firing 26cm and 15cm Krupp guns are replaced by 15.2cm Armstrong QF guns and the fighting tops, already lowered in consequence of the lessons of Sino-Japanese War, removed. Instead of the 25.4mm MG mounted on the tops and elsewhere heavier 47mm QF guns are distributed on both sides of the shelter deck. Note also the rangefinder mounted on a pedestal and the semaphore signal station shifted to the aft. The aft mast is not yet elongated so that apparently no wireless equipment is fitted. The ornament plates at the bow are removed with only the Imperial Chrysanthemum left (being the emblem of a warship of the IJN listed in the Gunkan *(Warship) category).*

The sisters are very hard to discriminate solely by their appearance. However, according to Mr. Nakagawa Tsutomu the number of bull-eyes between the second and third sponsons is different. Naniwa *had apparently seven,* Takachiho *only four – this is the main reason why the ship pictured in photo 8 is identified as* Naniwa *and why there are doubts if photo 5 really shows* Naniwa *and not* Takachiho. *However, the quality of the photos is insufficient to allow a definite identification.*

This photo was supplied to the late Hans Dresseler by the late Shizuo Fukui in exchange of photos of warships of the former Imperial German Navy and War Navy.

equipment with him. The installation of the new equipment progressed and the production was to begin, albeit slowly.

In July 1891 the powder engineer (in Japanese his title was *Kayaku Seizo Gishi* = Powder Production Engineer) Heinrich Blumenstein and a chief worker[60] came to Japan to instruct about the production process. At that time the new powder production facilities were much progressed and the expansion of Meguro Powder Factory was completed on 21 October 1891 to begin test production and trials in the following month. Japanese sources ('*Nihon Kaigun Kayaku-Shi*' = History of Naval Powder in Japan) do point out that from the start the high technical levels enabled perfect production, resulting in favourable firing tests. The key factors were the quality of the German equipment and the supervision of the installations and instruction of the production techniques by the German engineers. (Blumenstein returned home in the following year but the date for the chief worker is not known by this author.)

Based on the German instructions, three kinds of brown coloured hexagonal powder were produced without difficulties.[61]

In February 1892 the trial firing of the large calibre guns was conducted using brown coloured hexagonal type powder. On 1 July *Takachiho*'s 35cal 26cm main guns were test fired in Suruga Bay with favourable results using No 1 brown powder having the following particulars: height 25mm, width 40mm, one hole in the centre, weight 43 grams, density 1.84.

Based upon the results of the trials the order to supply No 1 and No 2 brown powder to the guns was given on 4 February 1893.

Therefore, in the Sino-Japanese War *Naniwa* and *Takachiho* used brown powder, generating less smoke than black powder, and the British built cruiser *Yoshino* was the only ship using smokeless British cordite, which is double base of nitro-glycerine and nitro-cellulose.

Changes of Armament

Examining the results of the Battle of Yalu, on 13 October 1894 the Naval General Staff requested the Navy Ministry to replace the 15cm Krupp slow firing guns with 6in (152.4 mm) QF guns. The Navy Ministry agreed and ordered them from Armstrongs in November 1894.[62] On 1 April 1895 the Navy Ministry ordered Kure and Sasebo Naval Stations to replace the guns, but the work for *Takachiho* was changed to Yokosuka Naval Station on 17 July 1895. *Takachiho* completed the replacement of the secondary guns in April 1896, *Naniwa* followed in May and left Kure shipyard.[63]

In company with the change of the secondary guns the anti-torpedo boat armament was strengthened by the replacement of four 25.4mm quadruple Nordenfelt MG with four 3pdrs on *Naniwa* and two 3pdrs and two 6pdrs on *Takachiho*.[64] The replacement had been requested by the Naval General Staff to the Navy Ministry on 1 August 1895 and the latter, in response to this request, had ordered Yokosuka Naval Station to replace the MG on 30 August but the order for *Naniwa* was changed to Kure Navy Yard in January 1896. It is said that these guns were supplied from the stock available in the Weapon Storage Office.

The four 11mm ten-barrelled Gatling MG were withdrawn sometime in 1898 but the definite date is uncertain.[65]

Then, in July 1898, the Navy General Staff requested the Navy Ministry replace the 26cm Krupp main guns with two 8in (203.2mm) Armstrong QF guns, but the Navy Ministry did not respond so quickly and before the order was given the Naval General Staff changed its mind and on 26 February 1900 requested changing two 8in QF guns to four 6in QF guns, arguing that the handling of the 8in guns was too heavy for the average Japanese sailor.[66] On 19 March the Navy Ministry recommended the reduction of the 6in QF guns to two and the Naval General Staff agreed on 20 March.

On 11 May 1900 the Navy Ministry ordered Kure Naval Station to change *Naniwa's* 26cm main guns to 6in QF guns and six 25.4mm Nordenfelt MG to four 3pdr and two 2.5pdr, during the replacement of the boilers. As for *Takachiho* the same order was given to Sasebo Naval Station on 7 June 1900.

The conversion and the re-arming of *Naniwa* was finished by September 1900 and that of the *Takachiho* by February 1902. As the result of these changes the ships were armed with eight 40cal. 6in Armstrong QF guns[67] as main guns (fitted with protective shields) and ten 3pdr and two 2.5pdr as anti-torpedo boat weapons.

The aforementioned changes are summarised in table 3.

In company with the refitting of the armament several modifications were carried out, such as (1) shifting of the semaphore signal equipment and its station aft, (2) adoption of 1.5 metre Barr & Stroud rangefinder upon the ceiling of the steering house, (3) removal of the bow decoration, (4) renunciation of the fighting tops.

Table 4 provides some essential date of the guns mounted aboard of *Naniwa* and *Takachiho*.

Machinery

Although Elswick built the ships, design and production of the engines were made by the well-known firm of

Table 3: *SUMMARY OF CHANGES OF ARMAMENT*

Type of Gun	Original Condition (1886 - 1889)	After re-armament (1900 - 1902)	*Takachiho* as Minelayer (1911)
35cal 26cm Krupp	2 (100)	removed 1900-1902	–
35cal 15cm Krupp	6 (75)	removed 1895-1896[3]	–
40cal 15.2cm Armstrong QF	–	8 (150)[4]	1 (bow)[5]
40cal 7.62cm Armstrong QF	–	–	10 (distr. on upper deck)
57mm (6pdr) Nordenfelt QF	2 (355) *Naniwa*[1]	–	
heavy 47mm (3pdr) Hotchkiss QF	2 (400) *Takachiho*	10 (400) *Takachiho*	removed[6]
heavy 47mm (3pdr) Yamauchi QF	–	10 (400) *Naniwa*	–
light 47mm (2.5pdr) Yamauchi QF	–	2 (400)	2[7]
25.4mm Nordenfelt IV MG	10 (6,760) *Naniwa*[2] 10 (5,670) *Takachiho*	replaced by 3pdr	–
11mm Gatling MG	4 (ca. 10,000)	removed in 1898	–
355.6mm Schwartzkopff TT	4 (12)	4 (12)	removed

Notes:

1 Changed to two 3pdr in 1896.

2 Four MG were replaced by 3pdr in 1896 (also in *Takachiho*).

3 The guns were used as follows: *Takachiho* 4 units for defence of Sasebo port, 2 units for Sasebo Kaiheidan (Naval barracks); *Naniwa* 4 units for training ship of Kure Kaiheidan, 2 units for port defence (?), 2 6pdr mounted on *Katsuragi* as side guns because her forward main gun had been destroyed by hit in the SJW.

4 When, in 1896, six guns were mounted the stock of ammunition per gun was 130.

5 4 guns were mounted on *Hashidate*, then training ship of Naval Gunnery School, in place of 12cm guns.

6 6 QF were mounted on *Hashidate*.

7 A total of 5 mounts were available, namely each 2 naval mounts (deck of the ship) and boat mounts and 1 landing mount. This means that the same guns were used by the ship, the ship boats and also the landing force.

Aside from the guns listed here there were also 12 *Hiroki shiki* (Hiroki Type) *Shoju Kokei* (Rifle Calibre) *Gaito-ho* (Outside-of-the-bore Gun). This was a sub-calibre gun fixed on a real gun for gunnery practice to save on the expensive projectiles.

Table 4: *PRINCIPAL PARTICULARS OF GUNS MOUNTED ON* NANIWA *AND* TAKACHIHO

			Gun		Shell/Round		Powder	Vo.	Penetration
Type	**Calibre** (mm)	**Barrel length** (mm)	**Total length** (mm)	**No. of lands**	**Weight** (kg)	**Explosive weight** (kg)	(kg)	(m/sec)	**Power at muzzle** (mm)
26cm	260	8,320	9,100	60	275	3.2	87	530	571
15cm	149.1	4,810	5,220	36	51	0.78	17	530	323
15.2cm	152.4	6,096	6,331	28	45.36	2.013	6.804	670	430
7.62cm	76.2	3,048	3,139	16	5.67	0.27	0.737	680	206
6pdr	57	2,479	2,721	24	2.722	0.115	1.418	655	147
3pdr	47	1,881	2,048	20	1.5	0.05	0.8	610	105
2.5pdr	47	1,401	1,558	20	1.115	0.045	0.2	450	51

Source: *Ships of the World*, 6/2000, p.109 (Vo. = muzzle speed).

Hawthorn, Leslie & Co.[68] and it was not only due to their excellent design, performance and arrangement that the world's navies focused their attention on these ships as the fastest cruisers afloat. The engines were typical products of their time, belonging to the surface condensing, horizontal, compound, direct-acting, two cylinder, double expansion steam type. The ships were fitted with two engines; one set placed in the fore and aft engine room respectively and driving one screw propeller. The engine rooms were described as 'unusually spacious and roomy, access being easily obtained to every part of the engines' and this was pointed out to be 'a great advantage in the case of a vessel which may be expected to pass much of her time in hot climates'.

This type of engine was characterised by the direct delivery of the action of the piston to the propeller shaft through the crank.

The diameter of the high pressure and low pressure cylinders (HP/LP cyl) was 1,219mm and 2,159mm res. With a stroke of 914mm, piston speed was 223.11m/min, corresponding to 3.72m/s. With 122 rpm corresponding to 7,500ihp the designed speed was 18 knots.

Designed by Mitchell, the engines were said to have been of exceptional lightness and compactness, combined with the requisite strength, and this must be attributed to the great experience of this British engine producer. Regrettably, no data about weight were found in the sources available to the author.

The starting and reversing gear of both engines (Marshall gear, the same as in *Tsukushi* and *Izumi*) was arranged close together to greatly facilitate efficient control on entering or leaving port, and if needed both sets could be easily started or stopped (reversed) by one man.

Steam was supplied by three single-ended and double-ended low cylindrical boilers made of steel (including tubes) and having a diameter of 5.79m, a length of 3.35m, with a total heating surface of 1,404.6m^2.[69] The boilers worked at 6.3 bar steam pressure which was reduced to 1.96 bar as the mean pressure in the LP cyl. The total weight of the boilers was 214.64 tons, that of water in the boilers at normal level was 91.53 tons.

The stokeholds were fitted to be worked in plenum system, air being forced in by fans of sufficient power to maintain air pressure of not less than 51mm of water.

In addition to the main boilers there was also one auxiliary boiler to supply steam for the capstan, winch and steering engines as well as to various pumps in case of necessity.

The propellers were made of manganese bronze and had three blades. The diameter was 4.27m, pitch 5.64m.

As stated earlier the ships were fitted with two military masts but carried no sails. Therefore total independence from wind power was obtained and 800 tons of coal were stowed to give a radius of nearly 9,000 miles at a speed of 13 knots. The abolishment of sails was well noticed by the Royal Navy and the influential magazine *Engineering* congratulated the Japanese for 'cutting themselves adrift from the obsolete tradition which still deforms and encumbers so many of our purely fighting ships with masts and yards'.

At the official trial *Naniwa* obtained a mean speed of 18.72 knots with 7,235ihp thus exceeding the planned value for nearly one knot despite a lower output than designed. *Takachiho* ran 18.77 knots with 7,604ihp.[70]

Conversion of Takachiho *to Minelayer*

In 1903, when Russia shifted two minelayers (*Kiraifusetsukan*) to Port Arthur, the IJN felt it was high time to prepare for this kind of warfare. The Shipbuilding Division of Yokosuka NY quickly test produced a simple minelaying device[71] and this was experimented aboard of *Fuso*. Afterwards three ships, including *Takachiho* were to be refitted to minelayers.

In January 1904 *Takachiho* was fitted with this device in Kure Navy Yard but after laying 24 mines off Vladivostok on 29 April it was removed because minelaying was shifted to converted merchantmen (special service ships).

The mine was successfully used in the Russo-Japanese War and in 1909 the Naval General Staff, following the example of the Royal Navy, wanted to have regular minelayers which were to belong to the fleet as standard ships. In peace time they were to carry out minelaying exercises and investigations about mine defences, and in time of war they should be deployed immediately after the declaration. For this purpose *Naniwa* and *Takachiho* were chosen and in October the Naval General Staff asked for their conversion demanding (1) removal of all QF guns and TT except the gun at the bow, (2) removal of the aft bridge[72] and installation of a light deck and bulwark from fore bridge to the position of former aft bridge, (3) mounting of eight to twelve 3in guns on the upper deck and four 60cm searchlights, and (4) necessary conversions for the storage of more than 200 mines. Irrespective of the considerable weight of the mines 70 tons of ballast had to be stored in the hold to compensate the weight decrease by the removal of guns their ammunition to maintain GM with a lowered centre of gravity.

The Navy Ministry agreed and decided to convert *Takachiho* within the budget of FY 1910. In September 1910 Yokosuka Naval Station (*Chinjufu*) was ordered to construct the new minelaying equipment. This time the standard type (the fitting of minelaying rails on the upper deck) was chosen and fitted on *Takachiho*, registering her as the IJN's first minelayer on 1 April 1911. In peace time 200 mines could be stored in each of the newly fitted mine storages on the middle and lower deck, which were equipped with hoists to transport the mines to the rails on the upper deck. After the conversion *Takachiho* was mainly used as training ship of the Underwater Weapon School (*Kaigun Surai Gakko*).

The conversion of the *Naniwa* was to be carried out during 1912 in Yokosuka NY. However, she sank in that year by accident before the completion of this work and on 29 July her conversion to a minelayer was abandoned.

Abridged Chronology

	Naniwa	*Takachiho*
Laid down	27 March 1884	10 April 1884
Launched	18 March 1885[73]	16 May 1885
Completed	15 February 1886	26 March 1886

Naniwa sortied from Newcastle-upon-Tyne on 28 March 1886 and arrived at Shinagawa on 26 June passing through the Suez Canal. The transfer voyage was made under the command of Captain Ito Yuko, the C-in-C of the Japanese Combined Fleet in the SJW and his vice was the still more famous Commander[74] Yamamoto Gonnohyoe who twice held the post of Navy Minister. She was the first ship brought from England to Japan by a Japanese transfer crew and was enrolled in the Standing Fleet in July.[75]

Takachiho sortied from Plymouth under the command of J M James and a crew collected by him in England on 10 May 1886 and arrived at Yokohama on 3 July via Suez Canal. She was enrolled in the Standing Fleet on 7 August and sortied from Yokohama on 13 October with several officials aboard to Tomitsu and Kannonzaki after which she cruised in Tokyo Bay.

On 26 November the Emperor and Empress reviewed the launching of torpedoes off Yokosuka, afterwards cruising to Yokohama from Nagaura.[76]

On 1 December *Naniwa* sortied from Yokohama for Kobe with the Prime, Army, Navy, and Justice Ministers aboard, then Tsushima Ozaki Bay to Pusan and returned to Yokohama on the 13th via Moji and Kobe. *Takachiho* sortied Kamonzaki on 4 December with the Imperial Doyen aboard and followed *Naniwa*.

On 19 January 1887 both ships sortied from Yokosuka for Kyoto with the Imperial Doyen aboard and returned to Yokosuka on the 19th.

On 25 January they sortied from Yokohama for Kyoto with the Emperor and Empress aboard who visited Takedoyo on 23 February. The ships cast anchor in Yokohama the following day.

On 1 March they sortied from Yokohama with the Imperial Doyen aboard but she was landed on 3 March because of a storm, boarded again on 11 March and returned to Yokohama on the 12th.

On 22 August both ships sortied and participated in the 'Great Manoeuvre' around Shimazu, Tateyama and returned to Shinagawa on 5 September.

On 8 November they sortied from Yokosuka with four other ships (among them *Tsukushi* and *Katsuragi*) to cruise around Japan (Kobe, Kagoshima, Hizen, Nagato, Aki, Inland Sea etc.) and returned to Kobe via Tosa on 17 and 13 December respectively.

On 28 December *Takachiho* cruised to Taketoyo.

On 17 June 1888 *Naniwa* became the flagship (of the Standing Fleet) and both ships sortied from Shinagawa to Okinawa and Taiwan via Nagasaki and arrived at Wonsan on 14 July, and Chifu on 16 August where the Japanese ships (*Fuso*, *Tsukushi*, *Kaimon*, and *Musashi*) were received by the Chinese Northern Squadron's most formidable ships *Ting Yuen*, *Chen Yuen* and *Lai Yuen* under the command of Admiral Ting, but disease spread to the ships and they returned to Nagasaki for disinfecting.

Later Premier Ito Hirobumi and Navy Minister Saigo Tsugumichi boarded *Naniwa* and the ships cruised to Chemulpo via Pusan, then to Genzan where they sortied on 17 September to cruise to Vladivostok via Posiet Bay. Both vessels returned to Maizuru on 1 October and the officials departed.

On 15 October *Naniwa* became the Emperor's ship to attended the launching ceremony of the cruiser *Takao* in Yokosuka Navy Yard.

Takachiho sortied from Maizuru for Kagoshima and arrived there on 8 October where both ships met on the 28th and returned to Shinagawa on 11 November via Kobe (arriving there on 2 November).

In 1889 *Naniwa* belonged to Yokosuka Naval Station and Standing Fleet while Takachio belonged to Sasebo Naval Station and was the flagship of the Standing Small Fleet.[77] On 2 July they sortied from Shiagawa for a cruise around the domestic coast together with *Fuso*, *Musashi*, and *Katsuragi* (*Naniwa* and *Katsuragi* were bound north; *Takachiho*, *Fuso* and *Musashi* were bound for the west; they rendezvoused at Miyazu on 20 July where C-in-C Inoue aboard of *Takachiho* changed the name of the fleet from *Jôbi-shô-kantai* to *Jôbi-kantai*) and arrived at Maizuru on 5 August, departed on the 12th and arrived at Aomori on 13th, at Ominato on 14th, departed on 5 September and arrived at Vladivostok on 26th, sortied 1 October to Gorgewitch Bay and Odeshima,[78] sortied on the 3rd and arrived at Pusan on the 7th via Wonsan. Afterwards they participated in minor manoeuvres. They sortied from Pusan on 14 October for Takeshiki and arrived at Sasebo on the 17th. On the 30th they arrived at Chifu via

Photo 11. Naniwa *anchoring in Sasebo naval port early in February 1905. Note the replacement of the main guns upon the closed barbettes by 40cal 15.2cm Armstrong QF and the remarkable elongation of the aft mast fitted with a wireless antennae. At that time the sisters had been in service with the IJN for 20 years but her condition and fighting power were still considered sufficient to participate in the Battle of Tsushima forming the Fourth Division of the Second Fleet together with domestically built cruisers* Akashi *and* Tsushima; Takachiho *flying the flag of Vice Admiral Uriu Sotokichi. It seems that photos taken after 1905 no longer exist.*

This photo was presented to the late Mr. Erich Gröner by the late Mr. Fukui Shizuo in exchange of photos of former Imperial German Navy and Kriegsmarine. One part of Mr. Gröner's collection is available in the Library of Contemporary History at Stuttgart but a remarkable number 'disappeared' before the collection was sold by Mrs Hilde Gröner to Prof. Jürgen Rohwer, then director of the library. However, it is also printed in Fukui Shizuo Japanese Naval Vessels Illustrated, 1869-1945, *Vol. 2 'Cruisers, Corvettes & Sloops', p.36, (Bestsellers Publishing Co. Chiyoda-ku, Kanda Jimbocho 2-10 Tokyo, 1980 and Fukui Shizuo Collection* Japanese Naval Vessels 1869-1945, *p.150, same publisher, 1994).*

Nagasaki and Talien Bay and sortied that harbour on 5 November to arrive at Saddle Group outside the mouth of Yangtze on the 9th, Wusung on the 12th, and sortied again on the 25th. The ships arrived at Nagasaki on 28 November[79] and anchored at Kobe on the 13th via Kagoshima,[80] left Kobe on the 18th and arrived at Shinagawa on the 20th.

In 1890 *Takachiho* remained as the flagship of the Standing Fleet. On 25 March, both ships participated in the Great Manoeuvre around Tateyama by the co-operation of the Imperial Japanese Army and the IJN. On 8 April the manoeuvre forces joined at Kobe. On the 13th the ship was reviewed in the presence of the Emperor. Afterwards the Emperor went to Ujina and returned to Yokohama on 7 May.

Naniwa sortied from Yokohama on 8 June and navigated along the east coast of Korea and then the Vladivostok area, returning to Shinagawa on 6 July.

Takachiho sortied on 4 August and carried out firing practice in Aomori Bay on the 20th. *Naniwa* arrived at Aomori on 10 September and met the fleet. On 4 October the ships sortied into the Inland Sea and arrived at Shinagawea on the 10th. Afterwards they carried out firing practice near Tokyo Bay and came back to Shinagawa on 8 November. On 23 August both ships were re-classified as 'Warships which are good for battle and high sea navigation' (*Dai-ichi Shu*).

In 1891 *Takachiho* was still the flagship of the Standing Fleet.

Naniwa sortied from Yokosuka on 2 July with the fleet, arrived at Genzan on 26 August, sortied on the 18th and arrived at Maizuru on the 29th. Later she visited Aomori, Hashidate, Yamada, Ofuna, Watori and returned to Shinagawa on 28 December.

Takachiho sortied from Shinagawa on 5 August, arrived at Wei-hai-wei on the 13th, Port Arthur on the 17th and navigated to Taku (the C-in-C Arichi Shinanojo went to Tientsin to see Viceroy Li Hung-chang), sortied on the 23rd and arrived at Maizuru on the 29th via Chifu and Pusan. She sortied again on 12 September, and, after the Futami Bay Accident[81] on 4 October, she towed *Tsukuba* and arrived at Kure on the 22nd, Shinagawa on the 31st.

Both ships sortied from Shinagawa on 2 February 1892 for Hong Kong via Kobe, Nagasaki and arrived there on the 19th, sortied on the 17th to come to Sasebo on 17 March via Malaga Okinawa, Oshima. Weighed anchor at Nagasaki on 30 March and participated in the 'Great Manoeuvre' off Kyushu, returning to Shinagawa on 25 July.

Naniwa became the flagship of the Standing Fleet on 25 July and *Takachiho* was classified as reserve ship on 18 October due to being repaired.

Naniwa sortied Shinagawa on 10 October and navigated to Aomori, Hashidate, Maizuru, Sasebo, Hakata, Nagasaki to return to Shinagawa on 15 November.

Naniwa sortied from Yokosuka on 4 February 1893 and arrived at Hawaii on the 23rd for the protection of the Japanese living there. She finished this service in May and

Photo 12. *A portrait of Captain Wada Kensuke who commanded* Naniwa *all through the Russo-Japanese War (a portrait of Captain Mori Ichibei, the commander of* Takachiho, *is lacking). Reproduced from 'The Russo-Japanese War Fully Illustrated' No. 4, September 1904, p.507 (Kinkodo Shoseki Kabiushiki Kaisha, Honcho, Nihonbashiku, Tokyo, 1904).*

The actions of both ships in the Russo-Japanese War are described very well in Sir Julian Stafford Corbett's Maritime Operations In The Russo-Japanese War, *(reprinted by USNIP, Annapolis, Maryland and Naval War College Press, Newport, Rhode Island, 1994), unfortunately without the numerous maps and charts of the confidential British edition of 1914. Corbett had access to both official and confidential histories of the Russo-Japanese War and also to the official Russian one. Both official histories were also translated into German but for Curt Baron von Maltzahn who sometimes severely criticises the official histories (the Japanese more than the Russian one) in his three-volume* Der Seekrieg zwischen Rußland und Japan 1904 bis 1905 *(The War At Sea Between Russia And Japan 1904 to 1905, Mittler und Sohn, Berlin, 1914) the confidential Japanese history was not available so that the conclusions of Corbett have to be regarded as the definitive ones. It may also be of some interest to note that Captain (later Rear Admiral) Togo Kichitaro's (a nephew of Admiral Togo Heihachiro) book* The Naval Battles Of The Russo-Japanese War, *(Gogakukyokwai, Tokyo, 1907), does not contain some of the 'failures' of the official Japanese version criticised by Corbett for the Battle off Ulsan (compare p.442 of Vol. 1 of* Maritime Operations *and p.32 of* The Naval Battles*).*

The sinking of the Russian armoured cruiser Rurik, *already crippled by the Second Division (four armoured cruisers commanded by Rear Admiral Misu Sotaro) of Vice Admiral Kamimura Hikonojo's Second Fleet, is described in Captain Togo's book, pp.32-44 by both the Japanese and the Russian side and pp.444-45 in Vol. 1 of the Corbett history. Vol. 4 of* The Russo-Japanese War Fully Illustrated, *deals with this action on pp.504-510. The names of the two war deeds mentioned on p.445 of Corbett's Vol. 1 may be found on p.33 of Togo's book, those of the wounded officers on p.509 of Vol. 4 of* The Russo-Japanese War *while the 15 ratings wounded are not individually listed.*

In sharp contrast to the cruel behaviour of Rear Admiral Iessen's Vladivostok-based cruisers when they sank the Japanese troop transports Hitachi Maru *and* Sado Maru *the Japanese cruisers* Naniwa, Takachiho, Niitaka, Tsushima, Chiyoda *and TB of the 9th and 14th Divisions rescued 625 officers and ratings out of a complement of 825 (*Naniwa *took aboard four officers and 129 bluejackets). However, as stated on p.540 of* The Russo-Japanese War *seven of the 16 officers were wounded with 169 more midshipmen, warrant officers and bluejackets.*

The fierce resistance of the Rurik *was 'worth of undying admiration' and caused Vice Admiral Uriu's orders to rescue as many of the helpless men as possible as soon as the bow of the armoured cruiser, laying nearly vertical in the water, went down on 14 August 1904 at 10:40 about 45 miles from Ulsan.*

The finishing of Rurik *was the highlight of the actions by both 20-year-old protected cruisers in the Russo-Japanese War.*

returned to Japan, and afterwards cruised together with the fleet, including her sister ship.

Takachiho was enrolled in the fleet on 21 April. She sortied from Shinagawa on 1 June and arrived at Chifu on 4 July. She departed on the 7th to Taku and arrived there on the 10th. On the way there was the heavy fog and she used the fog signal. The C-in-C Ito Yuko visited the Viceroy. She sortied on the 13th and came to Chempulpo on the 19th via Chifu, and Haiyang Island.[82] Then, she sortied on the 17th and arrived at Nagasaki on the 30th via Komun Island. She became the flagship of the Standing Fleet on 13 August and came to Vladivostok on the 26th via Pusan and Wonsan. She met *Naniwa* before the departure on the 30th and the ships arrived at Shinagawa on 8 November via Otaru, Chishima Island, Miyako Bay and Moji.

Then *Naniwa* sortied from Yokosuka on 17 November and arrived at Honolulu on 2 December (sortied on 2 April 1894 and came back to Yokosuka on the 15th).

Takachiho sortied from Yokosuka on 6 March 1894 and arrived at Honolulu on the 21st to release her sister, stationed there since 2 December 1893.

Naniwa returned on 15 April and was enrolled in No. 1 Flying Squadron under the command of Rear Admiral Tsuboi Kozo on 19 July. On 25 July she participated in the Sea Battle off Phung-do, firing the first shot on the Japanese side in the then still undeclared Sino-Japanese War and later on that day sinking the British steamer *Kowshing*, navigating under the Chinese flag.[83] She was commanded by Captain (later full Admiral) Togo Heihachiro, the C-in-C of the Combined Fleet in the Russo-Japanese War.

Takachiho returned from Honolulu and arrived at Yokosuka on 10 July. Cadets departed her at Sasebo on the 18th. She was enrolled in the Main Squadron (*Hontai*) on the 22nd, and changed to the First Flying Squadron (*Daiichi Yugekitai*) about 30 July. At that time Captain Nomura Tadashi was her commanding officer (he had been appointed on 26 February and had taken over command early in March).

Both ships participated in the Sea Battle off Yalu (Battle of the Yellow Sea) on 17 September 1894 According to the *Confidential History of the Sino-Japanese War* complied by the Naval General Staff the ammunition consumed, damages due to hits and casualties of crews in this battle were as shown in Table 5.

In 1895 they participated in all naval operations (i.e. the attack of Wei-hai-wei which ended on 17 February)

Photo 13. *The Second Division of Vice Admiral Kamimura's Second Fleet anchoring in an unidentified bay. From right: armoured cruiser* Izumo, *(commander Captain Ijichi Sueyoshi) armoured cruiser* Azuma *(supposed commander Captain Fujii Koichi), armoured cruiser* Iwate *(commander Captain Taketomi Sadakuni) and armoured cruiser* Tokiwa *(supposed commander Yoshimatsu Shigetaro) far behind of armoured cruiser* Azuma. *The Second Division was commanded by Rear Admiral Misu Sotaro, later Admiral, Baron and vice-chief of the Navy General Staff. The Chief of Staff was Captain Kato Tomosaburo, later Admiral, Navy Minister and Premier and the senior staff officer was Commander Sato Tetsuraro, the 'father of the Japanese naval strategy'.*

and also the Taiwan campaign (including the occupation of Pescadores Island). For the latter campaign they sortied from Sasebo on 15 March 1895. At first they escorted Army troops, then fired at enemy batteries in Pescadores Island and Taiwan, and dispatched landing forces. *Takachiho* returned to Nagasaki on 10 July and was excluded from the Standing Fleet on the 18th. *Naniwa* returned to Yokosuka on 20 October and retired from the Standing Fleet on 10 November.

In 1896 both ships were mainly in repair and conversion.

In 1897 *Naniwa* sortied from Yokosuka on 20 April for a training cruise to Hawaii and returned on 26 September.

In 1898 both ships were classified to 2nd class cruisers (*Dai-ni to Junyokan*) on 21 March. This was the first legal classification of the IJN's ship kinds. To obtain information on and impressions of the American-Spanish War, *Naniwa* sortied Sasebo on 3 May and returned on 28 August.

In 1899 *Takachiho* guarded Taiwan and the South China coast. *Naniwa* saluted German Fleet Commander Prince Heinrich at Yokohama on 29 June.

In 1900 *Takachiho* sortied Sasebo on 14 August due to the Amoi Incident and returned on 18 October.

In 1901 *Naniwa* was in North China waters till May (since December 1900).

In 1902 *Takachiho* changed her home port to Yokosuka Naval Station (Chinjufu) from her original Sasebo Naval Station on 1 April.

In 1904-05, in the Russo-Japanese War, the ships were already old and fought in the 'second line'. Both were enrolled in the Fourth Division of the Second Fleet, the *Naniwa* flying Rear-Admiral Uryu Sotokichi's flag.

From 7 to 16 January 1904 *Takachiho* was fitted for minelaying in Kure Navy Yard.

On 9 February 1904 they fought against the Russian cruiser *Varjag* at Chemulpo (Inchon) which retreated to the port and destroyed herself. It is said that *Takachiho* laid some mines off Chemulpo.

Then, they attacked Port Arthur on 10 March, and left the Korean West coast on 16 April to arrive at Chinhae on the 18th. The *Takachiho* loaded 24 mines from *Nikko Maru* on the 19th and both ships sortied on the 20th for Vladivostok, arriving there on the 29th, and the *Takachiho* laid the mines off the entrances. They arrived at Tsushima on 8 May.

On 14 August 1904 they fought against the Russian Vladaivostok cruisers at Ulsan but were late and were left to sink the crippled *Rurik*. Both ships sighted the *Rurik* at 08:30 and began to fire at her at 6,800m to 3,500m. After a while *Rurik* became silent, so they ceased fire at 10:05. The *Rurik* disappeared completely at 10:42 and both ships began to rescue survivors.

On 27-28 May 1905 at the Battle of Tsushima they operated at the rear of the main battle line and fired at Russian cruisers, destroyers or transports in the afternoon. The *Naniwa* was hit below the waterline at about 17:00

Table 5: *PROJECTILES FIRED AT THE BATTLE OF THE YELLOW SEA, 17 SEPTEMBER 1894*

Name	Projectiles Fired						Damage		Personnel Losses	
	26cm	15cm	57mm	47mm	25.4mm	11mm	Hits	Grade	Dead	Wounded
Naniwa	33	154	258	–	1,084 (!)	1,084 (!)	9	Small	0	2
Takachiho	22	89	–	155	1,899	401	5	Small	1	2

Note: Mr. Takasu doesn't believe that *Naniwa* fired the same number of rounds from her 25.4mm and 11mm MG. He points out that, despite the official nature of the *Confidential History of the Sino-Japanese War*, the work is often not trustworthy. However, no source of a more detailed nature is at present known.

and had some water inrush. After emergency repair she was able to chase the enemy again and ceased fire at 18:50.

In 1906 *Naniwa* belonged to the Second Fleet from March to November and operated off the coasts of Korea and China. *Takachiho* belonged to South China Fleet (*Nanshin Kantai*) and operated in South China.

In 1907 *Naniwa* was also enrolled in the South China Fleet in May. Her sister *Takachiho* operated in Shaghai and Foochoo (Fuchow) and retired from that fleet on 13 June.

In 1908 *Naniwa* was also excluded from that fleet on 23 June. Afterwards both ships participated the 'Grand Manoeuvre' under the First Fleet in October.

In 1909 *Naniwa* was a reserve ship and *Takachiho* became submarine deport ship in April. Then she must have been overhauled.

In 1910 the status of *Naniwa* remained unchanged and also *Takachiho* was used as depot ships for the IJN's young submarine force.

In 1911 *Naniwa* made survey operations and acted as a fishery guarding ship in the North Pacific from March to October. The *Takachiho* must have been under conversion to minelayer[84] in Yokosuka NY in the first half of the year and then operated as training ship for the Underwater Weapon School (*Kaigun Surai Gakko*).

In 1912 the *Naniwa* was designated to Guard and Survey Ship on 1 April and operated as a fishery guarding ship in the North Pacific. Due to strong fog she ran on to a reef off Drotona Island[85] belonging to Uruppu in the Kurile Islands on 26 June and, after beaching, sank completely on 18 July.[86] Stricken from the register of Imperial Japanese Warships on 5 August the wreck was sold and handed over on 26 June 1913.

Takachiho was re-classified as 'Second Class Coast Defence Ship' (*Dai-ni to Kaibokan*) on 28 August 1912. Otherwise she must have used for the same tasks as in 1911.

In 1913 *Takachiho* must have continued the co-operation with Underwater Weapon School and practised minelaying.

This must have also been her task in 1914[87] but on 8 August Japan declared war on Germany and the following day she was ordered to take on mines and practised this by loading 120 at Yokosuka and again at Sasebo. The Second Fleet, to which *Takachiho* belonged, sortied from Sasebo on the 23rd. After cutting the submarine cables between Tsingtao and Shanghai and Tsingtao and Chifu the ships escorted the convoy transporting the troops from Japan to conquer Germany's only colony in China. Late on 18 October *Takachiho* was torpedoed by the German torpedo boat S-90 off Tsingtao (Kiachow Bay[88]) and sank quickly through the explosion of her mines. Therefore, personnel losses were exceptionally high. She was stricken from the register of Imperial Japanese Warships on 29 October.

Figure 14. A contemporary artist's impression of the crippling of Rurik *by the Japanese Second Division. At that time* Naniwa *and* Takachiho *were stationed outside of the firing line and approached* Rurik *when the Japanese armoured cruiser chased the Russian armoured cruisers* Rossia *and* Gromoboi. Takachiho *began firing about 08:30 and until the sinking of the* Rurik *both ships expended 650 15.2cm shells. (Figures 13 and 14 were reproduced from 'The Russo-Japanese War Fully Illustrated' No. 4, September 1904).*

Table 6: *Summarisation of Important Technical Data*

Type	Protected Cruiser (protective deck 51mm at flat, 76.2mm at slopes)
Designer of hull	W H White
Builder of hull	Armstrong, Mitchell, and Co., Ltd., Newcastle-on-Tyne
Displacement	3,708 tons
Dimensions	91.44m (Lpp) x 14.02m (Bmoulded) x 5.64m (draught)
Characteristics	High freeboard, moderate ram, two military masts, one funnel, each one main gun mounted on centreline directly fore and aft of the superstructure, each three secondary guns mounted on sponsons amidships
Type of main engine	2-horizontal, direct-acting, two cylinder double expansion steam engine
Builder of main engine	R and W Hawthorn
Boiler	6-low double-ended cylindrical
Performance	7,500hp (designed with forced draught), *Naniwa* 7,235 IHP = 18.72 knots; *Takachiho* 7,604 IHP = 18.77 knots
Propeller	Twin screw; diameter 4.27m, pitch 5.64m
Coal	350 tons (normal), 800 tons (max)
Radius	About 9,000 miles at 13 knots with maximum load
Armament (as built)	2-35cal 26cm Krupp; 6-35cal 15cm Krupp; 2-57mm Nordenfelt QF (*Naniwa*); 2-heavy 47mm Hotchkiss QF (*Takachiho*); 10-25.4mm quadruple type Nordenfelt MG, 4-11mm ten-barrelled Gatling MG; 4-35.6cm Schwartzkopff TT; 4-Gramme type searchlights; 4-Gramme type electric generators

Notes:

1 The hydraulic Armstrong type three-cylinder engine for training the 80-Year Type 35cal 26cm Krupp main guns was situated below the protective deck. The movement was transmitted via a vertical turning shaft and gun carriage and gun were trained together by a toothed gear arrangement until the final point (120° to either side from the centreline; each 60° left and right to the aft were dead angles) was obtained.

2 To add some more data of the main gun: the weight of the barrel amounted to 27.7tons; the elevation and depressing angles were +14° to –5°, the loading angle was fixed at 0° horizontal; the recoil was regulated by Vavasseur compressors; the grooves made one turn in 25cal; the length of the shell was 1.04m (4cal); the propellant was Type 82-Year brown coloured hexagonal powder and at 2,000m distance a 433mm thick iron plate was pierced.

3 According to *All The World's Fighting Ships 1860-1905*, (Conway Maritime Press: London, 1979), p.226, there was a cellular double bottom which could be flooded to adjust trim for the operation of the guns. However, this statement could not be verified by Japanese sources. Also, there is doubt that the wing passages (viz. drawing of midship section) below the protective deck abreast the machinery spaces were used as coal bunkers to afford additional protection

Acknowledgements

This monograph could not have been written without the outstanding help of former Rear Admiral (ret.) JMSDF Takasu Koichi. Having special knowledge of the IJN in Meiji period as the fruits of long-time research work, he contributed a wealth of information taken from official documents and semi-official publications in the Historical Section of JMSDF that otherwise could not have been explored. The late Mr. Takasu kindly answered numerous questions and read both the original draft and the revised one, gave invaluable advice and offered opinions which resulted in still more revisions. His suggestions, continuously received in the course of writing this and other several manuscripts, provided the necessary encouragement not to give up but to complete this article.

Every error still included is due to my mistaken understanding and insufficient professionalism and solely my responsibility

Notes:

1 At that time *Kobusho* (Ministry of Industry) still managed Nagasaki and Hyogo shipyards though Nagasaki was lent to Mitsubishi in July 1884 and Hyogo was lent to Kawasaki to become Mitsubishi Nagasaki Shiyard and Kawasaki Kobe Shipyard respectively. Navy Yard (NY) is the equivalent to the Japanese *Kaigun Kosho* but this status (comparable also to the German '*Marinearsenal*') was not effective before 10 November 1903 and before that several names were used for the Yokosuka plant from the end of the Bakumatsu period until that date. In order to avoid confusion NY will be used uniformly.

2 *Katsuragi* (1st generation) and *Musashi* (2nd generation) were composite (wood-iron) ships with keel, frames, beams and so on made of iron, wooden skin, and sheathed. The third sister, *Yamato*, was laid down in E C Kirby's shipyard at Onohama on 23 November 1883. As Kirby committed suicide by pistol on 10 December 1883, the Yokohama Branch of Hongkong - Shanghai Bank which was Kirby's creditor solicited Navy Ministry for the purchase of his shipyard. So his works became Onohama *Kaigun Zosenjo* (Shipyard) on 25 January 1884 and continued to build the *Yamato*.

3 This tendency almost brought about the exclusion of the armoured ship for a while

4 According to Brassey's *The British Navy*, 3, p.546 Sir William Armstrong had recommended to build large numbers of small, speedy, and heavily armed ships to the Committee on Designs for Ships of War already in 1871 because armour could not secure invulnerability in view of improvements of guns, projectiles and underwater weapons and, hence, should be abandoned, except a few particular positions and compensated for by watertight subdivision. The fundamental princi-

ple underlying this idea was, to some degree at least, comparable to the later developed idea of the French Navy's *la jeune école* under the leadership of Admiral Aube, replacing gun power by torpedo power and substituting three protected cruisers by a much larger number of smaller but faster and quicker manoeuvring torpedo boats which, in a diversified attack, should sink an armourclad by destroying its unprotected underwater hull with their 'devil's weapon'.

5 This is the English spelling of the Chinese name *Chen-yüan*, the Japanese reading is *Chin'en*. When she became a war prize on 17 February 1895 the IJN did not change the name. They must have followed the Royal Navy's fashion, which did not change the spelling of captured ship's names but gave them English reading.

6 All three vessels were 1st generation ships.

7 At that time the French influence upon ship design and construction was still remarkable in Japan and even after that time there was a period (from about 1885 to about 1890) in which French ideas were predominant until before the Sino-Japanese War (1894-95), the change to British design and construction techniques was eventually taken. This shift was influenced by the poor offensive power of *Sankeikan* (*Matsushima* class), the loss of the cruiser *Unebi* on her transfer cruise to Japan and the sinking of the despatch vessel *Chishima* by collision with the steamer *Ravenna* in the Inland Sea.

8 When Captain John Ingles RN, was in Japan (from about 20 October 1887 to the middle of October 1893) his opinion about these ships, in 1887, was 'the best fighting ships, either 'offensive' or 'defensive' it is possible to have'. According to his view, the ship type represented by *Naniwa* class was the most efficient and destructive fighting ship of the day for the IJN and therefore recommended the possession of ten ships of this class to form a cruiser fleet which was to be bolstered with a large number of small gunboats. In 1889 the C-in-C of the British China Fleet still found the *Naniwa* class vastly superior to his ships in many respects and the purchase of the drawings of this class from Armstrong by the USN furnishes another proof of the opinion that they were perhaps the finest ships of their type in the world.

9 The torpedo-gear of Yarrow type torpedo launches built during the 1870s has been described in a contemporary source as follows 'When the pole (torpedo-spar) is out to its fullest extent it projects 25ft (7.62m) from the bow, and the torpedo itself is 10ft (3.48m) below the surface of the water'.

10 This factor imperative for obtaining favourable tactical positions or escaping superior enemies and a great number of small and smaller units were to secure the defensive power hitherto manifested in the thick armour of the battleship.

11 This, in fact, was a great misunderstanding of the primary objective in naval warfare, namely to obtain and secure control of the sea by the annihilation of the enemy's naval force.

12 This refers to the theories of the *la jeune école* as expressed in the books *Charmes Les Torpilleurs Autonomes* and *La Reform de la Marine* only and does exclude the later countermeasures in the construction of capital ships such as double and triple bottoms, longitudinal torpedo bulkheads, narrow watertight subdivision and so on.

13 If this is compared to Armstrongs conviction the characteristics mentioned in the 'Introduction' as (1) and (3) were incorporated in full while with regard to protection the second part (indirect protection) was taken up only. By the irony of fate the latter item was obtained sufficiently but speed and offensive power failed due to technical obstacles and defective design.

14 The *Kaigun Kansei Honbu* was officially established on 20 March 1900 as a central organisation outside the Navy Ministry. Before that date the section about ship design, construction, maintenance of all naval vessels and naval weapons (in the broadest sense) belonged to numerous organisations as follows (1) Warship Building Bureau (*Zosenkyoku*, 15 August 1871 to 12 October 1872, (2) Warship Office (*Shusenryo*, 13 October 1872 to 30 August 1876, (3) Warship Bureau (*Shusenkyoku*, 31 August 1876 to 29 January 1886), (4) Warship Administration Bureau (*Kanseikyoku*, 30 January 1886 to 6 March 1889), (5) No. 2 Bureau (*Dai Ni Kyoku*, 7 March 1889 to 19 March 1893), (6) Bureau for Military Affairs (*Gunmukyoku*, 20 March 1893 to 19 March 1900) Here, it will always be called Naval Technical Department in order to avoid confusion. It was comparable to the Bureau of Ships of the USN.

15 *History of IJN Systems* (*Kaigun Seido Enkaku*), Vol. 8, compiled as confidential books in 1941 and reprinted (by Hara Shobo) in 1971. By the way, this proposal led to the order of armoured torpedo boat *Kotoka* to Yarrow but the remainder of the armoured torpedo boat flotilla was suspended, accepting the advice of the French naval architect Louis Emile Bertin, hired as adviser of the Navy Ministry from February 1886 for four years.

16 In a personal letter of 28 October 2000 Mr. Takasu particularly stressed this fact and pointed out that the 'young school' did not influence the 1883 Program. He also recommended to delete this paragraph in order to avoid confusion among readers. However, I believe to have sufficiently made clear that the IJN maintained their official policy unswervingly and proposed not to delete it in order to show the considerable difference between the points of view of technicians and tacticians around that time.

17 President's address to the meeting of the Institution of Civil Engineers, but the origin of this idea dates back as far as 1871 as reported later by Lord Brassey.

18 In 1882 the IJN wanted to purchase the Peruvian warships *Socrates* and *Diogenes* then under construction in Germany. The contract of purchasing these ships under guaranteed speed of 15kts was signed on 24 January 1883. Then the foremost Japanese naval architect Saso Sachu (later Vice Admiral, naval constructor) left Yokohama for London to supervise their final fitting. The trials of the *Diogenes* were held at Stokes Bay on 23 February but the result averaged 14.25kts, which was reported to Navy Ministry. Saso arrived in London on 12 March and inspected both ships at once and reported that they were only dispatch vessels. Then he visited the Walker Yard to survey the Chilean *Arturo Prat* and he saw the *Esmeralda* on the slipway. When he looked at the latter ship he could understand the rationality of her design philosophy and preferred her at once to the Peruvian *Socrates* and *Diogenes*. Basing on Saso's reports and recommendation to buy her instead, Navy Ministry Kawamura took two actions on 26 March. First, he requested Foreign Minister to cancel the contract of Peruvian ships due to the lack of guaranteed speed and insufficient hull strength for the required armament. Second, he ordered Ito Toshiyoshi (later Rear

Admiral) and Saso to negotiate about the purchase of *Arturo Prat* (later *Tsukushi*) with Chile and petitioned Premier Sanjo Sanetomi to change to buy her on 1 May and got approval on 3rd. Then Kawamura decided to purchase the *Esmeralda* in June.

19 As will be described later, this was one of the reasons which led to the change of the heavy Krupp guns to lighter Armstrong QF guns in *Naniwa* and *Takachiho*.

20 This motion became known as the 'Fourth Naval Expansion Bill' in '*Kaigun Kansen Kakucho Enkaku*' (Outline of the Warship Expansion of the Navy' compiled by the General-Secretariat of the Navy Ministry (*Kaigun Daijin Kanbo*) in July 1904 but in '*Kaigun Gunbi Enkaku*' (Outline of the Armament of the Navy), compiled in 1922, these ordinal numbers of naval expansion were no more assigned.

The background of this motion was the Chinese order of armourclads from Germany. When *Fuso*, *Kongo*, and *Hiei* arrived in Japan in the middle of 1878 the IJN was superior to the Chinese Navy. When it was revealed that Chinese Navy had ordered two ironclads from the Vulcan Works, Stettin, the balance was destroyed and favor turned to Chinese Navy because the IJN had no expansion program since the construction of the above three ships had been admitted by providing extraordinary expenditures. In order to reverse this imbalance and turn the situation in favor of the IJN again the fourth bill was prepared.

21 It is very interesting to note that these 60 ships were not chosen from strategical/tactical viewpoints but from the personnel available for manning in those days. At that time the existing manpower available for crews was 480 officers and warrant officers and 4,569 petty officers and men. Assuming that an average of eight officers and warrant officers would belong to the crew of one ship, they could crew 60 ships. Assuming that a ship requires 150 petty officers and men on average to complete the complement, the existing personnel were for only about 30 ships or half of the demanded number, but the Naval Technical Department expected to recruit the remainder men in case of the outbreak of a war. In peace time 24 ships were planned to be on duty. Each 12 of them were to compose East Sea Fleet and West Sea Fleet, the other 36 ships being in reserve. Should the situation become critical, the crews would be recruited and each 12 ships were to be distributed to East, West, South, and North Sea Fleets and also the Expeditionary Fleet. Furthermore, 4 to 16 ships were to be transferred from the 'Sea Fleets' to the Expeditionary Fleet depending upon the circumstances. The term (20 years) of the proposed program was selected by then valid calculation of the service life of a ship.

22 About the second period was to be decided after the end of the first one. Other than this the construction of a shipyard was proposed to fulfil the goal of the first period because Yokosuka dockyard was so much engaged in the repair of domestic and foreign ships that even the completion of one warship each year was impossible. Another motion, dated also 20 December 1881, assigned the assistance of private shipyards and shipping lines for the supplementation of the naval forces by excellent mercantile ships and paved the way for building warships in entrepreneur-managed shipyards.

23 This was the total expenditure for 20 years summed up by 2,007,017 Yen yearly. This amount was the building cost of three ships of which hull and engines were estimated total 1.5 millions of Yen and armament 507,017 Yen. The estimation of hull and engine was averaged the actual costs of the foreign-built corvettes *Kongo* and *Hiei* and the domestic built sloops *Kaimon*, *Amagi* and the Imperial yacht *Jingei* (but the latter is somewhat doubtful) in round numbers.

24 This plan was likely to be based on an amateur idea. Irrespective of the unrealistic term and content Sanjo Sanetomi rejected this bill not for the reason of this idea but due to the financial problems. In those days financial priority was given to fostering the national resources and to liquidate the debt caused by Seinan War in 1877. Aside from non-realisation the real value of this motion was the impulse given to future naval expansion.

25 This amount of annual cost in silver was a par with 6,432,000 Yen of paper money as of 11 November 1882.

26 On 23 July the 'Seoul Incident' had taken place and by this *coup d'etat* China's strong influence upon Korea was revealed. The Office of the Premier (*Dajokan*) and Premier (*Dajo daijin*) Sanjo himself felt the crisis and perceived that the time was overripe to expand armament. This was the background to the Fifth Naval Expansion Programme.

27 The total expenses of Kawamura's original motion amounted to 32,160,00 Yen as warship construction expenses and the maintenance expenses in the eighth year (when the 48 ships were to be completed) amounted to 5,557,171 Yen 20 Sen. The building cost of a warship (1,800 tons. 200 men) was estimated at 670,000 Yen of silver while that of a gunboat (1,500ts, 17kts, 120 men) was calculated to be 487,000 Yen (also in silver). The estimated costs were higher than in the previous year because the hulls etc., were to be iron-built and the armament was to be strengthened by torpedo, Nordenfelt machine guns and searchlights. These expenses could not be paid by the hitherto opened revenues. Therefore the Finance Ministry calculated the increase of the national budget by 7,500,000 Yen per year by taxing alcohol and tobacco and declared the reduction of the annual warship construction costs to 3 millions of Yen. The period of the programme was not changed because eight years had been designated by the Office of the Premier for the following reason: The Emperor (*Tenno*) had declared in 1881 that the Diet was to be open in 1890. So the government had to open the budget for FY 1891 to the Diet and this procedure necessitated the completion of shipbuilding according to this programme before that FY, i.e. it had to end in FY 1890. The scheme reported by Finance Minister Matsukata to Prime Minister Sanjo on 26 December 1882 was as follows:

Fiscal Year	Ship-building	Ship Maintenance	Army	Total	Revenue
1883	3,000,000	500,000	1,740,000	5,240,000	7,500,000
1884	3,000,000	1,000,000	1,740,000	5,740,000	7,500,000
1885	3,000,000	1,500,000	2,340,000	6,840,000	7,500,000
1886	3,000,000	2,000,000	2,340,000	7,340,000	7,500,000
1887	3,000,000	2,500,000	2,340,000	7,840,000	7,500,000
1888	3,000,000	3,000,000	2,740,000	8,740,000	7,500,000
1889	3,000,000	3,500,000	2,340,000	8,840,000	7,500,000
1890	3,000,000	4,000,000	2,340,000	9,340,000	7,500,000
Grand Total	24,000,000	18,000,000	17,920,000	59,920,000	60,000,000

Note: Army expenses were funds for recruitment, construction of forts at Tokyo Bay etc.

Sanjo showed this scheme to Kawamura and ordered him

also to include in that amount the price of two Peruvian ships, which was 1,287,360 Yen of paper money (these were *Socrates* and *Diogenes* but as stated in footnote 18, purchase was not realised).

28 In addition, the average annual maintenance expenses for one new ship were estimated to be 115,386 Yen 30 Sen.

29 The Navy Ministry's planning was to distribute 48 ships to four Naval Stations and to take 12 ships in reserve. This could not be realised due to the reduction of the expenditures from 32 to 24 millions of Yen so that the number of ships had to be reduced accordingly. Before the policy of naval expansion was adopted, Navy Ministry had already submitted the FY 1883 budget book to Finance Ministry, in which *Kansen Seizo Hi* (Warship and Ship Construction Expenses) was 330,000 Yen, *Kansen Shufuku Hi* (Warship and Ship Repair Expenses) 186,000 Yen. Kawamura proposed to add these 330,000 Yen to 'Matsukata's' 3 millions every year and this was approved by Sanjo on 13 February 1883. That is why the total of the new budget item *Gunkan Seizo Hi* (Warship Construction Expenses) amounted to 26,640,000 Yen estimated to be sufficient for the construction of 32 ships.

30 After the naval expansion began, there appeared successive proposals of revision of the programme such as new ironclad fleet, new torpedo fleets not including ironclads and the fleet which laid priority upon gunboat construction. See the proposals mentioned under the headline 'A Short Excursus...'. The 19 May 1884 proposal was for an 'ironclad fleet' and the 21 February 1885 one for a 'non-ironclad fleet'. Unfortunately, there is no description of the types of ironclads in the proposal but the cruiser and torpedo boats included in the second proposal were to be 1st class types faster than 17 kts as *Fuso*, *Naniwa* etc., 2nd class cruisers were faster than 15 kts of 2,500t with protective deck, 3rd class cruisers were faster than 13 kts similar to *Kongo*, *Hiei*, *Kaimon*, *Katsuragi*, *Tsukushi* etc, gun boats were to be faster than 11 kts. Torpedoes were to be fitted: 8 on 2nd class cruisers and armoured torpedo boats and 4 on 3rd class cruisers and 2nd class torpedo boats. In addition, there are indications that a Coast Defence Fleet (Gunboat fleet) was studied in the former half of 1884 but there seems that this plan was not completed. However, receiving the Navy Ministry's FY 1886 budget book the Finance Ministry could not secure the revenue for them.

A volcano on Krakatau Island in Indonesia erupted in August 1883. The eruptive smoke and ashes enveloped the Earth for three years, shutting off the sunshine, by which crops were damaged across the world. In Japan the influence of this catastrophe increased gradually. In 1886 Japan had to import some rice and cotton for the first time. Such being the case, sake and tobacco taxes could not be collected as expected by the Finance Ministry (footnote 27). If the Government continued the policy to appropriate this tax for naval expansion, the red ink of Warship Construction Expenses would rise above 10 million Yen in FY 1890. As for Finance Minister Matsukata himself, he could not give up naval expansion, because of security fears from the Royal Navy constructing a naval base near Japan, while Russia was watching for an opportunity to construct a naval base in Tsushima. Therefore he made up his mind, to give up tax and to raise a loan instead for carrying out the existing shipbuilding scheme.

On 22 December 1885 the Japanese Government shifted to the Cabinet System and in this system the FY was to begin on 1 April. On 23 March 1886 Matsukata reported the situation to new Premier Ito Hirobumi. As the Cabinet council agreed with him, he made up the plan of floating Naval Loan (*Kaigun Kosai*) and reported Ito on 3 May as follows:

'The balance of Warship Construction Expenses to be appropriated from FY 1886 is 16,736,508 Yen...In the budget of FY 1886, Warship Construction Expenses should be all deleted and instead the public loans of 17 million Yen should be raised from FY 1886 to 1888...'

This plan passed the Cabinet on 1 Jun and the act of *Kaigun Kosai* was promulgated on 12 Jun. This fund was called Special Expenses (*Betto Hi* in FY 1886 and *Tokubetsu Hi* from FY 1887) and some of this money was spent for the construction of *Naniwa* and *Takachiho* as shown in Table 2 and the actual payment of Warship Construction Expenses was partially transferred to the following FYs.

31 Reed, formerly the chief naval architect of the Royal Navy, had already designed and supervised the construction of the armoured frigate *Fuso* and the belted corvettes *Kongo* and *Hiei* and had visited Japan in 1879. The events in Korea also brought about the IJN's decision to adopt Whitehead torpedoes, rapid-firing machine guns, and searchlights.

32 Minister Mori of London reported to the Ministry of Foreign Affairs on 26 August 1882 that Chile was going to sell her for the total amount of £90,000 for the hull, machinery, and armament. The IJN took no action for her purchase at once, because priority was placed on the Peruvian cruisers *Diogenes* and *Socrates*.

33 The *Tsukushi* left Newcastle on 11 July and arrived at Yokohama on 19 September. She was commanded by J M James who had been hired in February to arrange the voyage of the Peruvian ships but he actually selected the crew for the *Tsukushi* and insured her. The handing over to Tokai Naval Station was finished on 5 November the between time being used for cleaning, inspection and introducing machinery and so on to the Japanese crew.

34 This was probably at the beginning of September.

35 The sending of the drawings of the 5,200ts type protected cruiser to London for inspection is uncertain.

36 Particulars of this design are dealt with in the author's unpublished manuscript 'Eight British-Built Japanese Pre-Dreadnought Battleships'.

37 This and other reports were made by telegraph by the name of the Minister of the Japanese Legation at London to Minister of Foreign Affairs at Tokyo via St. Petersburg and then were notified to the Navy Ministry.

38 Kawamura informed rather laconically 'Kotetsukan will be changed to *Mersey* class' and in the budget the ships were designated as '*Kotetsukan Ko Go* and *Kôtetsukan Otsu Go*' even if they were not armourclads but protected cruisers.

39 When *Fuso*, *Kongo* and *Hiei* were under construction in British shipyards some students were also ordered to 'supervise' their construction. The purpose was to see and learn actual construction and naval architecture and other sciences in Britain.

40 This was reported in *Japan Weekly Mail*, 13 July 1886.

41 The reason why only this ship was transferred by a Japanese crew is explained by Mr. Takasu that the young IJN could not afford skilled officers and men for bringing two ships to Japan at the same time, without having to lay up active ships.

42 See the photograph taken a few days before launching.

43 The steering gear was of the Elswick pattern and could be operated either hydraulic or hand. Consequently, besides the hydraulic steering wheel there was also a hand-operated one placed in the wheel-house beneath the conning tower.

44 In case of necessity the ship boats could be armed with a 25.4mm Nordenfelt MG and there were also 2 torpedo launching devices (*Gyorai Hassha-kyo*, i.e. a frame work containing a torpedo, in case of launching it was lowered into water from the side of the boat) and 6 minesweeping gears (*Hansô Suirai*, i.e. this gear was composed of several mines, anchors, buoys, cables & etc. and was used aboard of launches or pinnaces to sweep areas in harbours suspected to be defended by mines. This 'countermine' was planted in a manner similar to laying controlled mines and fired electrically by pushing the firing switch) for demolishing enemy mines.

45 Besides the engine rooms, stokeholds, magazines and many other compartments below the protective deck, including the coal bunkers, were illuminated by incandescent lamps.

46 This defect led to the adoption of a thin side (belt) armour in the last group of the 'Elswick Cruisers'.

47 Mr. Takasu Koichi has published an excellent study in 'Ships of the World' (*Sekai no Kansen*' 6/2000 (No. 569), pp.108-113, entitled 'Japanese Protected Cruiser *Naniwa* & *Takachiho*: The Transition of Their Armaments' The following description relies heavily on this study and the correspondence in 1999 and 2000.

48 As stated before, the 2nd class cruiser *Mersey* of the Royal Navy was the template, but instead of the 15 ton main gun of this class the larger calibre Krupp gun was demanded under the premise that these ships had to fight a decisive battle against the Chinese armourclads.

49 *Teikoku Kaigun Kikan Shi* (History of Engines of Imperial Warships), the most authoritative Japanese source for engines, boilers, auxiliary machinery etc., known to the author, regrets that there are no data left and refers to Richard Sennet's *The Marine Steam Engine*, (London, Longmans, Green, and Co., 1882).

50 It must also be remembered that the application of hydraulic power in the middle of the 1870 was mainly due to Rendel.

51 In the purchase report of 20 January 1886 there are listed each 2 gun directors of improved type for *Naniwa*, *Takachiho*, and *Unebi*. These directors were installed not only for gun laying but also for director firing because the thick smoke developed at firing considerably hindered next aiming at local firing. Therefore director firing became popular in Western navies and the IJN wanted to adopt this system, too. It is supposed that Armstrong added the electric firing mechanism to the Krupp guns. According to the request of the commanding officer of *Naniwa* to C-in-C Yokosuka Naval Station on 9 March 1891, the electric firing circuit of primary batteries had been installed only for director firing and he wanted to expand it to independent firing because he feared that the time lag would critically affect hitting probability as the speed of the ships and also firing distance increased.

52 The Navy Ministry wanted the mounting of some Krupp guns of 15cm or 17cm calibre but White proposed to take six 15cm guns and the Ministry informed the agreement on 15 February 1884 to the supervisor in Britain. At that time Armstrong Co. also produced a trustworthy breech-loader and the supervisor, Rear Admiral Ito Toshiyoshi, sent a comparison table to Tokyo and recommended strongly to mount Armstrong guns but the Navy Ministry refused on the grounds not to extend the types of guns. However, Armstrong breech-loaders were mounted on the cruiser *Tsukushi* (ex *Arturo Prat*). It may be of interest to repeat that with the order to Ito to supervise the building work of later *Naniwa* the dispatch of supervisors (*Kantoku-kan*) was begun.

53 However, when *Naniwa* sortied for Japan these guns were not yet fitted and were transported by the cruiser *Unebi*, which departed Le Havre in October for Japan and were lost when this ship disappeared without a trace in the South China Sea. The guns were ordered again after the insurance money had been paid and were mounted in 1889 (exact date unknown, trial firing before installation took place on Etchujima proving ground in June 1889).

54 The Navy Ministry wanted the installation of 25.4mm Nordenfelt MG and ordered the investigation for mounting to the supervisor in April 1885. Being too heavy for fighting tops the mounting of smaller calibre MG was agreed and 8 units were ordered to Armstrong.

55 Naval student Ijuin Goro (later Vice Admiral, weapon specialist, inventor of 'Ijuin fuse') was involved in the armament of the *Naniwa* class. It was by his proposal in September 1884 that the TT were installed (in company with this the mounting of searchlights was also decided on). The mounting of TT required the alteration of one part of the hull by the installation of TT rooms fore and aft upon the protective deck, cutting of openings in the hull sides, mounting of torpedo hatches, and fitting of torpedo delivery stations on the upper deck and was the most extensive revision to be carried out during the construction. In the course of the change of the secondary guns to QF in 1895-96 the height of the TT had to be increased by 0.6m because owing to the increased draft their muzzles were only a few cm above the waterline in full load condition.

56 Taken from the author's unpublished manuscript 'Japanese Naval Powder and Explosives' whose compilation was possible by the generous supply of data about events in Meiji (1868-1912) and Taisho (1912-1926) eras by Mr. Takasu Koichi.

57 Mixture of nitrate, half-burnt charcoal, and sulphur by which the burning speed compared to black powder using pure charcoal was remarkably reduced and better controlled. In addition it was not as aggressive as the latter thus elongating the life of the barrel.

58 Saigo and his suite had left Yokohama for San Francisco on 13 July 1885. After visiting numerous towns in the USA he went to Europe for a trip through England, France, Germany etc. and returned to Japan on 30 June 1887.

59 The contract stipulated the delivery of all the equipment necessary for the production of powder, sending of engineers for the installation and teaching of manufacture process and so on.

60 While Blumenstein is mentioned in the *Werksarchiv* (Company Archive) of Krupp Co. (IXa 134) the name of the chief worker is not stated. It may be of interest to note that Krupp was involved again.

61 According to the report of the Naval Weapon Factory (*Kaigun Zoheisho*) #1 is for 35cal/26cm, 25cal/24cm, and 30cal/17cm, #2 (density 1.82) is for 'Old Type' (*Kyu shiki*) 21cm, 35cal/15cm, heavy 25cal/17cm, heavy 25cal/15cm and

light 25cal/12cm. #3 (density 1.79) is for 'Pre-80-Years-Type' (80 *nen zen shiki*) 17cm and 12cm and 'Old Type' 15cm, 12cm, and light 25cal/12cm and new type (*shin shiki*) 40pdr Armstrong gun (all, except the latter, were Krupp guns).

62 Armstrong (the IJN abbreviated this Co. as 'An') QF guns were adopted without the usual comparison test on the basis of the resolution of the Ordnance Board.

63 The change of the secondary guns was not as simple as described here and brought about several problems like strengthening of the gun foundations, alteration of the magazines and ammunition hoists, reduction of the coal storage for 71 tons, reduction of the ammunition for the main guns (to 70 shells from 100), landing of each one, anchor and minesweeping gear etc. The reductions and landings were, of course, to maintain the centre of gravity and metacentric height (GM). However, as stated before, draft increased and the position of TT had to be raised. The previously mentioned study of Mr. Takasu does deal with these problems in detail.

64 The armament of *Takachiho* became the same as *Naniwa* by the conversion stated below.

65 In the armament book of these ships, corrected up to 1900, the 11mm MG were deleted. In company with the renunciation of these MG the fighting tops were removed.

66 The experiments with the 8in gun mounted on the cruiser *Takasago* had brought about this result and had shown that the function as a rapid fire gun could not be maintained because both the weight of the shell and the powder bag were too heavy. In addition the erosion in the barrel of the 8in gun was excessive and in November 1899 the Naval General Staff had proposed the mounting of each 2-6in QF guns fore and aft in parallel. However, in company with the disappointing result of the *Takasago* experiment the Weapon Section (*Heikika*) pointed out the hindrance of the guns each other in parallel arrangement which might result also in the loss of the QF capability and also personnel losses. These were the backgrounds for the agreement to each one 6in gun (in company with the increase of the stock of ammunition to 150 from 130 per gun).

67 In spite of the reduction of the calibre of the main guns the total weight of shells to be fired in one minute was remarkable heavier due to the incomparable higher firing speed.

68 At that time still R and W Hawthorn.

69 This is Vice-Admiral Miyabara's data, *Teikoku Kaigun Kikan Shi* gives 1,450.8m^2.

70 At the trials Naval Attaché Lt. Cdr. Hatta Yujiro, Haji S., Miyabara Jiro (later Vice Admiral Eng., inventor of Miyabara watertube boiler) and acting captain J M James were aboard. In case of *Naniwa* Hatta did not participate but since the *Kaiko-in* (members bringing a warship to Japan) of *Naniwa* arrived at Newcastle after July 1885 some of them must have been aboard during the trials. It is also said that Japanese stokers operated the boilers.

71 A sketch of this gear, called *Kencho* (hanging) *Kido* (track) *Shiki* (type) *Fusetsu sochi* (laying equipment), is published in *Ships of the World* 6/2000, p.113.

72 In 1913 it was decided to install the bridge again due to serious communication difficulties.

73 Prince Yamashina-no-miya attended the launching ceremony.

74 Kaigun Shosa. After September 1897, when the rank of *Chusa* (Commander) was taken in the military rank system, Shosa was translated as Lt. Cdr.

75 At that time both ships were classified as 'Second class warship' (*Dai-ni to kan*).

76 If no name is given the event refers to both ships.

77 The *Jobi-sho-kantai* was organised by the Navy Minister's directive of 28 December 1885, and abolished and reorganised to Standing Fleet (*Jobi-kantai*) by Imperial edict of 22 July 1889 and enforced on 29 July.

78 In *Photo History of IJN Warships* (*Shashin Nihon Gunkan-Shi*) published by Umi-to-Sora sha in 1936, the names are written as 'Gasukebitchi Bay' and 'Odeshosu Ura'. Mr. Takasu was unable to locate these places on his map. Therefore they may be wrong. The author hopes that the names can be clarified with the help of readers.

79 This is in contrast to *Photo History*... but this data was checked by Mr. Takasu using the Bureau of Accounts 'Record for Addition of Allowance' which was complied by that Bureau in order to clarify the additional pay for crews in foreign voyage. In addition, *Takachiho* reported to have conducted outrigger torpedo practice off Nagasaki on 29 and 30 November.

80 *Takachiho* reported the launching of fish torpedoes off Kagoshima on 6, 7, and 9 December.

81 When the *Takachiho* was at Aomori, she received the report that that *Tsukuba* had damaged her bottom and screw on account of a heavy storm at Futami Bay, Sadoshima. So, the C-in-C moved his flag to *Naniwa* and *Takachiho* left Aomori for Futami Bay. She arrived there on 4 October and departed on the 13th, towing *Tsukuba* for Kure for repair.

82 This group of islands became famous neighboring the area of the Battle off Yalu and were also used as base of the Japanese Combined Fleet in the Russo-Japanese War.

83 The sinking caused a sensation and it took some time until it was accepted to be in conformity of international law, i.e. within the right of Captain Togo.

84 The conversion of *Takachiho* was classified a military secret and the very few existing records (examined by Mr. Takasu) do not provide a clear picture what has done and when. The fact that she was a minelayer was also concealed by the reclassification as coast defence ship and her loss was explained in the contemporary naval magazine *Kaigun* (Navy) by touching a mine from an enemy mine barrage and sunk by subsequent mine detonations, i.e. her use as minelayer was even concealed after the loss and Mr. Takasu, in his letter dated 26 November 2000 points out 'that the *Takachiho* was a minelayer was left unannounced as long as the IJN existed'.

85 North of Tokuma suido near Kitashima.

86 Jentschura Jung, Mickel *Die Japanischen Kriegsschiffe, 1869-1945*, p.166 give the position of beaching as 46°30'N/15°10'E.

87 There is a remarkable lack of data for the years 1910 to 1914. Again, the author hopes to be able to close numerous 'blank spots' with the assistance of readers.

88 The Japanese called this Koshu wan and the position of sinking is given as 5°S ca. 6sm W of Daikoto in Fukui Shizuo (et. al.), '*Nihon Kaigun Zen Kantei Shi-Shiryo Hen*' (*Complete History of All The Japanese Warships-Data Volume*; this volume complied by Nakagawa Tsutomu).

ARMSTRONGS' CONTRIBUTION TO THE NEW UNITED STATES NAVY

America's 'New Navy' began in 1883 with the so-called ABCD ships, three cruisers and a dispatch vessel. Their antiquated designs were much criticised, and the navy turned to Britain and Armstrongs for the latest practice. **Peter Brook**'s last article traces the influence of the Tyneside firm's cruiser drawings and, more than a decade later, the Navy's acquisition of actual Armstrong-built ships.

The great shipbuilding firm of Armstrongs built no warships directly for the USN but seven cruisers, all designed by Armstrongs, and four built by the firm, actually served in the navy. How did this come about? Three of these ships, *Charleston*, *Baltimore* and *Philadelphia*, were built in the United States using detailed drawings purchased from Armstrongs; these ships were important in shaping the 'New Navy' building programmes of the late 1880s. Two cruisers, *New Orleans* and *Albany*, were bought from Brazil just prior to the outbreak of the Spanish-American War of 1898, with the first playing an active part in operations in Cuban waters. The last pair, the Spanish *Isla de Cuba* and *Isla de Luzon*, were sunk at the battle of Manila Bay, 1 May 1898, subsequently salved and taken into US service as gunboats. Each of these ships will be looked at in more detail including design, construction and career and in particular the political infighting surrounding the first three.

Cruiser Designs for the US Navy

At the close of the American Civil War, the USN was, in terms of numbers of ships, one of the largest in the world. But by the early 1880s years of corruption, neglect and pork barrel politics had reduced the navy to a collection of unseaworthy monitors and full rigged wooden cruising vessels whose armament were mainly muzzle loaders. In his annual report for 1888, the Secretary of the Navy, William Whitney, a Democrat, described the fleet thus: 'In March 1885 the United States had no vessel of war which could have kept the seas for one week as against any first rate fighting power and was dependent on English manufacturers for the forging of guns, for armor and for secondary batteries'. The Secretary cancelled all foreign orders and encouraged domestic producers, notably the Bethlehem Iron Co to make steel by the Siemens process.[1] Whitney had taken over office from his Republican predecessor, William Chandler, in March 1885: at that time the first four modern warships built for the USN, three cruisers *Atlanta*, *Boston* and *Chicago* and the dispatch vessel *Dolphin* were under construction. In his first annual report of 1886 Whitney vigorously criticised their designs because they represented 'a simple abandonment on the part of the department of any attempt to reach the condition which should have been attained'. By this he meant high speed, regarding this as an indispensable feature of small cruisers.[2] All four designs were old fashioned, carrying sailing rig; all except *Chicago* had only single screws; *Chicago*'s machinery was remarkably similar to a vessel built 30 years previously, while her boilers were much the same as those powering sawmills in the backwoods. The cruisers had a partial deck covering boilers and machinery only and none could do better than 16 knots on trial.[3] Matters were made worse by the builder, John Roach of Chester, Pennsylvania, going bankrupt after *Dolphin* was criticised by Whitney as she failed to make her speed, her shaft broke on trials, her main gun could not be fired straight ahead and she could not withstand a heavy sea. Whitney deplored the granting of early payments to Roach, contrary to contract provisions, to save him from bankruptcy and said finally of *Dolphin* (earlier described as a 'pleasure boat rather than a dispatch (sic) boat') that if she proved strong enough 'other matters of dispute can probably be settled out of court'. The government then had to complete all the cruisers in poorly equipped Navy Yards with the result that the first pair were not commissioned until 1886 and *Chicago* in April 1889.[4] *Dolphin* was eventually accepted. Whitney decided to go abroad for further cruiser designs although domestic policy made it essential for them to be built in the United States. Interestingly his Republican predecessor in his last report had stated that 'great efforts had been made to gather plans of the latest work of eminent naval constructors of other navies'. In his 1886 report Whitney revealed that the department had purchased detailed drawings 'of the two most recent productions of Sir William Armstrong and Co' that is the *Naniwa* and *Takachiho*. A sub-committee of the 'Select Committee on Ordnance and Warships' had visited Armstrongs Yard in August 1885 when they must have had the opportunity of inspecting the almost complete *Naniwa* and were shown plans of a '19 knot steel protected cruiser'; this design, reproduced in the committee's report, was modified to form the basis of *Baltimore* and the hull form of *Philadelphia*. What the committee did not state was that the plans were based on Armstrongs submission for a competition for a first class cruiser for Spain; this competition was won by the Clydebank firm of Thomson later in 1885.[5] In November 1885 a contract was entered into for Armstrongs to supply the US government with designs and complete working drawings of hull and engines for two types. One 'was in all respects the same' as *Naniwa* and *Takachiho*, the other was 'to be based on a first class cruiser design submitted to Spain'; Humphrys Tennant were to supply the drawings of the engines of the latter ship.[6]

USS Charleston

The machinery plans were altered by Union Iron Works but *Charleston*'s first trials were a failure because of a number of design faults. The crosshead guides were solid steel while the slippers were of cast iron; this combination was satisfactory for slow running machinery but not for quick running ones. The air pumps were too small to provide a satisfactory vacuum and the thrust bearings overheated because of unsatisfactory design. After the first trials the necessary design changes were made and the second trial resulted in a speed of 18.2 knots which made her the fastest vessel in the US Navy. Although the IHP did not reach the contract figure the Bureau of Steam Navigation recommended that the ship be accepted as *Naniwa*'s IHP of 7650 was maintained for 30-45 minutes only, with steam pressure then falling off. Altogether it was concluded 'that she is a faster ship than the *Naniwa-Kan* and a more economical one to run'.[8]

Naniwa had mounted a 10in gun fore and aft but *Charleston* was, for cruiser work, more appropriately armed with 8in guns. *Charleston* was the first US warship to mount the 8in Mark 3, which fired a 260lb shell with a 43.8lb black powder charge giving a muzzle velocity of 2100ft/sec with a maximum range of 16,000 yards at an elevation of just over 20 degrees. Because of delays in delivery of the 8in *Charleston* was, for a short period, armed with two 6in guns in place of each of the 8in. A contemporary writer, an assistant engineer at the time of *Charleston's* trials, concluded that the machinery designs were those of *Etna*, an Italian built sister of *Giovanni Bausan* but with details drawn from that vessel, the Japanese *Naniwa* and probably the Chilean *Esmeralda*. Whether true or not *Charleston*'s weakest point was that, by the time of completion, triple expansion engines had completely replaced the compound type.[9]

Career

From 1890 to 1893 *Charleston* served as flagship of the Pacific Squadron and for a time of the Asiatic Squadron. While with the former she took part in the search for the

USS *Charleston* CRUISER NO.2

Builder	Union Iron Works San Francisco
Laid down	Jan 20 1887
Launched	July 24 1888
Trials	May 1889
Commissioned	Dec 26 1889
Designer	WH White
Displacement	3730 tons, (3580 tons on trials)
Dimensions	(Feet) 300pp (312 wl, 320 oa) x 46 x18ft 6in
	(Metres) 91.4pp (95.1 wl, 97.5 oa) x 14.02 x 5.64
Armament	2-8in BL 35 cal, 6-6in BL 30 cal, 4-6pdr RF, 2-3pdr RF, 2-1pdr RF
	4-37mm Hotchkiss revolving cannon, 2 Gatling machine guns
	Designed for 4-14in above water torpedo tubes but these were not fitted
Armour	Deck: 3½in on slopes, 2in on flat, 2in loading stations to 8in guns, 2in conning tower
Machinery	Two sets horizontal compound by Union Iron Works, Cylinders: 44in and 85in, Stroke 36in
	Six cylindrical boilers
Designed IHP	ND 5000, FD 7000
Designed speed	18 knots with FD
Trials	FD=6666 IHP=18.2 knots on a six hour trial
Coal	323 tons at normal draught, 622 tons full capacity
	Nominal radius of 7477 miles at 10 knots, 2960 miles at 16 knots
Complement	34 officers, 296 ratings, 30 marines
Metacentric Height	2.92ft at full load with displacement 4390 tons and draught 20ft 11in[7]

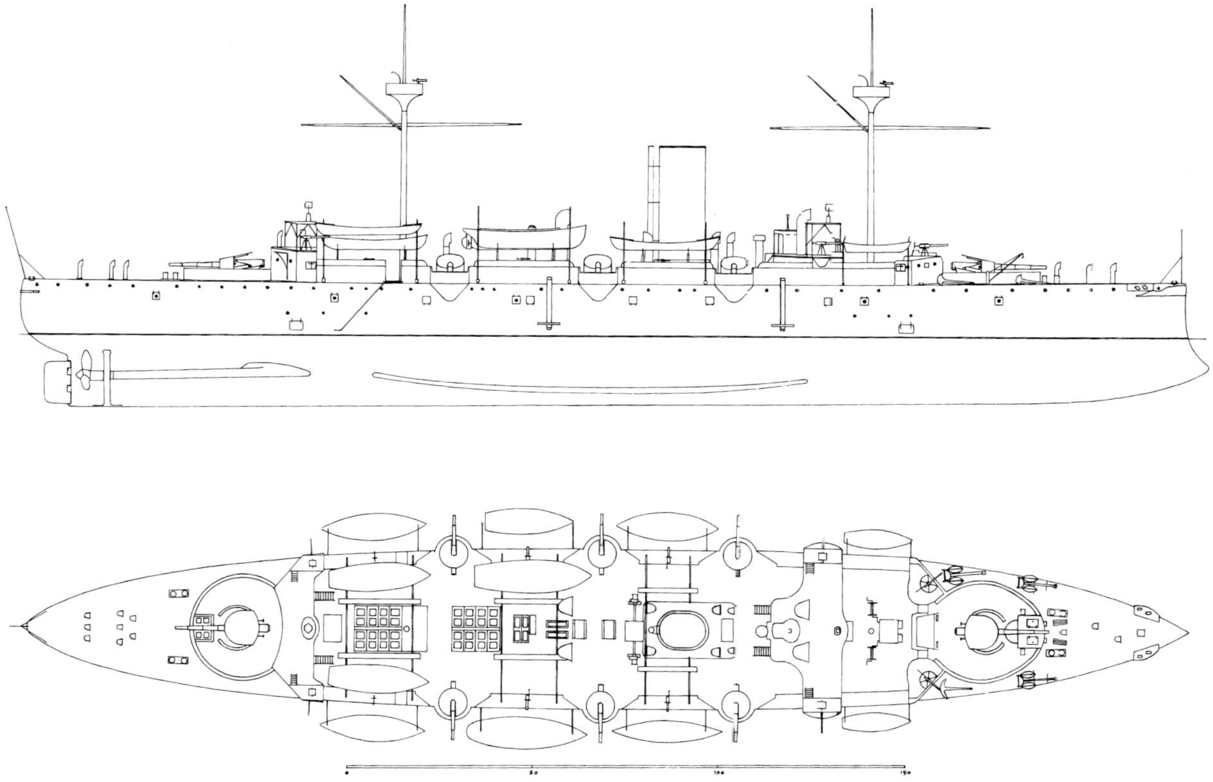

USS Charleston. *Side and Deck plans.* (Ian Sturton)

Chilean steamer *Itata* which had flouted neutrality laws during the course of the Chilean civil war of 1891. An interesting account of the voyage south through the Pacific was given by one of her engineers, Ira Hollis. Her coal was of poor quality and even under forced draught speed was only 14 knots; there was much trouble with leaky boiler tubes together with a number of other problems, so that by the end of the voyage speed had dropped to 12 knots.[10] After service in the Atlantic and Pacific over the next few years, *Charleston* was decommissioned in 1896. Recommissioned at the outbreak of the Spanish-American war she saw little service, although, *en route* to join Admiral Dewey's squadron in the Philippines she captured the island of Guam, meeting with no resistance. She took part in action against

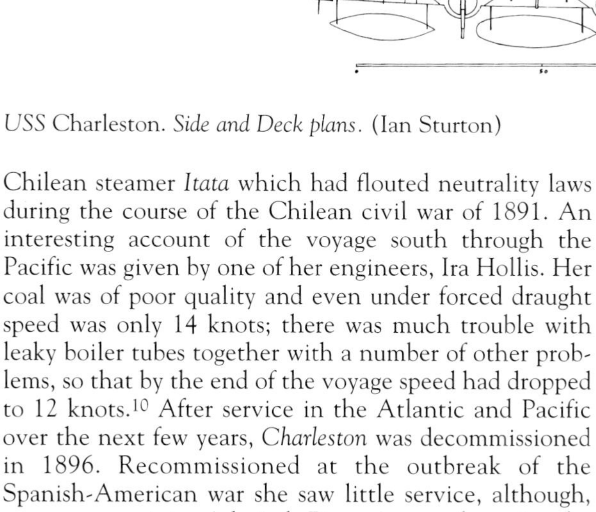

USS Charleston *at Hong Kong in 1898.*(USN NH 61039)

Filipino insurgents and while on this duty struck an uncharted reef 10 miles east of Camiguin Island on the morning of November 2 1899 becoming a total loss but thankfully with no casualties.[11]

USS Baltimore

The plans provided by Armstrongs were based on their unsuccessful design for Spain, while the machinery drawings were provided by Humphrys Tennant. The successful tender was made by Thomsons for the *Reina Regente* but this ship had low freeboard fore and aft and was grossly over weighted with four 9.4in guns mounted high up instead of the original 8in. The ship foundered near the Straits of Gibraltar in 1895 with the loss of all hands.[13] In contrast *Baltimore* had a high amidships freeboard of 14ft with a freeboard at bow and stern of about 24ft.[14] First trials were not a success but after relatively minor modifications such as extra bracing to the forecastle because of excessive vibration, overhauling the pumps and increasing the pitch of the propellers, the second trial, run in half a gale, was most satisfactory: the Secretary of the Navy waived any penalty due because of the designed IHP not having been attained. *Baltimore* was then the fastest cruiser in the USN and remained such until *Olympia* commissioned in 1895.[15] *Baltimore*'s first commander, Captain W S Schley in his initial report described her behaviour as most satisfactory, the workmanship excellent, stability good and generally that in

USS *Baltimore* CRUISER NO.3

Builder	Cramps Philadelphia
Laid Down	May 5 1887
Launched	Oct 9 1889
Trials	Jan 7 1889
Commissioned	Jan 7 1890
Designer	WH White
Displacement	4400 tons, designed, 4563 tons on trial
Dimensions	(Feet) 315pp (327ft 6in wl, 335 oa) x 48ft 6in x 19ft 6in
	(Metres) 96pp (99.8 wl, 102.1 oa) x 14.78 x 5.9
Armament	4-8in BL Mk 3 35cal, 6-6in BL 30 cal
	4-6pdr RF, 2-3pdr RF, 2-1pdr RF
	4-37mm Hotchkiss Revolving Cannon
	Designed for 5-14in above water torpedo tubes but not fitted
Armour	Deck: 4in slopes, 2½in flat, 2in shields to 8in guns, Conning Tower: 3in, 1in roof, 3in tube
Machinery	Two sets horizontal triple expansion by Cramps, Cylinders: 42, 60 and 94in, Stroke, 32in
	Four double ended, two single ended boilers
Designed IHP	ND 7500=17 knots, FD 10750=19 knots, final trials 4hr FD 10064=20.1 knots
Coal	400 tons designed, 1144 tons max, nominal radius of 12000 miles at 10 knots
	In service, 7212 miles at 10 knots in 1901 and 5300 miles at 10 knots in 1909
Metacentric Height	2.1ft at 4400 tons and 19.6ft draught
Complement	35 officers, 350 ratings[12]

her class there was no superior ship in the world. He did, however, make some criticisms, calling for better coaling facilities, modified ash chutes, improved davits, repositioning of the tops, better speaking tubes, more light quick firing guns and an improvement in the ammunition supply to the poop 8in guns. He had little to complain about the machinery except the pumps, main condensers and the draining system. He pointed out that in actual practice coal consumption was much greater than had been expected and in consequence the real steaming radius was smaller than calculated.[16]

Career

Baltimore's first duty was to convey the body of the great inventor, John Ericsson, back to his native Sweden. She then continued as flagship of the North Atlantic Squadron, afterwards serving in the Atlantic and Pacific being flagship of the Asiatic Squadron from 1893 to 1895. Decommissioned in 1896 but recommissioned in October of the following year, she was then stationed in Hawaii joining Commodore Dewey's squadron at Hong Kong just before the outbreak of the Spanish-American war, taking

USS Baltimore, anchored stern to the reef at Honolulu, c.1897-98. (USN NH 61697)

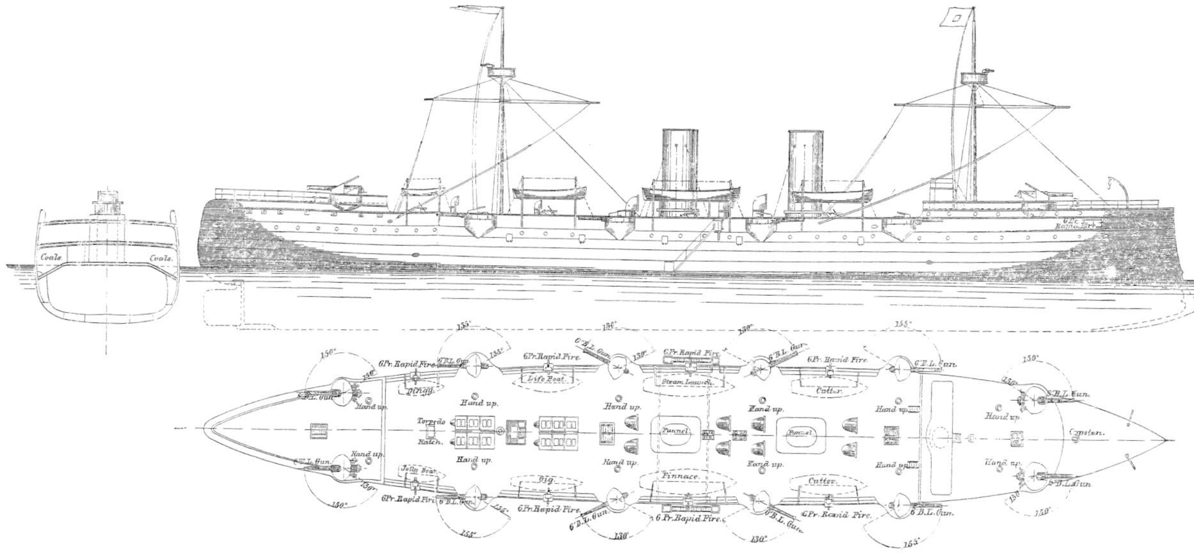

19 knot Protected Cruiser. (Report Select Committee)

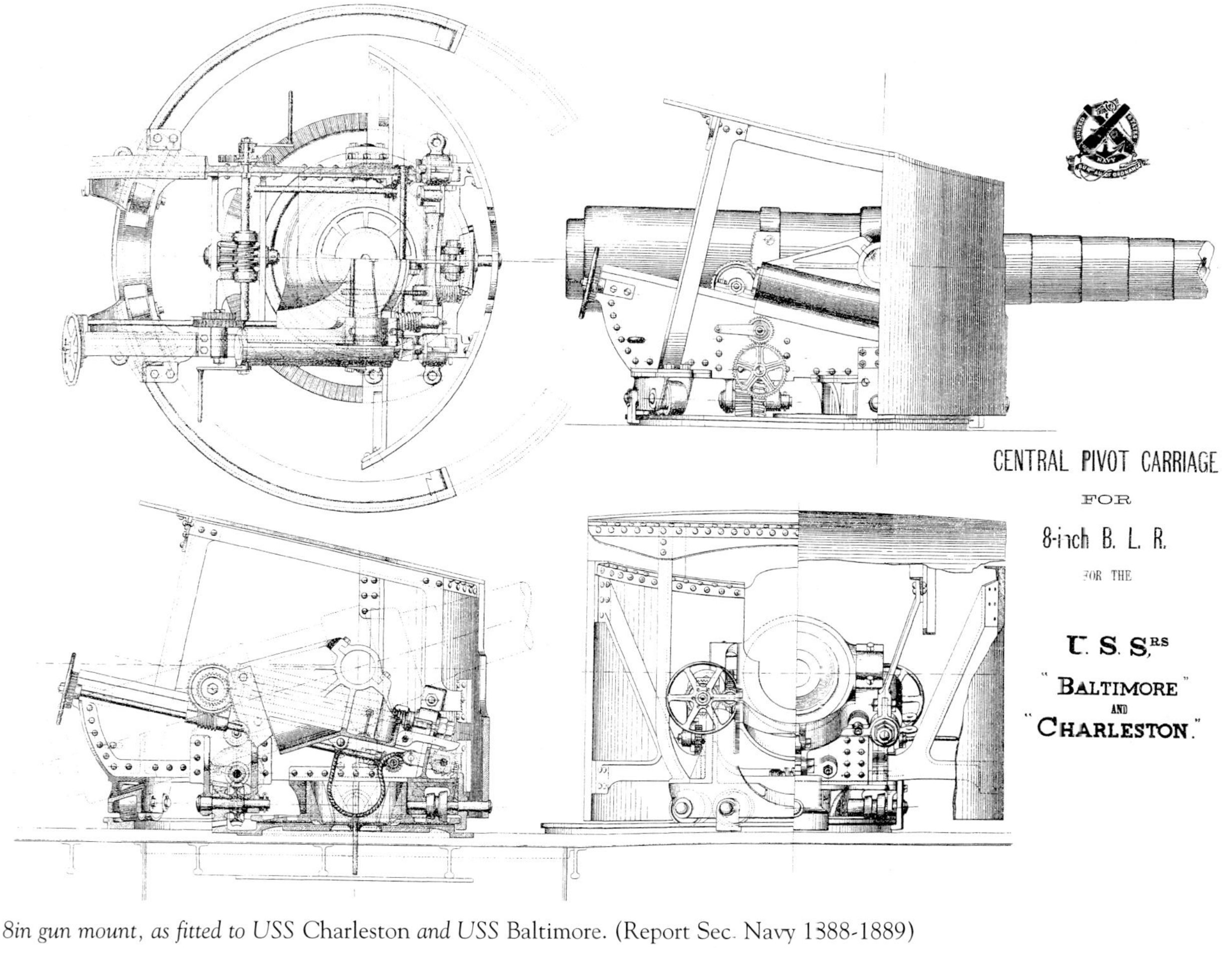

8in gun mount, as fitted to USS Charleston *and USS* Baltimore. (Report Sec. Navy 1388-1889)

USS Baltimore *in dry dock, Mare Island Navy Yard, during the 1890s.* (USN NH 71051)

USS Baltimore *in New York Harbour c.1903, after re-armament.* (USN NH 83962)

part in the destruction of the Spanish squadron at Manila Bay on 1 May 1898 and sustaining seven casualties.

Between 1900 and 1903 *Baltimore* was refitted in the New York Navy Yard losing her tops, and re-armed with twelve 6in 40 cal RF of a modern type, not fitted with shields; the guns were disposed one each side of forecastle and poop and four each side in the waist. She underwent another major refit during 1913-14 when converted to a minelayer, reclassified AM 1 and armament reduced to four 6in. In the First World War *Baltimore* took part in laying the Northern Mine Barrage in the North Sea, armament then being four 5in 51 cal and two 3in AA. Her value as a minelayer was limited as she only carried 175 mines. She was re-boilered with Babcock and Wilcox watertube boilers probably during her major 1913-14 refit.

She joined the Pacific Fleet in 1919 then decommissioned on 15 September 1922, at Pearl Harbor. When surveyed on 24 March 1937 the hull, main engines and boilers were considered to be in good condition, the auxiliary machinery was in a semi-dismantled state, crew accomodation was practically non existent, officers accomodation in poor shape all ordnance and navigation equipment had

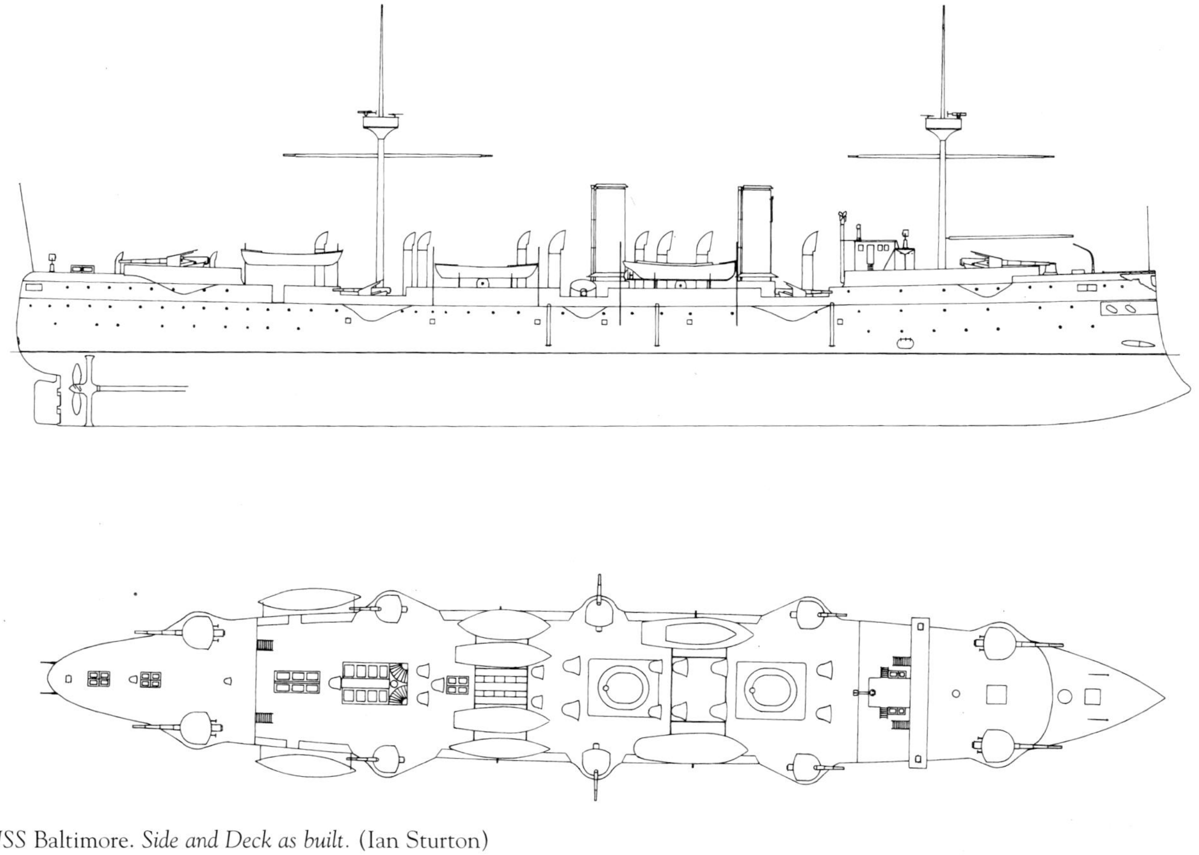

USS Baltimore. *Side and Deck as built.* (Ian Sturton)

USS Baltimore *converted to minelayer. Hampton Roads, Virginia, 10 December 1916.* (USN NH 54427)

Mine handling operations on board Baltimore, *1920. Note what appears to be a mine elevator at left.* (USN NH 56330)

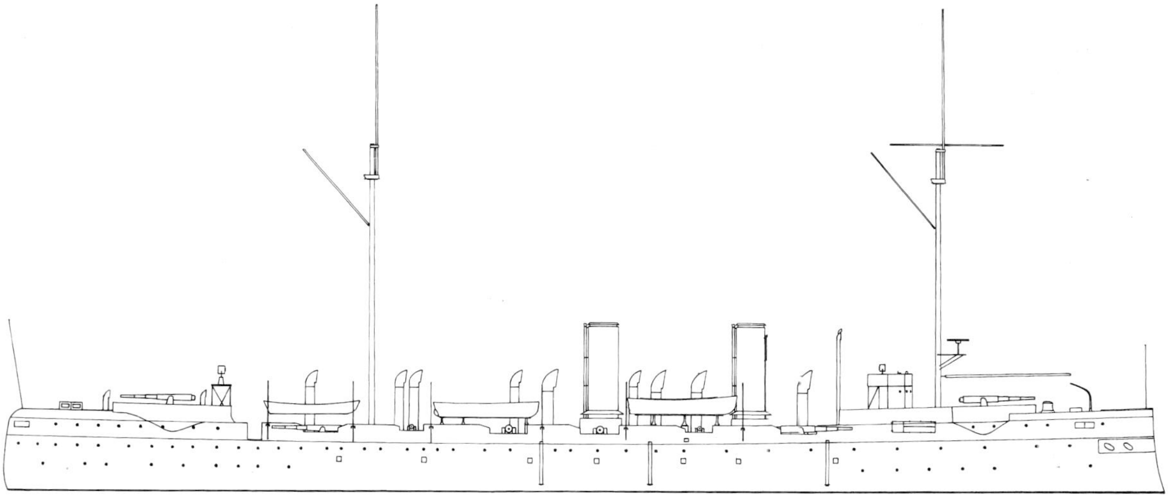

USS Baltimore. *Side as re-armed.* (Ian Sturton)

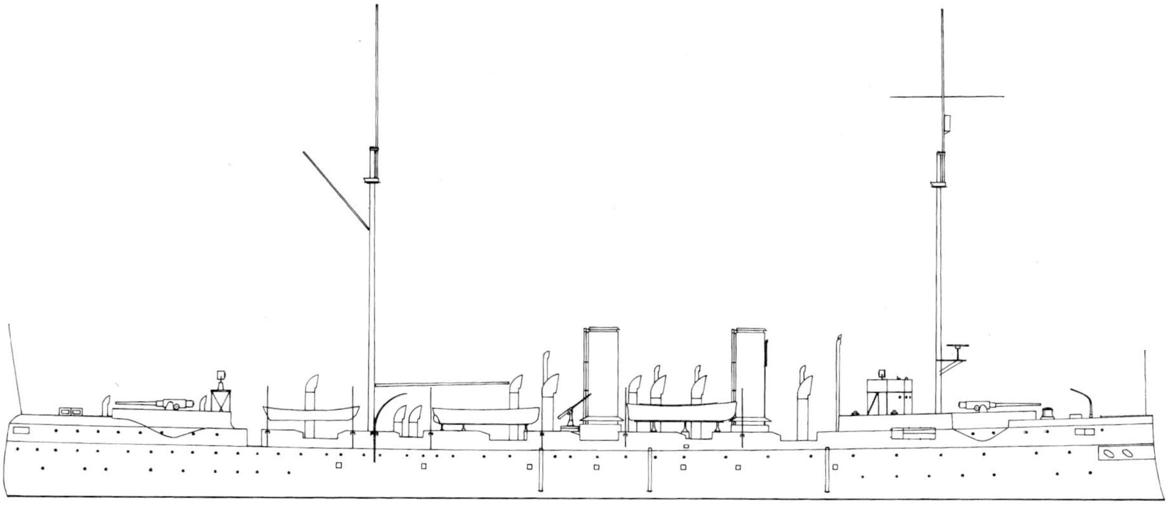

USS Baltimore. *Side as minelayer.* (Ian Sturton)

USS Baltimore *rusty and derelict in Pearl Harbor in late 1941.* (USN NH 52421)

USS Philadelphia *as a receiving ship at Bremerton. (US Navy photograph.)*

been removed and there was no wireless installation while the foremast was rotten. It was clear that *Baltimore* had no future as a combatant ship but it was not until February 1942 that she was sold for scrapping by auction to a Honolulu firm for $6,500.

USS Philadelphia

The hull form of *Philadelphia* was the same as *Baltimore* but her engines were quite different being Cramps' own design; the armament was a uniform 6in BL two each on poop and forecastle and with four on each side of the waist. One design reversion was having three masts, schooner rigged with tops on the fore and main masts. The mixed origin of *Philadelphia*'s design is made clear in the Secretary of the Navy's statement in 1887 that 'the plans purchased abroad constituted the basis for the plans submitted for competition but by the modifications made and being made they are now beyond identification. Thus the result will be as originally contemplated viz adopting at the outset the best known methods, native invention will enable us to improve upon them and to keep pace with the most forward'.[19]

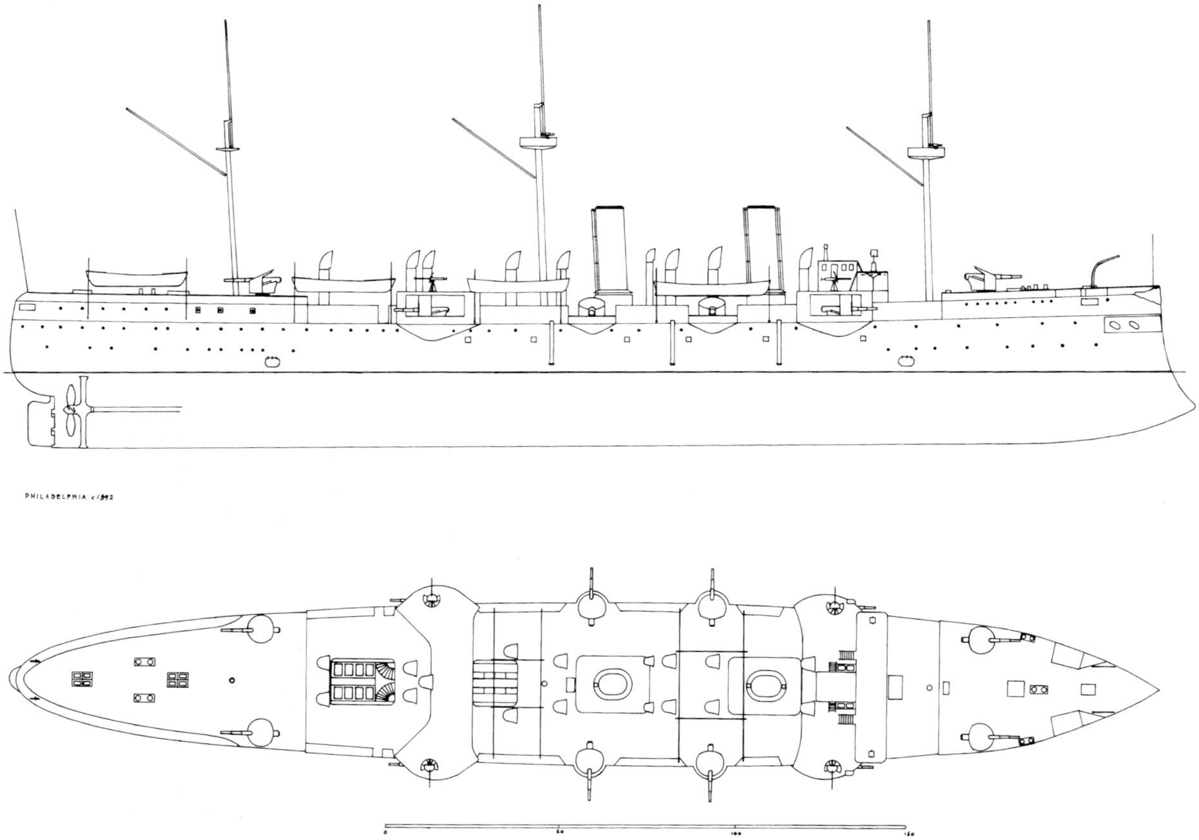

USS Philadelphia. *Side and Deck as built.* (Ian Sturton)

USS *Philadelphia* CRUISER NO.4

Builder	Cramps Philadelphia
Laid Down	March 22 1888
Launched	Sept 7 1889
Completed	June 1890
Commissioned	July 28 1890
Designer	WH White
	Engine design by Cramps
Displacement	4325 tons
Dimensions	(Feet) 315 pp (327ft 6in wl, 335 oa) x 48ft 6in x 19ft 2in
	(Metres) 96 pp (99.8 wl, 102 oa) x 14.78 x 5.84
Armament	12-6in BL 30 cal, 4-6pdr RF, 4-3pdr RF, 2-1pdr RF
	1-37mm Hotchkiss Revolving Cannon, 4 Gatling MG
	Designed for 4-14in above water torpedo tubes but not fitted
Armour	Deck: 4in slopes, 2½in flat, 3in Conning Tower
Machinery	2 sets horizontal triple expansion engines by Cramps, Cylinders: 42in x 58in x 85in
	4 double ended and 1 single ended cylindrical boilers
Designed IHP	FD 10500=19 knots, 4hr FD trials, IHP 8815=19.7 knots
Coal	400 tons at normal draught, 850 tons maximum
Metacentric Height	2.2ft at 4324 tons and 19ft 2½in draught
Sail Area	5600 sq ft of fore and aft canvas[18]
Complement	34 officers, 350 ratings

USS Philadelphia, *after removal of tops and mainmast c.1892.* (USN NH 42603)

USS Philadelphia. *Bow view showing three masted rig.* (Library of Congress Prints & Photographic Division, Detroit Publishing Co.)

From 1890 to 1893 *Philadelphia* was flagship of the North Atlantic Squadron and from 1893 to 1897 was flagship to Commander in Chief, Pacific Station. Out of commission from October 1897 to May 1898 when wooden fore and mizzen masts replaced the original steel ones; the mainmast and the fore fighting top were removed. She took no active part in the Spanish-American war but was present at the ceremonies marking the annexation of the Hawaiian Islands. She remained in the Pacific until 1901 when surveyed at Mare Island on 29 November with repairs estimated to cost $9,109. She arrived at Bremerton in August 1902 and was placed out of commission on 22 September 1902: 'work was begun February 15 1903, in accordance with the report of a board of survey ordered to ascertain the repairs and changes necessary to fit the *Philadelphia* as a receiving ship for this navy-yard.' Her engines were described as 'good' in 1902 and 'fair' in 1903. Work on the housing over was completed and she became a receiving ship at Puget Sound Navy Yard on 12 May 1904, then a prison ship on 4 November 1912, reverting to a receiving ship on 10 January 1916 until struck from the Navy List on 24 November 1926 and sold for scrapping in the following year. Why she ceased to be a fighting ship so early in her career remains a mystery as older ships such as Newark remained seagoing for much longer.[20]

Conclusion

Both *Charleston* and *Baltimore* attracted much adverse criticism when built and these criticisms were repeated in various publications until the 1980s. *Charleston* was, by the time she completed, out-dated and her machinery required modifications, although these were not as expensive as alleged; *Baltimore* was, after the relatively minor modifications made by the builders after initial trials, a highly successful ship. Possibly politics played a part in these criticisms, as they were built during a Democratic administration following the bankruptcy of John Roach who was a prominent contributor to Republican Party campaign funds. Roach's ships were heavily criticised by the Democrats when they were in office; the British

USS *New Orleans* EX USS AMAZONAS, USS *Albany*, EX ALMIRANTE ABREU

	New Orleans	*Albany*
Builder	Armstrongs, Elswick	Armstrongs, Elswick
Laid down	Feb 6 1896	Dec 8 1897
Launched	Dec 4 1896	Jan 14 1899
Final trials	Aug 19 1897	Jan 8 1900
Commissioned	March 27 1898	May 29 1900
Designer	Phillip Watts	Phillip Watts
Displacement	3438 tons	
Dimensions	(Feet) 330 pp (354ft oa) x 43 x 16ft 10in (Metres) 100.6 pp. (108.1 oa) x 13.1 x 5.1.	
Armament	6-6in QF 50 cal, 4-4.7in QF 50 cal, 10-6pdr QF, 4-1pdr pom-pom, 4-1 pdr QF, 4-0.30in Colt MG 3-18in torpedo tubes above water	
Armour	Deck: slopes 3½in, flat 1½in, glacis plates 4in, Conning tower 4in	
Machinery	2 sets VTE by Humphrys Tennant, Cylinders: 31in x 46in x 70in, Stroke 30in, 4 cylindrical boilers Designed IHP ND 6500=19 knots, FD 7500=20 knots	
Trials	IHP ND 6100=19.52 knots, FD 7520= 20.5 knots	
Coal	*New Orleans* 400 tons normal, 808 tons maximum *Albany* 350 tons normal, 1135 tons maximum	
Complement	22 officers, 42 marines, 301 ratings Designed for a complement of 260[22]	

designed warships unsuccessful first trials provided Republican Party supporters with ammunition for their riposte.[21]

The Purchased Cruisers

This pair were two of four cruisers built to Brazilian specifications but the first, *Ministro Zenteno* which mounted a uniform 6in armament was sold to Chile; the remaining three had a mixed 6in and 4.7in armament. All were sheathed and coppered. *Amazonas*, recently completed, and *Almirante Abreu*, laid down three months previously, were sold to the USA on 16 March 1898 (five weeks before the outbreak of hostilities with Spain on April 21) being renamed *New Orleans* and *Albany* respectively. On paper, *New Orleans* and *Albany* were, for their size, well armed with exceptionally powerful guns, fast and with a reasonable steaming radius. In reality the experience acquired by the US Navy revealed that far too much had been attempted on a relatively small displacement. They lacked the 3ft deep raft body above the protective deck which had been a feature of the forecastle and poop type

USS New Orleans *off Santiago in 1898.* (USN NH 85648)

of cruiser designed by Armstrongs since the *Yoshino*. This omission resulted in a freeboard of only 9ft at normal draught and 7½ft at full load, producing a wet waist, diminished protection and coal bunkers obtruding into an already cramped crewspace. Designed for a complement of 260 the pair had a crew of 365 in USN service and this together with American standards of accomodation for ratings resulted in complaints of cramped, poorly

New Orleans *arriving in New York harbour after her maiden voyage, April 1898. To the left is the receiving ship USS* Vermont. (USN NH 75495)

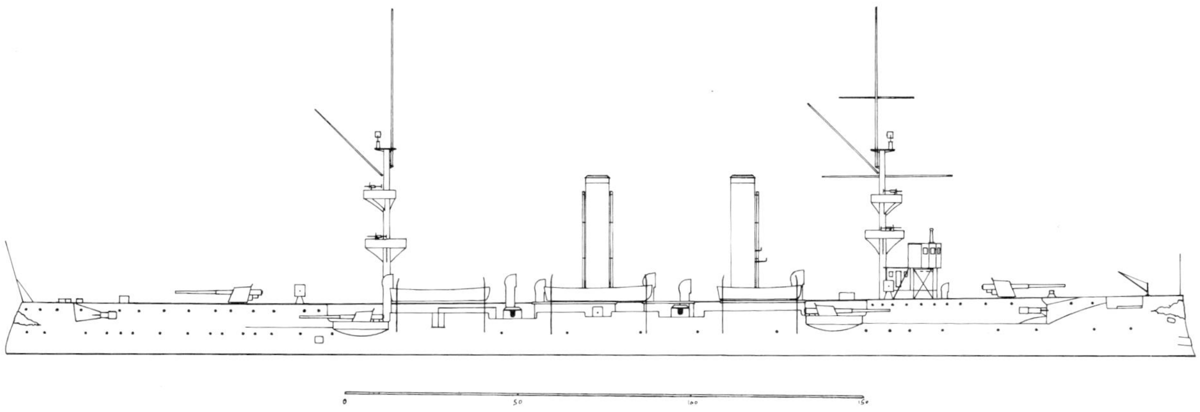

USS New Orleans. *Side view as built.* (Ian Sturton)

ventilated crew spaces and with quite inadequate sanitary arrangements. Their speed was 20 knots but this was achieved under forced draught which could not be sustained for long before the boiler tubes began to leak. Their continuous sea speed was only about 17 knots, reflecting the lower percentage of displacement (16.81 per cent), devoted to machinery compared with a contemporary, *Takasago*, with 25.8 per cent. Armstrongs had built far better cruisers and this over gunned and ill-balanced design was almost certainly due to Brazilian demands for maximum qualities on as small a displacement as possible to keep the cost down.[23]

New Orleans *refitting at Olangapo Naval Station Pl, after re-arming with 5in guns, reduced and disarmed tops.* (USN NH 71574)

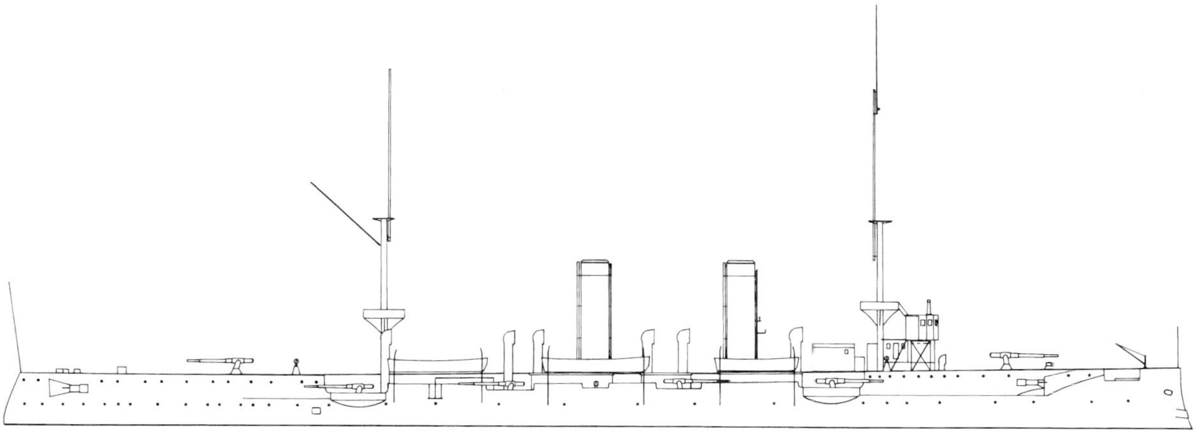

USS Albany. *Side. All 5in armament.* (Ian Sturton)

Careers

New Orleans left the Tyne on 3 March 1898 under the Brazilian flag for Gravesend and was sold to the USA on 16 March; commissioned as USS *Amazonas* she sailed for New York on 18 March with a steaming crew provided by USS *San Francisco*. She spent three weeks undergoing minor repairs and having hatches cut and davits fitted for ammunition supply as the electric hoists were unprotected and considered to be too slow. *New Orleans* was part of Commodore Schley's Flying Squadron off Santiago de Cuba bombarding ships and batteries on three occasions but missed the battle of 3 July when the Spanish fleet was annihilated having been detached to Key West to refuel. She subsequently took part in the Cuban blockade until the end of the war. From October 1898 to May 1899 she had a major refit in the New York Navy Yard to deal with the large number of complaints made about her construction and fittings. These included inadequate sanitary fittings, overheating of the magazines, inadequate ventilation of wardroom, cabins and crew space, particularly the quarters for the marines, poor drainage to gun sponsons and scuppers and the replacement of the 2½in fire main with a 5in one entirely under the armour deck. The comment was made that maximum coal had been obtained by coal bunkers obtruding into four crew berthing spaces rising to within 3½ft of the spar deck above and extending 9½ft inboard so that some sailors had to sleep directly on top of the bunker. It was recommended that the bunkers be cut down to 7in above the floor of the berth deck; by

USS Albany *off the Tyne after acceptance in 1900. Note that her funnels are thicker and lower than* New Orleans. (Cambridge University Library, Vickers Archive 2000)

USS Albany. (Author's collection)

using the oil tanks at the forward end of each engine room for coal there would only be a loss of 100 tons capacity.[24]

Most damning was a report of May 1899 saying that in light condition the ship was unstable. News of this reaching Armstrongs produced a strongly worded rebuttal from Sir Andrew Noble, enclosing a report from Phillip Watts, the chief naval architect, pointing out that inclining experiments on *Albany* had been perfectly satisfactory. A second inclining trial was made in September which revealed a negative metacentric height but it was finally concluded that the original calculations were faulty and that the September inclining test was quite invalid and *New Orleans* was allowed to sail to the Pacific in October where she served as flagship of the cruiser squadron of the Asiatic fleet for the next five years. Complaints about design and fittings continued to be made but the final blow was a report that the poor condition of the double bottom plating meant that it would only be safe for a further five months. She left for the US in December 1904 undergoing a long and leisurely refit at Mare Island from February 1905 until late 1909. The most obvious changes were the substitution of ten unshielded 5in RF in place of the mixed battery of 6in and 4.7in, the removal of the upper fighting tops and the mounting of two searchlights in each of the lower tops.[25]

New Orleans cruised the Orient until early 1912 when she was decommissioned until the end of 1913 when she patrolled the west coast of Mexico. At the beginning of the First World War, after overhaul, she took part in Atlantic convoys until January 1918 when she returned to the far east. From July to December 1919, she was station ship at Vladivistock supporting allied forces in Siberia. She spent two spells in Vladivostock in 1920 and 1922. *New Orleans* returned to the US in September 1922 decommissioning in the October, was struck off the Navy List in November 1929 and sold for scrapping on 11 February 1930.[26]

Albany's completion was delayed by a fire in the Elswick works which destroyed a 4.7in gun and dynamos. After service in the Pacific and Mediterranean from 1900 to late 1902, she returned to the US, joining the Asiatic fleet in August 1903 until May 1904, undergoing a long refit when the 6in and 4.7in guns were replaced by ten 5in RF. Recommissioned in 1907, she served in North and South American waters, including acting as flagship for the Nicaraguan Expeditionary Squadron. She served in the Far East until 1914 then joined the Pacific Fleet off the Mexican coast from May to November 1914. In 1916 she patrolled the Pacific and Atlantic coasts of Mexico from May to December. During the First World War she took part in escort duty in the Atlantic from July 1917 to November 1918 then saw service at Vladivostock during 1919 and 1920. She was decommissioned in the US in October 1922 and sold for scrapping on 11 February 1930. On the evidence of Wright and Fisher, *Albany* was never plagued by all the troubles experienced by *New Orleans* probably because of modifications made by Armstrongs while completing.[27] Despite their slow speed the pair remained in service for many years reflecting the almost total neglect by the USN of fast cruisers until the laying down of the first of the *Omaha* class in 1920.

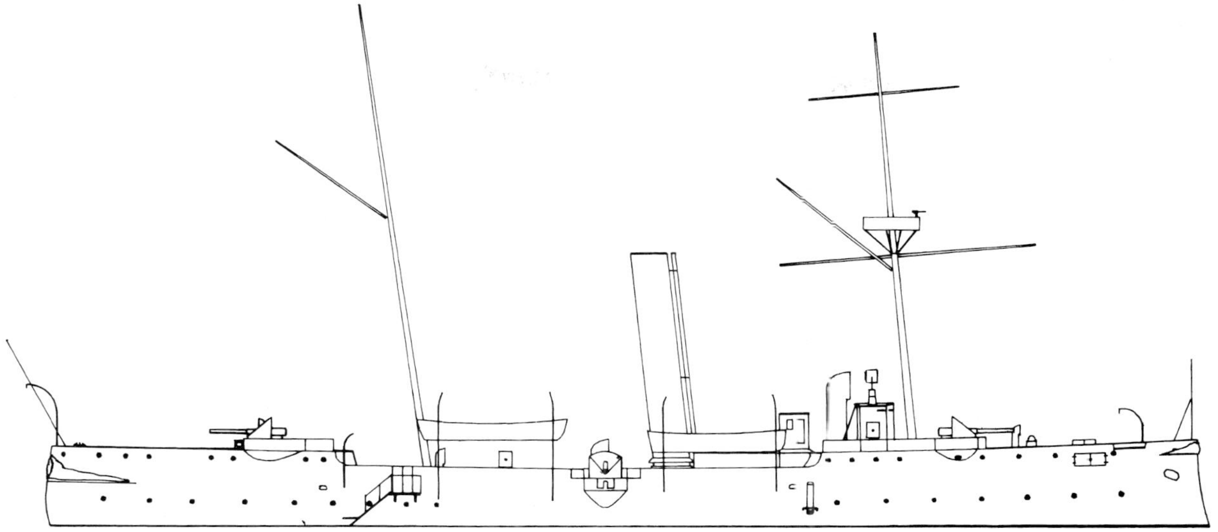

Isla de Cuba. *Side view as built.* (Ian Sturton)

The Captured Cruisers Isla de Luzon *and* Isla de Cuba

These small, slow, poorly armed cruisers were more appropriately rated as gunboats by the USN after their capture. Entering Spanish service in November 1887, they left for the Pacific in 1897 to become part of Rear Admiral Montojo's Philippine Squadron which was annihilated by Commodore George Dewey's Asiatic Squadron at the battle of Manila on 1 May 1898. During the battle the two ships were at the right of the Spanish line but somewhat behind, circling at speed. When the flagship *Reina Cristina* was disabled Admiral Montojo shifted his flag to *Cuba* which stood in and anchored behind Cavite arsenal where she was scuttled and later burnt by a party from the *Petrel*. Struck four times by 6pdrs she sustained little damage and had two wounded. *Luzon* was also scuttled behind the arsenal and later set on fire by a detachment from *Petrel*. During the battle the two forward guns were disabled by a large shell but apart from that she suffered no significant injury with only six of the crew injured.[29]

USN Careers

On 26 November 1898 Admiral Dewey reported that *Cuba*, *Luzon* and an unprotected cruiser *Don Juan de Austria* had been raised, docked and would shortly leave for Hong Kong under their own steam.[30]

After repairs in Hong Kong when she was rearmed with four 4in RF *Isla de Luzon* was commissioned into the USN on 31 January 1900. She served in the Philippines until August 1902, taking an active part in action against the Filipino insurgents, blockading the island of Samar and

Isla de Luzon, Isla de Cuba

	Isla de Luzon	*Isla de Cuba*
Builder	Armstrongs, Elswick	Armstrongs, Elswick
Laid Down	Feb 25 1886	Feb 25 1886
Launched	Nov 13 1886	Dec 11 1886
Final Trials	Sept 22 1887	Sept 22 1887
Designer	WH White	WH White
Displacement	1038 tons, 1053 tons on trial	
Dimensions	(Feet) 185 pp (197 oa) x 30 x 11ft 6in. (Metres) 56.4 pp (60 oa) x 9.14 x 3.5. Freeboard amidships 5ft	
Armament	Initially 6-4.7in BL, reduced to 4-4.7in BL, 4-6 pdr QF, 2-1in MG, 2 MG 3-14in torpedo tubes, above water	
Armour	Deck: slopes 2½in, flat 1½in, 1in at ends	
Machinery	2 sets horizontal triple expansion by Hawthorn Leslie, Cylinders: 18in x 29in x 43in, Stroke: 24in 2 single ended cylindrical boilers, designed IHP ND 1700=14 knots, FD 2200=15 knots	
Trials	*Cuba*: ND 1897=14.93 knots for 8 hours, FD 2827=15.82 knots on the measured mile *Luzon*: ND 14.19 knots, FD 15.49 knots on the measured mile	
Coal	100 tons normal, 200 tons maximum	
Complement	156 in Spanish service[28]	

supporting land operations. In December 1903 she was attached to the Louisiana State Militia and subsequently to the Illinois State Militia serving on the Great Lakes. Between 1908 and 1911 Babcock and Wilcox tubular boilers were installed and two tall thin funnels fitted in place of her original single one. During the First World War she was re-armed with four 3in RF and based in Chicago as a training ship. She served at the Naval Torpedo Station at Narragansett Bay from November to December 1918 having torpedo tubes installed, possibly removed during her major refit at Hong Kong. She was sold in March 1920 to the Bahama and West India Trading Co, renamed *Reviver* and used as a merchant salvage ship until scrapped in 1940.

After repair at Hong Kong, when she was re-armed with four 4in RF, *Isla de Cuba* was commissioned into the USN on 11 April 1900. Until her departure for the US in 1904 she took an active part in putting down the post war Philippine insurrection acting as a supply ship, transport, blockader and survey ship. After her return she underwent

The ex-Spanish Isla de Cuba *and* Isla de Luzon *salvaged from the shallows of Manila Bay, with temporary thatched roofs to provide shade during their refit for US naval service.* (Author's collection)

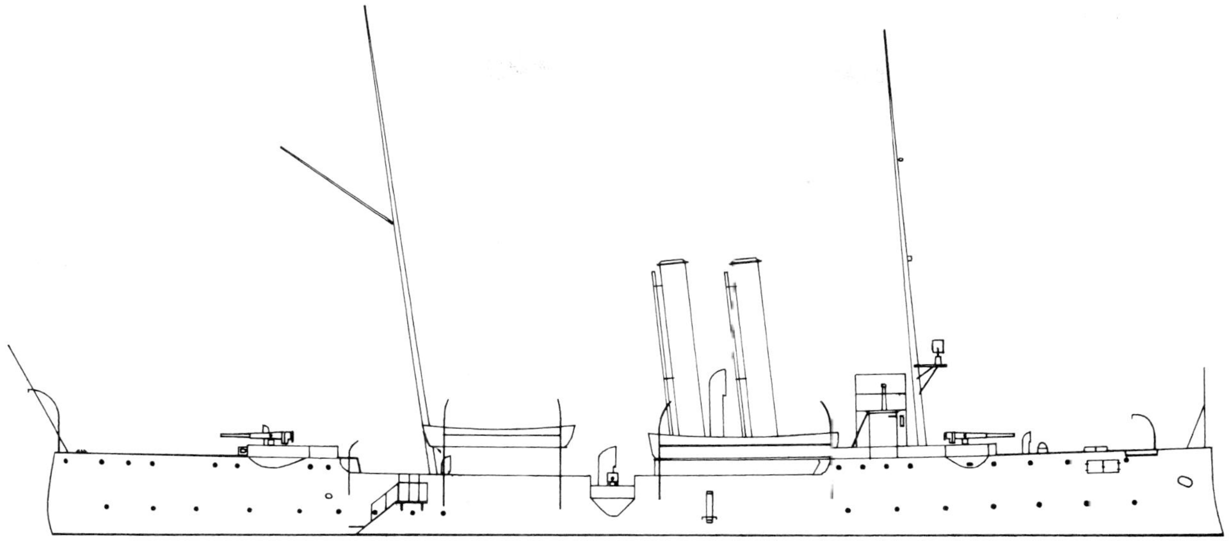

Isla de Cuba. *Side view, re-boilered and re-armed.* (Ian Sturton)

repairs until 1907 during which time Babcock and Wilcox boilers replaced the cylindrical ones and had two tall thin funnels fitted like *Luzon*. She served with the Naval Militia of Maryland as a school ship until 1912 when she was sold to Venezuela on 2 April 1912 and renamed *Mariscal Sucre*.[31] She was finally scrapped in 1940.

Acknowledgements

I am most grateful to Christopher C Wright, editor of *Warship International*, for checking references in the US. I owe a deep debt to Ian Sturton for his elegant and accurate drawings and for a productive visit to the Admiralty Library at Portsmouth to search Reports of the Secretary USN.

References

1 Report of the Secretary US Navy, 1888-1889, (Washington GPO, 1889), p.iii.
2 Report, Secretary USN, 1886, pp.5-6.
3 F M Bennett, *The Steam Navy of the United States*, (Westport Conn., 1972 reprint) p.781; *Conway's All The Worlds Fighting Ships, 1860-1905* (London, 1979), p.150.
4 Report, Secretary USN 1886, pp.xix-xxiv; G T A Davis, *Navy Second To None*, (New York, 1940), pp.43-44.
5 Report, Secretary USN 1885, p.xvii; Report Secretary USN 1886, p.7; Report of the Select Committee On Ordnance & Warships, (Washington GPO, 1886), pp.43-44.
6 Elswick Yard Report Book, 1, Vickers Archive 1157, Cambridge University Library, p.43.
7 N Friedman, *US Cruisers: an Illustrated Design History*, (London, 1985) pp.458-459; G W Melville, 'Notes on the Machinery for New Vessels of the United States Navy', *Transactions of the Society of Naval Architects and Marine Engineers*, 1893, 1, Table facing p.162; *Dictionary of American Naval Fighting Ships*, (Hereafter *DANFS*) (Washington GPO, 1964, 2nd ed.), 1, p.204.
8 Report of the Secretary USN, 1888-1889, pp.613-615.
9 N Friedman, *US Naval Weapons*, (London, 1983) p.239; Friedman, *US Cruisers*, p.23; Bennett, pp.789-790.

The wrecks of Isla de Cuba *and* Isla de Luzon *off Cavite Navy Yard after having been scuttled and set on fire.* (USN NH 902940)

10 I N Hollis, 'An American Cruiser on Service', *Engineering*, (London, 1894), 1, pp.281-283.

11 *DANFS*, 2, 1963, p.82.

12 Friedman, *US Cruisers*, p.459; Melville, facing p.162; *DANFS*, 1, p.204.

13 P Brook, 'Two Unfortunate Warships: *Unebi* and *Reina* Regente', *Mariners Mirror*, 87, Feb 2001, pp.56-62.

14 T D Wilson, *Steel Ships of the United States Navy*, estimated from Plate 11.

15 Report Secretary USN, 1888-1889, p.614.

16 W S Schley, 'Report on the *Baltimore*', *Proceedings of the United States Naval Institute*, 18, No.2, 62, pp.235-250.

17 *DANFS*, 1, 1964, p.89; *The Northern Barrage and Other Mining Activities*, (Washington GPO, 1920) p.70; C C Wright, *Warship International* 3, 1982, pp.294-301. This answer to a question in INFOSER gives much detail about the 20 years when *Baltimore* was laid up.

18 Friedman, *US Cruisers*, p.460; Melville, facing p.162.

19 Report Secretary USN, 1887, p.viii.

20 Friedman, *US Cruisers*, p.27; Report Secretary USN, 1902, p.103. Report Secretary USN, 1903, pp.855, 1015; *DANFS*, 5, 1970, pp.282-283.

21 J R Spears, *History of the United States Navy*, (New York 1908) p.256; J D Long, *The New American Navy*, (New York 1903), 1, pp.38-40; D Mitchell, *History of the Modern American Navy*, (New York, 1947) p.17; W R Herrick, *The American Naval Revolution*, (Louisiana, 1966) pp.30, 35; Friedman, *US Cruisers*, pp.23, 25.

22 P Brook, *Warships for Export: Armstrong Warships 1867-1927*, (Gravesend, 1999), pp.86-87.

23 *Ibid.*, p.47; C Wright and E Fisher, 'USS *Albany* and *New Orleans*, The American Elswick Built Units', *Warship International*, 4, 1971, pp.343-366 (this is an important contribution drawing heavily on USN archival material).

24 Brook, *Warships for Export*, p.86; Wright and Fisher, pp.343-354.

25 Wright and Fisher, pp.349-356.

26 *DANFS*, 5, 1970, pp.66-67.

27 Brook, *Warships for Export*, p.88; *DANFS*, 1, 1964, pp.22-23; Wright and Fisher, *passim*.

28 Armstrong Warships Particulars Book, 1, National Maritime Museum, Brass Foundry Greenwich, pp.30, 102; Brook, *Warships for Export*, pp.65-67.

29 Jm Ellicott, 'The Effect of the Gunfire of the United States Vessels in the Battle of Manila Bay', Office of Naval Intelligence, War Notes No V, Information From Abroad, (Washington GPO 1899), pp.10-11, 13.

30 Annual Report of the Navy Department For the Year 1898, Appendix to the Report of the Chief of the Bureau of Navigation (Washington GPO, 1898), p.69.

31 *DANFS*, 3, 1963, p.466; Brook, *Warships For Export*, pp.66-67.

Cuba *at Cavite Naval Base October 1903 after re-arming with 4in RF.* (Author's collection)

Luzon as training ship with the Illinois Naval Militia 1913. Re-boilered, twin funnels and 3in guns. (USN NH 75672)

Dr C Peter Brook (1927-2003)

It is with great regret that we record the death of Peter Brook, after a long illness. Peter trained as a medical doctor, retiring as a consultant psychiatrist after service in the NHS at Brentwood, near London, and at Cambridge. In his early career he became concerned about the training of young psychiatrists, and conducted research on the subject. Later he specialised in the psychiatry of old age, and was involved in research in Cambridge. As a teaching hospital consultant he taught Cambridge University medical students. He published papers in the *British Medical Journal* and the *British Journal of Psychiatry*.

Warship readers will remember Peter for his studies of Armstrongs (Sir W G Armstrong and Co), the great Tyneside armaments and shipbuilding conglomerate. He started with a series of articles on Armstrong warships, published in *Warship International* in the 1970s and 1980s. The articles comprised factual data and brief career summaries, and included a number of rare photographs. Later, he used the extensive Armstrong archival material in the Cambridge University Library, the Tyne and Wear Archives and the National Maritime Museum to refine and greatly expand the scope and detail of this early work. His book, *Warships for Export: Armstrong Warships 1867-1927* was published as a World Ship Society Monograph in 1999.

The book contains design and in-service histories of each ship built, from the 'flat-iron' gunboats of the 1870s to post-Washington Treaty capital ships, together with details of various aborted projects. In many cases Armstrong designers showed the world what a naval architect untrammelled by the demands of naval staffs could achieve; the long line of 'Elswick Cruisers' brought particular renown. Armstrong dreadnoughts and dreadnought designs were an important feature of pre-First World War South American and Near Eastern arms races. The Chief Designer often doubled as chief salesman; three successive Chief Designers would go on to become Directors of Naval Construction at the Admiralty. In addition to their biographies and a short history of the firm, the book includes 160 photos (some not previously published), numerous line drawings, a table of Armstrong guns and a full bibliography.

Peter completed the Armstrong story with four articles in *Warship*, two describing the contents of design portfolios in the National Maritime Museum and two the firm's contributions to the nineteenth century Italian and United States Navies. Consideration of the operational histories of Armstrong warships worldwide led to three further *Warship* articles on less familiar naval battles, namely the Yalu (1894), Santiago de Cuba (1898) and Ulsan (1904); of the five navies taking part in these actions, four used Armstrong ships. In contrast, a 1999 article in *Mariner's Mirror* dealt with the ill-fated cruisers *Unebi* and *Reina Regente*, lost at sea with all hands; these were not designed or built by Armstrongs.

I contributed line drawings to some of the articles, and was in frequent contact with Peter. He received each and every enquiry of mine, however incoherent or badly timed, with cheerful courtesy, and would send in response a generous package of photos, official drawings, reprints and drafts of articles. Maritime problems of my own were, after careful thought, answered with the benefit of his experience and the resources of that formidable library on the third floor.

His other interests included the history of Cambridge and of Cambridge University, and dinghy sailing. A dedicated family man, he was married to Joy for fifty years and leaves a daughter, a son, and two grandsons.

Ian Sturton

A CENTURY-LONG DREAM:

Single Purpose Engine Submarines of the Italian Navy, 1892-2003

In 2003 Italy launched *Salvatore Todaro*, the culmination of the nation's century-long quest to build a true underwater warship. In this article **Enrico Cernuschi** and **Vincent O'Hara** tell the story of Italy's design innovations, technological accomplishments, and the lost opportunities that marked her long voyage to build a single purpose engine submarine.

The Concept, 1892-1908

For a navy which has commissioned 293 submarines (twenty-two since the end of the Second World War) the trials ceremony held on 6 November 2003 for the *Marina Militare*'s new U212A type submarine, *Salvatore Todaro* would seem little more than a routine exercise. However, *Todaro* is something none of her predecessors were: she is a 'true' submarine. Powered by nine proton-exchange membrane hydrogen/oxygen fuel cells, she has a top speed of 20 knots submerged; she can stay under water for weeks, running at slow speed and her fuel cell engine multiplies by many times her 'discretion coefficient' and her subsequent military value. She is the latest step in 111 years of progress and development.

The story of Italy's quest to reach this point is full of innovation and technological accomplishments, surprising associations and missed opportunities. It is a story that has never been told in English.

Delfino, *1896. Her lines recall the attractive and futuristic shape of the USS* Albacore, *launched fifty-eight years later, the first modern American submarine designed entirely for underwater operation.* (Collection of Erminio Bagnasco)

The modern, 'true' submarine, designed to sail and fight submerged, was conceived at the end of the nineteenth century. In fact, the lines of the *Regia Marina*'s first underwater warship, *Delfino*, commissioned in 1896, recall the attractive and futuristic shape of the USS *Albacore*, launched 58 years later, the first American submarine designed entirely for underwater operation. But the bulky batteries required for electric underwater propulsion systems, their slow speed and limited endurance-rendered electric engine 'true' submarines like *Delfino* virtually useless, discouraging this construction philosophy and retarding their development worldwide for nearly five decades until the first German Type XXI U-boat entered service in 1944.

Constrained by the technological limitations, submarine designers created follow-up boats that grew ever larger. They set aside the ideal of building true submarines in favor of submergible torpedo-boats, a different type of unit altogether, optimised for surface navigation. By virtue of two different types of engines, petrol and later diesel for surface and electric for submerged operations, these boats had the ability to submerge principally for self-protection, creeping along underwater for several hours (and, later on, for up to three very painful days); but they sailed, and for the most part they fought, on the surface.

The Italian *Glaucos* class of 1903, a radical departure from the *Delfino*, were a good example of the new design policies gradually adopted by navies worldwide over a period of forty years, evolving from dangerous petrol surface engines (called, for good reason, '*benzinari*' or 'juice bars') to their successors, the safer and more reliable diesel, the navy's 'engine *par excellence*'.

In 1908 the *Regia Marina*'s chief of staff, Admiral Giovanni Bettolo, decided to pursue the development of

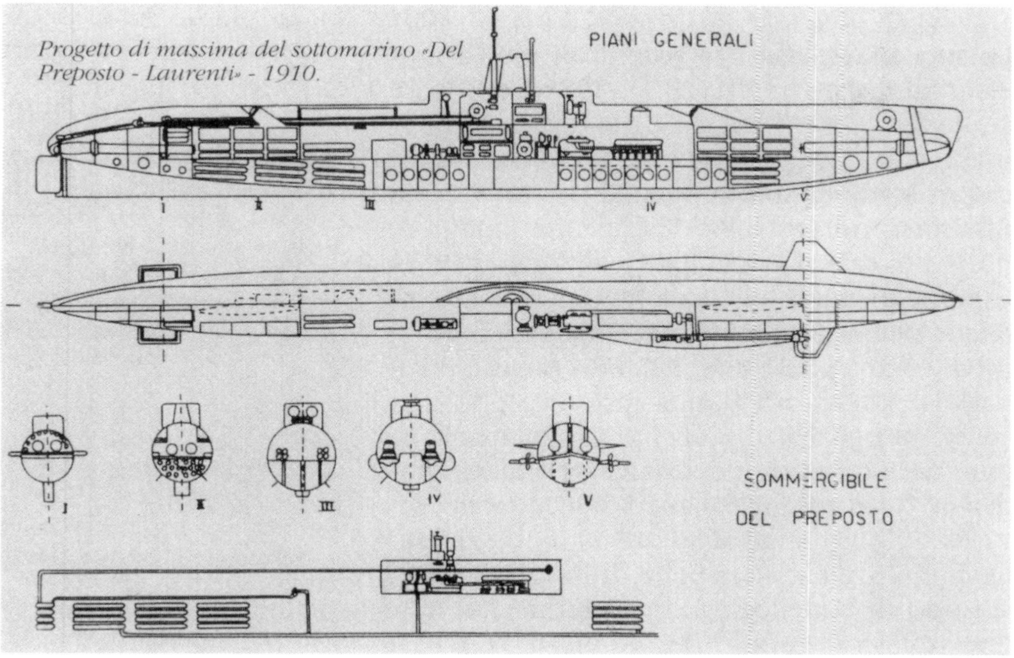

Giuseppe Del Preposto's proposed 1910 design for a boat of 435 tons equipped with a 1,700hp single function engine estimated to be capable of 16.5 knots submerged using both diesel and compressed air engines. (Rivista Marittima)

a high seas submarine. He had the innovative idea of using a new generation of advanced submarines to offset the *Regia Marina*'s unavoidable inferiority in battleships to the French navy. His program called for more capable propulsion systems. Once again the concept of a submarine powered by a 'single purpose engine', which could serve for surface as well as underwater navigation (and which had better submerged speed and endurance and used far less space), became relevant. Admiral Bettolo's idea rapidly took hold pushing the navy to dedicate a fraction of its meagre budget for this purpose.

First Steps, 1909-1915

The *Regia Marina* had a large pool of designs to choose from, some more, others less feasible, among the many continuously submitted to the navies of the world by a clamorous army of inventors as brilliant solutions to the on-going problem of underwater propulsion. The engineer Giuseppe Del Preposto presented the first design taken seriously under consideration in 1909.

Based on a diesel engine with a compressor connected to the engine's shaft (or 'shafthead') the boat in question would have had, when submerged, a series of cylinders fixed to the inside of the waterproof hull filled with air at 200 atmospheres and retained by a compressor acting as a thermal engine. When submerged the expansion of the air pressure in the tanks would activate the compressor pushing the air to fuel the thermal engine, thus ensuring the combustion necessary for operation.

As early as 1910 the engineer, Cesare Laurenti, Italy's leading submarine designer during the first decades of the twentieth-century, worked on this scheme and developed plans for a boat of 435 tons equipped with a 1,700hp single function engine that could develop, on paper, 16.5 knots submerged making simultaneous use of both diesel and compressed air engines. However, the *Regia Marina* did not take his design beyond the consideration stage as it wanted a blue water submarine, not another coastal boat.

In 1911 the Navy ordered two conventional submarines, *Giacinto Pullino* and *Galileo Ferraris*. The naval architect Virginio Cavallini designed these with classic subsurface features and a strong double hull capable of withstanding higher pressures (50 meters compared to the *Glaucos*' operational limit of 20 meters). The boats were armed with six 450mm torpedo tubes on an overall displacement of only 355 tons. They were very handy and, with a submerged speed of a good 10 knots sustainable for more than two hours, they were the fastest (underwater) boats of the Italian navy until the 'Toti' class of the Sixties. The 'Pullino' class compared quite well with foreign boats of the same period excepting only the controversial British 'R' class of the First World War, which could achieve 15 knots submerged for less than an hour.

In the same period the *Regia Marina* gained valuable new experience in their quest for a fast 'true' submarine when the arsenal of Venice constructed, in great secrecy, two small electric semi-submersibles named *Alpha* and *Beta*. Completed in 1913, these boats, hardly six meters long, had just one propeller and were intended to supply Laurenti with the hull and rudder data he needed for a successor submarine of 1,000t capable of 16 knots submerged.

Concurrent with these activities, the *Regia Marina* was developing a dual-purpose diesel engine for their future oceanic subs, the 'Micca' class. In 1912 the Navy tested diesel engines proposed by FIAT and Tosi aboard two oil tankers and in 1915, after an initial cycle of laboratory tank experiments conducted at La Spezia, a new oil tanker, the *Acheronte*, received a diesel engine modified with a connected compressor as proposed by Del Preposto to test operation in oxygen free conditions.

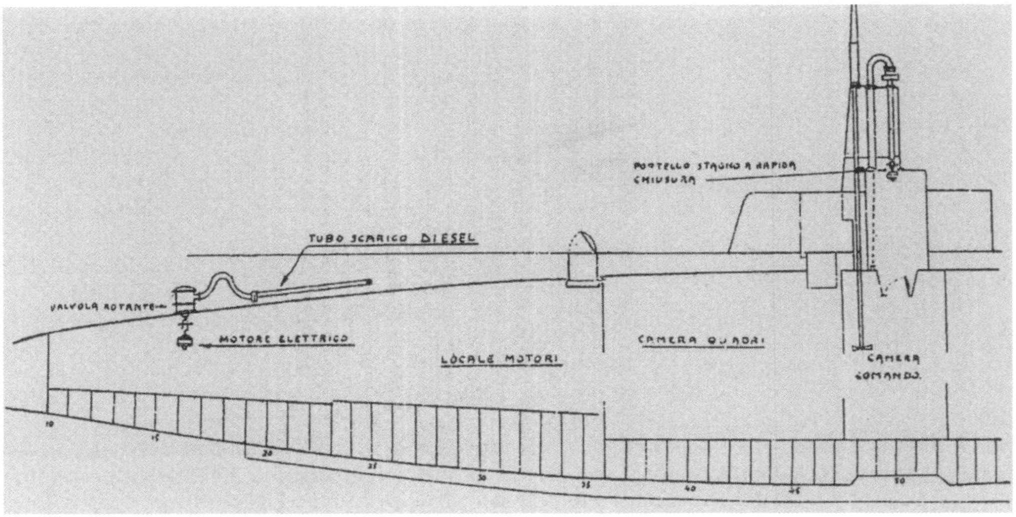

Outline of the Ferretti apparatus (snorkel) as fitted in the Royal submarine H3 *in 1926. The diesel exhaust tube may be seen emerging from the hull aft (fixed to a rotating value driven by a small electric motor) while the air intake tube is located atop the conning tower.* (Gino Galuppini, Lo schnorchel Italiano)

However, by 1914 Naval command's progressive experience and ever deeper study into the theory of the single purpose engine led to a general cooling of enthusiasm for Del Preposto's design. Adapting a diesel engine to serve for both above and below surface propulsion was proving more complex than originally believed. First, there was the telltale wake of bubbles produced by the compressor during submerged navigation; then there was the more critical problem of onboard venting of combustible gases at depth. Finally, a careful and realistic study showed the endurance of the boat in its final 1,000 ton version would be far below presumed (and required) values because of the huge volume of air it required to operate the engine.

Nevertheless, the *Regia Marina*'s sincere interest in a fast, deep sea submarine propelled by a single use engine continued unabated (and this in spite of a merry-go-round of three ministers and four chiefs of general staff that alternated in power between 1911 and 1914.) In the spring of 1914 the Ministry asked Germany to share the benefits of their experiments conducted along the same lines that had produced a design called the 'Krupp System', based on regeneration of the products of a diesel combustion engine working in immersion by means of oxygen addition.

Cooperation seemed ensured given German good will toward the Italians (Italy had, after all, been an ally for nearly a half century first with the Prussians and the Empire thereafter), but a few weeks later the unexpected eruption of a new European war ended the possibility of Italy adopting the Krupp System.

As a possible replacement to the German option the General Staff studied a proposal by Laurenti for a refinement to his last design based, this time, on a steam propulsion system. The chorus of opposition from submariners, mindful of the great unhappiness this type of machinery had caused their French colleagues and Italy's entrance into the war stopped the *Regia Marina*'s experiments and studies just when she was in sight of ordering, finally, her first 'true' experimental submarine prototype.

The expediency of the snorkel, 1919-1935

Three years later, despite the Great War's legacy of loss and exhaustion, the decisive intervention of the Navy Corps of Engineer's Major Pericle Ferretti, Italy's true father of the modern single purpose submarine engine, rejuvenated Italian interest in underwater navigation by means of a diesel drive system. He first improved the technique of using, while surfacing, the so-called 'fireplace',

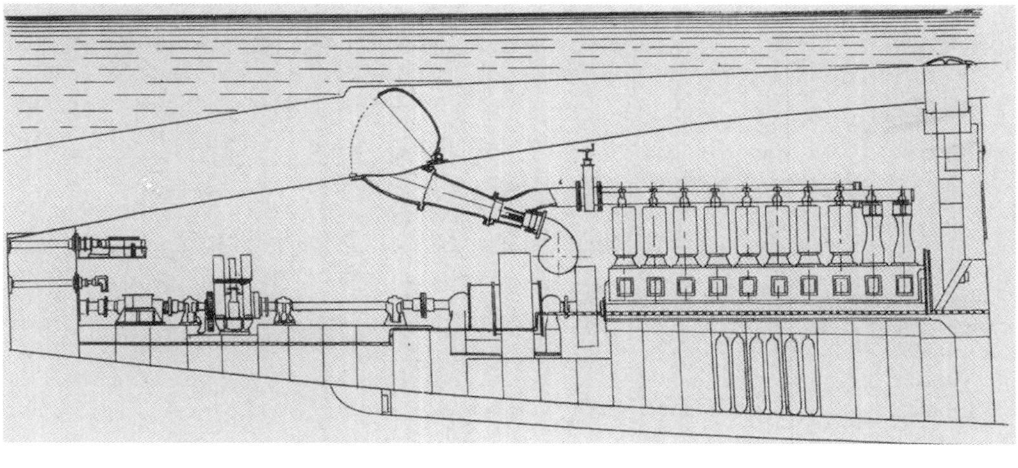

Outline of Ferretti's hydraulic ejector. This solved the problem of underwater emissions and prevented the accidental re-entry of water. (Gino Galuppini, Lo schnorchel Italiano)

which was a characteristic feature of the excellent American 'Holland' boats acquired by the *Regia Marina* (and by the fleets of half the world) in 1916. He accomplished this with a hydraulic ejector that solved the problem of underwater drainage through the exhaust manifold and prevented accidental reentry of water. Moreover, between 1925 and 1926 he designed and tested the first prototypes of the 'Ferretti Apparatus' destined to receive the more appropriate name of 'Italian snorkel' from Admiral Gino Galuppini in his official history of this pioneer device.

The *Regia Marina*'s Grand Admiral Thaon di Revel, who was already a supporter of the 'true' submarine from 1913 when he was chief of the general staff, demonstrated great interest in this revolutionary device. In the end, however, the *Regia Marina* failed to adopt Ferretti's invention. A snorkel is, and always will be, nothing more than a 'hole in the hull' and as such it was regarded with considerable suspicion by submariners throughout the world (with the possible exception of the Dutch). This disregard, along with the inevitable mechanical and operational limitations in the initial versions of the device, was sufficient to offset the interest of Admiral Ernesto Burzagli, the Italian Navy Chief of the general staff from 1927 to 1931 and a strong supporter of classic solutions without frill or fancy.

Starting in 1932, however, interest in the Ferretti Apparatus was resurrected by the perception of a growing English threat menacing Italy's future, compounded by a potentially dangerous Germany, unexpectedly released by London from the debatable but effective Versailles web of military restrictions. Foreshadowing current technology, Ferretti had improved his snorkel adopting a turbine instead of the 'water closed' ball-cock solution still used worldwide into the Sixties. This new version he called 'ML', a mysterious acronym which was, simply, the initials of his wife, Maria Luisa.

In 1935 the degeneration of relations with London, provoked by the war in Ethiopia, moved Ferretti to propose to the Ministry plans for a new single purpose engine of revolutionary design.

The return of the single purpose engine submarine, 1935-1937

Ferretti's concept came into its own with the support of the Italian naval chief of the general staff, Admiral Domenico Cavagnari. He allowed Ferretti and his collaborators to commence an initial cycle of experiments on the engine mounting before the end of 1935 and later to test the new engine itself inside a special tank constructed at Naples.

In his own practical and strongly traditional way Cavagnari quickly came to realize (as did Ferretti) that the construction of an oceanic 'true' submarine, if such was really feasible, would require too much time. This conclusion followed the assessment of at least two other alternative designs by MARICOMINAV, the Naval Planning Committee Plan, based on an apparatus that used boilers fitted with special generators whose spray

Major (GN) Pericle Ferretti, Italy's father of the modern single purpose submarine engine. (Gino Galuppini, Lo schnorchel italiano.)

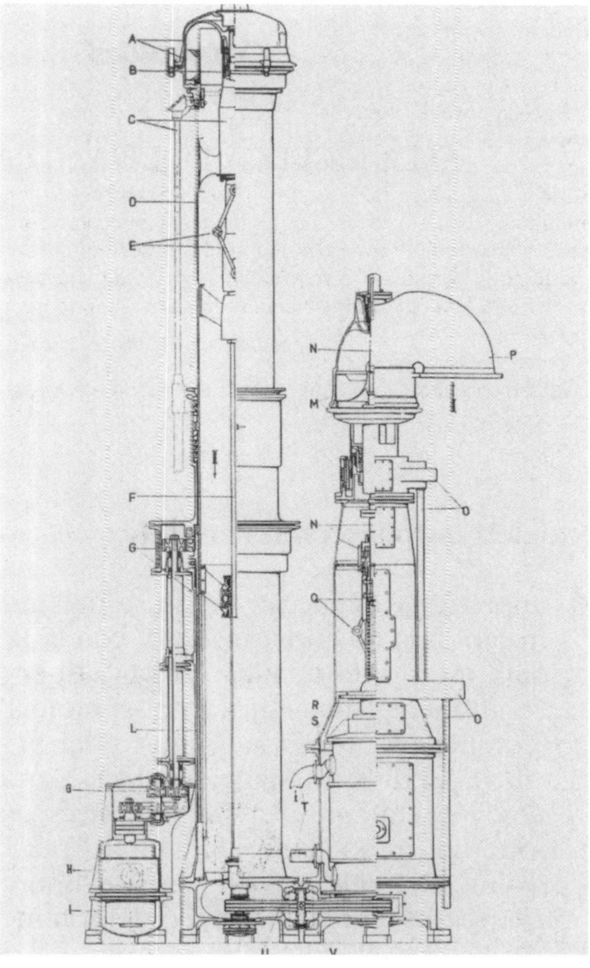

The improved Ferretti apparatus. This uses a turbine rather than the traditional water closed ball-cock method. The device had the mysterious name 'ML', which was nothing more than the initials of his wife, Maria Luisa.
(Gino Galuppini, Lo schnorchel Italiano)

Uarsciek, *a classic Italian boat of the thirties. Technically, it was a good submarine for underwater patrol, but slow in comparision to the German VII types used by the* Kriegsmarine *for wolf pack night surface actions and a dead end in the face of Allied ASW tactics in use by 1943.* (Collection of E. Cernuschi)

tubes, embedded in an aluminum setting, would thermodynamically recycle heat previously stored in the same tubes. Ferretti's experiments then became directed (beyond accumulating data for future developments) toward the rapid construction of a 30 ton underwater high speed attack 'mini-submarine'. Because of its ability to independently operate on the high seas, deploying from bases close to enemy transit points, and its remarkable submerged speed, which could be used to escape after making an attack, this weapon seemed more practical than other similar systems under development or consideration.

Ferretti's project was similar to one conceived in the same years by the Imperial Japanese Navy. They developed their own 40 ton electric mini-submarines, progenitors of the 'A' class; these could reach 19 knots submerged for less than an hour and were intended to be launched from a class of fast, specially designed mother ships.

The independent Italian version of this concept enjoyed, at least on paper, some considerable advantages over its Japanese cousin. First was the decision to use an experimental 250hp Isotta Fraschini internal combustion engine fueled by alcohol and using oxygen as the combusting agent. The exhaust gases would have been recycled thereby assuring the pressure required for combustion. This allowed the planners to avoid the major pitfall of previous schemes: the requirement for a volume of air up to five times greater than that needed by the 30 ton

Another view of the Uarsciek *underway.* (Collection of E. Cernuschi)

Boats of the Mameli, Settembrini *and* Calvi *classes, built at the end of the twenties and the beginning of the thirties, docked at Naples in 1938.* (Collection of Erminio Bagnasco)

project's new engine system to deliver similar speed and endurance.

Tests of the Isotta Fraschini motor made in 1936 were encouraging, but they did not assure that the 500hp motor destined for the operational boat would have the necessary reliability.

The end of the Ethiopian crisis and the following period of tentative *détente* with Great Britain that began in 1936 and lasted through to August 1937 also ended the impetus for the Ferretti plan, although Cavagnari decided to continue theoretical studies on the basis of the remarkable amount of experience and information collected during the year before.

In 1936 Captain Raffaele de Courten, Italian naval attaché in Berlin and himself an old submariner, learned of German advances in the development of lightweight batteries. This encouraged the Ministry to pursue, once again, a single engine submarine and to bring to the shipbuilding industry a new design for an electric boat. Contrary to their own conservative tradition the CRDA society of Monfalcone proposed, in December 1936, a small assault craft design with dimensions of 12m x 1.52m, displacing 13 tons, with a crew of two and a 450mm torpedo in the bow. Equipped with a small diesel of barely 50hp and an electric drive system fed by 204 48volt batteries of the type recently introduced aboard the new and much publicized 'Littorine' fast railway locomotives, this mini-submarine would have been able to maintain 12 knots submerged for a quarter hour. This would facilitate escape from an ambush zone after an attack. The small unit would then surface, facing a slow and difficult voyage home.

Limitations in the design of the 13 ton boat combined with the hope of obtaining examples of the new German batteries encouraged the Ministry and the CRDA to plan a follow-up electric boat of 100 tons in 1937 (known also as *Viola-Moschini*, after the names of its first supporters). Four units were to have been secretly constructed and sent, in two pairs, to the Navy bases of La Spezia and Augusta along with six crews, where they would be held ready to respond to any sudden emergency. Not even this secret weapon went beyond the drawing board, however, because the Germans produced nothing but a constant stream of empty promises. These same batteries were destined to represent the heart of the future type XXI and XXIII *elektroboote* of 1942, the progenitors of the modern non-nuclear submarine, at least until the advent of new air independent propulsion (AIP) systems.

By 1938 the *Regia Marina* General Staff and the Submarine Command had lost practical hope of constructing their own 'true' submarine anytime in the near future. Conscious as they were of the vulnerability of the classic submarine-torpedo boat which formed their current submarine force, the Italian admirals concentrated

The launch of the Dandolo *on 20 November 1937. She was the only member of the* Marcello *class to survive the war. While the so called coastal submarines of the 600 class confirmed their limitations in 1940 against modern British ASW experience and tactics, these big Italian oceanic boats were able (when used correctly) to obtain good results against Allied shipping in the Atlantic and Indian Oceans.* Dandolo *crippled the cruiser* Cleopatra *and sank or damaged five freighters, totalling 16,142grt.* (Collection of Erminio Bagnasco)

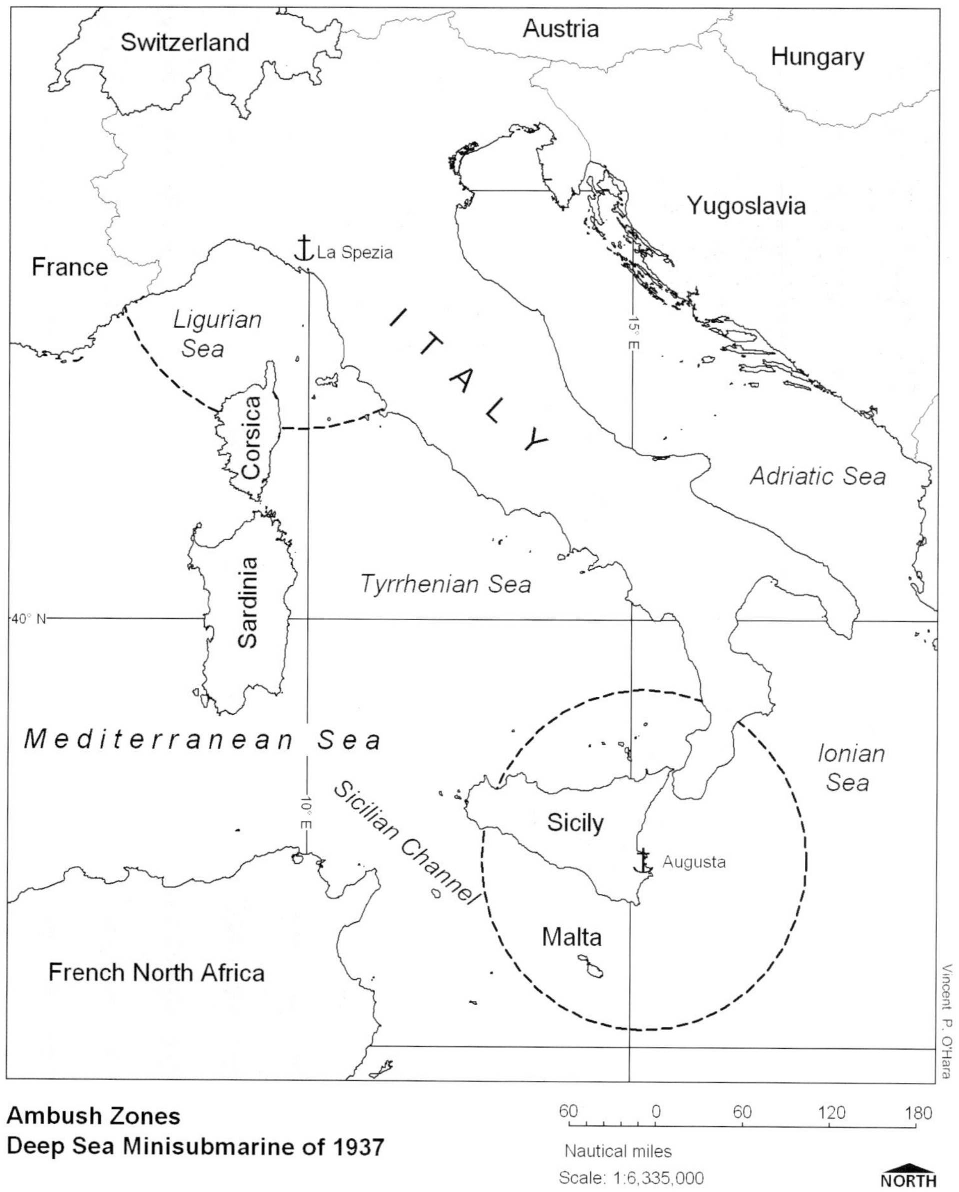

The proposed high speed 100t mini attack submarines of 1937 would have been an effective sea denial boat in the vital choke points of the Central Mediterranean and Ligurian Seas. (Vincent P. O'Hara)

Below: *a* Caracciolo *class boat in 1941. They were the biggest and best conceived oceanic submarine cruisers of the Regia Marina.* (Collection of Erminio Bagnasco)

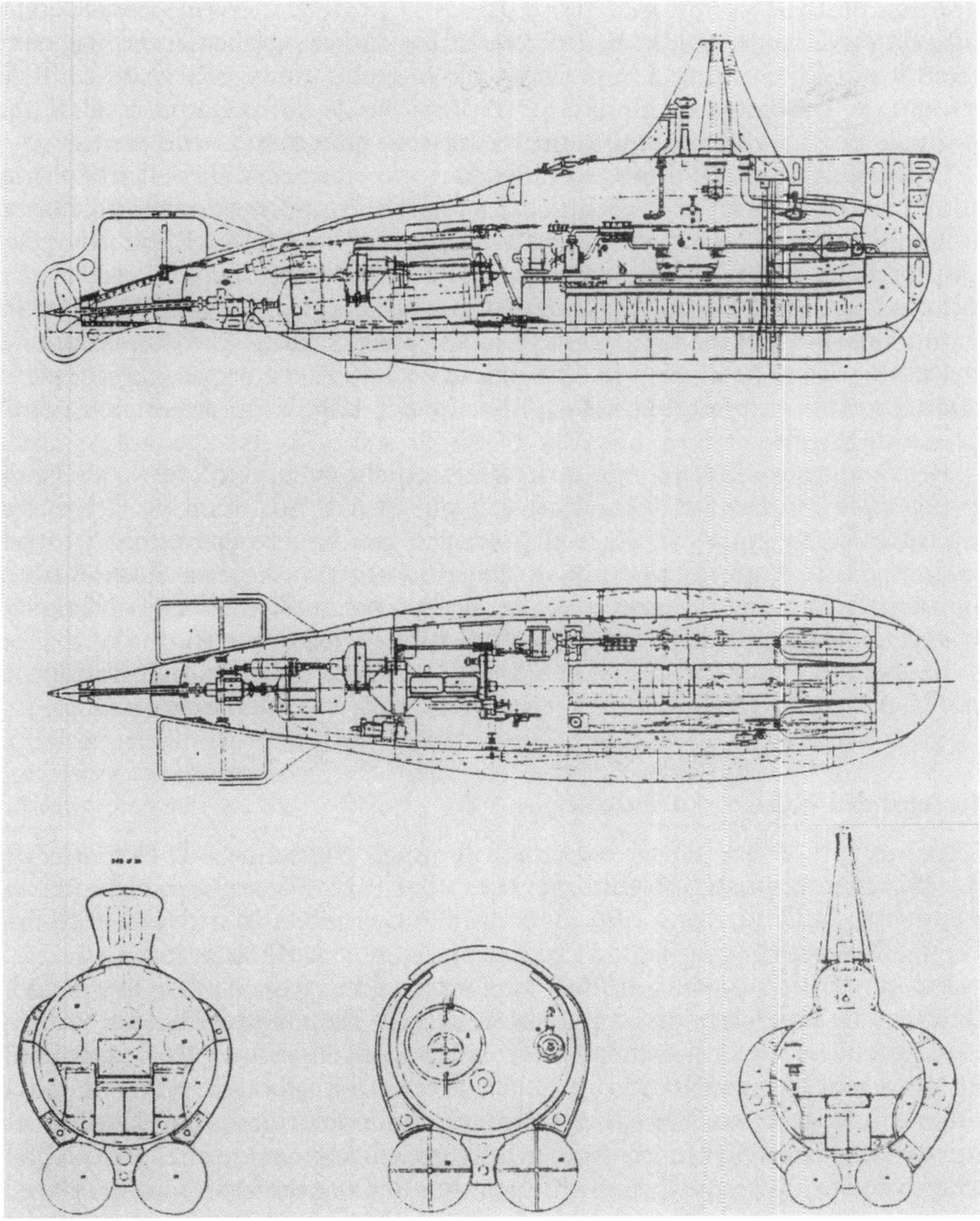

Further proof of Italy's inventive submarine design philosophies of the thirties was the S3. This classic midget diesel/electric boat was further developed and in 1939 became the 'CB' class which was used extensively by the Regia Marina in the Gulf of Naples, the Black Sea, in Calabrian waters and in the upper Adriatic by the post-1943 RSI's Marina Nazionale Repubblicana. (Associazione Navimodellisti Bolognesi)

on the Navy's efforts to realise a 'blind launch' system for the planned '800' type boats which, beginning in 1942, were to replace the forty-six units of the classic '600' utility type commissioned between 1932 and 1938. This system was intended to provide the ability to launch a salvo of four or six torpedoes from 20m underwater, practically without resort to the periscope, by using a mechanical calculator, the excellent Italian hydrophones and the newly developed 'ecogoniometro' (sonar) for aim and accuracy. In the event, these new techniques and operating doctrines were put to the test by the larger, wartime 'Flutto' class at the end of 1942. During the course of the following year they revealed themselves to be a simple palliative compared to the overwhelming antisubmarine superiority achieved on all seas by the Anglo-Americans.

The War, 1940-1945

Once ignited, the Second World War's unexpected prolongation pushed the Navy Ministry in December 1940 to reconsider the never forgotten Ferretti motor of 1935. The basis for this was a new, very original design elaborated by General (AN[1]) Eugenio Minisini. The goal was a small, 13 ton attack submarine called *SA1* but soon nicknamed '*Sandokan*' after a popular Italian movie hero by the workers and technicians at its construction site, the Baia Torpedo plant.

SA1's lines were clearly inspired by torpedo design. She was intended to be transported near the enemy by a destroyer mother ship and was characterized by a pair of forward counter rotating propellers. *SA1* was completed

The X1, *one of the first mini-submarines to use the anaerobic propulsion system.* (Rivista Marittima)

Opposite: *salvage operations at the Royal Italian Torpedo Works in Baia, October 1943. This photo was taken by the United States Navy team examining the* 'Sandokan' *attack submarine.* (FDR Library)

The Flutto *class boat* Tritone *on sea trials in July 1943. This class employed the Italian navy's 'blind launch' system that used hydrophones and sonar to aquire data that a mechanical computer used to calculate firing solutions.* (Collection of Erminio Bagnasco)

by 1942 and was immediately followed by a twin, *SA2* (nicknamed '*Yanez*', Sandokan's step-brother in the original novel).

Sandokan demonstrated unsuspected powers of maneuverability, which excited admiration in an American evaluation made two months after the armistice. ('Many interesting discussions arose from these experiments, because some technical experts had previously believed that tractive propellers would prove unsuitable.')[2] Her Isotta Fraschini four stroke 350hp internal combustion engine effectively reached 15 knots submerged and was able to maintain this speed for two consecutive hours.

The persistent delicacy of the motor, notwithstanding two years of tests, pushed Ferretti, in collaboration with

Salvage operations at the Royal Italian Torpedo Works in Baia, October 1943. This photos shows the United States Navy teams examining the 'Sandokan' attack submarine.
(FDR Library)

Captain (AN) Cesare Sansonetti, to complete in 1942 plans for a new, more reliable closed circuit, two cycle diesel engine of reduced weight and volume, but equal power.

This motor used exhaust gases to dilute oxygen, which was discharged directly into the sea while the mixture remaining in the cylinders was freshly enriched with a direct injection of the correct quantity of oxygen to combust the charged diesel engine oil. Successfully tested at Baia in 1943, first in the lab and then in the tank, the motor was destined for the next boat, *SA3* (alias '*Kammamuri*', the faithful servant of '*Sandokan*' and '*Yanez*')

The Italian armistice of 8 September 1943 brought the entire programme to an abrupt end. In 1944, however, the USN resurrected the project, for experimental purposes only, taking advantage of the collaboration, (authorised by the Italian Ministry) of Minisini and, subsequently, of Ferretti himself after these men were liberated, first from the hands of the Germans and, subsequently, from the almost equally disliked British.

Concurrent to Baia's involvement with *SA1-3* it should be noted the Navy entertained a number of other plans, some more, some less feasible, even if all were enthusiastically endorsed by Mussolini personally. These ranged from the Campini/De Bernardi design of 1942 to its ambitious follow-up, the failed 'Dux', to the private venture *Delfino* by Pietro Vassena (the creator, after the war, of the brilliant bathyscaph C3) to, finally, the *Sassaroli* conceived and put on the slipway after the armistice by the Fascist Italian Social Republic. Finally, in 1943 Ferretti, on his own, conceived on paper the same Walter turbine the Germans began constructing some years before.

Partnership with the United States, 1943-1958

In 1947 problems in the British Walter turbine prompted renewed interest in the Ferretti/Sansonetti closed circuit diesel engine in Italy and beyond. Even as early as 1943 many considered this engine a way of achieving the long awaited single purpose engine submarine; it was not as brilliant a solution as the closed circuit hydrogen peroxide boat, but it was far more reliable.

The classified history of the successful collaboration between the Italian and American Navies between 1947 and 1957 remains largely unexplored, despite an abundance of source material in both Italian and American archives. This collaboration began with experiments, pursued at first separately and then jointly, aimed at constructing a mini-submarine of approximately 30 tons for penetration of harbor defences (and in the case of Italy, with the further aim of arriving at a real attack submarine of 900 tons).

According to the wishful thinking of the time, this ambitious classified programme would have let the *Marina Militare* (the *Regia Marina*'s Republican incarnation) remove in one flick of the wand post war handicaps imposed by the peace treaty on its traditional doctrine of denial of sea superiority. The Italians were going to use the old *Bario* as a prototype. This was a submarine launched at Monfalcone in 1944 and never completed, but recovered by the *Marina Militare* after the war in order to reconstruct it as a purely experimental closed cycle boat by means of the Ferretti/Sansonetti system.

This boat was finally completed as a conventional experimental unit after development of the Ferretti/Sansonetti system was deprioritized in 1957 in favor of a new, very ambitious Italian program (with assistance from the USN) for a class of nuclear submarines similar to the contemporary *Skipjack* class. In 1961, close to its delivery, the *Bario* at last received its definitive name of *Pietro Calvi*.

The Italian dream of a closed circuit diesel engine was finally shipwrecked in February 1958 when the small American experimental submarine *X1*, constructed around a revised and improved version of the Ferretti/Sansonetti system, suffered an explosion in the area of the engine, killing some of the crew and breaking the craft into three pieces.

The Blind Alley, 1957-1975

The next stop in the long history of Italy's quest to build a 'true' submarine was an ambitious 1957 program for a three unit class of attack 'nukes'. After an encouraging start facilitated by the favor of the Eisenhower administration, a new and more prudent foreign nuclear policy enacted by the American Congress put an end to these dreams of glory just after President Kennedy's assassination in 1963. This was after the first boat, *Guglielmo Marconi* had been incautiously and prematurely announced by the Italian government in July 1962. In any case, the *Marina Militare* was not in a position to welcome such expensive warships, engaged as it was in a furious budget battle with the government for sufficient funds to just maintain the existing fleet.

After this disappointment, the *Marina Militare* and, even more so, the Rome government seriously considered a French proposal in the first half of the 1960s to construct in partnership a flotilla of 4,000 ton nuclear attack submarines. However, political considerations and veiled American pressure ensured this proposal went nowhere. A further French offer along the same lines was renewed throughout the 1970s for what would become, finally, the *sousmarin nucléaire de chasse* of the 'Rubis' class.

After the nuclear fiasco Italian development of a 'true' submarine became a monopoly of private business, first by Sub Sea Oil Services of Milan and subsequently by another association, Maritalia, which from 1970 through the beginning of the 1990s endeavored to develop a new, closed circuit diesel engine based, this time, on the dilution of oxygen in carbon dioxide (rather than helium as in Ferretti's engine). The engineer Guido Santi developed this system and coupled his new idea to the innovative solution of a torus hull structure to store oxygen without reducing the always inadequate space available aboard the boat.

The notable success of some small underwater craft projected and built by these two Italian companies (*PH-X.02*, *Phoenix 1350-1250*, *IMI-35* and *CEE-22 gst*), all based on these new concepts renewed, once again, the interest of the USN for a 'green nuke' submarine, considered ideal for use by its Sea Air and Land (SEAL) Special Force teams.

The success of private industry also encouraged the Italian Naval General Staff to try, once again, the now

A further view of the Baia salvage operations. The dimensions of the submarine are readily apparent. (FDR Library)

seventy year-old means of achieving a 'true' submarine. In the late 1980s they planned to delete the *Attilio Bagnolini* of the 'Toti' class to replace one of her diesel engines with a new closed circuit apparatus, opportunely placing the required oxygen containers on her deck. This experiment was, in any case, stopped at the very last moment by a further development.

The German Route, 1995-2003

The experimental nature of the aforementioned closed circuit diesel engine, judged suitable for civilian use, but not reliable enough for a warship, and a comparative study of the thermal efficiency available in alternative off-the-shelf solutions (the Stirling motor developed in Sweden

and the German Siemens fuel cell) finally induced the *Marina Militare* in 1995 to select the German solution. This decision gave life to the submarines of the new *U212 Todaro* class.

This was a difficult choice in many respects, not least in light of Italy's long and often illustrious history of innovative submarine design. However, it is inaccurate to say that with this decision Italy 'surrendered its submarine design capability to Germany' (see *Warship 2000-2001*, p.166). On a simply historical basis it is equally valid to conclude that Italy's decision to base its next class on German technology is only the fulfillment of Italo-German collaboration promised in 1914 and again in 1935-43, but never realised.

This cooperation is, in fact, the first step in the development of the design process for an innovative and very ambitious next generation boat, the so called 690t 'Razza' ('Skate') class, now on the drawing boards; a new kind of boat destined, in the hopes of many, to bring to final fruition the promise implied in Italy's very first submarine, *Delfino*, in 1896.

Bibliography

Bagnasco, Erminio, *I sommergibili della seconda guerra mondiale*, (Albertelli, Parma 1973) and *Submarines of World War Two*, (Cassell & Co. New York: 2000).

Bagnasco, Erminio and Cernuschi, Enrico, *Le navi da guerra italiane 1940-1945*, (Albertelli, Parma: 2003).

Cernuschi, Enrico, 'Il sottomarino italiano, storia di un'evoluzione non conclusa, 1909-1958', Supplement to *Rivista Marittima*, April 1999.

—'Il regio sottomarino Sandokan', *Rivista Marittima*, August-September 2002, pp.95-112.

Franklin D. Roosevelt Presidential Library, 'Salvage Operations at Royal Italian Torpedo Works', File A/16, Box 166.

Gardiner, Robert, (ed), *Conway's All the World's Fighting Ships 1860-1905*, (Mayflower, New York: 1979).

—*Conway's All the World's Fighting Ships 1906-1921*, (Naval Institute Press, Annapolis: 1985).

—*Conway's All the World's Fighting Ships 1922-1946*, (Mayflower, New York: 1980).

Galuppini, Gino, *Lo schnorchel italiano*, (Ufficio Storico della Marina Militare: Rome, 1986).

Preston, Antony, 'Soviet and Russian Air-Independent Submarines', *Warship 2000-2001*, (2000), pp.146-147.

—'Navies in Review 2000-2001', *Warship 2000-2001*, (2000), p.166.

Puglisi, G, 'Il sommergibile da lavoro 'Phoenix' con diesel a circuito chiuso', *Rivista Marittima*, December 1981, pp.35-50.

Rastelli, A 'Il sommergibile d'assalto *Delfino*', *STORIA Militare*, November 2001, pp.27-32.

Santi, G, 'Il sottomarino di nuova generazione', *Rivista Marittima*, March 1987, pp.33-44.

Sieche, Erwin, 'Austro-Hungarian Submarines', *Warship II*, 1980, pp.14-27.

Turrini, A, 'Almanacco dei sommergibili', Supplement to *Rivista Marittima*, January, February, March 2003.

—*La conquista degli abissi, storia del battello subacqueo da aristotele al sottomarino nucleare*, (Vittorelli, Gorizia: 1995).

—'Minisommergibili con motore a circuito chiuso', *Rivista Marittima*, March 1986, pp.85-87.

—'Quale futuro per la tecnologia subacquea italiana', *Rivista Marittima*, November 1992, pp.69-76.

—'Il battello subacqueo, nuova capital ship alle soglie del duemila', *Rivista Marittima*, March 1994, pp.35-43.

—'Una nuova concezione per lo sviluppo delle unità subacquee', *Rivista Marittima*. February 2001.

—'Nuovi concetti costruttivi per il sommergibile convenzionale', *Rivista Marittima*, February 1990.

—'La silenziosità, principale caratteristica del battello subacqueo', *Rivista Marittima*, February 1989, pp.39-53.

—'Sommergibili del futuro', *Rivista Marittima*, July 1986, pp.17-24.

—'Possibili sviluppi futuri della tecnologia subacquea italiana', *Rivista Marittima*, April 2003.

Notes

1 AN: Armi Navali or Naval Weapons

2 'Salvage Operations at Royal Italian Torpedo Works', 18 November 1943, p.10. FDR Library.

Another view of the Baia salvage operations, taken bow on and showing the forward counter-rotating propellers. (FDR Library)

MINELAYER *CLAS FLEMING*

An Early Gas Turbine Ship

The Swedish minelayer *Clas Fleming*, built in 1914 was originally propelled by Parson's direct-drive turbines. Heavy coal consumption led to her being laid up in 1917 and sparse commissionings thereafter, until in 1940-41 when she was rebuilt, gas turbines driven by exhaust gases from diesel engines being fitted. In 1945 the British Admiralty showed a mild interest in this gas turbine system. **Daniel G. Harris** describes this example of the Swedish Navy extensively modernising an old hull when funds for new ships were not available.

The mid-1900 journals of the Swedish Royal Society for Naval Sciences contain articles about the mine's use as an offensive weapon with special reference to its results in the Russian-Japanese war of 1904-1905. The journals suggest offensive mining could be suitable for Swedish defence. One contributor's article proposes that, to be used effective offensively, mines should be laid in overlapping rows.

Knowledge of the Russian-Japanese war's events probably influenced the Swedish Board of Admiralty, in 1908, to apply to the cabinet for funds to construct a high-speed vessel with good seakeeping qualities able 'under cover of darkness, to lay offensive minefields, some close to an enemy's coasts'. In 1909, the Crown in Council authorised the release of funds for the construction of a turbine-driven minelaying cruiser. The new vessel's purposes were to include not only minelaying, but also those of a cruiser to search for the enemy and to report back to the main fleet. The Admiralty Board decided the vessel's name was to be *Clas Fleming* after a seventeenth century Swedish Admiral who, in the reign of Gustaf II Adolph (1611-1632), was responsible for the creation of that monarch's powerful fleet.

The Construction

The *Clas Fleming*'s dimensions were: length 80m; beam 10.4m, and draft 4.3m. Steam turbines would enable the vessel to steam at over 20 knots. Two 12cm guns, one forward and one aft, were its original armament. *Clas Fleming* was to carry at least 190 mines. Displacement fully loaded was 1850 tons. The hull design had similarities to the German *Albatross* minelayers built in 1907.

Early in 1910, the board requested tenders from Götaverken of Göteborg, Kockums of Malmö and Bergsund Finnboda of Stockholm. The competing yards offered three different types of turbines. Götaverken's offer proposed De Laval, Kockums AEG-Curtiss and Bergsund's, Parsons 6500hp direct drives.

The Admiralty Board accepted Bergsund's tender, dated 21 January 1910, which was the lowest. It proposed to build the vessel at a total cost of 1,493,350 kronor. The contract, dated 17 May 1910, between the board and the yard, was given the highest level of secrecy. Under its terms, Bergsund agreed to build the vessel, with 7000hp turbine engines capable, in light wind and smooth sea conditions with full load, of steaming for three hours at an average speed of 20 knots. Bergsund was to report 'Cardiff smoke-free coal' consumption at speeds of 20 and at 14 knots during trial runs. No specifically-skilled stokers were to be employed for the acceptance trials.

The contract contains the following stipulations: that first-class Swedish materials were to be used where possible; the hull to be ready for launching eighteen months from 21 January 1910; all mild steel used shall meet Lloyd's Register's requirements for merchant vessels; rivets shall be to the standards of the '*English* Admiralty'; the total weight of 'engines, propeller shafts, pumps, condensers, and ten-ton fresh water reserve tank shall not exceed 227,700 kilos'. Finally, all costs of launch, for which 14 days notice must be given, were to be met by the builder.

Payment for the ship's construction was to be in eight instalments: on signing the contract; raising the frames; completion of plating, bulkheads, hause holes and installation of propeller shafts and rudder; laying of the main decks with winches; construction of deck houses, gun platforms and bridge; inspection of boiler material and forged cast turbine parts; completion of engines, boilers and funnels; lastly, following the installation of all machinery. Following acceptance trials, the board would pay the remaining costs.

The Bergsund contract gives particulars of the material for different sections of the hull. The keel comprised

11mm thick plates in the bow and stern, 10mm elsewhere. The keelson from frames, 5 to 117, was to be built of 12mm thick plates and the remainder of 10mm. Fourteen watertight compartments to the height of the orlop deck were to be placed at frames 5, 12, 15, 17, 23, 31, 43, 45, 78, 98, 104 and 111. Twelve and fifteen were to be of 6mm plate, the others of 5mm. The frames were of angle bar 130 x 65 x 10mm. The hull plating was to meet Lloyd's standards for merchant vessels and be 10mm thick at the bow and stern, and 11mm amidships. All plating was to be double riveted. Bergsund was to make certain all plate edges were clean before use and free of rust before painting.

The stern post was to be of cast steel, annealed after casting. The stem post was of cast steel, flat in the vertical and in V form to receive hull plates. The balanced rudder frames were of forged steel and its side plates were 8mm thick. Red lead painted wood was to fill the open space.

The deck armour, 16mm midships and 25mm at the ends, was of nickel steel, having a yield point of 35kg per kvm, tensile strength of 55kg per kvm and elongation of 22 per cent of normal length. Bergsund provided test pieces to withstand 25mm and 16mm shells.

The conning tower sides were to be 75mm thick, its roof of 30mm thick oil-hardened steel. Test pieces were to withstand 75mm shells. The bridge was of 3.5mm steel, with 10mm thick cork was to line the wheelhouse, for which the builder would provide one sofa, two chairs and a table. The deckhouses, with the forward, containing fan room and galleys at the main administration and chart room, were of 3mm plate. All roofs were to be lined with 10mm of cork. The yard was to make a rack for 30 rounds of 12cm shells and place it close to the stern gun.

Clas Fleming's hull carried bilge keels one third of the length at a height of 500mm, width at base 200mm, of 7mm plate, attached by 100 x 65 x 8 corner iron and double riveted. Hause holes suitable for Tyzacks anchors were to be pierced in the bow.

Delay in completing the hull was caused by the failure, on 10 December 1912, of steel under test delivered by the Domnarvet Works. The material was supposed to meet Lloyd's Register's norms of 46.1-50.4kg per kvm.

Eight coal-fired water-tube boilers with a heating area of 1200kvm, grate area 22kvm, in three watertight compartments supplied the steam at a pressure of 17kg/cm^2. The coal bunkers held a maximum of 265 tons. The Admiralty Board stipulated that the Yarrow-type boilers be of Swedish Martin steel, tensile strength 43-47kg per kvm, and at least 28 per cent elongation per 200mm. The boiler tubes inner diameter was to be 1⅛ English inches and a thickness of 2.34in. Those closest to the firebox were to be 2.64in thick. The boilers' mantles were to be of galvanized Swedish steel.

The Motala Works, under licence, manufactured two 3500hp ahead and reverse turbines. The former were capable of operating at 550rpm. The contract contained specific instructions about the material to be used to make the turbine blades, which were to be 67-70 per cent copper. One turbine house burst on test and was replaced. The turbines were to have separate compartments. Motala was responsible to supply the intermediate and tail shafts. Under test, these failed to meet the specifications, but were accepted provided Motala replaced them within two years. Siemens of London supplied Hopkinson patent torsion meters for the propeller shafts. The condensors were to be able to withstand 2.5kg per kvm

Bergsund ordered two 3-blade propellers of Atlas Manganese Bronze to turn outwards from Henry Walker of Newcastle at a price of £86 each. The blades were to be finely polished, sharp and balanced. No manufacturer's name was to be stamped on the propellers. Lloyds' Register's survey certified the propellers as in order for £2. Parsons argued the template gauges to the arms had an error of ½ of 1 per cent. That was ignored.

De Laval provided 8hp turbines for the electricity generators made by Luth & Rosén. The contract required the yard to provide a 90cm searchlight to be mounted on the bridge's roof, and a 60cm to be mounted on the bridge aft. Harfield's electrically-driven windlass with two cable lifters for 28mm links was to be installed on the bow, and a second windlass aft.

Clas Fleming *as built, 1914-15.* (Courtesy of Sjohistoriska Museet, Stockholm)

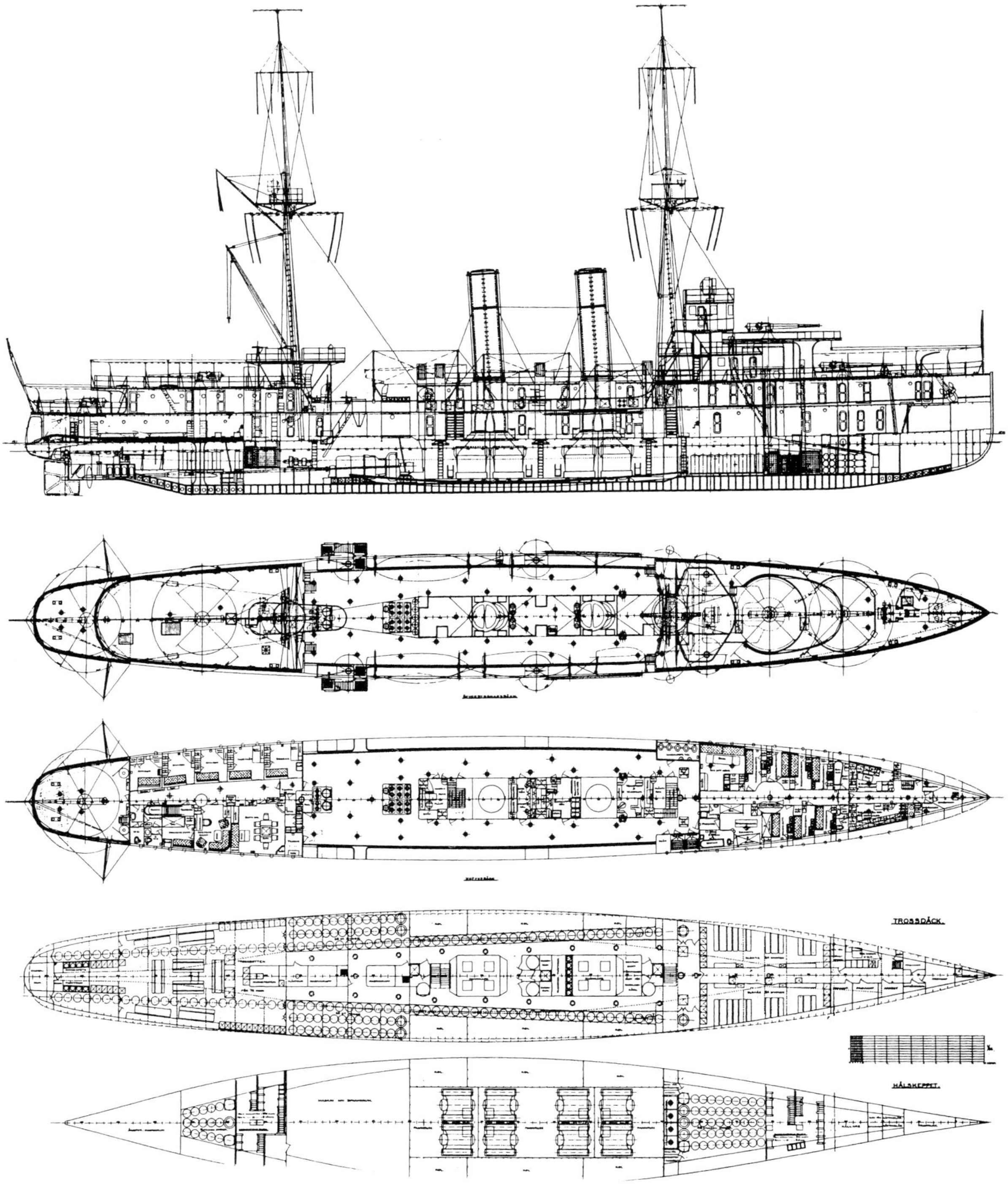

Original plans of Clas Fleming. (Krigsarkivet, Stockholm)

The steam-driven steering gear (no particulars in the contract) was to ensure that the rudder would not exceed an angle in excess of 35 degrees. The German Fitzner Laura supplied the two masts and spars of mild steel 34/41 to meet Germanischer Lloyd's norms.

Clas Fleming was to carry 190 mines, of which 60 were to be held on rails fitted to the main deck and laid through the stern's doors. 130 mines were to be held on the orlop deck and raised by Pater Noster equipment. Armament comprised one 12cm gun mounted on the centre line ahead of the conning tower and the second placed aft on the quarter deck. In addition, the vessel was to carry six machine guns, forty cutlasses and 12 rifles. A three-metre stereoscopic range finder was placed on the wheelhouse roof.

The ship's complement comprised eight officers, twenty-three non-commissioned officers and 130 men. The former were accommodated with bunks, the other ranks in hammocks on the orlop deck. The commanding officer's cabin was to have a curved sofa; furniture for officers was to be of pine with mahogany veneer; for warrant officers, oak; for other ranks, pine without 'American polishing'.

The new minelayer was only able to join the active fleet in the summer of 1914 owing to delays in construction and lengthy trials. *Clas Fleming* was the navy's only vessel available to carry out offensive mining that was considered operable. By mid-1917, the command decided defensive mining was to consist of controlled minefields laid by old gunboats and operated by the coastal artillery, a branch of the navy; offensive mining by the *Clas Fleming*, destroyers and the 4000 ton cruiser *Fylgia*, the latter to be fitted with rails for mines. In addition, the command held all light craft, destroyers and the torpedo cruisers ought to have minelaying capabilities.

The First Commissions and First Refit

In the summer of 1915 *Clas Fleming* carried out limited neutrality patrols in the Åland sea within territorial waters and in the Northern Stockholm Skerries. Owing to lack of fuel, coal had to be imported from Britain or Germany. British restrictions on coal exports to Sweden were part of the Western Allies' blockade of the central powers. The fuel shortages limited the minelayers' activities to two days per week. The Navy Board also made the unpleasant discovery that *Clas Fleming*'s fuel consumption was higher than expected. Owing to the turbines' lack of gearing, the high rate of propellor turns had only limited effects. Consequently, in the last quarter of 1917, *Clas Fleming* was paid off and placed under dockyard control in Stockholm for alterations. Sea time experience proved that the mine doors were too close to the water, which brought a risk of flooding in a stern sea. That could have unfortunate effects on the vessel's stability. The solution was to rebuild the stern increasing the doors' height above the water, with the mine tracks altered to cause the mines to mount an incline before leaving the hull During the 1918 refit, the positions of the 12cm guns were changed and given shields; one was retained on the forecastle, one on the poop. Two additional 12cm were added amidships on either side. In the 1920s, three 25mm Vickers anti-aircraft guns replaced the 6.5mm machine guns, two aft, and one on the roof of

Clas Fleming *after the first reconstruction, which was carried out during 1918-19.* (Krigsarkivet, Stockholm)

the conning tower. A lighting top was placed on the foremast.

The engines' high fuel consumption, not revealed during acceptance trials, brought various proposals to replace the Parsons direct-drive turbines with modern geared turbines. Nonetheless, in the 1920s and early 1930s, when defence expenditures were kept to the minimum, no action was taken. Left in dockyard control on minimum maintenance, the vessel's condition deteriorated. In spite of poor condition, *Clas Fleming*, in the autumn of 1939, was commissioned to lay mines in the Åland Island area and then returned to dockyard control.

The Second Reconstruction

In 1933 the Götaverken shipyard, Göteborg, had proposed an alternative to new steam turbines. One of its engineers, Erik Johansson, had been experimenting with a system in which a mixture of compressed air and diesel engine exhaust gases drove a type of gas turbine engine. The shipyard had installed Johansson's system in one of its tugs, and in the Fisheries Department's inspection vessel *Skagerack*. The interest from Swedish naval engineers in gas turbine development is apparent from an article published in *Tidskrift i. Sjöräsendet* for 1913. It details the Swiss Stodola & Zoelly experiments and those of Holzwarth in Mannheim, Germany. In addition, it mentions Brown Boveri's trials with a 1800hp turbine where temperatures reached 400°C. Götaverken offered to build a system similar to *Skagerack*'s, suitable for the larger *Clas Fleming*. In addition, Götaverken would lengthen *Clas Fleming*'s hull and provide a new bow. Götaverken requested funds for design and experimental work. The Navy's budget had no funds available to meet the shipyard's needs. In 1934, the Navy Board learned that the Social Affairs Department was willing to subsidise Götaverken's activities with funds allocated by parliament for unemployment relief.

Contract negotiations between the Navy Board and Götaverken began in the late 1930s. A final agreement was signed in December, 1939. The refit costs, including lengthening the hull by six metres amidships, a new bow, improvements to the stern mine doors, installation of oil fuel tanks in coal bunker space, extension of the orlop deck to the vessel's sides, conversion of the two forward boilers to oil fuel to provide steam for auxiliaries, were estimated at 889,300 kronor. Costs rose to over 1 million by the end of 1940. Differences arose during contract negotiations. The Board had included a stipulation that should the new engines fail to meet specifications to provide a speed of over 20 knots with full load, Götaverken would remove them and restore the old steam turbines and boilers to their former positions. The yard rejected those conditions as impossible and risible, since the old equipment and boilers would have been cut up during removal and thus had become scrap. The Navy Board agreed to delete that stipulation.

Two De Laval geared impulse turbines replaced the Parsons direct drive steam, each to drive one propeller. Together these were to provide 6500hp for ahead operations. The propellers were to turn at 360rpm to provide a

Clas Fleming *after her second reconstruction, pictured in 1940.* (Courtesy of Krigsarkivet, Stockholm)

Clas Fleming *after her third refit, 1940.* (Courtesy of Krigsarkivet, Stockholm.)

maximum speed of 20 knots, the vessel drawing 3.6 meters. For astern movements, the astern turbines turned the propellers at 220rpm for a maximum of fifteen minutes. The new engines guaranteed an ahead speed of 20 knots with a fuel consumption of about 1300 kilos per hour. At the cruising speed of ten knots, consumption should decline to 200 kilos per hour.

Two turbines for ahead operations and those for astern movements had common exhaust, and were the type in which the heated air/exhaust gas mixture expanded to about 4 akms. All had force-feed lubrication. Turbine operation was controlled by varying the gas pressure. During normal speed, it could be controlled by reducing the generators' fuel and during other operations, by chocking the turbine main stop valves.

The gas hot-air generators comprised four three-cylinder double-acting piston compressors connected to four six-cylinder, two-stroke reversible diesel engines with direct fuel injection and scavenging pumps. The diameter of the cylinders was 370mm and the stroke length 480mm. The compressors supplied compressed air at about 4 atm, which had to pass into the driving engine cylinders through apertures in the linings. The mixture of compressed air and exhaust gas from the diesel engines at a temperature of 400-500°C and was led to the turbines.

For full speed of 20 knots, the generators operated at 350rpm. When stopped, the generators fell to 75rpm and the gas, after passing through a muffler, was released to the open air by the after funnel. The system start was carried out by two 2-stage compressors capacity, 1m^3 of air was to be compressed to 50kg/cm^2. The compressors were not to exceed 1000rpm. A 15hp electric motor drove one, and a single-cylinder steam engine drove the other. One was placed in each turbine room. The connected reservoirs capacity of 1.9m^3 was capable of starting a main generator four times. The reservoir pressure of 50kg/cm^2 was to be reduced before use to 25kg/cm^2.

The gas turbine rotors were of forged steel and the turbine houses of cast steel. The bearings were of cast steel lined with white metal. The air compressors' pistons were of steel and the cylinders and cover of cast iron. The crankshafts were of Siemens Martin steel to be forged in one piece (i.e., drop forged). The oil cooling system for each generator was to consist of one oil cooler with a cooling surface of about 50m^2. Exhaust gases were vented through the after funnel.

Four steel propellers made by the Swedish Kohlswa Works replaced the original bronze. Two were kept in reserve in the Stockholm dockyard. Steel propellers were more able than bronze to withstand the ice in the Baltic. A diesel-driven electric power plant was located in each engine room to provide for all power needs.

The contract contained the following procedures for testing the ship and its new engines.

The trials were to begin with the engines cold. Each unit was to be started separately, and the operating of each noted; also when two, three, and four were in use. The revolutions of the propeller shafts were to be recorded with the ahead turbines, during operation of one, two, three or four generators. Similar procedures were to be followed for the astern turbines employing two, three and four generators. The *Clas Fleming* was to operate at full speed for six hours, and at 10 knots for the same period. The inspectors were to make careful notes of the fuel consumption at both speeds. They were to observe closely the astern turbines at 200rpm. In addition, the trials included 'steaming' at full ahead. On reaching maximum speed, with 6400hp effort, the four generators were to put to full astern and the time to bring the vessel to standstill recorded.

A report of the trials held in May refers to difficulties with personnel unfamiliar with *Clas Fleming*'s unusual operating system. Apparently, the trials were more successful when a certain D. Morosoff, a former Imperial Russian naval engineer employed by the inventor Johansson, in sober condition, took charge of engine room operations! Difficulties were found with the start-ups. One Swedish naval officer held that they were like starting a car with a frozen engine!

Clas Fleming's four 12cm guns were given higher elevations and personnel shields. The higher elevations increased the range of the four guns to 16,000 meters.

Clas Fleming *as part of the neutrality guard force in the Baltic, 1942*. (Courtesy of Krigsarkivet, Stockholm)

Three Bofors 40mm AA automatic guns replaced the Vickers 20mm; one on the roof of the conning tower and two on the poop. Two depth-charge mortars aft completed the armament. The magazine was to hold one hundred depth charges.

The foremast length was reduced and the fighting tops lowered. The main mast was also removed. An additional range finder was placed behind the after funnel. For some unknown reason, the Navy Board decided that a third dummy funnel be set up between the other two. It gave the vessel an unusual silhouette. The forward funnel vented the fumes from the two boilers retained to provide steam for auxiliary equipment.

Owing to gasoline shortages, Götaverken was to have the engines from the ship's boats adapted to operate with producer gas plants, using charcoal chips.

Trials lasted from May to August 1940. In September, *Clas Fleming* became part of the active fleet in the Baltic and gave fairly satisfactory service until May 1945. She was then paid off and laid up in the old Stockholm dockyard, and placed on minimum maintenance for the next fourteen years. In 1959, after removing of usable equipment, the hull was used as target. In 1960 it was sold for scrap.

The Johansson patented hot air and diesel exhaust gas turbine system gained no other customers, so it joined the company of unsuccessful inventions. The experiment proved that Swedish steel makers could produce steel able to withstand the high temperatures for gas turbine operations. (Throughout the Second World War, the Ljungström turbine plant secretly produced heat-resisting rotors for the British aircraft engine builders shipped out by the clandestine air service.) Nonetheless, when a small nation's funds for new buildings were limited, the Swedish Navy Board's technical staff was able to adapt an obsolete hull to use Johannson machinery to meet the pressing needs of a national emergency. Apart from 2½ years active service during the First World War and five in the Second, *Clas Fleming* seems to have been under dockyard control for thirty-seven of her forty-five year career.

Sources

Published:

Borgenstam, C B (et. al.), *Kryssare* (Stockholm, 1993).

Halldin (et. al.), *Svensk Skepps Byggeri* (Malmö, 1965).

Tidskrift i. Sjöräsendet, issues 1904-1913 (Karlskrona).

Unpublished:

Marin Forvaltning, *Skepps byggnads Grupp 148* 1908-12, Krigsarkivet.

– Diverser Riksarkivet.

– *Clas Fleming* Files 1910-1959, Krigsarkivet.

Bergsund Contract & Specification Schedules 1910, Krigsarkivet.

Götaverken Contract & Specification Schedules, December 1939.

PROJECT 69: THE *KRONSHTADT* CLASS BATTLECRUISERS

Starting in the mid-1930s the Soviet Union embarked upon an ambitious shipbuilding program. A central element in these plans was the construction of large cruisers, usually described as battlecruisers in western publications. **Stephen McLaughlin** describes the tortuous design history of these ships.

The Political Background

By the early 1930s Iosif Vissarionovich Stalin had secured his position as absolute dictator of the Soviet Union, eliminating all potential rivals by the technique of forming alliances with a group to bring down the most dangerous opponent, then betraying his former allies by aligning himself with another bloc. But if Stalin had achieved absolute security domestically, the international situation was far more uncertain. In the east, Japanese involvement in China caused growing concern, while in the west the rise of Hitler, and the indecisiveness of the Britain and France in the face of a resurgent Germany, suggested that the entire European order might be in for radical change.

Faced with these threats, Stalin was determined to turn the Soviet Union into a great military and naval power. This of course required a strong industrial base, and a number of draconian measures were taken to accelerate the process of industrialisation. Great progress was indeed made, at a tremendous cost in human suffering, but the statistics showing skyrocketing production were largely based on optimistic or even fraudulent figures provided by managers at all levels, who were quite literally under the gun to demonstrate their successful performance. Each year the target figures, based on the previous year's inflated reports of extraordinary industrial achievement, were raised to even more unrealistic levels, and each year industry proved incapable of meeting the targets. This fundamental problem goes a long way toward explaining why Stalin's warship building programmes were constantly being 'corrected' and 'refined.' At a time when industrial productivity was supposedly growing by leaps and bounds, it was time and again necessary to reduce the scale of the shipbuilding programmes. The barest outline of the changes in the number and types of ships to be built gives some idea of the fluid and unrealistic nature of Stalin's naval plans.[1]

	June 1936	Sept. 1937	Feb. 1938	Aug. 1939	July 1940	Oct. 1940
Battleships: Type 'A'	8	6	15	15	6	3
Battleships: Type 'B'	16	14	-	-	-	-
Heavy Cruisers	22*	10*	15**	16**	4**	2**

*Armed with 250 or 254mm (10in) guns
**Armed with 305mm (12in) guns

In addition to constant changes in the number of ships to be built, the size of individual ships also fluctuated wildly, the type 'A' battleships swinging between 35,000 and 60,000 tons, while the type 'B' battleships ranged from 26,000 to 48,000 tons. Trying to extract some underlying rationale for these fantasy figures is a pointless exercise; the only constant in the morass of these plans was Stalin's overwhelming desire to create a 'great sea-going and oceanic fleet' that would impress potential allies and frighten potential enemies.

The Soviet Design Process

Before launching into the story of these cruiser designs it is necessary to outline how Soviet ships were designed in the 1930s.[2] The most important point to bear in mind is that the Soviet navy did not design its own ships. Both merchant vessels and warships were designed by the various design bureaux of the Main Administration of Shipbuilding, which was itself a part of the People's Commissariat of Heavy Industry. Relations between the navy and the Shipbuilding Administration were governed by a formalized process that usually began with the navy establishing the broad requirements (*operativno-takicheskoe zadanie*, or OTZ) for a new design. These spelled out the missions the new ship was supposed to fulfil. The navy's own shipbuilding organization would then work out very preliminary designs that were intended to demonstrate the feasibility of the requirements. As a result of these design studies, the navy would formalize the tactical-technical requirements (*taktiko-tekhnicheskoe zadanie*, TTZ), indicating the desired displacement, the number and calibre of the guns, the level of protection and the speed. These characteristics would then be handed over to the Shipbuilding Administration, which would assign the project to a design bureau for the development of a 'pre-sketch design' (*predeskiznyi proekt*). In the case of important projects like battleships and battlecruisers, two bureaux would work out competitive proposals, and the navy would select the one it considered superior. The chosen design bureau would then work out the 'sketch design' (*eskiznyi proekt*). Despite its name, this was actually a fairly elaborate piece of work, complete with all necessary calculations for stability, trim and buoyancy. Once the navy had approved the sketch design, the work would start on the 'technical design' (*tekhnicheskii proekt*), which was equivalent to the contract design in the USN or a detailed design in the Royal Navy. When this was approved, it would be turned over to one of the shipyard drawing offices, where the actual working drawings (*rabochie chertëzhi*) would be composed.

That at least was the process in theory. It rarely proceeded so smoothly in practice. To begin with, it usually required several iterations of the pre-sketch and sketch-design phases before the navy and the design bureau reached an agreement. This inevitably involved a good deal of correspondence between the navy and the Shipbuilding Administration, and usually a good deal of friction as well. And the entire process could be derailed by political interference. For major classes of warship, every important stage in the design process would have to be approved by the Defence Committee of the Counsel of People's Commissars, headed by Stalin. Although Stalin had a fairly sound grasp of many technical matters, he demonstrated a woeful ignorance of naval strategy and tactics, and also had a habit of radically altering a ship's characteristics mid-way through the design process, thereby negating months of design work.

Starting about 1936, as the Great Purge got underway, the governmental structure underwent a frenetic series of reorganizations and re-namings. Thus in December 1937 the navy, which had been part of the Red Army since the 1920s, became a separate service with its own People's Commissariat. This was more than a paper change, for it gave the navy an independent voice in the highest levels of the government, whereas previously its needs and ideas had to filter upward through the army high command. In early 1939 the Commissariat of Heavy Industries was broken up into a number of more specialized bodies, one of which was the new Commissariat of Shipbuilding. These high-level changes led to reshuffling and re-naming of the ship design organs as well, but by and large the design process remained the same as before.

'Large Cruisers'

Initial Soviet interest in big warships centred on large cruisers. These studies were paralleled in other nations, where the idea of building 'cruiser killers' that could overtake and overwhelm 10,000 ton 'Treaty' cruisers were investigated from time to time in the inter-war period.[3] But the fact that such 'super-cruisers' would use up a portion of a nation's limited capital ship tonnage usually made them unattractive. The Soviet Union, however, was not bound by these treaty limits, and so in the early 1930s the Red Navy expressed considerable interest in the construction of *istrebiteli vashingtonskikh kreiserov* – 'Washington [Treaty] cruiser hunters.' The first set of requirements for such a ship was issued sometime in 1934, and called for a ship that would fulfil the following general roles:

- Independent operations on the high seas
- Operations against the enemy's coasts
- Support of Soviet light forces that were operating at a distance from their own bases

More specifically, the ship was to carry a main battery powerful enough to destroy any enemy ship having a higher speed, while its protection should be able to resist cruiser gunfire and medium high-explosive bombs. Speed was set at 38 knots, and enough aircraft were to be provided to allow the ship to scout over a 50nm radius. Although the ship was not intended to face enemy capital ships, it was to be able to inflict 'serious' damage on battleships or battlecruisers if the need arose.

Calculations showed that, in order to have a decisive superiority over the *Panzerschiffe Deutschland* or the Japanese *Atago* class heavy cruisers, a gun of 220-225mm was necessary. Taking into account the fact that more heavily protected cruisers might appear in the future, it was decided to adopt a 240mm/60 gun firing a 235kg shell at a muzzle velocity of 900m/s, and the Leningrad

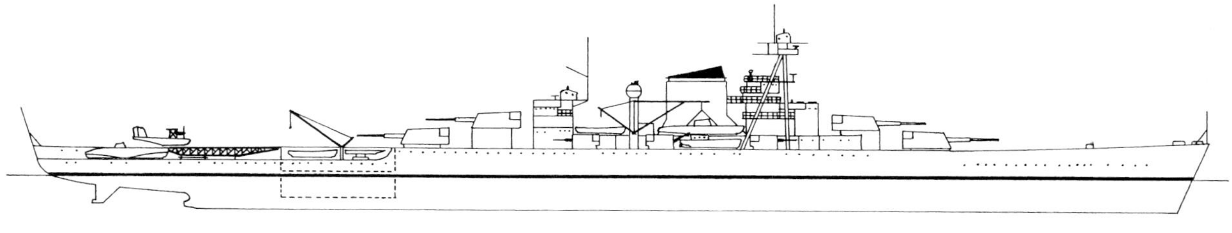

Fig. 1. *Large Cruiser 'X', May 1935. Note that the small torpedo boat/submarines of the 'Blokha' type were to be stowed just aft of the catapult, one on either beam. They were to be launched from gravity davits. Also note the large, two-level hangar just abaft 'Y' turret (shown in broken lines).* (Drawing by the author)

Metallicheskii Works drew up a sketch design for a triple turret for this gun. It featured a maximum elevation of 60°, and the rate of fire was to be five rounds per minute, dropping to 2.7 rounds per minute at higher elevations, since it took longer for the gun to be lowered and raised from its fixed loading angle.

The development of a design to meet the navy's requirements was assigned to the Main Administration of Shipbuilding's TsKBS-1 (*Tsentralnyi konstruktorskii biuro spetsialnogo sudostroeniia*, Central Design Bureau for Special Shipbuilding – 'special' in this case meaning warship design). The chief constructor on the project was V P Rimskii-Korsakov.[4] His design, dubbed Large Cruiser 'X' (*Bol'shoi kreiser* 'X'), was submitted to the naval authorities for review on 21 May 1935. This was only a few days after the *Scharnhorst* and *Gneisenau* were laid down, so no account could be taken of their characteristics, which at the time were still being described as *Panzerschiffe*, that is, pocket battleships. Large Cruiser 'X' was therefore only powerful enough to tackle a treaty cruiser with reasonable confidence in the outcome of the engagement.

Displacement:	15,518 tons (standard) 17,350 tons (normal) c.20,000 tons (full load)
Dimensions:	233.6m wl, 236m oa x 22.3m x 6.6m (normal) 766ft 5in wl, 774ft 4in oa x 73ft 2in x 21ft 8in (normal)
Armament:	12-240mm (9.45in)/60 (4 x 3; 110 rpg) 12-130mm (5.1in) (6 x 2; 200 rpg) 6-45mm (6 x 1; 500 rpg) 4-12.7mm MG (12,000 rpg) two triple 533mm (21in) torpedo tubes one catapult, nine seaplanes
Protection:	main belt: 115mm (4.5in) main battery turrets: 150mm (5.9in) faces, 100mm (3.9in) sides, 75mm (3in) roofs, barbettes 115mm (4.5in) conning tower: 152mm (6in) upper level, 75mm (3in) lower level, 100mm (3.9in) roof deck: 75mm (2.95in)
Machinery:	three shafts, geared turbines, six boilers; 210,000shp
Speed:	38 knots
Range:	900nm at full speed; 5,000nm at ? knots
Complement:	728

One of the most striking features of the design was the large number of aircraft contemplated, as many as some hybrid cruiser-carrier schemes. In fact there is a passing resemblance between Large Cruiser 'X' and the Swedish *Gotland*. With only one catapult, the launch rate would have been fairly slow, so it is likely that the main role seen for the aircraft was reconnaissance rather than offensive strikes. There was a below-decks hanger abaft the after 240mm turrets, with four aircraft stowed on each of two levels. One more aircraft would be kept on the catapult.

Another unusual feature of the design was the provision of two small submersible torpedo boats of the 'Blokha' type, an idea suggested by the head of TsKBS-1, V L Bzhezinskii. These strange craft were to have a surface speed of 29 knots and were intended for coastal operations.

The high speed required led Rimskii-Korsakov to propose using the advanced boilers designed for the Project 45 destroyer *Sergo Ordzhonikidze* (launched in December 1935; renamed *Opytnyi* in 1940). This machinery plant was inspired by the high-pressure boilers Bzhezinskii had recently seen during a trip to Germany. The *Ordzhonikidze*'s boilers, designed by L K Ramzin, pushed the steam conditions to the limit, the designed pressure was 75kg/cm^2 (1,069lbs/in^2) at a temperature of 450°C (842°F). The twin-shaft plant of the destroyer was designed for 70,000shp per shaft; Rimskii-Korsakov simply added a third shaft to achieve a total of 210,000shp. The design speed of 38 knots was to be maintained on a twelve-hour trial at the normal displacement of 17,350 tons; however, the *Ordzhonikidze*'s power plant proved disappointing in service (to put it mildly) so it is doubtful if Rimskii-Korsakov's Large Cruiser 'X' could ever have achieved her designed speed.

Apparently Large Cruiser 'X' didn't fully satisfy the navy, and a larger ship, with a more powerful armament, was asked for. The new design was also worked out by Rimskii-Korsakov, assisted by V A Nikitin, and was completed before the end of 1935. The design repeated the power plant of Large Cruiser 'X' but had a more powerful main battery and considerably heavier protection:

Displacement:	19,500 tons (standard) 20,500 tons (normal) c.24,000 tons (full load)
Dimensions:	240m oa x 24m x 7.45m (normal) 787ft 5in oa x 78ft 9in x 24ft 5in (normal)
Armament:	9-250mm (9.84in) (3 x 3) 12-130mm (5.1in) (6 x 2) 12-45mm two triple 533mm (21in) torpedo tubes one catapult, nine seaplanes
Protection:	main belt: 200mm (7.87in) decks: 25mm (0.98in) upper deck, 100mm (3.9in) armour deck
Machinery:	210,000shp
Speed:	36 knots
Range:	5,000 at ? knots

By December 1935 several other large cruiser designs had been submitted to the navy for review, but information on these projects is very incomplete. Sizes apparently ranged from 23,000 to 30,000 tons, with main battery guns of up to 305mm (12in) calibre. Also studied were designs for hybrid 'cruiser-carriers' (*kreisera-avianostsy*) ranging in size from 21,500 to 28,500 tons, with 305mm guns and carrying 49-60 aircraft. Despite this wide range of cruiser studies, however, the navy was still not satisfied, and in early 1936 it asked for a new design, which was eventually designated Project 22. This called for a 23,000 ton ship armed with 254mm (10in) guns, but little else is known about this design. In any event, by June 1936 the series of large cruiser designs had been superseded by a new concept, the small, fast battleship.

Battleship 'B'

In September 1935 the Naval Academy (that is, the naval war college) had carried out a series of studies of 'large armoured artillery ships' – a euphemism for battleships, a term that was at the time still out of favour in Soviet naval circles. These outline designs, which were intended to explore the tactical possibilities of such ships, featured 305mm main batteries arranged as in HMS *Nelson*, with all three triple turrets forward of the superstructure. The conclusion reached by the Naval Academy was that two different types of battleships were required, a large type intended primarily for operations in the Pacific, and a smaller ship for use in the restricted waters of the Baltic and Black Sea. The big battleship (designated 'A') eventually evolved into the *Sovetskii Soiuz* (Project 23) class. The initial requirements for the smaller 'B' type battleships called for ships capable of destroying Treaty cruisers or pocket battleships – in other words, the same roles considered for the large cruiser designs. But by the time the navy's requirements were completed, battleship 'B' had somehow grown into a 35,000-ton ship armed with 406mm guns, large enough, it would seem, to keep it distinct from the big cruiser studies. Then in May and June of 1936 the Soviet Union entered into negotiations with Britain for a bilateral naval agreement that would have imposed the Washington Treaty limits on ship size on the Red Navy's battleships. In expectation of this, the two battleships were 'downsized': battleship 'A' was now to be a 35,000-ton ship, while battleship 'B' reverted to 26,000 tons and an armament of 305mm guns. Given the fact that battleship 'B' and the Project 22 large cruiser were now about the same size, the cruiser studies were cancelled in June 1936 and attention was focused on battleship 'B'.

The navy's requirements were issued on 12 July 1936, calling once again for a ship that could destroy Treaty cruisers and pocket battleships. These specifications were issued to both TsKBS-1 and the design bureau at the Baltic Works, KB-4. But even as the design teams set about their work, the Naval Academy was conducting new studies, and on 3 August the navy again changed the characteristics, leading to a ship in the 30,000-ton range rather than the 26,000 tons originally specified. In November 1936 TsKBS-1 was awarded the design of Battleship 'B,' now dubbed Project 25, while KB-4 was assigned the development of the larger Battleship 'A'.

The design team at TsKBS-1 was the same that had worked on the large cruiser designs – Bzhezinskii, Nikitin, Rimskii-Korsakov and A I Maslov, a fact which had probably given them an edge in the competition with KB-4. In addition to the earlier large cruiser designs, the construc-

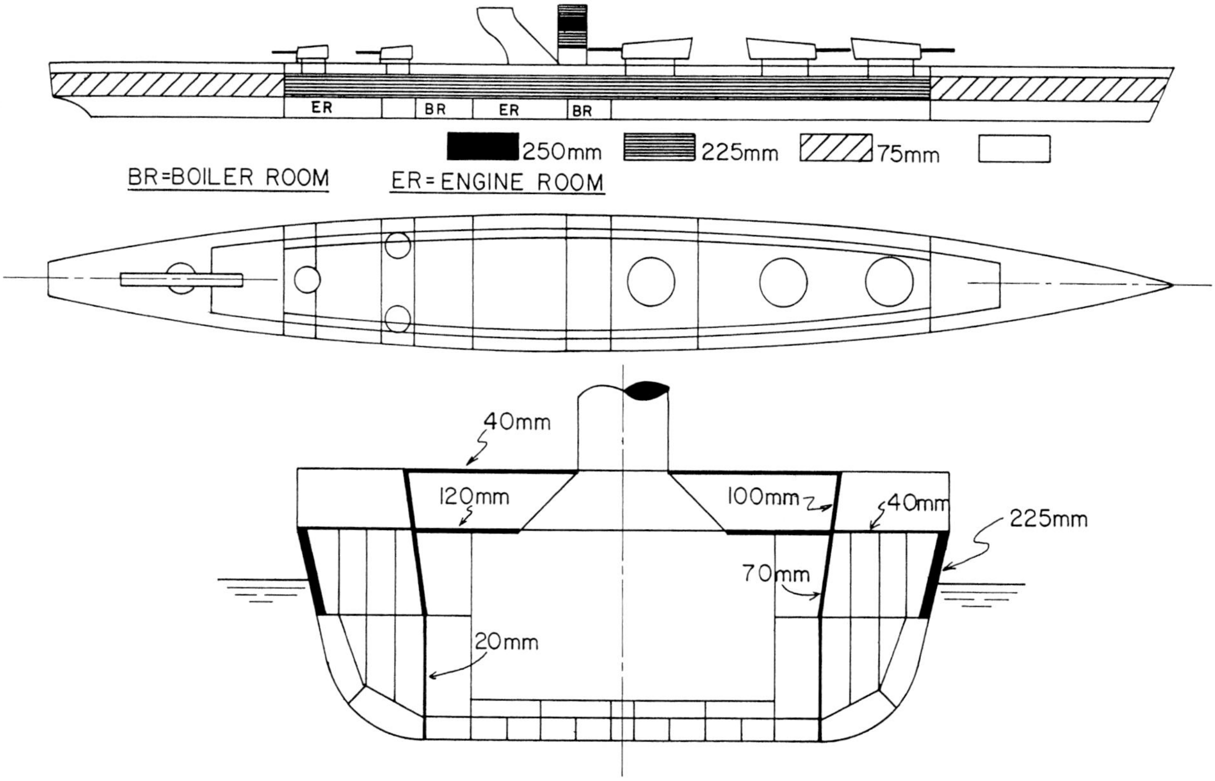

Fig. 2. *One of the notional 'large armoured artillery ships' studied by the Naval Academy in September 1935. Particularly noteworthy is the peculiar arrangement of protection shown in the cross-section, which would have allowed shells on some trajectories to reach the vitals by penetrating the 40mm deck at the side and the 70mm bulkhead below.* (Drawing by the author)

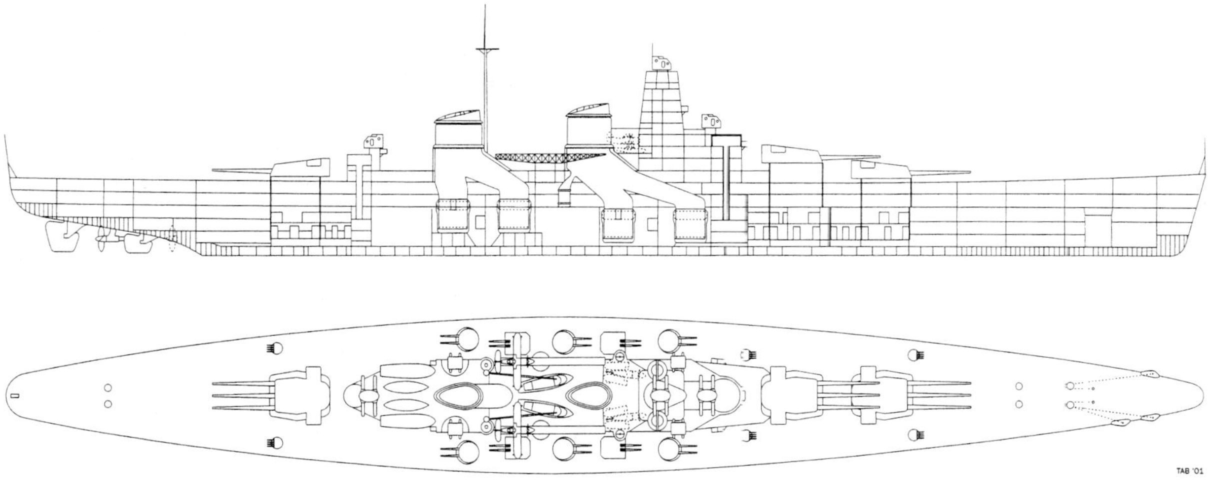

Fig. 3. *Battleship 'B', Project 25, late 1936. This is the penultimate version of the design, before the decision was made change to a three-shaft propulsion plant in order to use the same turbines as the Project 23 (Sovetskii Soiuz) class battleships. The round turrets on the side-decks are for the 130mm guns, while the squarish gunhouses are for the 100mm HA guns. The unusual arrangement of the 130mm and 100mm guns was apparently adopted so that the catapults could train outboard over them.* (Drawing courtesy of Thomas A Burns)

tors made use of a pair of Ansaldo designs that Bzhezinskii had brought back from Italy in 1936. Drawn up at the same time as the well known UP-41 battleship, one design was for a large cruiser very similar to the earlier Soviet studies (22,000 tons, 37 knots, nine 250mm guns), while the second was for a small battleship (27,900 tons, nine 345mm guns). The Italian designs proved useful in developing the hull lines and general arrangements. One feature adopted from them, for example, was a bulbous bow – a feature developed, ironically enough, by a Russian naval architect, V I Iurkevich, before the First World War. TsKBS-1's initial Project 25 design had the following characteristics:

Displacement:	30,900 tons standard, 37,800 tons full load
Dimensions:	250m oa x 30.6m x 7.5m 820ft 3in oa x 100ft 5in x 24ft 7in
Armament:	9-305mm (12in) 12-130mm (5.1in) 8-100mm (3.9in) 24-37mm two catapults, four seaplanes
Protection:	main belt: 200mm (7.9in) turrets: 230mm (9.1in) faces conning tower: 230mm (9.1in) upper deck: 40mm (1.57in) splinter deck: 20mm (0.79in) armour deck: 100mm (3.9in)
Machinery:	four shafts, 240,000shp
Speed:	35 knots
Range:	7,000 at ? knots
Complement:	1,253

As was the norm in Soviet shipbuilding, however, the specifications were soon changed. The belt armour was increased to 250mm (9.8in) and the armour deck to 125mm (4.9in). An even more radical change was the switch from a four-shaft to a three-shaft propulsion plant. This revision resulted from the work of a commission headed by Flag Officer 2nd Rank S P Stavitskii[5], which recommended that as many components as possible be standardized between the big and small battleship designs to simplify production. Despite these major alterations, the technical design for Project 25 was completed by the summer of 1937.

Everything now seemed ready for the start of construction, and in fact the ships had already been ordered. As early as 22 November 1936 (that is, when work on the design was really just getting started), plans were made for the construction of six ships, but this was reduced to four ships in January 1937. Two were to be built at the A. Marti Works in Leningrad, and another pair at the 61 Kommunara yard in Nikolaev. All four were supposed to be laid down in late 1937 and early 1938.

But things were never simple in Stalin's Russia, and just as the Project 25 design was completed the bloodletting of the Great Purge descended upon the navy It began with the arrest of the head of the navy, V M Orlov, in August 1937, and before long officers and technicians at every level were being arrested, tortured, executed or sent to the Gulags of Siberia. Project 25 was soon declared 'wrecked', that is, sabotaged. Bzhezinskii, Rimskii-Korsakov, and P O Trakhtenberg, all associated with the design, were arrested, and Trakhtenberg and Rimskii-Korsakov were both executed before a year had passed.

The primary charge against Project 25 was that it was weak compared to foreign ships, so the new Chief of Naval Forces, Fleet Flag Officer 1st Rank M V Viktorov, ordered the main battery increased. By August-September 1937 a new set of requirements had been issued calling for a much more powerful battleship. Designated Project 64, it was to be armed with 356mm (14in) guns and protected against 16in shellfire. These specifications were clearly

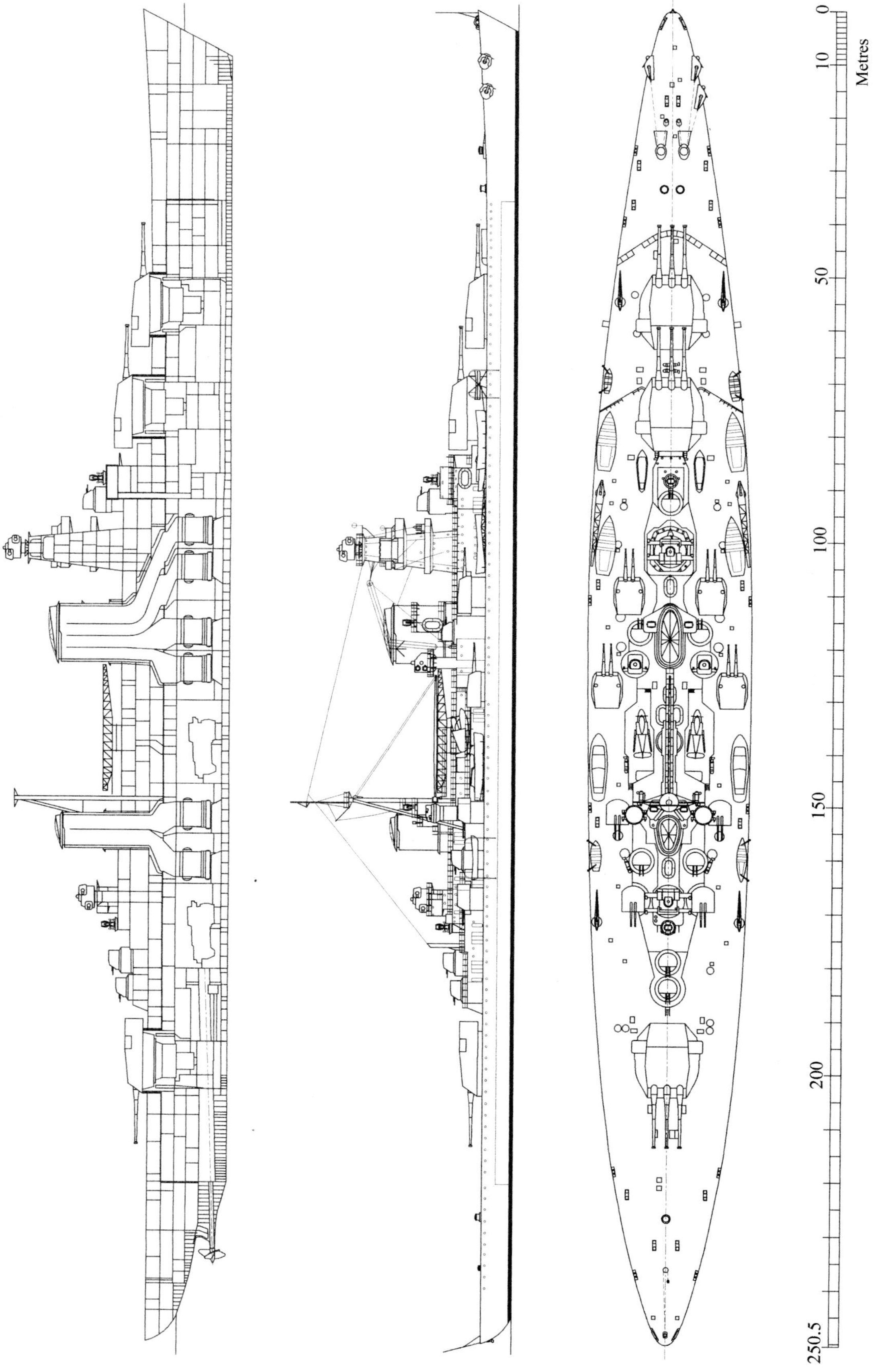

Fig. 4. *Project 69, sketch design, early 1939. The design was subsequently altered slightly, the 37mm quad mounting atop the conning tower being replaced by a third HA director.* (Drawing courtesy of John Roberts)

incompatible with a 'small' battleship, and by the end of 1937 the design had reached a displacement of 48,000 tons standard. There was no clear rationale for building such large second-class ships, and in early 1938 the decision was made to abandon the whole Battleship 'B' project and simply build a larger number of the more powerful *Sovetskii Soiuz* class battleships.

Heavy Cruisers: Project 69

But the idea of a small, fast capital ship refused to die. In August 1937, just as Project 25 was declared wrecked, a new requirement for a large cruiser designated Project 69 was prepared. The ships were now being referred to as 'heavy cruisers' (*tiazhëlye kreisera*). Although sometimes considered a Soviet attempt to deceive other nations into thinking these were 8in-gunned ships, within the Soviet scheme of classification the description made sense. The Russian term for 'battlecruisers' was *lineinye kreisera*, literally, 'cruisers of the line'. This was a fitting description for the *Izmail* class ships laid down before the Great War, which were really fast battleships. But the much more lightly protected Soviet 'heavy cruisers' were hardly fit to lie in the line of battle, and the roles foreseen in the original requirements were in fact classic cruiser duties. Since the Soviet Union was not a signatory to the Washington Treaty, the term 'heavy cruiser' was a logical one for these ships.

The initial requirement was composed after reviewing both the earlier 'large cruiser' designs and the Ansaldo designs, and outlined the following tasks for the new large cruiser:

- In a fleet action, to oppose the enemy's cruisers, especially his heavy cruisers, in support of the light forces
- Supporting the action of light forces in distant areas
- Independent operations on the enemy's lines of communication

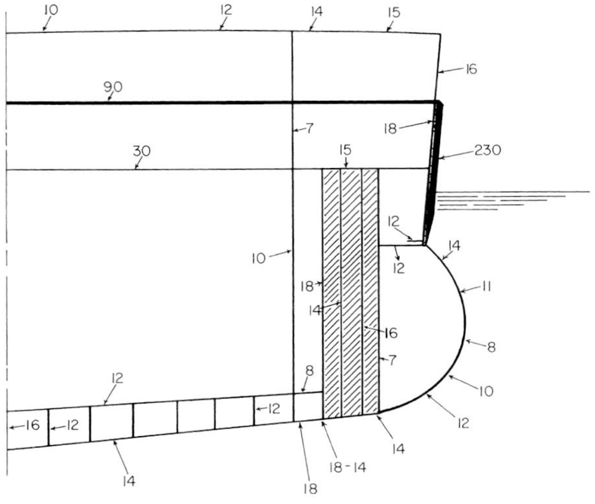

Fig. 5. *Project 69, cross-section. The figures represent armour and plating thicknesses in millimetres. Note that the beam is greater over the bulge than at the level of the upper deck.* (Drawing by the author)

In other words, the new heavy cruiser had exactly the same tasks as the initial concept of Battleship 'B'. Its characteristics were also similar:

Displacement:	'not to exceed' 22,000-23,000 tons standard
Armament:	9-254mm (10in) 8-130mm (5.1in) 8-100mm (3.9in) 16-37mm 6-533mm (21in) torpedo tubes two seaplanes
Protection:	To be protected against 203mm (8in) shellfire at ranges greater than 60 cables (12,000 yards) on bearings of 40-50° and 130-140° (measured from the bow), with deck protection to withstand 203mm shells out to 150 cables (30,000 yards) and 250kg bombs dropped from 4,000m
Speed:	34 knots
Endurance:	6,000nm at 20 knots, 8,000nm at 'economical' speed

In addition, the silhouette was to be similar to that of Battleship 'B'.

The responsibility for the design was again assigned to TsKBS-1, which had been redesignated TsKB-17 in January 1937. By this time the bureau must have had a whole library of aborted big cruiser/small battleship projects to draw upon, which probably assisted in the design work. The first attempt was worked up by one of the few survivors of the Project 25 team, V A Nikitin, and was ready by June 1938, almost a year after the initial order. The delay can probably be attributed to a combination of a heavy workload on the staff, and to the general confusion caused by the ongoing purges, which were destroying the navy's experienced command staff.

As usual, the specifications had proven overly ambitious, and the navy had to make a number of concessions to keep the displacement down. The torpedo tubes were deleted, the ammunition stowage for the 254mm guns was reduced from 150 to 125rpg, and range at 20 knots was reduced to 4,500nm. Even so, Nikitin was unable to keep the ship's size within the specified limit, and the speed was also less than desired.

Displacement:	24,450 tons (standard) 26,200 tons (normal)
Dimensions:	232m oa x 26.6m x 7.64m (full load)[6] 761ft 2in oa x 87ft 3in x 25ft 1in (full load)
Armament:	9-254mm (10in) (3 x 3) 8-130mm (5.1in) (4 x 2) 8-100mm (3.9in) (4 x 2) 24-37mm one catapult, two seaplanes
Protection:	main belt: 140mm (5.5in) turrets: 210mm (8.26in) faces decks: 80mm (3.15in) armour deck, 20mm (0.79in) splinter deck

Machinery: 210,000shp
Speed: 33.3 knots
Range: 4,500 at 20 knots

The design was reviewed by the Defence Committee, headed by Stalin, in June 1938. By this time the first details of the *Scharnhorst* class were known, and as might have been expected Nikitin's design was seen as too weak in comparison with the German ships. As a result the Defence Committee changed the requirements. The ship was now to be armed with nine 305mm guns, the belt was fixed at 250mm, speed at 31-32 knots and the standard displacement was to be 30,000-31,000 tons. The navy subsequently specified that the ship should also be armed with eight 130mm, eight 100mm, twenty-four 37mm guns and should carry two aircraft. The protection had to be able to resist 280mm (11in) shells at ranges between 70 and 120 cables (14,000-24,000 yards) on bearings of 40-50° from the bow. It is interesting to note that, unlike the earlier 254mm-gunned design, no corresponding bearings abaft the beam were specified.

Work now moved forward on Project 69 at a very rapid rate, in part because the constructors were able to take a short cut by using the 'wrecked' Project 25 design of the Battleship 'B' series as a starting point. By October 1938 TsKB-17 had worked out a sketch design with a standard displacement of 32,870 tons. The design was evaluated by the Naval Academy, where it was gamed against the *Scharnhorst*, *Dunkerque* and *Kongo*. These potential opponents were generally based on the following strategic scenarios:

In the Pacific, the ship would conduct raiding operations in Japanese waters and on Japanese maritime communications, with the goals of interrupting trade and distracting the Japanese navy from offensive operations in the Sea of Okhotsk or the Sea of Japan.

In Arctic waters, the cruiser would carry out raiding operations in the northern areas of the North Sea and Atlantic. This role may have reflected Soviet concerns over the possibility of German landings in the Arctic.[7]

In the Black Sea, the ship would counter the Turkish battlecruiser *Yavuz*, which was considered too fast to be effectively dealt with by the battleship *Parizhskaia kommuna*. In the event of more powerful enemy forces appearing in the Black Sea, the ship would carry out raiding operations to keep the enemy 'in constant tension'.

The results of the games indicated that while the ship would be superior to the *Kongo* at ranges of 50-90 cables (10,000-18,000 yards), it would be inferior to the *Dunkerque*. Of course, the most pertinent comparison was with the *Scharnhorst* class, and here the Academy's gaming indicated that the Soviet design would possess some advantages. It is very likely, however, that at this time the Soviets were unaware of the true characteristics of the German ship. The displacement of the *Scharnhorst* and *Gneisenau* had been publicly announced as 26,000 tons standard, but in fact their design displacement was more than 31,000 tons, and as completed they were even heavier, although varying figures are given.[8] Certainly the Soviet design had a heavier main battery with a longer range than that of the *Scharnhorst* class, and also had a slight edge in speed. In terms of armour protection, however, it clearly yielded to the German ships, having a belt of only 230mm compared to 350mm.[9] In addition, the *Scharnhorst* had 105mm slopes from the armour deck to the lower edge of the armour belt, a very substantial reinforcement to her belt protection. Against this must be weighed the fact that the *Scharnhorst* was seriously overloaded as completed, leaving her armour deck almost exactly at the design waterline and 730mm (2ft 5in) below the full load waterline. Thus any damage to her sides near the waterline could have led to flooding above the armoured deck, with a potentially serious effect on her stability.

In addition to the Naval Academy's comparisons, the design was also evaluated by a special commission of the navy's own Shipbuilding Administration. The commission believed that the 130mm secondary battery was inadequate both in number and calibre, and recommended replacing it with 152mm guns of the same type planned for the Project 23 battleship. It also wanted to see heavier armour on the conning tower, the main and secondary battery turrets, and on the forward transverse bulkhead. Improvements were also desired in the underwater protection. To compensate for all these additions, the navy was willing to reduce the ship's range, which was considered to be in excess of that required for its specified strategic roles. Even so, it was recognized that the correction of all the faults noted would require a growth in displacement of about 1,500 tons, and in fact the revised design prepared by TsKB-17 at the end of 1938 weighed in a 35,000 tons. This sketch design was finally approved by the navy and was presented to the Defence Committee in January 1939.

But at this stage it would appear that some opposition arose within the navy from officers who thought that the 'heavy' cruisers were *too* heavy. Among them was a rising young officer, Flag Officer 2nd Rank N G Kuznetsov, commander of the Pacific Fleet and soon to be appointed Commissar of the Navy. Kuznetsov criticised the heavy cruisers at a conference in early 1939. Afterwards he was quietly advised by A M Redkin, an official of the Shipbuilding Commissariat, to be careful, since Stalin had promised to punish anyone opposing the construction of the heavy cruisers.[10] In case anyone had lingering doubts on that score, in a speech in March 1939 at the XVIII Congress of the Communist Party, I F Tevosian, commissar of the shipbuilding industry, pointed out that 'Stalin had threatened to mete out severe punishment to anyone objecting to heavy cruisers.'[11] Since Tevosian specifically mentioned heavy cruisers but apparently made no reference to other large surface ships, it seems likely that battleships and smaller cruisers were generally accepted but that there were those in the naval hierarchy who, like Kuznetsov, opposed the big cruisers. As Kuznetsov noted in his memoirs, Stalin had 'a special and curious passion for heavy cruisers.'[12]

With Stalin's wishes made clear, opposition evaporated, and in May 1939 the navy drew up the requirements for the technical design, based on the sketch design already worked out by TsKB-17. The basic concept was that the ship should be superior to the *Scharnhorst* and fast enough to escape from the *Bismarck*. According to these requirements, the ship had to be able to:

- Cause decisive damage to the German battleships of the *Scharnhorst* class at battle ranges of 72-122 cables [c. 14,400-24,400 yards] on bearings of 33-50° from the bow
- Destroy all light and heavy cruisers, excluding those which have an advantage in speed, without receiving hits in the vitally important areas from 203mm shells at battle ranges greater than 55 cables [c.11,000 yards] on all bearings
- Engage the modernized battleships of the *Giulio Cesare* class at ranges of 96-120 cables [c.19,200-24,000 yards] on bearings of 33-50° from the bow

The inclusion of the Italian ships in the list of potential opponents was probably based on concerns that the Italians might break through the Turkish Straits and threaten the Soviet Union's Black Sea coasts.

Especially noteworthy are the bearings defined in the requirements; the intention was for the Soviet ships to fight with the enemy on forward bearings, which led in the final design to a heavy forward transverse armour bulkhead. The main armament was still somewhat uncertain, and studies were apparently made of ships with 254mm, 280mm and 305mm guns, but work seems to have been concentrated on the 305mm designs.

At about this time a major change in the horizontal protection was adopted. The previous designs had placed the heaviest armour deck at lower deck level, with lighter protection on the upper and middle decks above it. In 1937 bombing trials were carried out in the Black Sea using an old merchant ship fitted with differing deck protection arrangements, and these showed that a 500kg bomb would usually penetrate both a 40mm upper and 50mm middle deck before exploding on the main armour deck. It was therefore better to move the heaviest deck up to middle-deck level, with a splinter deck below it to catch any fragments resulting from the bomb explosion. This entailed extending the main belt up by one deck level to close the sides of the armoured citadel, further increasing the weight of the armour protection.

Meanwhile, Nikitin, as both head of TsKB-17 and leader of the Project 69 design team, was overworked, so in February 1939 F E Bespolov was assigned to head the project. Bespolov had previously worked on Battleship 'B' and the Project 22 heavy cruiser, so he was a good choice for the job of completing Project 69. Assisting him were constructors N K Gorbatenko and T L Dzhelomanov. The characteristics of the design at this point were as follows:

Displacement:	35,240 metric tons standard, 38,360 metric tons trials, 41,539 metric tons full load
Length:	240m wl, 250.5m oa (787ft 5in wl, 821ft 11in oa)
Beam:	29.4m wl, 31.6m oa (96ft 6in wl, 103ft 8in oa)
Draught:	8.88m trials, 9.45m full load (29ft 1in trials, 31ft full load)
Armament:	9-305mm (12in)/54 (3 x 3; 100rpg) 8-152mm (6in)/57 (4 x 2) 8-100mm (3.9in)/56 (4 x 2) 28-37mm (7 x 4) 8-12.7mm MG (4 x 2) one catapult, two KOR-2 seaplanes
Protection	main belt: 230mm (9in) bulkheads: 330mm (13in) forward, 275mm (10.83in) aft turrets: 305mm (12in) faces, 125mm (4.9in) roofs barbettes: 330mm (13in) conning tower: 330mm (13in) decks: 14mm (0.55in) upper deck, 90mm (3.54in) middle deck, 30mm (1.18in) lower deck
Machinery:	twelve watertube boilers, three turbine sets, 201,000shp full, 231,000shp (forced draught, two hours trial)
Speed:	32 knots full (245rpm), 33 knots forced (252rpm)
Endurance:	2,920 tons oil normal, for a range of 1,100nm at full speed; 5,570 tons oil maximum; 8,300nm at 14.5 knots, 6,900nm at 16.5 knots
Complement:	1,837

The design showed a ship with a flush-decked hull of riveted construction with a modest sheer forward and none aft, the upper deck height above the baseline being 16.3m (53ft 6in) forward and 14.3m (46ft 11in) amidships and aft. The framing was on the 'mixed' system, with longitudinal framing throughout the citadel and transverse framing fore and aft of it, and the hull was divided into twenty-five main compartments by twenty-four transverse bulkheads. The total reserve of buoyancy was 80.5 per cent, the armoured reserve was 37 per cent, and the counterflooding system was to enable the ship to recover from an 8° list in ten minutes. Amidships the beam over the anti-torpedo bulges was greater than the width of the upper deck. Metacentric height was 2.8m (9.19ft), the condition of loading not being specified. There were two rudders, placed in the races of the outboard shafts, and tactical diameter was five ship-lengths, or about 1,200m. The weight breakdown was as follows:[13]

Hull (not including torpedo protection):	11,100.6 tons	31.5 per cent
Armour:	12,369.24 tons	35.1 per cent
Torpedo protection:	1,198.16 tons	3.4 per cent
Armament:	4,616.44 tons	13.1 per cent
Ammunition:	881 tons	2.5 per cent
Machinery:	3,911.64 tons	11.1 per cent
Supplies:	563.84 tons	1.6 per cent
Margin:	599.08 tons	1.7 per cent

Armament: The main battery consisted of three MK-15 triple turrets for 305mm/54 B-50 guns; these turrets were based on the MK-2 turrets designed earlier for the 'wrecked' Battleship 'B'.[14] Maximum angle of elevation was 45°, and

Table 1: Gun Mountings of the Project 69 Battlecruiser

Guns					
Designation	38cm SKC/34	B-50	B-38	B-54	37/67.5
Bore	380mm	304.8mm	152.4mm	100mm	37mm
Weight including BM	111000kg	733000kg	11999kg	2680-2713kg	65kg
Length oa	19630mm	16810mm	8935mm	5795mm	2510mm
Length bore	18405mm	16460mm	8690mm	?	?
Length rifling	15982mm	13077mm	6980mm	4625mm	2053mm
Number of grooves	90	40	40	40	16
Twist	1 in 36 to 1 in 30	1 in 30	1 in 30	1 in 30	1 in 30
Approximate barrel life	250	300	450	800	2000
Projectiles					
Type	AP	AP	AP	AA Shrapnel	AA Shrapnel
Weight projectile	800kg	470kg	55kg	15.6kg	0.732kg
Propellant charge	212kg	182kg	24kg	5.3kg	0.210kg
Muzzle velocity	820m/s	900m/s	950m/s	900m/s	880m/s
Working pressure	3200kg/cm^2	3200kg/cm^2	3200kg/cm^2	3000kg/cm^2	2800kg/cm^2
Maximum range	194 cables	260 cables	164 cables	118.8 cables	46 cables
Maximum vertical range	N/A	N/A	N/A	10000m	5000m
Mountings					
Designation	Drh LC/34	MK-15	MK-4	MZ-16	46-K
Number of guns	2	3	2	2	4
Maximum elevation	+30 deg	+45 deg	+45 deg	+85 deg	+85 deg
Maximum depression	–5.5 deg	–3 deg	–5 deg	–8 deg	–10 deg
Loading angle	+2.5 deg	+6 deg	+8 deg	All	All
Revolving weight	1064 tons	1024 tons	146 tons	See note	16 tons
Ball track diameter	8750mm	9000mm?	4400mm	3200mm	2240mm
Barbette internal diameter	10000mm	9700mm?	4680mm	?	?
Distance apart gun axes	3750mm	2360mm	1300mm	700mm	?
Recoil distance	1050mm	1200mm	550mm	600mm	185mm
Max elevating speed	6 deg/sec	10 deg/sec	13 deg/sec	10 deg/sec	15 deg/sec
Max training speed	5.4 deg/sec	5.1 deg/sec	6 deg/sec	12 deg/sec	20 deg/sec
Rate of fire	2.3 rounds/min	3.24 rounds/min	7.5 rounds/min	16 rounds/min	145 rounds/min

Note: The MZ-14 twin 100mm mounting of the Project 23 battleships, which differed from the MZ-16 only in having somewhat heavier armor, had a rotating weight of 65 tons.

the rate of fire was intended to be 2.36-3.24 rounds per minute. The difference was due to the fixed loading angle, so that the rate of fire was slower at higher elevations. Main battery fire control included two KDP-8-III directors, each with two 8m rangefinders; the main director was located atop the tower mast (29m above the waterline), with a 360° field of view and a visual range of 213 cables (c.42,600 yards). The second main battery director, located on the after superstructure, was 14.2m above the waterline, had a visual range of 178 cables (c.35,600 yards) and a field of vision of 300° across the stern. There was a Central Artillery Post (*Tsentral'nyi artilleriiskii* post, equivalent to the RN's Transmitting Station or the USN's Main Battery Plot) forward, with another aft.

The eight 152mm/57 guns were to be mounted in four twin MK-4 turrets. Their disposition was unusual and clever, with the forward turrets being mounted inboard of, and higher than, the after turrets. This provided very good arcs of fire, especially on forward bearings. To control these guns there were two KDP-4t-II directors, with 4m rangefinders. The directors were 14m above the waterline, with a visual range of 178 cables (c.35,600 yards) and had a field of view equivalent to the training arcs of the 152mm guns themselves, approximately 180°. There was a separate central post for controlling the 152mm guns.

The heavy anti-aircraft battery of eight 100mm guns was arranged in four MZ-16 enclosed gunhouses, and like the 152mm turrets they were disposed in an unusual manner, all four being toward the after end of the superstructure. Well separated from the 152mm guns, they had good sky arcs. They were controlled by two gyro-stabilized directors with 3m rangefinders. These were 14m above the waterline, and were credited with a visual range of 75 cables (c.15,000 yards). Compared to foreign capital ship designs of similar size, the heavy anti-aircraft battery seems somewhat weak. The light anti-aircraft battery, on the other hand, was impressive. There were no less than seven quad 37mm (model 46-K) anti-aircraft mounts, one on a pedestal above the conning tower, two abreast the forward funnel, two just abaft the after funnel, and two superimposed on the centreline at the after end of the superstructure. As was the case with the 100mm gun locations, this disposition led to a somewhat greater concentration of AA firepower aft. In early 1940 the navy insisted on replacing the 37mm mounting atop the conning tower with a third director for the 100mm guns, since the other two directors were blocked on forward bearings by the superstructures. From this point on the light AA battery consisted of only six 37mm quad mountings. In partial compensation, at about this time four twin DShK-2 12.7mm machine guns were added. This number was later increased, but it is not clear what the final total was to be.

The aviation outfit consisted of two KOR-2 seaplanes and a single catapult located between the funnels. Six 90cm searchlights were provided, one atop the conning tower, two on the forward funnel, two on the mainmast and one aft above the centreline 37mm mounts. The ships would also have carried hydrophones and an early form of infrared detection gear.

Armour: The scale of the protection was relatively modest. The main belt was inclined at 6° and was 230mm thick, tapering toward the lower edge. It was 5m high, of which 1.6m was to be immersed at the design displacement. The belt was 185m long, and ran from frame 62 forward to frame 431 aft, covering 76.8 per cent of the waterline. The citadel was closed off fore and aft by transverse bulkheads, the forward bulkhead being 330mm thick and the aft bulkhead 275mm. Forward of the main belt a 20mm 'ice belt' extended to the stem; this presumably also served as a splinter belt. The upper deck was 14mm over the main magazines and was intended to defeat light bombs and initiate fuse action on shells, while the main armour deck, which rested on the upper edge of the armour belt, had a thickness of 90mm. Below the main armour deck was a 30mm splinter deck, which was reduced to 15mm toward the sides where it covered the torpedo protection system. The 305mm turrets had 305mm faces and backs, with 125mm sides and roofs, and their barbettes were 330mm. The secondary turrets had 100mm faces with 50mm sides and roofs, with 75mm barbettes, while the 100mm gunhouses were 50mm, with 40mm barbettes. The conning tower had 330mm sides and a 125mm roof, with a 230mm communications tube running down to the armour deck. High in the tower mast the admiral's bridge was protected by 50mm plate. All of the directors, main, secondary and heavy AA, were provided with 14mm splinter protection, as were the 37mm mounts. The funnels had 20mm protection right up to their caps. There was a small box of 50mm armour aft protecting the smoke-generating apparatus.

Underwater Protection: The anti-torpedo system was based on the 'American' system, the Soviet term for the multi-bulkhead style of protection, as opposed to the Pugliese system used in the *Sovetskii Soiuz*. It was designed to survive a hit from a 500kg charge of TNT. The system consisted of a bulge and four longitudinal bulkheads, with a fifth bulkhead forming the boundary to the ship's interior. It covered 61.5 per cent of the ship's length and had a total depth of 6m amidships, reducing to 4m forward and aft as the hull lines grew finer. The middle three spaces in the system were intended to be liquid-loaded with fuel or water. Five main compartments (out of a total of twenty-five) could be flooded without endangering the ship's buoyancy or stability.

Machinery: The propulsion plant occupied an expanse running from frame 175 forward to frame 351 aft. It was laid out *en echelon*, with eight boilers in the two forward fire-rooms, followed by an engine room with the turbines for the two wing shafts, then four more boilers in a single fire-room, and finally the centre shaft turbine. The boilers were of the 7u-bis type, a designation that indicates that they were a second series (*bis* is a Russian borrowing of a French word meaning 'repeat' or 'encore') of an improved (*uluchshennyi*) version of an earlier boiler. Working at a pressure of 37kg/cm^2 and a temperature of 380°C, their steam production was 90 tons/hour. The turbines were of the same type intended for the *Sovetskii Soiuz* class, the total output of the three shafts being 210,000shp for a speed on trials of 32 knots, while forced draught would boost power to 231,000shp for an additional knot. At 70,000shp per shaft, the shaft-loading in these ships was very high, and has been questioned by some western experts.[15] It is generally held that propulsive efficiency begins to fall off somewhere around 50,000shp due to cavitation; nevertheless, the triple-shaft plant was a deliberate choice on the part of the Soviet designers, intended to reduce citadel length in the *Sovetskii Soiuz* class, where the three turbines could be arranged side-by-side. In the narrower Project 69, however, this arrangement was not possible, and a second longitudinal compartment was necessary for the centre shaft's turbines.

In theory, economical speed could be achieved with two boilers and cruising speed on four boilers. If the predicted steaming ranges were based on this type of operation, the ships would actually have had a considerably shorter range in wartime service, since it was usually necessary to keep most, if not all, of the boilers fired at all times so that maximum speed would always be readily available.

The electrical plant consisted of four turbogenerators (1,200kW each) and four diesel generators (650kW each), all working at 220V. There were also two small boilers for harbour service and for running auxiliary machinery.

Project 69-I

Work on the Project 69 technical design had begun almost immediately after the sketch design was completed, despite the fact that the Defence Committee had yet to approve the design. That approval finally came on 13 July 1939, and approval of the technical design followed on 12 April 1940. Long before that date, however, it was clear that the development of the 305mm guns and turrets for these ships had fallen so far behind schedule that the entire battlecruiser programme was in jeopardy. The 406mm guns and mountings of the *Sovetskii Soiuz* class battleships had a higher priority, and had absorbed the attention of the armaments works.[16] But then an unlikely

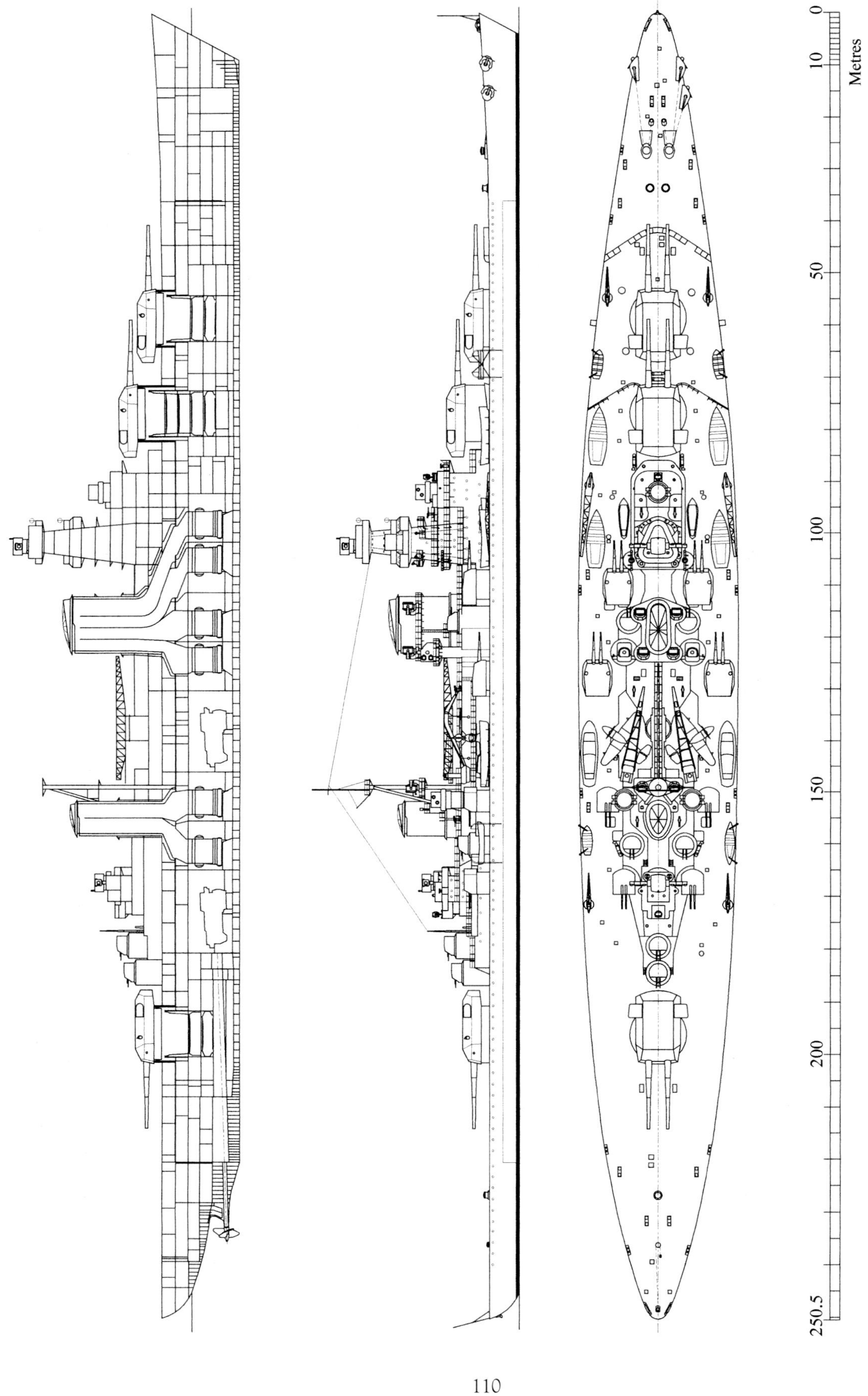

Fig. 6. Project 69-I, October 1940. A considerable number of changes were necessary to accommodate the German 38cm turrets: 'B' turret had to be raised to clear 'A' turret, which in turn led to the conning tower being raised a deck level; the 37mm quad mountings on the centerline above 'Y' turret also had to be raised. There are some indications that the original drawings were prepared in a hurry, since there are discrepancies between the profile and plan view in the immediate vicinity of the funnels. (Drawing courtesy of John Roberts)

solution to this problem appeared: guns from Nazi Germany.

This possibility had come up during negotiations over a trade agreement following the signing of the Nazi-Soviet Non-Aggression Pact in August 1939. During talks held in Moscow on 8 February 1940, Stalin himself asked the German delegates if triple 283mm turrets of the type mounted in the *Scharnhorst* could replace the 305mm turrets of the Project 69 class. The Germans replied that 283mm turrets were no longer in production, but new ones could be manufactured.[17] Stalin then asked whether it would be possible to mount twin 380mm (15in) turrets in place of the triple 305mm planned for the new battlecruisers. Not surprisingly, the German negotiators expressed some uncertainty over the technical issues involved, but agreed to obtain the relevant information.

By a curious coincidence, the Krupp firm just happened to have some spare 380mm guns and turrets on hand.[18] These had originally been ordered by the *Kriegsmarine* for re-arming the two *Scharnhorst* class ships, a project planned for 1940-1941. This re-arming was cancelled sometime before the war, apparently because it was considered unwise to have the ships out of service in a time of rising international tensions. The guns and mountings were now earmarked for the 'O' class battlecruisers, but the construction of these ships was likewise cancelled in early 1940, so Krupp was left with several guns and turrets in various states of completion. Their sale to the Soviets probably seemed like a good way of making some money to Krupp.

Later in February 1940, when Shipbuilding Commissar I F Tevosian travelled to Germany to sign the trade pact, a preliminary agreement with Krupp was reached for the purchase of the 380mm guns and mountings, and the order for twelve guns and six twin turrets was finalized in November 1940.[19] The contract provided for the following delivery dates for the turrets:

1 October 1941 to 28 February 1942
2 December 1941 to 31 March 1942
3 February 1942 to 30 April 1942
4 May 1942 to 30 November 1942
5 August 1942 to 31 December 1942
6 November 1942 to 28 March 1943

The order with Krupp also included 10m rangefinders and 150cm searchlights for the ships. The fire control gear was to be manufactured by Siemens, with Krupp acting as intermediary on behalf of the Soviets.

The negotiations for purchasing the turrets were well advanced before any studies of whether the change was even feasible had been undertaken. It was only on 17 April 1940 that the navy and the Shipbuilding Commissariat were able to report that the conversion to 380mm guns was technically possible. In May the Naval Academy carried out tactical studies of the Project 69 battlecruiser armed with 380mm guns, gaming it against the standard opponents, *Scharnhorst* and *Dunkerque*. The results were favourable; although the lesser number of slower-firing 380mm guns meant fewer hits, this was offset by improved armour penetration and the greater destructive effects of the bigger shells. On the basis of these reports, Navy Commissar N G Kuznetsov approved the development of a sketch design for re-arming the first two Project 69 ships with German-made guns and turrets.

In this the Soviet designers faced a difficult task, since many details of the German equipment were only vaguely known – even such basic data as the weight of the turrets was uncertain. In addition, the twin 380mm turret was too large for the triple 305mm barbettes and so many changes were required between frames 62-175 forward and 351-431 aft. Moreover the German turrets were taller than the original 305mm ones, so the barbette for turret number 2 had to be raised to keep its guns clear of the lower turret, which in turn made it necessary to raise the conning tower by one deck level. In a somewhat similar fashion, the greater height of the after 380mm turret forced the designers to raise the two 37mm mounts superimposed above it, as well as the after main battery director's structure. It was necessary to increase the output of the turbogenerators to 1,300kW to handle the greater electrical load required. The ultimate effect of all these changes was to increase displacement by more than 1,000 tons. The sketch design, designated Project 69-I (*Importnyi* = imported) was ready by 16 October 1940. In the explanatory memorandum accompanying the design it was noted that the German turret plans were urgently needed to complete the work.

Kuznetsov, who had criticised the heavy cruiser design back in 1939, still thought it was too large and expensive, and in early October 1940 he suggested that work on the battlecruisers be halted altogether so that the resources devoted to them could be used to build more Project 30 destroyers. Stalin rejected the proposal, and instead a decree dated 19 October 1940 cancelled one of the four Project 23 battleships, the resources released by this being devoted to speeding up the construction of the battlecruisers.[20] Their launch date was advanced to the third quarter of 1942, with entry into service planned for 1944.

On 11 February 1941 Kuznetsov and I I Nosenko, the new Commissar of the Shipbuilding Industry (in 1940 Tevosian had been made commissar for the Metallurgical Industries), presented the sketch design to the Defence Committee. But both men had doubts about the supply of German materials, which they expressed in a joint report to the Defence Committee in early April. Nevertheless, Stalin believed that the Germans would eventually deliver the guns, and so on 10 April the Defence Committee ordered that the first two ships of the class, by this time named *Kronshtadt* and *Sevastopol*, be armed with six 380mm guns. Subsequent units of the class were to be built with Soviet-made 305mm guns, and some publications indicate that the third ship would have been named *Stalingrad*. Kuznetsov and Nosenko pointed out that if the German guns were not delivered, the two lead ships could revert to the original Project 69 design, although many internal changes would be necessary and their completion would be delayed.

The Project 69-I technical design was scheduled to be completed by 15 October 1941. The sketch design's characteristics, approved at the 10 April meeting, differed from the original Project 69 design in the following areas:

Displacement:	36,250 metric tons standard, 39,660 metric tons normal, 42,831 metric tons full load
Length:	242.1m (794ft 4in) wl
Draught:	9.13m (30ft) normal, 9.7m (31ft 10in) full load
Armament:	6-380mm (15in)/51.66 (3 x 2; 95rpg)
Protection:	turrets: 360mm (14.2in) faces, 130mm (5.1in) roofs
Complement:	1,819

The waterline length was increased by 2.1m not because of any change in the ship's hull, but because the sharply raked stem and spoon-shaped stern were more deeply immersed at the new displacement. The metacentric height was now 2.58m, a reduction of 0.22m, due to the heavier turrets and the need to raise turret No. 2 as well as the conning tower. The total reserve of buoyancy dropped from 80.5 per cent to 75 per cent and the armoured reserve decreased from 37 per cent to 33 per cent. Internally, the side protection system had to be extended by 9m to cover the increased length of the magazines. Despite the increase in displacement and draught, speed remained unaltered because a more efficient propeller form had been developed. There were also a number of more or less cosmetic changes to the superstructure, including the replacement of the aircraft-handling boom by cranes on the German pattern, as well as a rearrangement of the searchlight platforms.

Construction

It had originally been planned to lay down the first two battlecruisers in November 1938, but by that date not even the sketch design was ready. In March 1939 it was hoped that an immediate start on construction would allow the first two ships to be delivered to the navy in 1943. But that plan reckoned without the need for improvements at the shipyards, and the Council of People's Commissars agreed to postpone the start of construction until 1 September 1939. In the end, work was actually started on the first two ships in November 1939, and even then the technical design had not yet been approved by the Committee on Defence.

The lead ship of the class, the *Kronshtadt*, was laid down at Yard No. 194, the Marti Yard on Galernyi Island in Leningrad, on 30 November 1939, with S M Turnunov acting as supervising constructor. The slipway at Galernyi Island was too short for the *Kronshtadt*'s hull, and the ship's stern was built separately next to the main portion of the hull on the same slipway. The *Sevastopol* was actually laid down a few weeks earlier, on 5 November, at Yard No. 200 (61 Kommunara Yard) at Nikolaev, with G V Babenko as constructor.

The short slipway in Leningrad was only one of many problems that plagued the construction of the two battlecruisers. By 1940 it was clear that Stalin's attempt to create a major shipbuilding industry by decree was a failure, as difficulties were encountered in the production of virtually every component of the ships. Attempts to make good the failures of domestic industry by ordering material abroad were almost uniformly unsuccessful.[21]

At the most basic level, there was a shortage of shipyard workers. This problem was so bad that at one point Shipbuilding Commissar Tevosian had proposed that Red Fleet sailors be sent to the shipyards to assist with the work, a suggestion rejected by the navy. By June 1941 there were 24,700 and 28,600 workers at the yards in Leningrad and Nikolaev, respectively, less than half the workers that had been specified in Stalin's plan for the creation of a vast fleet.

Steel was another problem. Actual production consistently fell below the unrealistic targets set by the government, leading to intense competition between the army and the navy for the limited supply of steel that was available. In the end, steel had to be ordered from abroad, but this did not solve the problem. Mario Zampi, an Italian engineer from the Odero-Terni-Orlando firm, who was in Leningrad as a technical advisor in the construction of the *Chapaev* class cruisers, was told that work had been suspended on the *Kronshtadt* on 1 February 1940 due to the non-delivery of 14,000 tons of steel and armour ordered in the United States.[22] It is very likely that the American deliveries were halted after the Soviet invasion of eastern Poland on 17 September 1939.

The situation with armour production was even worse. Problems with the manufacture of cemented plate were so bad that in November 1940 the decision was made to abandon attempts to manufacture cemented plates greater than 200mm in thickness. This decision had serious implications for the level of protection of the ships. Many nations, including the United States and Japan, made extensive use of non-cemented face-hardened armour, but the Soviets made a fundamental error in the specifications for their plate. They apparently tried to compensate for the lack of a cemented face by increasing the overall hardness of the plate, which led to increased brittleness, and the plates proved susceptible to cracking and breaking in trials. Thus all the heavy armour of the *Kronshtadt* class ships would probably have been of considerably less protective value than foreign armour of equal thickness.[23]

And this was only one part of the armour problem. In June 1940 a joint memorandum from the navy and the Shipbuilding Commissariat to the Commissariat of Foreign Trade summed up the situation:

> ...for the construction of ships in 1940 the armour industry of the USSR should produce, at a minimum, 45,000 tons...in reality it will be 30,000-32,000 tons. In 1941 about 87,000 tons of heavy armour will be needed, whereas even taking into account the completion of plans for major work [at improving the armour plants] not more than 60,000 tons will be produced...[24]

The memo ended with a plea to secure a contract for heavy armour from Germany, but in the end Krupp turned down the proposal. Domestic production proved to be even worse than predicted; in 1940 a total of 27,438 tons was delivered, but 30-40 per cent of the plates had to be rejected after proving-ground trials.

Things were equally gloomy in the area of armament.

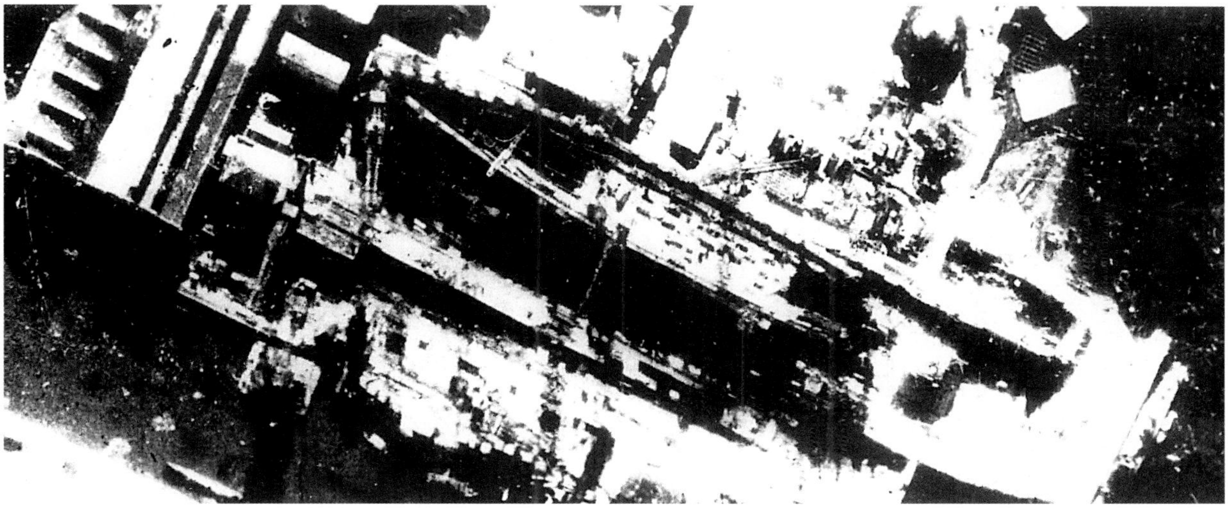

Fig. 7. *A famous aerial reconnaissance photo of* Kronshtadt*'s hull at Leningrad, taken by a German reconnaissance aircraft in the autumn of 1941. Note the ship's stern being built separately. Also evident is the large gap in the structure in the area of the forward main battery magazines, where progress was slow due to the lack of detailed drawings and specifications for the German 38cm turrets.* (Naval Historical Center, NH 79295)

The decision to use Krupp 380mm guns for the first two ships of the class bears witness to the fact that the design and development of the 305mm guns and mountings had fallen far behind schedule, and matters were equally bad with the smaller guns. By June 1941 not a single 152mm turret had been manufactured, and the prototype 100mm mounting was also incomplete. Matters were slightly better with the 37mm guns; the prototype quadruple mounting was completed in December 1940 and delivered to the proving grounds. It was later installed on the forecastle of the old battleship *Oktiabrskaia Revoliutsiia* in the spring of 1942. There were also delays in the manufacture of the fire control equipment.

As for the machinery, both the *Kronshtadt* class battlecruisers and the *Sovetskii Soiuz* class battleships were intended to have the same type of turbines, four of which were ordered from the Swiss firm of Brown, Boveri et Cie. Three were to be used in the battleship *Sovetskaia Ukraina* and one was to serve as a model for domestic production at the Kharkovskii Electromechanical and Turbogenerator Works (also known as the Stalin Works). Although three of the Swiss turbines were delivered to Archangel in 1940, the Kharkovskii Works was overloaded with other orders and refused to commit to any definite schedule of delivery for the turbines. In the end, the Kharkovskii Works did not complete a single turbine

The old battleship Oktiabrskaia Revoliutsiia, *pictured after her modernisation of 1931-34, with her sister ship* Marat *beyond.* (CPL)

before the war. The situation with regard to boilers is less clear, although it is known that there were problems and delays in the manufacture of a prototype boiler for the *Sovetskii Soiuz* class.

Even lesser components for the propulsion plant seemed cursed. Problems with the propeller shaft forgings led to an order for them being placed abroad, in this case with a Dutch firm. A few weeks later, Holland was overrun by the Germans. The rejection rate of many domestically manufactured components was another problem. For example, in 1938 it was reported that 'in the period from 17 January to 7 April, 187 cylinders were cast at the shipbuilding works, of which 160 were rejected'.[25]

At the time of the German invasion on 22 June 1941, the *Kronshtadt* was calculated to be 10.6 per cent complete, and the *Sevastopol* 11.6 per cent.[26] Work immediately stopped on both ships. In the autumn and winter of 1941, during the German siege of Leningrad, some of the *Kronshtadt*'s armour plate was used in defensive positions, and some material was apparently used to repair other ships. Her sister ship, the *Sevastopol*, suffered a somewhat similar fate, although at different hands – in August 1941 the Soviet retreat from the Ukraine was so rapid that they did not have a chance to destroy the hull and she was captured by the Germans undamaged on the slipway. The Krupp guns and turrets were, of course, never delivered, nor was sufficient documentation ever received to allow the areas around the magazines and barbettes to be designed, so these areas lagged behind the work on the rest of the ship. As a result the *Sevastopol*'s incomplete hull had no obvious internal structures identifying her as a big-gun warship, and the Germans thought she might be an aircraft carrier. Some of her armour and material was used by the Germans for defensive works, some was apparently shipped to Germany. When Soviet forces closed in on Nikolaev in March 1944, the Germans damaged the hull and slipway with explosive charges.

Thanks to the German demolition efforts the *Sevastopol* was a total loss, but the *Kronshtadt* was in reasonably good shape and construction could have been resumed after the war. But although Stalin had lost none of his interest in big-gun warships, she was not fated ever to be completed. TsKB-17 argued that she was outdated by wartime advances: her anti-aircraft battery was inadequate, her design made no provision for radar, and she lacked underbottom protection against non-contact mines and torpedoes.[27] The same, of course, could have been said of virtually every other capital ship in the world, and there is some reason to believe that the design bureau was deliberately pessimistic in its evaluation of the potential of both the *Kronshtadt* and the battleship *Sovetskii Soiuz*. It were already overloaded with work on new battleship, battlecruiser, cruiser and destroyer designs, and probably sought to avoid diverting precious time and energy to modernization plans for the prewar designs.

However, some thought was given to the idea of converting *Kronshtadt* to other uses. In April 1945 the navy's Scientific-Technical Committee (NTK) proposed that she be completed as an aircraft carrier, and it was optimistically forecast that she would be able to carry seventy-six aircraft. But this idea was rejected, since Stalin stubbornly opposed the construction of carriers of any description. Also rejected was a proposal to convert the *Kronshtadt* into a base ship for a whaling flotilla.

By a decree by the Council of Ministers dated 24 March 1947, it was directed that the Project 69 hulls be broken up. Dismantling work was begun on the slipways soon after, and both ships were dismantled during 1948.

Table 2: *FAST BATTLESHIPS AND BATTLECRUISERS, 1932-1940*

	Dunkerque	*Strasbourg*	*Scharnhorst*	O Class	*Renown*
Country	France	France	Germany	Germany	Great Britain
Laid down	1932	1934	1935	cancelled 1939	reconstr. 1939
Displacement, standard (tons)	26,500	27,300	31,053	32,300	30,750
Displacement, design (tons)	30,750	31,570	?	?	33,725
Displacement, full load (tons)	35,697	36,380	37,224	38,200	36,080
Length, wl (feet)	685.73	685.73	741.5	807.13	794.1
Beam (feet)	101.97	101.97	98.43	98.43	102.33
Draft (feet)	28.12 (design)	28.64 (design)	28.44 (standard)	31.5 (standard)	26.5 (standard)
Armament	8 x 13in/52 16 x 5.1in/45 10 x 37mm 32 x 13.2mm	8 x 13in/52 16 x 5.1in/45 8 x 37mm 32 x 13.2mm	9 x 11.1in/54.5 12 x 5.9in/55 14 x 4.1in/65 16 x 37mm	6 x 15in/51.66 6 x 5.9in/55 8 x 4.1in/65 8 x 37mm 6 x 21in TT	6 x 15in/42 20 x 4.5in/45 24 x 40mm 16 x .50 mg
Catapults	1	1	1	1	1
Aircraft	3	3	3	4	2
Belt armor (in)	8.86 at 11.8 deg	11.14 at 11.8 deg	13.78	7.09	9
Main Armor deck, mags (in)	4.92	4.92	4.14	2.36	4
Machinery power (shp)	135,585	131,960	161,164	176,000	120,560
Speed (knots)	31.06	30.9	31.65	33.5	29.93
Endurance (nm / knots)	7,850 at 15	?	10,100 at 19	14,000 at 19	6,580 at 18
Complement	1,381	1,302	1,669	1,965	1,200
Metacentric height (feet / displ.)	8.6 at 30,750	?	7.38 at 33,454	10.47 at 31,143	4.72 at 33,725

Note: Deck protection is difficult to determine, especially for the reconstructed ships where new plate was often laid on top of old plate. The f

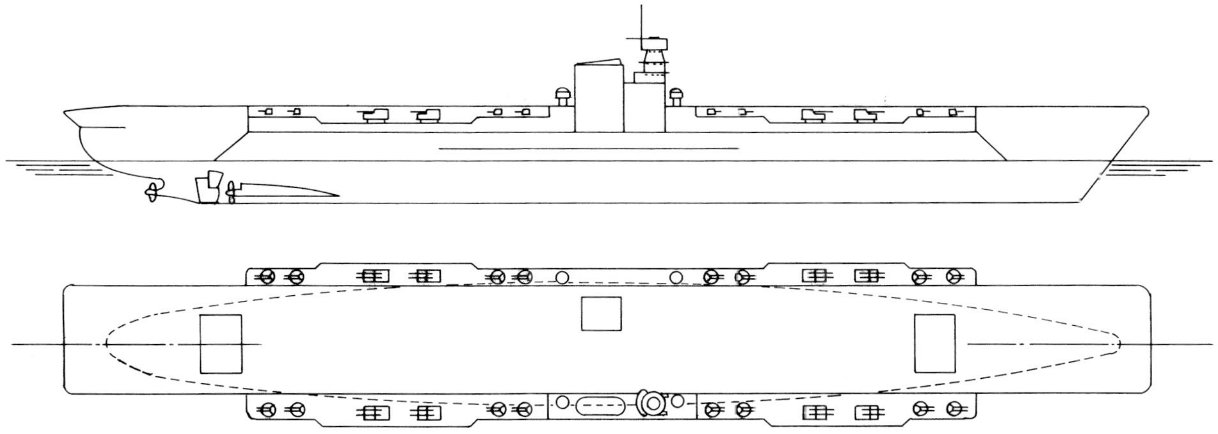

Fig. 8. *A 1945 proposal for converting the incomplete* Kronshtadt *into an aircraft carrier. This rough sketch, prepared by the navy's Scientific-Technical Committee (NTK), reflected the Soviet navy's interest in carrier operations, but Stalin rejected all proposals for the construction of aircraft carriers.* (Drawing by the author)

However, the separately built stern section of the *Kronshtadt* was seen moored on the river Neva as late as September 1950, perhaps to be used for tests of some sort.[28]

Comparisons

The *Kronshtadt* class design was one of a series of fast battleships or battlecruisers either built or planned in the decade prior to the Second World War, many of which had remarkably similar characteristics. Table 2 gives the basic statistics for these ships and some older ships that were reconstructed to a similar standard. Although she was the largest of all these ships, the *Kronshtadt*'s military characteristics were not exceptional in any regard. What is striking, however, is her tremendously powerful machinery plant. The Soviet design required about 60,000shp more than the German *Schlachtkreuzer* 'O' or the Japanese B-65 to achieve a similar speed. One factor here is the relatively poor hull form of the Soviet design, which had a block coefficient of about 0.61 compared to *Dunkerque* with a coefficient of 0.54, *Alaska* with 0.5266, and *Schlachtkreuzer* 'O' with about 0.52. Another factor was the poor propulsive efficiency of the overloaded three-shaft machinery plant. A four-shaft plant with reduced shaft loading would almost certainly have been more efficient, and probably would have allowed a better hull form as well.

Cavour Class	*Dulio* Class	*Kongo* Class	B-65	Design 1047	Project 69	*Alaska*
Italy	Italy	Japan	Japan	Netherlands	Soviet Union	United States
reconstr. 1937	recontr. 1940	reconstr. 1937	cancelled 1942	cancelled 1940	cancelled 1941	1941
?	?	32,156	31,400	27,988	35,240	27,000
27,726	28,700	36,610	34,950	31,396	38,360	32,774
29,032	29,000	?	?	?	41,539	34,253
ca.593	ca.593	730 oa	787.44	774.3	787.4	791.5
91.87	91.87	95.3	90.23	95.46	96.5	90.78
34.12	34.12	31.9	28.87	29.59	31.2 (normal)	30.77 (normal)
10 x 12.6in/44	10 x 12.6in/44	8 x 14in/45	9 x 12.2in/50	9 x 11.1/54	9 x 12in/54	9 x 12in/50
12 x 4.7in/50	12 x 5.3in/45	14 x 6in/50	16 x 3.9in/65	12 x 4.7in/	8 x 5.9in/57	12 x 5in/38
8 x 3.9in/47	10 x 3.54in/50	8 x 5in/40	12 x 25mm	14 x 40mm	8 x 3.9in/56	56 x 40mm
8 x 37mm	19 x 37mm	20 x 25mm	4 x 13mm	16 x 13mm	24 x 37mm	34 x 20mm
12 x 20mm	12 x 20mm		8 x 24in TT		8 x 12.7mm	
0	0	1	1	1	1	2
0	0	3	3	3	2	3
9.8 max	9.8 max	8in	7.48 at 20 deg	9.84 at 18 deg	9 at 5 deg	9 at 10 deg
3.9	3.9?	4.76?	4.92?	3.94	3.54	4.25
93,000	85,000	136,000	167,674	177,538	231,000	150,000
28.2	27	30.3	33	34	33	33
3,000 at 20	3,390 at 20	10,000 at 18	8,000 at 18	4,500 at 20	8,500 at 14.5	12,000 at 15
1,236	1,495	1,437	?	?	1,819	1,517
c.4.69	3.67 at 28,141	?	?	c.9.15	9.19	8.0 at 32,774

s given in the table are the best available.

It is hardly surprising to find that the larger and more modern Soviet design had a clear superiority over the reconstructed Italian battleships. Against its other most probable opponents, its advantages are by no means outstanding. In a duel with the *Scharnhorst* the Soviet design's heavier armament might have offset its much weaker protection to some extent, while in the case of the *Kongo* the situation was reversed, the Soviet ship having somewhat better protection but a less powerful main battery. Against *Schlachtkreuzer* 'O' the Soviet ship has just about equal speed, equivalent armament and superior protection.

But would the *Kronshtadt* class have actually achieved its designed performance? There is good reason for doubt. The armour protection was especially problematic, as described earlier. In all likelihood the level of protection provided by the heavy vertical armour would have been a good deal less than the designers had intended. The ships would almost certainly have been overweight as completed (the Shipbuilding Commissariat expressed concerns about this even before the war), which would have had an effect on speed. Given the problems suffered by other Soviet machinery plants, where extremely high steam conditions were combined with sometimes questionable workmanship, there is every reason to believe that the turbines and boilers would not have performed as designed, further reducing the ship's performance.

Conclusion

By the summer of 1937 a complete technical design for the Project 25 small battleship was ready, and construction could probably have been started in late 1937. It is not inconceivable that at least one ship might have been completed by June 1941. Although such a ship would have been of little service to the Soviet Union in its desperate war with Nazi Germany, its construction would at least have been an achievement of some note. But the purges swallowed up Project 25 and its designers, and another two years were spent developing the Project 69 design, which in the end had very similar characteristics to Project 25. The design was completed too late, and the construction of the ships was hobbled by industrial shortcomings and the squandering of scarce resources on too many overly ambitious projects. In fact the Soviet navy's 'heavy cruiser' designs were doomed by the constant changes in requirements, the deliberate destruction of the design staff during the purges, and the failures of Soviet industry. Every one of these problems can be traced back to Stalin's influence and interference. Although the dictator's regime accused many men of 'wrecking,' it was Stalin himself who sabotaged his own plans to build a seagoing navy.

Acknowledgments

I would like to express a great debt of gratitude to John Roberts, who provided drawings of projects 69 and 69-I of a quality far beyond anything I could hope to produce. John also read a draft of the article and provided valuable comments on it. I am also indebted to Thomas A Burns for the excellent drawing of Project 25. Tim Lanzendörfer provided help in obtaining German material, and Nathan Okun explained some of the fine points of cemented and face-hardened armour to me. As usual, Jan Torbet provided invaluable editorial assistance.

Sources

The best overall view of the complex development of the small battleships and big cruisers of the 1930s is found in *Istoriia otechestvennogo sudostroeniia*, vol. IV, *Sudostroenie v period pervykh piatiletok i Velikoi otechestvennoi voiny 1925-1945 gg.* (St. Petersburg: Sudostroenie, 1996), pp.278-282, 291-303. Also very valuable for many iterations of the design is N A Liasota and A B Morin, 'Tiazhelyi kreiser "Kronshtadt" (proekt 69)' (*Gangut*, no. 17 [1998], pp.59-78), a compilation of archival materials linked by a useful commentary. For technical details of Projects 69 and 69-I the most complete account is A A Chernyshev, 'Stalinskii favorit (tiazhelyi kreiser proekta 69 "Kronshtadt")' in *Superkreisera 1939-1945* (Modelist-konstruktor, 1995). Also useful are V Iu Usov, 'The *Kronshtadt* Class Battle Cruisers' (*Warship International*, vol. XXVIII, no. 4 [1991], pp.380-386), translated and with commentary by Evan Mawdsley; and V Krasnov, 'Kreisera tipa "Kronshtadt"' (*Morskoi sbornik*, no. 8, 1990 [August], pp.54-56). Where information comes from sources other than those mentioned above, an endnote has been provided.

Notes

1 For details of the various shipbuilding programmes, see Jürgen Rohwer, 'The Development of Strategic Concepts and Shipbuilding Programmes for the Soviet Navy, 1922-1953: Stalin's Battleships and Battlecruisers' (*The Northern Mariner/Le Marin du nord*, vol. VII, no. 3 [July 1997], pp.51-61).

2 For an overview of the Soviet design process in this era, see *Istoriia otechestvennogo sudostroeniia*, vol. IV, pp.247-248. See also the description and useful flow-chart in E A Shitkov, V N Krasnov and V V Balabin, *Korablestroenie v SSSR v gody Velikoi Otechestvennoi voiny* (Moscow: Nauka, 1995), pp.25-27.

3 Much of this section is based on L A Kuznetsov, 'Bol'shoi kreiser "X"' (*Gangut*, no. 18 [1999], pp.45-51. This design raises an interesting problem in transliteration: was the 'X' meant to be the Latin 'X,' used either for a mathematical unknown or the Roman numeral 10, or the Cyrillic letter 'X,' pronounced like the 'ch' in Bach?

4 It may be noted in passing that Voin Petrovich Rimskii-Korsakov was a member of the same naval family as the great composer Nikolai Andreevich Rimskii Korsakov. It is likely that Voin Petrovich was a grandson of the composer's brother, Voin Andreevich Rimskii-Korsakov, who attained the rank of rear-admiral before his untimely death in 1871.

5 After the Bolsheviks came to power, they eliminated the 'bourgeois' rank system and until 1935 used a somewhat fluid system that based an officer's rank on his position. On 22 September 1935 permanent ranks were again introduced similar to the system used in the tsarist navy, but the term 'admiral' was not used. Instead, the word *flagman*, literally 'flag officer,' was used. The ranks were Flag Officer 2nd Rank (rear-admiral), Flag Officer 1st Rank (vice-admiral), Fleet Flag

Officer 2nd Rank (admiral) and Fleet Flag Officer 1st Rank (fleet admiral). The term admiral was restored in 1940.

5 The dimensions of this design seem to be somewhat garbled in the table in *Istoriia otechestvennogo sudostroeniia*, p.302; the beam is given as 62.6m, while the draught is quoted as 76.4m – both figures are obviously errors. It seems most likely that in the beam the first two digits have been transposed, while in the draught the decimal point has shifted one digit to the right.

7 Soviet fears of a German amphibious attack in the far north are mentioned by Rohwer, 'The Development of Strategic Concepts and Shipbuilding Programmes for the Soviet Navy,' p.56.

8 As late as 1939 Sir Stanley Goodall, the DNC, thought the *Scharnhorst* might not exceed her announced displacement of 26,000 tons by very much. See F H Hinsley, E E Thomas, C F G Ransom and R C Knight, *British Intelligence in the Second World War: Its Influence on Strategy and Operations*, vol. I (London: HMSO, 1979), pp.505-507. The Soviets did not have access to accurate information about German ships until after the Nazi-Soviet Non-Aggression Pact was signed in August 1939.

9 This is the figure given by most published sources. Note, however, that M J Whitley, *German Capital Ships of World War Two* (London: Arms and Armour Press, 1989), p.38, says that it was actually 320mm.

10 Rolf Erikson, 'Soviet Battleships,' part 2 (*Warship International*, vol. XI, no. 2 [1974], pp. 115-133), p.130.

11 Robert Conquest, *The Great Terror: A Reassessment* (New York: Oxford University Press, 1990), p.210.

12 Quoted in Robert Waring Herrick, *Soviet Naval Strategy: Fifty Years of Theory and Practice* (Annapolis: Naval Institute, 1968), p.34.

13 The weights are based on Chernyshev, 'Stalinskii favorit,' p.10, where they are given as percentages of the normal displacement. The figures in tons are my calculations based on these percentages.

14 For details of Project 69's armament, I have relied on A V Platonov, S V Aprelev and D N Siniaev, *Sovetskie boevye korabli 1941-1945 gg.*, vol. IV, *Vooruzhenie* (St. Petersburg: Tsitadel', 1997) and A B Shirokorad, *Entsiklopediia otechestvennoi artillerii* (Minsk: Kharvest, 2000).

15 See William H Garzke, Jr. and Robert O Dulin, Jr., *Battleships: Allied Battleships in World War II* (reprinted with corrections and updates. Annapolis: Naval Institute Press, 1990), pp.329, 336, and Paul J Heine, letter to the editor, (*Warship International*, vol. XXIX, no. 2 [1992], p.114) for discussions of the shaft-loading question.

16 In fact the first prototype 305mm was test-fired at the proving ground near Leningrad only in the fall of 1940, with Navy Commissar N G Kuznetsov himself present to observe the trials. See Erikson, 'Soviet Battleships,' p.129.

17 Tobias R Philbin III, *The Lure of Neptune: German-Soviet Naval Collaboration and Ambitions, 1919-1941* (Columbia, SC: University of South Carolina Press, 1994), p.45. The following paragraphs are based on the same work, pp.45-51. Philbin, *Lure of Neptune*, following contemporary German practice, quotes gun calibres in centimetres; I have converted these (except in direct quotes) to millimetres for consistency's sake.

18 Rohwer, 'The Development of Strategic Concepts and Shipbuilding Programmes for the Soviet Navy,' p.57. See also Siegfried Breyer, 'Sowjetische Schlachtkreuzer mit Krupp-Kanonen' (Marineforum, March 1991, pp.301-303). The subsequent career of these sporadically homeless guns may be mentioned in passing. On 26 February 1942 *Gneisenau* was bombed by the RAF, causing an ammunition fire that burned out her forward turret, so the Krupp 380mm guns and turrets were now wanted for her reconstruction. But in February 1943 this too was canceled by Hitler, who was furious at the surface navy over the Barents Sea fiasco. In the end, the guns and mountings were used in coast defences. A complete summary of their final fates is provided by Philbin, *Lure of Neptune*, pp.49-50

19 Western sources usually indicate that sixteen guns in eight turrets were ordered. The reason for the differing figures has not yet come to light.

20 For the complete text of this decree, see Evan Mawdsley, 'The Fate of Stalin's Naval Program' (*Warship International*, vol. XXVII, no. 4 [1990]), pp.400-404.

21 For a scathing review of the failures of the Soviet shipbuilding industry in this period, see A M Vasil'ev, 'Nekotorye aspekty stroitel'stva lineinykh korabli tipa "Sovetskii Soiuz"' (*Sudostroenie*, no. 5, 2000, pp.65-72). The following paragraphs are based on this article.

22 Erikson, 'Soviet Battleships,' p.128. The general circumstances are confirmed by a US naval attaché report, which indicated that work on a 'battleship,' reputedly to be named the *Stalin*, had been halted in early 1940 due to the nondelivery of armour plate from the United States (quoted in Herrick, *Soviet Naval Strategy*, p.40).

23 I am grateful to Nathan Okun for information about the relative value of cemented and non-cemented plate (e-mail to author, 28 August 2001).

24 Vasil'ev, 'Nekotorye aspekty stroitel'sva...,' p.67.

25 V N Krasnov, 'Stalinshchina v VMF i korablestroenii' (*Sudostroenie*, no. 7, 1990, pp. 64-69), p.66.

26 Shitkov et al., *Korablestroenie v SSSR*, p.8.

27 V I Efimov and A B Morin, 'Proektirovanie i stroitel'stvo tiazhëlykh kreiserov proekta 82' (*Gangut*, 14 [1998], pp.33-55), pp.37-38.

28 Erikson, 'Soviet Battleships,' p.129.

THE DAWN OF THE *SALISBURY, LEOPARD* AND *WHITBY* CLASS FRIGATES

The new first classes frigates constructed for the Royal Navy in the mid-twentieth century embodied the hard-won experience gained during the Second World War and technical developments which evolved in the immediate post-war era. **George Moore** describes the story of their evolution.

Prelude

The 'Hunt' class dominated the escort force under construction at the outbreak of the Second World War.[1] They were initially to be armed with three twin 4in mountings and be capable of 29 knots. Endurance was, however, sacrificed with the ships designed to achieve 1350 miles at 25 knots and 2500 miles at 20 knots. This feature was adequate for operations in coastal waters but inadequate for service where endurance was a prime requirement. Also under construction were sloops of the *Black Swan* class also armed with three twin 4in mountings and capable of 19 knots.[2] The expected endurance was 7,500 miles at 12 knots, much more suitable for ocean going service.[3] The trade off between speed and endurance was graphically illustrated in the design of these two classes. The outbreak of war saw large orders placed for the very basic corvettes of the 16 knot 'Flower' class and trawlers which were built to merchant ship standards. However, they were never designed to fight submarines on the oceans and sea keeping left much to be desired. The anti-submarine armament in all these escorts was depth charges with asdic (sonar) to find the U-boats. In the first seven months of the war the Germans lost eighteen U-boats of which eleven were detected by asdic.[4]

By the Autumn of 1940 it was clear that the 'Flower' class corvettes were too basic a ship for the strenuous duty of escorting convoys in the Atlantic although a lack of more seaworthy vessels meant that their use on this task continued for the remainder of the war. In November it was decided that the ideal ship would achieve 22 knots, have one or possibly two single 4in mountings, displace at least 1500 tons with steam turbines developing 12,000shp. Length, a key parameter in gaining seaworthiness, should be between 300ft and 320ft. The 'River' class emerged which were a compromise. Virtually all the class had reciprocating engines producing 5,500ihp for industry could not build the numbers of turbines required. However, the overall length of 301ft 4in, long forecastle like the *Black Swan* and a high freeboard resulted in an excellent sea boat. The ships were built to merchant ship standards and although small numbers of the *Black Swan* class were produced to full warship standards the 'River' class and their successors the mass-produced 'Loch' class and the smaller 'Castle' class dominated the escort production programme. The 'Loch' class frigates were pioneers for considerable use was made of fabrication at structural engineers and equipment was produced under Admiralty contracts for the shipyards. The United States Navy meanwhile produced destroyer escorts and the 'Captain' class frigates, 78 of which served in the Royal Navy. Some of these flush decked 1,300 ton ships were capable of 24 knots but seaworthiness was never regarded as more than satisfactory until the bilge keels were enlarged and top weight added which improved matters.[5]

With the U-boat war at a peak in late 1942 and early 1943 when the 'Loch'/'Castle' class programmes were in production, Staff Requirements for a new escort were being formulated. What was wanted was a design on the lines of the prefabricated frigates but also incorporating the best features of the 'Hunt' and 'Captain' classes. They had to be capable of operating in the open oceans in adverse weather conditions and be highly maneuverable. An operational speed of 25 knots was wanted, which meant using 'Hunt' class machinery with endurance being 3000 miles at 15 knots. The armament was to consist of two twin 4in mountings both placed forward of the bridge, two 40mm Buster mountings and at least six 20mm Oerlikons. Two sided 6pdrs to attack submarines were also specified. The asdic equipment consisted of a housing dome set and a depth prediction set (types not specified) whilst an ahead throwing weapon was ultimately to be the anti-submarine armament.[6] This project died in the Summer of 1943 with victory essentially achieved in 'The Battle of the Atlantic', but its echoes emerged when frigate designs next came up for discussion.

Origins

The need for a new sloop design emerged in late 1944 with the matter coming before the Future Building Committee in January 1945 when the 1945 New Construction Programme was discussed. The Director of Anti-Submarine Warfare, Captain N A Prichard, although not a member of the committee was present. The minutes state that DA/SW pointed out the necessity for the provision of anti-submarine escort vessels (of a type to be considered later) in place of part of the Sloop programme. It was agreed to 'recommend that the two sloops to be built in a Royal Dockyard be cancelled and that four escort vessels of a type to be designed be substituted. In the meantime Staff Requirements would be considered.' At this stage the draft programme included five sloops, three of which were to be built at a slow rate in private yards. This aim was fulfilled by the orders for *Partridge*, *Waterhen* and *Wryneck*, which were ultimately cancelled shortly after the end of the war. The logic of building these ships according to the Director of Plans, Captain G Grantham, was the need for a warship 'which was designed to operate in an independent role and for this reason carry out many important duties on Foreign stations in peace time'. They were not expected to take part in the Japanese war.[7]

Although the Future Building Committee minutes and memoranda do not refer at this point to the increased underwater speeds said to be achieved by German submarines, the Director of Plans indicated to the Director of Naval Construction, Mr (later Sir) Charles Lillicrap, that to counter this threat a speed of 25 knots would be needed. The initial thought in mid-December 1944 was that just two of the new sloops would be wanted in the 1945 Programme.

The First Concepts

The first shot at producing a new design was made by Constructor M K Purvis who worked in conjunction with H S Pengelly, an Assistant Director of Naval Construction. Leading dimensions were on the lines of a modified *Black Swan* sloop but with a speed of 25 knots. The details are set out in Table 1. The most conspicuous feature was the large increase in shaft horsepower needed to achieve an additional five knots speed, which could only be gained with steam turbine machinery. It was anticipated that the new machinery would produce nearly four times the power of that fitted in the *Black Swan*

Sparrow *in 1946. Initial studies were based on a 25 knot development of this sloop design.* (World Ship Society – Kennedy Collection.)

Table 1: *9TH JANUARY 1945*

	Proposed 25 knot Sloop	1944 Modified *Black Swan* Sloop
Length water line	325ft 6in	295ft 6in
LBP	313ft	283ft
Beam	40ft 6in	39ft 6in
Depth	17ft 6in	17ft 6in
Standard Displacement	1,663 tons	1,429 tons
Standard draft	9ft 1in	8ft 10in
Standard G.M.	2ft 7in	1ft 6in
Deep Displacement	2,143 tons	1,910 tons
Deep draft	11ft	11ft
Shaft horsepower	15,000	4,300
Oil (tons)	415 tons	415 tons
Standard displacement		
Hull	900	791
Equipment	243	243
Armament	190	178
Machinery	300	217
Board Margin	30	-
	1,663 tons	1,429 tons

Source: ADM 138/830 (NMM)

class but it was less than twice the weight reflecting advances in practice and design. This also necessitated an increase in length, which in turn enabled the close range armament to be increased. The main armament of three twin 4in mountings remained as fitted in the *Black Swan* class. Fuel carried although identical to that achieved in the *Black Swan* class was expected in practice to improve without adding to the dimensions. The estimated cost was £500,000. This figure would have been subject to correction for even then a sloop in the 1944 Programme was costed at £510,000 and the new ships were clearly going to be more expensive.[8]

On 15 January 1945, Captain Prichard produced a memorandum entitled A/S and A/A Escort Vessels – 1945 Programme. This document was very clear about the nature of the opponent and the means by which he should be combated. The anti-submarine vessels wanted were divided into those required for fleet work and those required for trade protection. The type of U-boat with which the escorts had to compete was specified as the Type XXI, a boat said to have been designed with an underwater speed of 15-18 knots. The modern fleet destroyer was described as but a U-boat scarer, which was inadequate as the foe needed to be destroyed. It was therefore essential that a force of vessels should operate with the fleet, which was suitably equipped to hunt and destroy any U-boat detected. For trade protection duties a large number of escorts were required on the outbreak of war and it was considered necessary that any ship designed for

Brissenden *pictured in 1950. This Thornycroft version of the 'Hunt' class, which was capable of 25 knots, showed the value of a long forecastle.* (World Ship Society – Kennedy Collection.)

this purpose should be mass produced on the outbreak of hostilities. It would obviously simplify matters if one vessel could perform both functions. It was also advantageous if the hull could be designed so that a ship could be completed either as an A/S vessel or an A/A escort. Both types were to be capable of carrying out cruises on foreign stations thus carrying out the sloop function.

Staff Requirements were now formulated by both the Director of Gunnery Division, Captain Edden, and the Director of Anti-Submarine Warfare. The hull displacement desired by the Naval Staff was limited to 1,400 tons. The ships were to be capable of 25 knots and an endurance of 4,500 miles at 18 knots when out of dock for six months was wanted. It was hoped that the anti-submarine ship would carry one 4.5in twin and one 20mm twin but the gun armament was otherwise entirely subordinate to the A/S armament. They wanted the anti-aircraft ship to carry two twin 4.5in mountings, one twin 40mm and as many 20mm Oerlikons as can be mounted in the space available. The A/A vessels were also to carry an asdic set and depth charges for 'scaring' submarines but the A/A armament was the paramount feature. The twin 4in Mark XIX was also considered but the larger weapon was preferred as it was to be the future standard HA/LA gun whilst the 4in mounting could not be improved. DNC's Department produced a series of designs in the 1A to 4B series (Table 2) which set out the various alternatives and possibilities. There were clearly doubts about meeting the requirement on the displacement suggested especially in the case of the A/A vessel and when the Staff Requirements and design options came to be discussed in committee it was accepted that both versions would be heavier than suggested. The A/A escort would displace in the order of 1650 tons whilst the A/S version on the same hull would probably displace 1500 tons. The question of also incorporating aircraft direction facilities in the A/A escort was also now debated at some length. A reduced main armament in both versions to save dis-

Table 2: *21ST FEBRUARY 1945*

	1A AA Design	1B AS	2A AA	2B AS	3 AS	4A AA	4B AS
Length (WL)	335ft	335ft	325ft	*	320ft	310ft	310ft
Length (OA)	340ft	340ft	330ft		325ft	315ft	315ft
Beam	40½ft	40½ft	40½ft		40ft	39½ft	39½ft
Standard Displacement	1715 tons	1605 tons	1615 tons		1535 tons	1400 tons	1400 tons
Deep Displacement	2335 tons	2225 tons	2235 tons		2150 tons	1950 tons	1950 tons
SHP	23,000	23,000	23,000		24,000	19,000	19 000
Speed (Deep & Dirty)	25 knots	25½ knots	25 knots		25 knots	24 knots	24 knots
Speed (Standard & Clean)	28½ knots	29¼ knots	28½ knots		28½ knots	28¼ knots	28¼ knots
Oil Fuel	525 tons	525 tons	525 tons		525 tons	480 tons	480 tons
Endurance at 18 knots (Miles)	4500	4500	4500		4500	4500	4500
Armament: Gunnery	2-4.5in Twin	1-4.5in Twin	3-4in Twin		1-4.5in Twin	2-4in Twin	1-4in Twin
	1-40mm Twin STAAG	1-20mm Twin Oerlikon	1-40mm Twin STAAG		1-20mm Twin Oerlikon	4-20mm Twin Oerlikon	1-20mm Twin Oerlikon
	4-20mm Twin Oerlikon		4-20mm Twin Oerlikon				
	"Ben"		"Ben"				
Armament: Anti-submarine	4 D/C Throwers	6 Bidders	4 D/C Throwers		6 Bidders	4 D/C Throwers	6 Bidders
		1 Squid			1 Squid		1 Squid
		2 D/C Throwers			2 D/C Throwers		2 D/C Throwers

Notes:
1B – Anti-submarine design in 1A hull with same machinery.
2A – Design produced to reduced requirements.
2B – Anti-submarine requirements in 2A hull with same machinery. Differences between 2A and 2B generally as between 1A and 1B.*
4A and 4B – Designs on 1400 tons standard.

Source: ADM 138/830 (NMM)

Table 3: *20TH MARCH 1945.*

	A1 A/A Design	A2 A/S Design	B1 A/S Design	B2 A/A Design
Length (W/L)	330ft	330ft	325ft	325ft
Length (O/A)	335ft	335ft	330ft	330ft
Beam	40ft	40ft	40ft	40ft
Standard Displacement	1607 tons	1551 tons	1536 tons	1528 tons
Deep Displacement	2155 tons	2090 tons	2065 tons	2065 tons
SHP	22,000	22,000	21,000	21,000
Speed (Deep and Dirty)	25 knots	25 knots	25 knots	25 knots
Speed (Standard and Clean)	29 knots	29½ knots	29 knots	29 knots
Oil Fuel	400 tons	400 tons	390 tons	390 tons
Endurance at 15 knots (Miles)	4500	4600	4500	4500
Armament: Gunnery	2-4.5in Twin	1-4.5in Twin	1-4.5in Twin	3-4in Twin
	1-40mm Twin STAAG	1-40mm Twin STAAG	1-40mm Twin STAAG	1-40mm Twin STAAG
	4-20mm Twin Oerlikon	4-20mm Twin Oerlikon	4-20mm Twin Oerlikon	4-20mm Twin Oerlikon
	"Ben"			"Ben"
Armament: Anti-submarine	4 D/C Throwers	6 Bidders	6 Bidders	4 D/C Throwers
		1 Squid	1 Squid	
		2 D/C Throwers	2 D/C Throwers	

Source: ADM 138/830 (NMM)

placement was considered but not recommended.[9]

DNC's Department now produced designs 1A, 1B, 2A and 2B in February 1945, which were soon overtaken by new options designated A1, A2, B1 and B2 in March 1945 (Table 3). This activity was followed by a Naval Staff Conference on 16 April 1945 for which a further set of options was produced based on the earlier studies (Table 4). Particulars of the 'Loch', 'Bay' and 'Hunt' Type 2 class frigates were also provided. Prior to the conference DNC's Department considered issues which needed to be resolved. It was first of all pointed out that the difference between the new frigates and the earlier wartime designs was so marked that any comparison was meaningless. It was also felt that anti-aircraft armament had outstripped anti-submarine armament during the war. It was therefore wise to use the larger A/A hull for the A/S escort in order to have an adequate margin for future developments.[10] As a speed of 25 knots was wanted dimensions of both types would need to be virtually the same. Should a shorter hull be chosen for the A/S ship then all the weight saved in the hull would be lost in the machinery weight. The question of a need for an aircraft direction was also raised. At this time consideration was being given to using the "O" and "P" class destroyers in this role. They would lose a set of torpedo tubes in the conversion. The cost in an A/A frigate was expected to be the loss of a 40mm STAAG and Design "F" was drawn up showing this option. However the loss was not regarded as acceptable. To overcome this obstacle a new sketch design with an increased length of 12ft and extra displacement of 50 tons would be needed. The question of the need for a special Headquarters Ship for the senior officer of a convoy was also raised.[11]

At the meeting of the Naval Staff on 16 April 1945 it was agreed that the 1610 ton design should be adopted (Designs 2 and 2A in Table 4) and it was agreed that there was a requirement for an aircraft direction escort. The ship was needed to:

- Direct shore based fighters outside the range of shore based radar when accompanying convoys.
- To provide advance warning of low flying enemy aircraft during assault operations.
- To operate at a distance from important convoys to give advance warning and early interception of enemy aircraft.
- To enhance control of night fighters supporting a convoy.

DNC was asked to examine a design (Design 2B) on the same hull as Designs 2 and 2A. It was also agreed that a headquarter ship for the senior officer of a convoy to provide improved communications, facilities for control of anti-submarine aircraft and accommodation for his staff could be required. In this case DNC was asked to produce a new design (Design 2C) which should follow the specification of Design 2A as far as possible after the requirements of the prime function had been met. Also wanted was a smaller anti-submarine ship of the corvette type.

Table 4: *PRODUCED FOR CONFERENCE HELD ON THE 16TH APRIL 1945*

	1 A/A Design	2 A/A Design	2A A/S	3 A/S	3A A/A
Standard Displacement	1660 tons	1610 tons	1550 tons	1535 tons	1535 tons
Deep Displacement	2335 tons	2155 tons	2090 tons	2065 tons	2065 tons
Endurance at 15 knots (miles)	4500	4500	4500	4500	4500
Armament: Gunnery	2-4.5in Twin	2-4.5in Twin	1-4.5in Twin	1-4.5in Twin	3-4in Twin
	1-40mm Twin STAAG 4-20mm Twin Oerlikon	1-40mm Twin STAAG 4-20mm Twin Oerlikon	1-40mm Twin STAAG 4-20mm Twin Oerlikon	1-40mm Twin STAAG 4-20mm Twin Oerlikon	1-40mm Twin STAAG 4-20mm Twin Oerlikon
	"Ben"	"Ben"			"Ben"
Armament: Anti-submarine	4 D/C Throwers	4 D/C Throwers	6 Bidders	6 Bidders	4 D/C Throwers
			2 Squids	2 Squids	
			2 D/C Throwers	2 D/C Throwers	

Source: ADM 138/830 (NMM)

Note: Arthur Honnor RCNC points out that there is something inconsistent between Design 1 and the remainder. Variable load (difference between standard displacement and deep displacement) for Design 1 is 675 tons. The remainder vary between 530 tons and 545 tons.

Loch Achray *in 1946. The mass produced and effective 'Loch' class with their long forecastle were a significant influence on the early post war frigate designs.* (World Ship Society – Kennedy Collection)

Start Bay *in 1946. Mass produced anti-aircraft version of the 'Loch' class. The ability to alter design when under construction from an A/S ship to an A/A ship as achieved in the 'Loch'/'Bay' classes was wanted in the initial post war frigate studies.* (World Ship Society – Kennedy Collection)

The use of the new escort vessels in fleet operations was not felt to be of primary importance as fulfilment of this need would lead to far too costly a ship. Approval had been obtained to build four ships as part of the 1945 Programme and if it was practical the designs were to be developed with a view to obtaining war experience. By this stage however the war in the west had but a few days to run whilst the Japanese war was moving rapidly to its final outcome.[12]

The main anti-aircraft armament specified the new 4.5in Mark VI mounting in most of the design options considered. However between January and April 1945 consideration was given to the production of a new single 4.5in Mark VIII mounting for the 'Improved Frigates', the description given to them by the Director of Naval Ordnance. The design was to be based on the 4.5in Mark VI mounting so that equipment, drill and maintenance was standardised. The project probably died once the Naval Staff had decided on the basic specifications of the new frigates. The gun did not feature in any of the options considered which seems to indicate there was a lack of enthusiasm for the inevitable reduced anti-aircraft capability which the ships would have if armed with the new gun.[13]

These frigate designs were intended for mass production and during the Spring and Summer of 1945 relevant issues were considered. The wartime 'Loch' class programme had used mass production techniques, which involved the use of fabricated structures produced at structural engineers. The shipyards, however, had their own fabrication facilities and DNC considered that using their resource was better than relying on outside contractors for this work. The point was made that really rapid production depended on a properly balanced plan for the provision of hulls, machinery, gun mountings, gun control arrangements, internal fittings and labour. Ideally the yards should be laid out for this purpose but they were trapped by history. One answer to this problem was to put several frigates on a large slip at a major shipyard such as Harland and Wolff. This practice was used there to produce both frigates and minesweepers. The Engineer in Chief pointed out that the escorts needed turbine machinery which took 50 per cent more time to build that the reciprocating machinery hitherto used in virtually all the escort force. It was pointed out that there was a wide field of reciprocating machinery builders but there was no surplus turbine production capacity as all the existing resource would be needed to meet normal naval requirements in the event of war. The Director of Naval Ordnance noted that many items for which he was responsible would take longer to produce than the ship. He also commented on the likelihood that a shortage of electricians would have to be faced. As a way of perhaps partially combating this weakness the Director of Electrical Engineering believed that radar, wireless telegraphy offices and transmitting stations could be fitted out on shore and then lifted when complete on to the ship.[14]

Post War Progress

The paper outlining the 1945 New Construction Programme was produced for the War Cabinet on 29 June 1945. Included in the memorandum were 'four escort vessels of a new type each of about 1400 tons and with a speed of about 25 knots.' The text went on to say that 'these ships are largely for experimental purposes; two will be finished as A/S vessels and two as A/A ships.' The total cost of the programme was £2,700,000 (£675,000 each) with expenditure running until 1948. The document was destined not to be presented to the War Cabinet.[15] The four new escorts remained in the programme until November 1945. There was clearly strong pressure exerted on the Board of Admiralty to reduce the programme at this point in time for the Deputy First Sea Lord, Admiral Sir Charles Kennedy-Purvis indicated in a memorandum to the First Sea Lord that one of each of the four types of escort was needed to judge the effectiveness of the designs. The pressures were such, however, that on 12 November 1945 the First Sea Lord, Admiral Sir Andrew Cunningham, conceded and the programme was reduced to two ships, one fitted as an A/A ship, her consort as an A/S vessel. He reserved the right to insert the remaining pair in to the 1946 Programme. The two new escorts duly appeared in the revised programme the cost of each vessel now being assessed at £675,500 with expenditure running until 1949. The Cabinet approved the revised programme on 27 November 1945.[16]

The loss of the two frigates opened up a debate about the type of vessel to be built. On 14 December 1945 the Director of Tactical and Staff Duties Division drew up a memorandum which highlighted the case for and the case against building either an A/A frigate or an A/D frigate. He considered there was no case for building the A/A frigate, against was the lack of a suitable director and the associate control system for mounting in small ships observing that no useful knowledge was likely to be gained by fitting equipment already at sea in destroyers. In the case of the A/D frigate it was said that it was impossible to deny the need for ships of this type. The Type 960 and 277Q radar could be fitted now and still retain the defensive gun and anti-submarine armament. Later types were expected to have the same needs for space. The inevitable result of his analysis was that it was better to lay down one A/D frigate. The A/S version was needed to enable experimental work with new weapons to be carried out and there was a particular need to counter the fast submarine. By January 1946 it was decided that one A/S and one A/D frigate should be built. Displacement was now expected to be 1600 tons rather that the 1400 tons quoted in the memorandum presented to the Cabinet.

Detailed investigation into the characteristics of the A/A ship were undertaken at the close of 1945. The Engineer in Chief now expected the weight of the machinery to increase by 50 tons and even with welding saving 7½ per cent the displacement still came out at 1697 tons standard. To reduce to 1600 tons Constructor M K Purvis indicated that one twin 4.5in would need to be replaced by a 4.5in single or both twin mountings replaced by two 4.5in single mountings. The close range armament would be one 40mm Staag and two 40mm single Bofors. To add to the complexity of the situation, the Staff Requirements were now being reconsidered with additional aircraft direction facilities wanted which required more space whilst the A/S frigate was to have either two Pentad Bidder mountings or one mounting with re-load arrangements. This opened up four issues:

- Does the A/A ship really need to achieve 25 knots deep when six months out of dock in the tropics?
- The A/S ship presumably requires to achieve a high speed but is the 4.5in twin mounting really necessary?
- Does the A/D ship really require the high speed or heavy A/A armament?
- The Senior Officer Convoy Ship presumably also requires a high speed like the A/S ship but again is the heavy 4.5in mounting necessary?

The result of these deliberations was that it was decided to build both ships as A/S frigates. With displacement now expected to reach 1700 to 1750 tons it was considered possible that two types of hull would have to be adopted. Revised designs were duly prepared (Table 5) and duly produced at the end of May 1946. During July the designs were further refined (Table 6). The availability of armament for the new frigates was considered by the Director of Gunnery and Anti-Aircraft Warfare at the end of August. His memorandum indicated that assumed completion dates were expected to be 1950 for the first anti-submarine version, 1952 for the aircraft direction variant with the initial anti-aircraft type completing in 1954. New weapons being developed included a medium range mounting expected to be available in 1953/54 with an associated medium range control system (M.R.S.) to hand by 1951/52. A suitable guided weapon system (POPSY) under development to replace the STAAG 40mm mounting was however not expected to ready before 1956 and as a consequence was excluded from requirements. This was the last time that there was a mention of the requirement for a Senior Officer of a Convoy version.[17]

The Diesel Machinery A/A and A/D Frigates

Although ideally a common hull and machinery requirement should be in place for all designs placed in production, in practice this aim was impossible to achieve. These classes were wanted for rapid production in wartime and the industrial capacity just did not exist to enable the production of steam turbines for escorts as the works capacity would be needed to satisfy production of destroyers and larger warships should hostilities break out. There was also perceived to be a difficulty in finding skilled personnel to operate the machinery. The parting of the ways occurred in the Spring of 1947 when the Naval Staff concluded that common designs of about 1,700 tons should be confined to the A/D and A/A types. The initial proposals which were accepted involved the use of eight 2,000bhp standard diesel engines driving two shafts capable of developing a continuous rating of 14,400shp in the tropics, which, for short periods of up to eight hours, could be rated at 16,000shp. The penalty of switching to diesel power was that the ship was expected to achieve only 23 knots when she had been out of dock for six months in the tropics. It was still considered necessary for the anti-submarine version to be able to obtain 25 knots in this condition. The hull retained the dimensions of the earlier turbine driven designs in the first studies produced by W Paradise on the instructions of M K Purvis in April 1947. Priority was now given to the design of the A/A and A/D frigate designs and there was a call by the Engineer in Chief to virtually shelve the A/S variant for five years. The point was made that this was not practical as should hostilities break out there was a requirement for 180 A/S escorts which could only be met if the design was ready to place in production. There were thoughts of producing the design of an intermediate A/S frigate but they were not followed up at this time.[18]

By January 1948 the Sketch Designs of both the A/A and the A/D versions were placed before the Board of Admiralty (Table 7). The ships were designed for what was described as 'interim' armament and radar since the new 3in/70 twin mounting intended for ships of this type was still in the early stages of development. The aim was to achieve rapid production in wartime and methods of fabrication were to be developed so that this objective could be achieved. Standard range diesels were to be used for both main propulsion and for diesel generators. A three engine room arrangement was adopted to gain watertight subdivision.[19]

The possibility of producing these frigates in large numbers was soon to wane. The hull was constructed using a large number of longitudinals in the structure which were found to be difficult to assemble by the shipbuilders, which were initially two Royal Dockyards. The technique

Table 5: *Produced by 11th May 1945 to meet revised Staff Requirements*

	A/A Frigate	A/D Frigate "A"	A/D Frigate "B"	A/S Frigate
Standard Displacement	1632 tons	1597 tons	1629 tons	1595 tons
Deep Displacement	2078 tons	2035 tons	2075 tons	2033 tons
SHP (tropics)	18,000	18,000	18,000	18,000
SHP (temperate)	19,200	19,200	19,200	19,200
Speed Deep (six months Out of dock tropics)	25 knots	25¼ knots	25 knots	25¼ knots
Speed (Standard clean tropics)	27½ knots	27¾ knots	27½ knots	27¾ knots
Oil	305 tons	305 tons	305 tons	305 tons
Endurance	4500 miles	4550 miles	4500 miles	4550 miles
Displacement				
Hull	540	555	555	540
Hull incidentals	416	438	450	406
Equipment	122	124	124	122
Armament	227	153	173	200
Machinery	295	295	295	295
Board Margin	32	32	32	32
Standard Condition	1632 tons	1597 tons	1629 tons	1595 tons
Additional Armament	18	10	18	10
Additional Equipment	88	88	88	88
Oil Fuel and Diesel Oil	305	305	305	305
Reserve Feed Water	35	35	35	35
Deep Condition	2078 tons	2035 tons	2075 tons	2033 tont
Armament: Gunnery	2-4.5in RPC twin	14.5in RPC twin	2-4.5in RPC twin	1-4.5in RPC twin
	1-40mm twin STAAG 4-40mm single	1-40mm twin STAAG 4-40mm single Longshot	1-40mm twin STAAG	1-40mm twin STAAG 4-40mm single
Armament: Anti-submarine	Single Squid	10 Depth Charges	10 Depth Charges Mounting	2 Squids 1 Pentad Bidder 10 Bidders 15 Depth Charges Nightshirt
Radar	Type 291 Type 293Q	Type 960 Type 277Q Type 293Q	Type 960 Type 277Q Type 293Q	Type 291 Type 293Q

Source: ADM 138/830 (NMM)

was effective from a damage limitation point of view having been developed by E. W. Gardner who carried out explosive trials against the ex-German "Z" class destroyer *Nonsuch* (ex-Z38) which used similar principles in her construction. There was also elaborate electrical equipment which added to the complexity and by February 1951 it was said that there was no hope of completing the ships in large numbers quickly in wartime conditions unless this problem was solved. It meant removing a large proportion of the wiring and assembly from the shipyard labour.[20] The engine installation was also complex for in addition to the eight ASR 1 diesels driving the main engines (two in both the forward and aft engine rooms and four in the central engine room) there were four more driving generators located in both the forward (two generators) and after (two generators) engine rooms. Provision was also made for a small 60kW emergency generator to be fitted; it was located in the distinctive bow,

Table 6: *Revised Designs July 1946*

	All types on hull length 330ft (wl), 335ft (oa)		
	A/A Frigate	**A/D Frigate**	**A/S Frigate**
Standard Displacement	1611 tons	1588 tons	1591 tons
Deep Displacement	2057 tons	2026 tons	2029 tons
Deep Draught	10ft 3in	10ft 1in	10ft 1in
SHP (tropics)	18,000	18,000	18,000
SHP (temperate)	19,200	19,200	19,200
Speed			
Deep 6m out of dock tropics	25 knots	25¼ knots	25¼ knots
Deep Clean, tropics	25¾ knots	26 knots	26 knots
Standard 6m out of dock tropics	26¾ knots	27 knots	27 knots
Standard Clean, tropics	27½ knots	27¾ knots	27¾ knots
Oil Fuel	305 tons	305 tons	305 tons
Endurance at 15 knots six months out of dock, tropics (2550 SHP)	4500 miles	4550 miles	4550 miles
Displacement			
Hull	540	558	540
Hull incidentals	415	421	419
Equipment	122	126	122
Armament	207	156	183
Machinery	295	295	295
Board Margin	32	32	32
Standard Condition	1611 tons	1588 tons	1591 tons
Additional armament	18	10	10
Additional equipment	88	88	88
Oil fuel and diesel oil	305	305 tons	305 tons
Reserve feed water & overflow	35	35	35
Deep Condition	2057 tons	2026 tons	2029 tons
Armament: Gunnery	2-4.5in twin 1-40mm twin STAAG 1-40mm single Bofors	1-4.5in twin 1-40mm twin STAAG	1-4.5in twin 1-40mm twin STAAG
	…………Medium Range Rocket Illumination……………..		
Armament: Anti-submarine	Single Squid 10 salvoes	Single Squid 10 salvoes	2 LIMBO 25 salvoes 1 Pentad "Bidder" Mounting 10 Bidders Nightshirt
Radar	Type 291 Type 293Q	Type 960P Type 277Q Type 293Q Type 981	Type 972 Type 293Q

Source: ADM 138/830 (NMM)

Table 7: *Legends of Anti-Aircraft Frigate and Aircraft Direction Frigate 1945 Programme*

	A/A Frigate December 1947	June 1950	A/D Frigate December 1947	June 1950
Length Waterline	330ft	330ft	330ft	330ft
Length Overall	340ft	339ft 10½in	340ft	339ft 10½in
Breadth	40ft	40ft	40ft	40ft
Displacement (standard)	1770 tons	1835 tons	1665 tons	1738 tons
(deep)	2095 tons	2185 tons	2005 tons	2110 tons
SHP (temperate)	15,200	15,200	15,200	15,200
SHP (tropical)	14,400	14,400	14,400	14,400
Speed in Standard Condition 6 months out of dock tropics	23 knots	23 knots	23 knots	23 knots
Total Oil Capacity	200 tons	230 tons	220 tons	252 tons
Endurance at 15 knots 6 months out of dock tropics	4500 miles	4500 miles	5000 miles	5000 miles
Complement of Officers & Men	251	220	247	222?
Armour and Protection	none	none	none	none
Displacement				
General Equipment	255	224	255	224
Machinery	418	465	418	465
Armament	265	300	160	215
Hull	922	930	917	918
Board Margin	35	36	35	36
Fuel Oil	200	230	220	252
Deep Displacement	2095 tons	2185 tons	2005 tons	2110 tons
Armament				
Twin 4.5in Mark VI	2	2	1	1
Rounds per Gun	375	300	375	300
40mm twin STAAG	1		1	
Rounds per gun	1580		1580	
40mm Bofors Mark VII Single	2	2	-	1
Rounds per gun	1580	1200	-	1200
Single Squid (10 salvoes)	yes	yes	yes	yes
Sources:	Legends NCD 24 (NMM)	ADM 167/135 (PRO)	Legends NCD 24 (NMM)	ADM 167/135 (PRO)

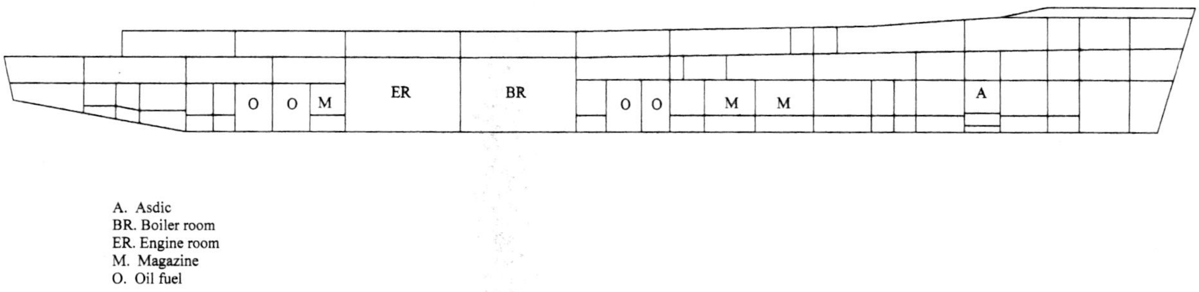

Anti-Submarine Frigate. Drawing dated 21 October 1949 showing disposition of bulkheads and compartments. Note the forecastle design that is reminiscent of the design featured in the contemporary Blackwood class. *Drawing by John Roberts based on drawing in Work Book 822/1, E Gardner.* (National Maritime Museum)

well away from the engine room. The original plan was for the engine exhausts to be led through the ships side at the waterline but this was superceded in 1951 when the exhausts were placed in the masts. The ASR 1 design evolved over a number of years having its origins in a high speed V16 diesel for submarines which was under development at Chatham Dockyard in 1939. There were thoughts about installing the design in the new 'A' class submarines but development only reached fruition after the war when the design was converted to direct injection and supercharged to become the ASR 1 diesel.[21] The new diesel installation was 100 tons heavier than the steam machinery originally specified and the loss of speed meant that the two frigate classes could not operate as effective units of the fleet but then this was not the intention when they were conceived. The major gain was endurance where the A/A and A/D versions could achieve 4,500 miles and 5,000 miles respectively at 15 knots. Less space was taken up by armament and ammunition storage in the A/D version which, in turn, meant more capacity within the hull was available for fuel.[22]

The plan in April 1949 was to lay down the two planned frigates in mid 1950 with the A/A version being built at Devonport and the A/D ship at Portsmouth. For some reason the plans were revised with Devonport building *Salisbury*, the A/D version and Portsmouth *Leopard*, the A/A ship. Two sets of machinery were ordered from Vickers Barrow in August 1948 with one set subcontracted to Peter Brotherhood of Peterborough. The latter firm in practice produced the machinery for generating electricity. Changes in the design between 1947 and 1950 were relatively minor and principally concerned the volumes of oil and ordnance carried. Proposals to produce the 'Stage Two' versions of the design with the 3in/70 twin mounting replacing the 4.5in Mark VI twin lingered on until June 1954 when it became clear that trials of the prototype would be delayed. Both classes carried a comprehensive radar fit with each carrying the Type 275 anti-aircraft fire control and Type 960 air warning radar. The A/A ship also carried the Type 262 close range anti-aircraft control system and the Type 992Q surface/low level search system, which reflected it's anti-aircraft role. The A/D vessel was fitted with Type 277 height finding, Type 960 air warning and Type 982 low air warning radar for its specialised task. Each class was fitted with Types 162, 170 and 174 sonar.[23]

The Anti-Submarine Frigate

With the main design effort concentrated on the new diesel powered anti-aircraft and aircraft direction frigates and the conversion of fleet destroyers to anti-submarine frigates throughout 1947, work effectively ceased on the anti-submarine frigate. When resumed in the Spring of 1948 the 25 knot version with the standard hull was still being considered. The Naval Staff however produced a study into the speed and endurance characteristics needed to counter a range of submarine threats. There were three types of submarine to oppose:

- The Second World War submersible with a full submerged speed of seven knots.
- The Intermediate B with a full submerged speed of 17/18 knots.
- An intermediate submarine with a full submerged speed of 25 knots.

The response to (a) was the 'Loch' class with a speed of 17-18 knots. To counter (b) a speed of 27 knots was needed while to oppose (c) 35 knots was required. The design of a 27 knot frigate now became important as the Intermediate B type submarine was seen as a potent threat. The Naval Staff required the new design to have an endurance of 4,500 miles at 12 knots an earlier requirement that 4,500 miles at 15 knots be achieved being too ambitious. In service, 5 per cent of the time at sea was expected to be spent at 27 knots, 15 per cent at 18 knots and 80 per cent at 12-14 knots. The Board of Admiralty approved preparation of the design in November 1948.[24]

The initial quest for a 27 knot frigate meant increasing the output of the machinery from 20,000shp to 30,000shp. The first studies in May 1948 utilised the standard hull but it soon became necessary to increase the

Table 8: *ANTI-SUBMARINE FRIGATE DESIGNS*

	27.5.48 25 knots Length 330ft	27.5.48 27 knots Length 330ft	9.2.50 Design 'X' Beam 40ft	16.2.50 Design 'Y' Beam 41ft
Hull	920	920	980	990
Equipment	255	265	280	290
Armament and Radar	220	220	240	244
Machinery	220	310	368	368
Oil	340	350	360	360
Reserve Feed water	35	50	18	18
Board Margin	35	40	40	40
	2025 tons	2155 tons	2286 tons	2310 tons
Sources:	Work Book 442/6, J W Harrington		Work Book 822/2, E Gardner (NMM)	

Salisbury *in 1957 when just completed.* (World Ship Society – Kennedy Collection.)

Leopard *in 1958 soon after completion.* (World Ship Society – Kennedy Collection.)

Whitby *in 1956. Note the distinctive funnel design.* (World Ship Society – Kennedy Collection.)

Rothesay *in 1960. A modification of the* Whitby *design to enable the ships to operate effectively with the fleet.* (World Ship Society – Kennedy Collection.)

waterline length by 30ft to 360ft. Two width options were considered, Design 'X' with an unchanged beam of 40ft and Design 'Y' with the beam increased to 41ft (Table 8). The latter option was soon chosen. The new Y100 design main machinery was ordered for the first ship in the Summer of 1948 construction of the first ship being authorised in the 1949 New Construction Programme. The hull was designed for rapid production by prefabrication methods the longitudinals being more widely spaced than those incorporated in the A/A and A/D designs. The hull was generally of all welded construction with 'S' quality steel used on highly stressed portions of the hull and mild steel elsewhere. The use of aluminium in the structure was avoided as far as possible on grounds of cost, quickness of building and an anticipated shortage of the material in wartime. The ship was designed to steam at full power in rough weather so she was given a fine forebody. The freeboard forward was also enhanced as far as possible with the hull given additional stiffening to counter possible damage from pounding in a seaway. The long forecastle deck, whilst increasing displacement, provided additional space, improved seaworthiness and adequate reserves of stability and buoyancy. Water ballast compartments were provided, which were independent of the fuel system to maintain stability when the ship was in light condition. The twin rudders provided good maneuverability whilst the new large 12ft diameter propellers achieved a reduction in noise and improved efficiency. Revolutions were in the order of 220rpm at full speed. The design was approved by the Board of Admiralty in December 1950 with first ship ordered in February 1951 and scheduled to complete in mid 1953 (Table 9).[25]

Table 9: LEGEND OF FIRST RATE ANTI-SUBMARINE FRIGATE DESIGN "Y" FEBRUARY 1950

Length between perpendiculars	360ft
Length overall	370ft
Breadth	41ft
Standard Displacement	1840 tons
Shaft Horsepower	30,000
Propelling Shafts	2
Speed in deep condition, six months out of dock in tropical waters	27 knots
Total Oil Fuel Capacity	360 tons
Endurance at 12 knots, six months out of dock in tropical waters	4500 miles
Complement of Officers and Men	283
Armament	
Twin 4.5in Mark VI UD Mounting	1 (375 rounds per gun)
STAAG (twin mounting)	1 (1500 rounds per gun)
Target Seeking A/S Weapons	4 Tubes (12 torpedoes)
Double Limbo	1 (20 salvoes)
Displacement	
General equipment	287
Machinery	377
Armament including Radar	240
Armour and Protection	Nil
Hull	988
Fuel	360
Reserve Feed Water	18
Board Margin	40
Deep Displacement	2310 tons

Source: ADM 167/135 (PRO)

Postscript

The *Leopard* (Type 41) and *Salisbury* (Type 61) class frigates proved to be a design cul-de-sac. They were complex designs, which took around three and a half years to build and their inability to operate efficiently with the fleet, particularly in the case of the Type 61, was a profound weakness. In service the diesel engines also proved troublesome. The *Whitby* class (Type 12) benefited to a degree from experience gained in the construction of the earlier classes in that the hull design was simplified. After the initial production of six ships the design went on to provide the basic concept for the successor *Rothesay* class which was modified to enable the ships to operate efficiently with the fleet. The highly successful *Leander* class general purpose frigate followed using the same basic hull, machinery and main armament, providing a fitting tribute to soundness of the Type 12 Design which had its origins in those far-off wartime concepts.

Acknowledgements

I would like to particularly thank David K Brown RCNC and Arthur Honnor RCNC who have both read the manuscript and provided many useful professional comments and anecdotes which have enhanced the work. I am also grateful to the staff at the Public Record Office and Bob Todd and his team at the National Maritime Museum for all their support. I must also thank Brian Hargreaves of the World Ship Society for providing the photographs and John Roberts for producing the drawing of the early *Whitby* class hull design.

References and Footnotes

1 J English, *The Hunts*, (World Ship Society).

2 A Hague, *Sloops 1926-1946*, (World Ship Society) and D K Brown RCNC 'Sir Roland Baker, RCNC' (*Warship* 1995).

3 ADM 167/99. 1937 Board of Admiralty Memoranda "Escort Vessels 1937 Programme" and 1939 Board of Admiralty Memoranda "Fast Escort Vessels 1939 Programme". (TNA)

4 Vice Admiral Sir Arthur Hezlet, *The Electron and Sea Power*.

5 ADM 229/24. Director of Naval Construction: Papers June 1940-March 1941. (TNA) and D K Brown, RCNC (ed) *The Design and Construction of British Warships 1939-1945*. The ships also suffered from insufficient freeboard due to the flush

In the mid 1960s the Leopards *were extensively re-fitted, most noticably gaining a new mainmast supporting the aerial for the Type 965 search radar. In 1978 and 1982 respectively* Jaguar *became* Ali Haider *and* Lynx *became* Abu Bakr *in the Bangladesh Navy.* Abu Bakr *is here shown leaving Portsmouth on 30 April 1982, just over a month after her transfer. (CPL)*

The ships have been good value to their new owners, and are still (2003) in service, albeit now in a training rather than operational capacity. Ali Haider *(ex-Jaguar) is here pictured at Penang in May 1990.* (Leo van Ginderen Collection)

Table 10: LEOPARD CLASS TYPE 41

Name	Programme	Job Number	Yard Number	Builder	Ordered	Laid down	Launched	Completed
LEOPARD	1945	FA01	-	Portsmouth	21. 8. 51	25. 3. 53	23. 5. 55	30. 9. 58
LYNX	1951	FA02	679	John Brown	28. 6. 51	13. 8. 53	12. 1. 55	14. 3. 57
PANTHER	1951	FA03	680	John Brown	28. 6..51	20.10.55	15. 3. 57	28. 3. 58
PUMA	1951	FA04	664	Scotts	28. 6. 51	16.11. 53	30. 6. 54	24. 4. 57
JAGUAR	1951	FA05	1476	Denny	28. 6. 51	2.11. 53	30. 7. 57	12.12. 59

Note. Eleven ships were planned in 1953, (*Vanguard to Trident*, E Grove) Further names suggested by the Ships Names Committee were *Cougar* and *Cheetah*. (Minutes are held in the Naval Library, Whitehall.) *Panther* was sold to India prior to completion and two further ships were built for them.

SALISBURY CLASS TYPE 61

Name	Programme	Job Number	Yard Number	Builder	Ordered	Laid down	Launched	Completed
SALISBURY	1945	FD01	-	Devonport	21. 8. 51	23. 1. 52	25. 6. 53	27. 2. 57
CHICHESTER	1951	FD02	771	Fairfield	28. 6. 51	25. 1. 53	21. 4. 55	16. 5. 58
LINCOLN	1951	FD03	772	Fairfield	28. 6. 51	20. 5. 55	6. 4. 59	7. 7. 60
LLANDAFF	1951	FD04	726	Hawthorn Leslie	28. 6. 51	27. 8. 53	30.11. 55	11. 4. 58

Note. Ten ships were planned in 1953, (*Vanguard to Trident*, E Grove) Further names suggested by the Ships Names Committee were *Truro, Winchester, Durham, Ely, Lichfield, Armagh* and *Canterbury*. *Exeter* (FD05) and *Gloucester* (FD07) were cancelled in 1957. *Coventry* (FD06) was replaced by *Penelope* (*Leander* class).

WHITBY CLASS TYPE 12

Name	Programme	Job Number	Yard Number	Builder	Ordered	Laid down	Launched	Completed
WHITBY	1949	FSA01	1229	Cammell Laird	2. 2. 51	30. 9. 52	2. 7. 54	19. 7. 56
SCARBOROUGH	1950 Sup	FSA02	142	Vickers - Tyne	6. 3. 51	11. 9. 53	4. 4. 55	10. 5. 57
TENBY	1951	FSA03	1233	Cammell Laird	6. 3. 51	23. 6. 53	4. 10. 55	18. 12. 57
EASTBOURNE	1951	FSA04	143	Vickers - Tyne	6. 3. 51	13. 1. 54	29. 12. 55	9. 1. 58
TORQUAY	1951	FSA05	1472	Harland & Wolff	6. 3. 51	11. 3. 53	1. 7. 54	10. 5. 56
BLACKPOOL	1951	FSA06	1473	Harland & Wolff	6. 3. 51	20. 12. 54	14. 2. 57	13. 8. 58

Note. Two ships intended for the Royal Navy were sold to India. Three were constructed for South Africa and four built in Australia. Twelve ships of the similar *Rothesay* class were ordered for the Royal Navy of which three were modified while under construction and completed as *Leander* Class frigates.

deck which contributed to the seaworthiness problem in the view of Arthur Honnor RCNC.

6 ADM 229/30. Director of Naval Construction: Papers June-August 1943 (TNA) The "Buster" was a computer controlled 40mm mounting designed by Vickers. 102 were ordered by the Admiralty but all bar one were cancelled after the war. (Vickers Archives, Cambridge University Library)

7 ADM 116/5151, Future Building Committee Minutes and Memoranda. (TNA)

8 ADM 138/830, Destroyers and Frigates General Cover. (NMM) The estimate of expenditure on the 1944 Programme *Black Swan* Class sloops is contained in a paper for the War Cabinet 'New Construction Programme 1944' dated 1 May 1944 held in CAB 66/49. (TNA)

9 ADM 138/830, Destroyers and Frigates General Cover. (NMM)

10 Arthur Honnor RCNC comments on this very interesting point. 'Although our escorts with ship mounted weapons did sterling service, the submarine menace was largely defeated by intelligence and the use of aircraft both shore based and carried on escort carriers. The result was the later development of aircraft (helicopters) carried in small carriers (*Invincible*) and the later frigates.'

11 ADM 138/830, DNC's departmental note also talks of the possibility of the new ships mounting the 40mm twin "Buster" mounting.

12 ADM 138/830, no particulars of Designs 2B and 2C have been found. Nothing was done about developing the small corvette design at this point bar the production of a sketch design in June 1945. The *Blackwood* Class eventually emerged to fill the niche for a small specialised anti-submarine escort. (G Moore, 'The *Blackwood* Class, Type 14 Second Rate Frigates', *Warship 2001-2002*)

13 ADM 138/830. The new gun would have been designed at Vickers Armstrong, Elswick. Their resources were committed to work on two pilot 5.25in mountings that were originally intended for the 1944 Cruiser. The first priority was for new 16in mountings for two battleships expected to be included in the 1945 New Construction Programme. The Mark VII 4.5in was a modified Mark VI mounting intended for the *Gibraltar* Class fleet aircraft carriers.

14 ADM 138/830. It took many months for the issue of a lack of turbine machinery production capacity to be grasped. (D K Brown has doubts about the perceived lack of capacity for Thornycroft had unused capacity during the war and firms constructing turbines for land power stations could have become involved.) The idea of producing fully fitted out offices was followed up and was incorporated in the initial designs but not carried through to the final designs. The idea did not die for it was utilised when the large missile direction

Appendix 1: *Draft Staff Requirements for an Anti-Aircraft Escort Vessel*

Dated 22nd February 1945 (Abbreviated)

SECTION A GENERAL

Function

1a. To provide A/A protection for convoys.
 b. To carry out minor offensive operations for which fleet destroyers are unsuitable.
 c. To assist in anti-submarine operations.

General Remarks

2. Vessel should be capable of directing coastal craft.

Speed

3. 25 knots in tropical waters under operational conditions six months out of dock in tropical waters.

Endurance

4. 4500 miles at 15 knots.

Displacement

5. Of the order of 1400-1600 tons.

Draught and Dimensions

6. Under consideration.

Special Features

7. To be fitted for service in tropical waters and cold climates.

SECTION B ARMAMENT

Main Gun Armament

8. 2-4.5in RPC mountings at least one forward.
9. Main gun to be capable of firing "Shark" missiles.

Close Range Armament

10. One "Ben".
11. One twin 40mm capable of blind fire.
12. As many handworked Oerlokons as can be mounted in space available.

Ammunition

13. Normal outfit including "Sharks".

Gun Control

14. Type of director under discussion.

Anti-Submarine Armament

15. Ability to fire 10 charge pattern. 50 depth charges.
 (Designed for one triple torpedo tubes as an alternative to depth charge armament.)
16. Consideration to be given to fitting "Hedgehog" instead of "Ben" if latter not available. 10 "Hedgehog" salvoes.
 Asdic Set.

---

radar offices were installed in the *Invincible* class.

15 CAB 66/67. The New Construction Programme 1945 (TNA). The programme at this point also included the battleships *Lion* and *Temeraire* (New design) and one experimental submarine.

16 ADM 205/52, First Sea Lords Papers. The right to insert the two deleted ships in the 1946 Programme was not exercised. Cabinet approval is recorded in CAB 128/2, the accompanying memorandum is held in CAB 129/4. (TNA)

17 ADM 138/830, Destroyers and Frigates General Cover. (NMM) See also Work Book 233/11 H S Pengally. (NMM) who raised the question of speed requirement in A/A and A/D frigates together with need for 4.5in twin mounting in A/S and SO Convoy versions. The new Medium Range Mounting was the twin 3in/70.

18 M K Purvis, RCNC, 'Post War Frigate and Guided Missile Destroyer Design 1944-1969'. (Paper read to Royal Institution of Naval Architects in 1974). See also Minutes of Sea Lords Meeting held on 11 April 1947, (ADM 205/67 (TNA) and Memorandum 'Future Construction' by Engineer in Chief, 1949. (DNC Papers Volume 77 held at NMM) The note by Purvis to Paradise dated 25.4.47 is held in ADM 138/830, (NMM). This file also holds notes on wartime A/S vessel requirement.

19 ADM 167/131, 1948 Admiralty Board Memoranda: A/A Frigate 1945 Programme Sketch Design and A/D Frigate 1945 Programme Sketch Design. (TNA)

20 Arthur Honnor RCNC who was closely associated with the designs commented on the difficulties experienced by the Shipbuilders. The difficulties with electrical work are recorded in the Ships Cover ADM 138/795.

21 ADM 265/1 holds a record of development in 1939. D K Brown RCNC provided the later history of the Admiralty Standard Range (ASR 1) diesel. The exhaust outlet location change is recorded in the Ships Cover. See alsom M K Purvis, RCNC, 'Post War RN Frigate and Guided Missile Destroyer Design 1944-1969' (1974 RINA).

22 Note to the author by Arthur Honnor RCNC.

23 ADM 138/795, 1945 Anti-Aircraft and Aircraft Direction Frigates. (NMM) In January 1948 when firms to build the engines were being sought, The Engineer in Chief found it very difficult to find interested contractors. (Volume 74 DNC Records held at NMM). For the history of Post War developments in Radar and Sonar see Hezlet *The Electron and Sea Power* and W Hackmann *Seek and Strike*.

24 Work Book 442/6, J W Harrington (NMM) and ADM

Appendix 2: *Draft Staff Requirements for Anti-Submarine Escort Vessel*

Dated 22nd February 1945 (Abbreviated)

SECTION A GENERAL

Function

1. To hunt and destroy U-boats.

General Remarks

2. This type of vessel is the core of the anti-submarine forces and should be capable of mass production.

Speed

3. 25 knots in tropical waters in operational condition six months out of dock.

Endurance

4. 4500 miles at 15 knots.

Displacement

5. Of the order of 1400-1600 tons.

Draught and Dimensions

6. No limitations

Special Featuresz

7. To be capable of operating Asdics in any weather in which anti-submarine escorts may be required to operate.
8. Good maneuverability is essential.
9. To be fitted for service in Tropical waters and cold climates.

SECTION B ARMAMENT

Main Gun Armament

10. One 4.5in twin RPC mounting forward.
11. Main gun armament to be capable of firing "Shark" projectiles.

Close Range Armament

12. One twin 40mm capable of blind fire.
13. As many hand worked Oerlikons as can be mounted in the space available.

Ammunition

14. Normal outfit including Sharks.

Gun Control

15. Type of director still under consideration.

Anti-Submarine Armament

16. Two – three barred Squids – 25 salvoes.
17. Ability to fire five depth charge pattern. 25 depth charges.
18. Two Mark "X" depth charges.
19. Six Bidders. Launching arrangements under consideration.

Asdic Set

20 Latest.

Note.

"Hedgehog"	An anti-submarine mortar firing contact fused projectiles.
"Shark"	A projectile fired against surfaced submarines at up to 800 yards range. Requirement was deleted from specification in November 1945.
"Bidder"	Anti submarine torpedo later code named Dealer B. Ultimately designated Mark 30 torpedo.
"Ben"	Short range anti-aircraft missile later codenamed "Longshot" and finally "Popsy". Project cancelled c.1950.

116/5632, Ship Design Policy Committee Meetings and Recommendations 1948-1952, (TNA). Harrington's Work Book (442/6) includes initial brief calculations dated 5.4.48 on what was needed to produce a 36 knot fast A/S frigate. Displacement 1800 tons, Length 320ft beam 40ft. No A/A armament. Limbo and Bidders specified. Machinery: three shafts, four 4000bhp Deltic diesels on each outer shaft, Four 5000shp Rolls Royce gas turbines on centre shaft. Total say 50,000shp.

25 ADM 281/149, DNC 1950 Annual Progress Report. (TNA) Although 'S' quality steel seems to have initially been specified for certain areas of the hull it appears that in practice mild steel was used throughout. Arthur Honnor RCNC comments: 'The hulls were not particularly highly stressed because they were designed with an extended forecastle. Also that separate ballast tanks were fitted because of wartime experience which showed that engineers were reluctant to put ballast water into oil fuel tanks because of the problems caused. This meant that destroyers especially were often operating with less stability than was really safe. The space occupied by the water ballast tanks was later used to good effect when the Type 12 design was updated to become the *Leander* class. By this time the type of fuel bought by the Royal Navy was not subject to the same problems and a different solution was possible. Regarding propellers, at that time, the noise reduction effect was more a hope than a reality. Subsequently, the programme of trials, experiments and theorizing that was led by the Admiralty Experiment Works, Haslar produced a considerable improvement and gave the Royal Navy the quietest frigate propellers in the World.'

Appendix 3: *Agreed Staff Requirements for 1945 Aircraft Direction Frigate*

Dated August 1945 (Abbreviated)

SECTION A GENERAL

Function

1. (a) To be capable of directing aircraft either carrier borne or RAF shore based by day and by night.
   (b) To act as air control ship for convoy and in amphibious operations when no other suitable ship present.

Secondary Function

   (c) To act as coastal force directing ship.
   (d) To assist in the anti-submarine protection of convoys and to be capable of self defence against submarines.
   (e) To assist in the anti-submarine protection of convoys or anchorages.

General Remarks

2. The ship to be capable of rapid production. After the aircraft direction requirements have been met (which are to have priority) the best possible anti-aircraft armament should be fitted.

Speed

3. 25 knots at deep load six months out of dock tropical waters with propeller silencing fitted but not working.

Endurance

4. 4500 miles at 15 knots.

Displacement

5. Of the order of 1600 tons.

Draught and Dimensions

6. Common hull with other types of 1945 design frigate is desirable.

SECTION B

Main gun armament

1. Provision for one new medium range mounting. Interim equipment one 4.5in twin RPC.

Close Range Armament

2. One Staag or one twin Bofors and simple tachometric director.

Main Gun Control

3. Provision for one MRS (Medium Range System). Interim equipment one Mark VI director and "Flyplane".

Aircraft Direction

10. Fitted for two day interceptions and one night interception.

SECTION C

Radar.

1. Provision for latest height finding radar. Interim 277Q.
2. Provision for latest WA set aft. Interim Type 960(P) on mainmast.
3. Provision of WS and height finding directing set forward. Interim 277Q.
4. Radar homing beacon Type 251 P/X.
5. Target indication.
6. Transponder.
7. Gunnery radar on director and Staag.

Appendix 4: *Staff Requirements for 1945 Frigate Fitted as Headquarters Ship for Senior Officer of a Convoy*

Dated 15th November 1945 (Abbreviated)

SECTION A GENERAL

Function

To provide accommodation and operational facilities for the senior officer of a convoy escort and his staff. To control anti-submarine aircraft.

General Remarks

The ship is to be capable of rapid production.

The vessel should be capable of directing coastal craft.

After the requirement for fulfilling the function have been met the armament should conform as nearly as possible to the 1945 anti-submarine frigate.

Speed and endurance – 25 knots.

Displacement of the order of 1600 tons.

Officers – plus nine.

Ratings – extra communications ratings and aircraft direction personnel.

Main armament – one twin 4.5in Mark VI.

Close Range Armament – One twin 40mm plus as many as possible twin 20mm hand worked Oerlikons.

THE SHIPS NAMED ANZAC

On 25 April 1915, troops of the Australian and New Zealand Army Corps landed on the Gallipoli Peninsula as part of the allied assault on Turkey. Despite the ultimate failure of the campaign, the valour of the troops shone like a beacon and there is no name more honoured in Australia than that of 'Anzac'. It is hardly surprising therefore that there have been several warships of that name in the Royal Australian Navy and Royal Navy. **Colin Jones** details their story.

The First Anzac

Strictly speaking, the first vessel named *Anzac* was a 68ft steam launch built for the Melbourne Harbour Trust in 1915 but renamed *Red Bird* in 1916 after the Australian government issued a regulation forbidding use of the name *Anzac*. A 40ft private New Zealand launch, the *Oban*, was also renamed *Anzac*. However, the first naval *Anzac* was a 135ft trawler of 317 tons gross, built in 1916 for the East Riding Steam Fishing Company of Hull and hired almost immediately by the Royal Navy. She was armed with one 6pdr gun and a 7.5in anti-submarine howitzer. In March 1917 she was renamed *Anzac II*, but her registered name remained the same.

It was a time of crisis in the war at sea, with the menace of German submarines looming very large, and patrol craft such as the *Anzac* were in great demand. Her most notable exploit was to tow the 951 ton Dutch steamer *Bernisse* to Kirkwall in the Orkneys in May 1917. The *Bernisse* had been intercepted by an auxiliary cruiser on blockade duty and sent to Kirkwall for examination, but on the way she was torpedoed by a German submarine. The *Anzac* took her in tow and delivered her safely to be beached before she sank. After the end of the war, the *Anzac* reverted to civil ownership in 1920 and was sold in 1922. Her name, however, had passed to a vastly more impressive ship.

The Second Anzac

During the Great War destroyers had increased markedly in size to become highly capable ships and between 1911 and 1917 the number of flotillas in the Royal Navy had doubled. Destroyer leaders, larger vessels, had replaced light cruisers for the senior officers. The second *Anzac* was ordered in December 1915 as an improved *Nimrod* type leader. Her keel was laid at Denny's Dumbarton yard on 31 January 1916, she was launched on 11 January 1917 and commissioned on 24 April 1917, one day short of two years from the event that her name commemorated. She was manned from Chatham. These are her particulars:

1731 tons deep
325ft oa (314ft 11in bp) x 31ft 10in x 12ft 1in max
4-4in QF Mk IV, 20° elevation, 120 rpg (144 common shell, 336 lyddite)
2-2pdr pompom
4-Lewis MG
4-21in TT, 4 torpedoes
Direct drive turbines, triple screw, 37,060 shp, 32.9 knots
Radius of action - 2500 miles at 15 knots or 850 miles at full power
Complement - 122

On completion she joined the 14th Destroyer Flotilla, attached to the Grand Fleet. At the time of the last sortie of the German fleet, on 23-25 April 1918 (that date again), there were 87 destroyers with the Grand Fleet. But there was no action.

The *Anzac* saw service in the northern part of the North Sea and was damaged by stress of weather while steaming slowly in August. Then, with the abolition of the Grand Fleet on 7 April 1919 she was laid up. It was not, however, to be for long, as that same month she was transferred as a gift to the Royal Australian Navy as the leader of its destroyer flotilla - five S class boats, also a gift, and the navy's existing six improved 'River' class. She commissioned again on 27 January 1920 and sailed from Plymouth a month later, catching up to the rest of the boats at Singapore, so that they all arrived together at Sydney on 29 April.

Many of her earlier commanders saw only short terms of duty, but a curiosity was the successive tenure of twin brothers, Commanders Reginald and Herbert Creer RAN, in 1922.

One moment of glory concerned the Royal Fleet Review on Port Phillip on 28 May 1920. The whole Australian fleet was drawn up in lines off the suburban beaches of Melbourne, the temporary national capital, for review by the Prince of Wales, but in foggy conditions, his ship, the *Renown*, had experienced difficulty in making the entrance to the bay and the destroyers were sent to find her. The Prince was taken on board the *Anzac* and

Anzac passes astern of HMAS Australia at the Prince of Wales' fleet review on Port Phillip, 28 May 1920. (Author's collection)

Flotilla leader Anzac during manoeuvres off Sydney. (HMAS Anzac Assoc.)

the destroyers then raced up the bay in formation, the swell from their coming causing severe embarrassment to watchers who had positioned themselves too close to the water. Louis Mountbatten, who was accompanying the Prince, expressed a mordant view that the fog was beneficial in concealing the relatively small size of the Australian fleet.[1] It was, however, to be something of a last hurrah, as the fleet suffered very considerable reductions in the stringent post-war climate in 1922, leaving its entire commissioned destroyer strength as just *Anzac*, *Stalwart* and *Tasmania*. The flotilla had no number, and the Commander (D) could be either in *Anzac* or the depot ship *Platypus*, or even the sloop *Marguerite*.

Australian recruits found her to be de facto an RN ship, with the associated benefits and problems:

> In those days we still received "hard layers" money. However we were a happy ship most of the two years I served on *Anzac* I. I just had to suffer a Pommy torpedo gunner and a t.g.m.[2]

In 1923 her men assisted with a bunker fire on the steamer *Hartington* in Brisbane and she visited New Guinea in 1924 and 1926 before being laid up in that August. *Anzac* recommissioned in January 1928 but with the economy in a very poor condition at the onset of the Great Depression by 1930 she was a lone destroyer to accompany the fleet's two cruisers and the seaplane carrier on the annual northern and southern cruises. For the sailors, the navy offered just the four ships in commission, but at least it was a secure job when so many of their mates ashore were on the dole. Indeed, by 1933 the navy boasted just two ships in commission, the *Australia* and *Canberra*. The big ships soaked up the manpower.

Lieutenant Commander John Collins became *Anzac*'s CO on 24 July 1930. Collins remembered the difficulties with the ship in heavy weather off Gabo Island in November 1930, when she was unable to continue with the flagship, but wallowed with the bridge knee deep in water. Bass Strait was again living up to its reputation as being equivalent to the Bay of Biscay and *Anzac* was the sort of ship where you could stand at the port rail and be seasick over the starboard side. Later there were turbine troubles at Townsville that almost put the ship ashore while berthing in a high wind. It may have been the engines and boilers that were crucial for her very limited future, nevertheless, Collins remembered her as 'a fine little ship and a first-rate ship's company.'[3]

The London Treaty of 1930 specified that destroyers laid down before 1 January 1921 could be considered to be over-age after 12 years. An official life of just 16 years was assumed (i.e., 1933 for this ship). She was laid up in reserve at Sydney 1931 and declared for disposal in March 1933. In fact the whole flotilla was replaced by destroyers of the V and W class and their leader, *Stuart*, in their own way, not significantly more modern and in the next war to be called the 'scrap-iron flotilla'. The new boats sank the *Anzac* as a target off Sydney on 7 May 1936.

Standing by to fire torpedoes. (HMAS *Anzac* Assoc.)

The ship's company of the second Anzac, *with Lieutenant Commander Reginald Creer at Sydney, 1922.* (HMAS *Anzac* Assoc.)

The Third Anzac

In 1945 the Royal Navy ordered from Vickers Armstrong at Barrow a submarine to be named *Anzac* but the ending of the war saw her cancelled before laying down, and the name was retained by the Royal Australian Navy for another destroyer. Although often passed over in books about British destroyers, the Australian *Anzac* and *Tobruk* were the only representatives of the last development of the 'Battle' class destroyer type (see *Warship 2002-2003*). They introduced, in particular, the first installation afloat of the radar-controlled 4.5in Mark VI twin mounting and there was considerable interest in its performance when it was used in Korea. The guns were officially credited with an unrealistic 25 rounds per minute (double that of the Mark IV), and were regarded as accurate to a range of ten miles.

Australia insisted on local production to strengthen its war industries, so there was no question of buying an existing destroyer from the RN. The *Anzac* was allocated to the Naval Dockyard, Williamstown, and the post-war labour conditions saw a relatively slow construction. She was ordered in October 1944 with drawings supplied by John Brown, Clydebank. Engines and boilers were supplied by Cockatoo Dockyard in Sydney. Laid down on 23 September 1946, she was launched on 20 August 1948 and commissioned on 14 March 1951 when Yeoman-of Signals D. Young attached the commissioning pennant to the metal slouch hat at the masthead. 'This is the finest ship in the R.A.N. and we'll look after her', said Commander John Plunkett-Cole.[4] On 21 March she undertook speed and gunnery trials in Bass Strait. Then the blue ensign was hauled down and the white ensign was raised as she was handed over to the navy. Unlike the guns of her sister *Tobruk*, which had been imported from England in 1948, the equipment for the *Anzac* had been built locally at the two ordnance factories in Victoria. 'They demonstrate that Australia can fulfil demands for the most complicated and delicate equipment.'[5]

These are her particulars:

3,360 tons deep
379ft 4in oa (355ft bp) x 41ft 1in x 15ft 9in max[6]
4-4.5in Mk VI, 300 rpg, 18 RPM, 80° elevation, 53lb shell
12-40mm, 1400 rpg (6in twin STAAG Mk II & 6 single Mk VII, 120 rpm)
10-21in TT, 10 Mk IX torpedoes
1 Squid, 10 salvoes, 400lb projectile (lethal at 21ft against a WWII sub)
Geared turbines, twin screw, 53,000 shp, 33 knots (31 kts sea speed)
Endurance - 2930 miles at 20 knots (6 months out of dock)
British Mk VI director
Asdic type 166 (Sonar Type 147B to determine depth for Squid) (unable to operate sonar above 12 knots owing to propeller noise)
291 air search radar (range of 40 miles but low accuracy due to 40° beam)
293 target indication radar (short range but above range of guns)
IFF antenna
Complement - 290

She was leader of 10th destroyer flotilla Compared with the navy's most modern earlier destroyers, the 'Tribal' class, she was much improved. She was fitted with all

The third Anzac *in Korean waters, 1951*. (C Thwaites)

electric ovens, the laundry had automatic washing machines and there were water fountains throughout the ship. 'A housewife's dream', the burly cook said.[7]

Like her predecessor, she was to go to war immediately. There were initial difficulties in preparing the 'Battle' class ships to go, but the *Anzac* was able to sail from Sydney via Brisbane and Hong Kong for Korea on 30 July 1951. She arrived at the allied base of Sasebo in Japan on 14 August. Korea was a hard environment but the Australian 'Battle' class were superior ships. As one who was there said, the 'wily Brits' had arranged for their newest mark of gun to be tested first by the Australians, and we had better be good.[8]

Initially she was assigned to the escort of the west coast aircraft carrier, first USS *Sicily*, and then HMS *Glory*, but she would also be involved in shore bombardment, such as the destruction of a command bunker at Haeju, west of the Han River, on 6 September, the first time her guns fired on an enemy. She then went to the east coast near Songjin, where she accompanied two US ships in the defence of the nearby island of Yang Do. During this time her guns destroyed a train, a task requiring the accuracy and speed of a sideshow shooting gallery. Her men were especially proud that 'she was putting her shells as much as seven miles inland and hitting things the size of a dunny'.[9] The story was also told of a practice anti-aircraft shoot in company with some American destroyers. The Australian gunnery was hitting the target so readily that the ship was told to go to the end of the line to give the others a chance. She rescued a pilot from the US carrier *Boxer* on 19 September. Back on the west coast, she supported a badly-managed raid by South Koreans on the town of Pong-ri.

On 26 September she arrived at Kure at the end of her time in the war zone. She had fired 1000 rounds from her 4.5in guns and, after escorting the *Glory* from Hong Kong, she returned to Sydney via Fremantle after steaming 23,000 miles. She refitted at Williamstown subsequently and then accompanied the *Australia* on the winter cruise to New Guinea and the islands in 1952. Then it was time to return to war.

Captain Galfrey Gatacre, DSC & Bar, became her second commander on 6 February 1952 and the ship was subsequently part of the ladder of promotion for coming men in the RAN. The *Anzac* sailed from Sydney on 1 September 1952 via Singapore and Hong Kong and relieved *Bataan*. She joined the West Coast Bombardment and Blockade Group with *Newcastle* and *Rotoiti* from 28 September.

Her time would usually be spent with six days bombardment and blockade then nine days on the carrier screen, on this occasion with *Ocean*, frequently in company with ships of the Royal Navy as well as Canada, New Zealand, the Netherlands and the United States. After returning to Sasebo and Kure, she deployed for three weeks with British destroyers for the defence of Sok To at

Two views of the third Anzac *refuelling from an aircraft carrier.* (D Oliver)

Cho Do. The latter housed an important radar station and tactical air defence centre.

She had a 23 minute duel with shore battery of four 3in guns at Cho Do on 16 November 1952, and lucky she was not hit or sunk. In these situations there is a 'narrow margin afforded by chance, when one's only allies were swift decision and the gods'. As Arleigh Burke, doyen of wartime American destroyermen said, the difference between a good officer and a poor one was 'about ten seconds'.[10] Captain Gatacre describes it:

> *Anzac* quickly opened rapid counter battery fire with her 4.5-inch guns, slipped and buoyed her anchor, and was immediately under way. Because of shoals, the ship could not steer to quickly open the range so a running fight developed. *Anzac* was first straddled by the enemy's third salvo as she was turning to head in a direction in which she could steam; one shell of the enemy salvo was seen to hit and sink our anchor buoy! *Anzac* fired 174 rounds in putting the enemy guns out of action; about 50 enemy shells fell near *Anzac* and it was unbelievable that the ship was not hit.[11]

After time as screen of the carrier *Glory*, she moved to the east coast, on which station the ship's company were disappointed in not having the opportunity to join the exclusive club of 'trainbusters'.[12] Then they were back at Cho Do in February to again 'work over' the Communist batteries. In the midwinter conditions there was severe icing, with the lowest temperature recorded on the ship of 9 degrees fahrenheit.[13]

One thing that concerned the crew was that the ship had no particular feature to show that she was Australian and not British, and so a kangaroo was cut from brass, as shiny as possible, and attached to the masthead.

The New Year of 1953 saw the ship on the defence of Yang Do, a duty shared with United States destroyers.

Back on the west, *Anzac* was briefly in command of whole west coast blockade force. She passed this duty on to the cruiser *Birmingham* and after some time in Sasebo, joined the *Glory* again.

After some welcome time in Hong Kong at the start of May, she returned to the east coast patrol at Yang Do with the US destroyers *Gurke* and *Maddox*. She was in Tokyo with the *Mounts Bay* to salute the coronation of Queen Elizabeth II. After escorting the *Ocean* for four days, she was relived by *Cockade* on 13 June and finally left the war behind her. She returned to Sydney on 3 July 1953 after steaming 57,865 miles. Gatacre, who had already moved on to another appointment, was awarded the DSO and Roberts, her first officer, the DSC.

The latter part of 1953 and early 1954 was a high point for the RAN, as it was operating its dream of two aircraft carriers together. *Anzac* was with *Sydney*, *Vengeance* and other units of the fleet in exercises off Queensland and also escorted the Royal Yacht *Gothic* during the Queen's first visit to Australia. She was replaced at this time by *Tobruk* as Captain (D). Activities during 1954 involved exercises with one or other of the aircraft carriers, as well as British and New Zealand warships, in Australian and New Guinea waters. Although officially earmarked for the ceasefire patrol in Korea in October 1954, she spent

Anzac *on her way up the Brisbane River in 1956.* (M Jones)

Training ship Anzac *in Melbourne, 1969. Classrooms have replaced B turret.* (D Robertson)

the time instead in manoeuvres with the Australian fleet.

Meanwhile, in view of developments in the political situation in Southeast Asia, a regional treaty association, SEATO, had been formed, and a commitment to base warships in Singapore on a continuous basis as part of what was called the Commonwealth Strategic Reserve. Between June 1955 and November 1959 *Anzac* saw four tours of duty in Singapore. These deployments would often see cruises to the Philippines, Hong Kong, Japan and Korea, with regular exercises with other Commonwealth warships in the South China Sea.

In company with *Tobruk*, her guns fired again in anger during the bombardment of Malayan terrorists on 29 September 1956, 15 miles south of Jason Bay, in the Kota Tingi district of Johore. The Royal Artillery observation officer in an aircraft reported 'the fire was most effective'.[14]

During Exercise Albatross in October 1956, in which a strong Australian force took part with units of five other navies, she was sent to Saigon as Australian representative for their National Day celebrations. The name *Anzac* was seen as most appropriate in the circumstances.

Anzac and *Tobruk* relieved *Queenborough* and *Quickmatch* on returning to the Strategic Reserve in mid 1957. From the vantage point of Singapore they were witness to the political turmoil in Indonesia, with rebellion in Sumatra and Borneo. Hostilities even extended to an attack on the British submarine *Aurochs* by Indonesian aircraft. Thus when the Dutch liner *Nieuw Holland* sailed in company with *Anzac* in January 1958, it was not strictly being escorted, but it provided a degree of reassurance. The two destroyers were again in Singapore in 1959, though with reduced complements, relieving *Queenborough* and *Quiberon*.

Exercises during this deployment included Sea Demon, the largest SEATO exercise so far held. It involved 30 ships and submarines, including HMAS *Melbourne*, HMS *Albion*, *Ceylon* and *Newfoundland*, USS *Yorktown* (from duty in Taiwan Strait and off Viet Nam) and HMNZS *Royalist*.

The destroyers returned home in time for Christmas. *Anzac* and *Tobruk* had seemed like inseparable sisters at this time, but at target practice off Jervis Bay in September 1960 an accident saw *Anzac* put a shell directly into *Tobruk*. For the latter ship it was time to pay off permanently and for *Anzac*, the future was to lie in becoming fleet training ship, allowing the old sloop *Swan* to retire. By 1962 a classroom had replaced some of the after guns and the torpedo tubes were removed. In 1965 another classroom replaced B turret, reducing her armament to two 4.5in, five 40mm and the squid.

On a lighter, but typical side of naval life, *Anzac* was declared 'Cock of the Regatta' at Hobart in February 1962, but the men of the defeated *Queenborough* crept on board in the middle of the night to steal the trophy from the masthead.

For the trainee officers there would be a regular round of visits to Australian ports as well as those in nearby countries, and there could be ceremonial too, such as the escort of the Royal Yacht *Britannia* in 1963, a cruise with the Governor General in 1964 and visiting Tonga for the Coronation in 1967. In 1965, 1966 and 1968 she helped escort the transport *Sydney* on voyages to Vietnam. There would also be regular training exercises with units of the Australian fleet, the Royal Navy and others, such as Tuckerbox II in 1962, and Coral Sands in 1968. During this last, involving landings on the Queensland coast by 3500 troops, the *Hermes* was not flying her aircraft at night and as a result the British forces fell into an ambush set by the Australian destroyers in the islands and most ships were declared sunk.

She took part in the search for survivors from the freighter *Noongah* which capsized in a gale off Smoky Cape on 26 August 1969 but just picked up the wreckage of a lifeboat.

In the context of a heightened Cold War, the four-navy Commonwealth exercises in November 1969 were actually monitored by Russian naval vessels off the Australian coast, an event which added a certain spice of unusual realism.

Anzac was at Williamstown to repair engineering problems for the first half of 1971 but was soon back participating in a varied and busy round of duties. In just one of these, *Anzac* participated in Exercise Planti Manua in March 1972 as command ship of ten patrol boats in Milne Bay area, a high point for the new navy of Papua New Guinea.[15] Following a last cruise to Fiji Anzac was to be replaced as training ship by the *Duchess*, and she returned to Sydney on 11 August 1974, flying a 500ft paying off pennant. She was sold on 23 October 1975, and towed away for scrap on 30 December. During her time she had steamed 693,000 miles.[16]

The Fourth Anzac

The name *Anzac* was now firmly and permanently the property of the Royal Australian Navy, and it became the name ship of a new class of frigate, built in Australia for the RAN and RNZN. The navy had a requirement for a 'light frigate' to replace the 'River' Class and in October 1987 started evaluation of the main contending designs - Meko 200 from Blohm & Voss in Germany and the M Class from Royal Schelde in the Netherlands. The German design, with appropriate modifications, was successful. Lessons from the Gulf War were incorporated in the design, especially in matters of survivability, and there was Australian input for arrangements fundamental to RAN/RNZN operational philosophy.[17] The building programme for ten vessels, the largest defence contract ever awarded in Australia, was agreed with New Zealand and contracts were signed on 10 November 1989.[18]

The new ship was to set a standard in efficiency in naval construction in Australia. The Transfield company (now called Tenix) had taken over the old Williamstown Naval Dockyard and built the new ships on a modular basis. The *Anzac* was wholly constructed at Williamstown but for the other ships, sections were brought in from elsewhere. The *Anzac* was laid down on 5 November 1993, launched on 16 September 1994 and commissioned on 18 May 1996. These are her particulars:

3,543 tons deep
387ft 2in x 48ft 7in x 14ft 5in (13ft 6in hull)
1-5in Mk 45 Mod 2, 54 cal automatic rapid fire, 20 RPM
1 Mk 41 vertical launch Sea Sparrow, 8 missiles
6-12.8in ASTT Mk 32 Mod 5 (for Mk 46 torpedo)
2-0.5in MG
1 Seahawk S-70B2 helicopter for surveillance & maritime strike
Gas turbine or diesel, twin screw, 30,172 shp, 27 knots (sustained at full load), special acoustic measures allow silent operation at low speed
Range - 6000 miles at 18 knots, 900 miles on full power
Radar - Raytheon SPS-49(V)8 air search, CelsiusTech 9LV 453TIR air/surface search & STN Atlas Electronic 9600 ARPA navigation
Sonar - Spherion-B
Complement - 163

She sailed from Sydney in May 1997 for Pearl Harbor to conduct missile firings on the Pacific missile range facility. Subsequently she took part in Exercise Kakadu with RN and other ships, followed by further work *en route* to her permanent base at HMAS *Stirling*, near Fremantle.

An early job for the *Anzac* was in the policing of Australia's exclusive economic zone in the Southern Ocean against two illegal fishing boats that had threatened, and even almost rammed, licensed Australian fishing boats on the lucrative Patagonian toothfishery. Accompanied by the support ship *Westralia* she sailed from Fremantle on 6 October 1997 for Heard Island. Operating in high winds, rough seas and freezing temperatures, the navy found the two ships, first the *Salvora* and then the *Aliza Glacial*, boarding them from a helicopter and escorting them back to Fremantle where their owners and officers were levied substantial fines by the court. The illegal profits were apparently worth the risk, the *Salvora* was again apprehended fishing in French Antarctic waters in 1999.

Inevitably for a new ship of a new class, there were problems in *Anzac*'s earlier years. These included trouble with the turbine blades that had been overcome before the end of 1998.

Anzac had been preparing for an exercise in Malaysian waters at the end of August 1999 when she was required at short notice to join the task force preparing for operations in connection with the tragic and violent events in East Timor. Although the Australian fleet provided the greatest force, it was joined by ships of the New Zealand, British, US, French and Singapore navies. With *Success* and *Darwin* she arrived off Dili on 20 September 1999. As the troops arrived, *Anzac* was guard ship, but fortunately, her guns were not required and she was able to put work parties ashore to assist in reconstruction work. The troops, living on their ration packs, were also cheered by the emergence from *Anzac*'s galley of 2800 'sticky buns'. Then, with a good job done, *Anzac* handed over the job of guard ship to HMS *Glasgow* on 29 September.[19]

Subsequently she has participated in exercises with other units of the fleet on both sides of the continent and in Southeast Asian and New Zealand waters. In the second half of 2001 she was deployed to the international

Frigate Anzac, first of a new breed. (RAN)

The ship's company of Anzac, *with Captain Nigel Coates, in tropical waters. Women in the crew indicate a major change from the old navy.* (RAN)

force on the blockade of Iraq in the Persian Gulf. The deployment was repeated in October 2002, resulting in the ship changing from blockade work to actual combat with the start of the war against Iraq in March 2003. The *Anzac* gave gunfire support for 30 minutes to a landing by Royal Marine commandos on the Al Faw peninsula on 21 March, with spotting from the ship's helicopter by a member of the Royal Artillery. Gunfire support continued during the next few days during the securing of the port area. She and the other Australian frigate on station, *Darwin*, returned to Australia in May, but first they shared the celebration of the 88th Anzac Day on their war station.

The newest *Anzac* has lived up to the reputation of her forebears. Every ship of the name has actually seen wartime action. Spanning a whole century, the ships named *Anzac* illustrate the changes that have taken place in modern warfare and the naval environment. For Australia they have always been, in many ways, the 'finest ship' in the fleet.

Notes

1 L Mountbatten, *Diaries, 1920-1922*, p.66.
2 Memories of J Tanner.
3 J Collins, *As Luck Would Have It*, (Sydney: Angus & Robertson, 1965), p.51.
4 *The Age*, 15/3/51.
5 Australian News & Information Bureau, *Australia in Facts and Figures* No.29, p.20.
6 Figures such as these vary, even in official sources, and for all three ships I have adopted those which I believe to have the most authority.
7 *The Age*, 15/3/51.
8 W. Roberts in *Navy News* 16/8/1974.
9 Memories of A Porter. The word dunny is Australian slang for an outhouse toilet.
10 M Isenberg, *Shield of the Republic*, (New York: St Martins, 1993), p.634.
11 G Gatacre, *Reports of Proceedings*, (Sydney: Nautical, 1982), p.250.
12 Commenced in July 1952, HMCS *Crusader* was the champion by 1953.
13 9°F = -13°C
14 HMAS *Anzac*, *Report of Proceedings*-September 1956, file 34/4 AWM 78.
15 'Planti Manua' is pidgin for 'many men of war'.
16 J Ware, official history in *Navy News* 16/8/74.
17 R Dunbar, 'ANZAC Ships from a Designer's Perspective', *Australia's Navy 1994-95*, pp.88-89.
18 H Carstens, 'The Anzac Frigate Project Underway', *Warship International*, 1997, pp.35-41.
19 Internet site http://www.navy.gov.au/9_sites/ffh150/timorhist.htm, visited 28/5/01.

WORLD NAVIES IN REVIEW 2003-2004

Conrad Waters, with **Martin Robson** and **Stephen Dent,** provide *Warship* readers with an overview of naval developments, construction and procurement in the preceding twelve months.

The last 12-months have been particularly busy for the world's navies. The new instabilities best illustrated by the ongoing 'war against terrorism' have posed a particular challenge to the NATO fleets that had been considerably eroded by the post-Cold War 'peace dividend'. Significant amounts are now being spent on reshaping naval forces to deal with the new realities of international relations and previously semi-dormant shipyards are starting to invest in the facilities and staff needed to meet this new demand, not least in the United Kingdom. However, the political will to provide additional resources to pay for this reshaping is by no means universal and many existing force structures are being scaled back as a result. There is also a general shift in spending, and thus capability, towards Asian markets, where better economic conditions and local rivalry are combining to produce considerable naval expansion. A final notable feature is the ongoing technological leadership of the United States, where imminent programmes such as the DDX destroyer and LCS littoral combat ship will serve to confirm that country's pre-eminence among the world's fleets.

European Navies

The European Navies continue their slow adjustment from previous Cold War force structures and the resulting, more adaptable fleets are better able to counter the threats posed by a world of new uncertainties. Whilst progress is being made in the right direction, lack of money continues to hinder the rate of change and the almost universal result is a general downsizing of force levels through the decommissioning of older vessels to pay for new equipment.

The major European Navies

France: The most notable naval development in France during 2003 was receipt of official Parliamentary approval for construction of a second aircraft carrier under the 2003-2008 defence programme. Less certain is the likely design of the new ship, with the somewhat problematic debut of France's nuclear-powered *Charles de Gaulle* and the potential for large savings through a collaborative approach leading to serious consideration of a derivative of the UK's new carrier design. The involvement of French defence giant Thales in the British carrier programme makes such a step more likely, albeit the actual UK design originated from British Marine Technology. Meanwhile *Charles de Gaulle* herself is scheduled to visit Portsmouth in June 2004 as part of celebrations to mark the centenary of the *Entente Cordiale*.

A collaborative approach is also being adopted for the French Navy's renewal of its surface fleet, with a memorandum of understanding signed with Italy in June for the construction of a total 27 new frigates under the programme designated '*frègates multi-missions*'. France's share of the project is planned to encompass no less than 17 units, of which the first will be ordered in 2004. The new vessels will be constructed in both ASW and general purpose versions, with France's immediate priority being the construction of new anti-submarine tonnage. In the meantime, DCN's main surface shipbuilding facility in Lorient is being kept busy building derivatives of the *La Fayette* stealth frigate for Saudi Arabia and Singapore.

Design work on the *Barracuda* nuclear attack submarine is also continuing and the order for the first of a projected total of six vessels to replace the current *Rubis* class is also likely to be placed during the coming year. The keel of the first of two new LHDs, *Mistral*, was laid on 10 July.

Italy: Construction of the new aircraft carrier *Andrea Doria* continues at Fincantieri's Riva Trigoso and Muggiano shipyards in a modular arrangement reminiscent of the division of labour involved in the UK's Type 45 programme. However, recent defence cutbacks have shelved plans to purchase more AV-8B Harrier aircraft and she will have to share an air wing with Italy's existing carrier *Giuseppe Garibaldi* when both ships are in commission. The same expenditure reductions have also put paid to plans to acquire a fourth member of the *San Giorgio* LPD class.

The frontline surface fleet continues to experience some shrinkage, with the veteran helicopter cruiser *Vittorio Veneto* and the last of the original batch of four *Lupos* being retired during the course of the year. However, commissioning of further 'Commandanti' class corvettes provided some compensation. Looking further into the future, construction has commenced on the second 'Horizon' class air defence frigate whilst co-operation with France will

The Italian LPD San Giusto. *Budget cuts mean a fourth vessel of the class will not now be ordered.* (Courtesy Vic Jeffery)

be further extended through collaboration on the joint frigate programme. The first of Italy's planned share of ten units, which will ultimately replace the eight *Maestrales* and four *Artiglieres*, will be ordered within the next 12 months.

Salvatore Todaro, the first of Italy's Type 212A class air independent propulsion (AIP) equipped submarines that are being constructed by Fincantieri in association with the German Submarine Consortium, was launched on 6 November. She will be delivered in mid-2005.

Spain: The Spanish Navy has steadily transformed itself into one of Europe's most powerful and professional fleets over the past 20 years, supported by a strong domestic shipbuilding base and close technological links with the United States. The most tangible recent evidence of this co-operation is the F-100 programme of Aegis-equipped air defence frigates, which envisages four of these powerful 6,000 ton ships being completed by 2006. Post-commissioning weapons trials saw first of class *Alvaro de Bazan* operating off the United States' Atlantic coast during the summer of 2003, whilst the second unit, *Almirante Don Juan de Borbon*, was commissioned at IZAR's Ferrol shipyard on 3 December. A follow-on order for an additional two class members is currently under consideration, possibly as an alternative to the mooted F-110 frigates. This would see an eventual fleet of 12 major surface combatants, with the *Santa Maria* class of modified FFG-7 *Perry* class frigates making up the balance.

Amphibious capabilities form a key aspect of Spanish maritime strategy, which, as for the United Kingdom's Royal Navy, is increasingly focused on power projection in the littoral. A very tangible sign of the Spanish Government's commitment to this approach has been the order for a new amphibious assault ship (known as a strategic projection ship in Spanish circles), which, at some 27,000 tons displacement, will be the Navy's largest ever warship. Capable of accommodating 12 helicopters in the hangar and four LCM-8 type landing craft or a US LCAC in a stern well dock, the new ship is also able to operate Harrier STOVL fighters and is intended as a 'stand-in' when Spain's only aircraft carrier, the *Principe de Asturias*, is undergoing refit. When combined with the two recently built *Galicia* class landing platform docks (LPD), the new ship will give Spain a powerful amphibious force when she is delivered in 2008.

Also benefiting from modernisation is the Spanish submarine force, which saw four new S-80 diesel-electric submarines approved in September. A larger and more capable version of the Franco-Spanish *Scorpènes* ordered by Chile, the S-80s will replace the four members of the *Delphin* class that have already started to decommission. A further four vessels could be ordered later in the decade to give Spain a homogenous submarine fleet.

United Kingdom: The United Kingdom's renewed focus on seaborne power projection was given a stern test in the early stages of the invasion of Iraq. An amphibious assault group, centred on the aircraft carrier *Ark Royal* (operating in her secondary amphibious role) and including the helicopter carrier *Ocean* and logistic landing ships from the Royal Fleet Auxiliary (RFA), played a key part in seizing the vital Al Faw peninsula in the early stages of the campaign. The

Alvaro de Bazan *undergoing weapons trials off the United States coast, June 2003.* (Norman Whittington)

HMS Ark Royal *transits the Suez Canal on deployment to the Gulf.*

RFAs Ford Austen *and* Diligence, *with* Fort Victoria *and* Orangeleaf *beyond, in the Gulf during the war in Iraq, 2003.* (All images on this page Crown Copyright)

RFA *Sir Galahad* subsequently brought the first humanitarian aid supplies to the port of Umm Qasr on 28 March after clearance by an Anglo-American mine countermeasures force. The Royal Navy's ability to fire Tomahawk land attack missiles was also much in demand, with the nuclear powered attack submarines *Splendid* and *Turbulent* being deployed to the Gulf for this purpose.

Away from Iraq, the Royal Navy's ambitious fleet modernisation plans have continued to make headway in spite of increasingly apparent pressure on the defence budget and poor performance at a number of shipyards that has resulted in programmes such as the *Astute* class nuclear-powered attack submarines, *Albion* class LPDs and 'Bay' class auxiliary LSDs falling behind their planned delivery dates. A notable and encouraging exception has been Vosper Thornycroft's self-financed construction of three 'River' class offshore patrol vessels, with delivery of the final class member, *Mersey*, at the end of 2003, permitting the transfer of the old 'Island' class *Lindisfarne* and *Guernsey* to Bangladesh. An additional order for two enlarged 'Rivers' as a replacement for the RN's other remaining offshore patrol ships, *Leeds Castle* and *Dumbarton Castle*, is currently being considered.

In spite of the aforementioned

HMS Liverpool *escorting HMS* Ocean *during operations in the Gulf.*

The aviation training ship RFA Argus *was used for logistic support in the Gulf.*

An artist's impression of the Thales CVF design adopted for the Royal Navy's new aircraft carriers, to be called Queen Elizabeth *and* Prince of Wales. (Thales Design)

The new LPD Albion, *commissioned in 2003.* (Crown Copyright)

HMS Tyne, *the first of three River class offshore patrol vessels, leased from the VT Group.* (Conrad Waters)

delays, there was a welcome stream of new vessels entering service during the course of the year, of which the most significant commissioning was undoubtedly that of the 18,500 ton landing platform dock *Albion* on 19 June. Amphibious forces also benefited from completion of the remaining 'Point' class Ro-Ro ferries (for a total of six), which are operated under the Red Ensign by AWSR Shipping Limited on behalf of the Ministry of Defence. Other new ships included the survey vessels *Echo* and *Enterprise* and the RFA fleet tankers *Wave Knight* and *Wave Ruler*. The most notable decommissioning was that of the submarine *Splendid*, paid off as planned shortly after her return from operations against Iraq.

Looking forward, the future is somewhat mixed, with plans to decommission an unspecified number of older ships as part of plans to ease the current defence overspend confirmed at the start of December. Whilst no firm information is available, press commentary has centred on withdrawal of the remaining three Batch I Type 42 class destroyers and, perhaps, two of the Type 23 frigates, leaving a force of 26 major surface combatants. Numbers of minehunters and attack submarines may also be trimmed. Savings will help finance construction of the new Type 45 *Daring* class destroyers (the first of which commenced construction at BAe Systems' Govan yard on 28

March), although total class numbers are likely to fall to ten or less from original plans for 'up to twelve.' More positively, the future carrier programme looks set to escape the threat of major shrinkage, with the carrier alliance of BAe Systems and Thales currently finalising plans for the construction of two 65,000 ton giants of around 285m in length. It was announced in November that the new ships will be named *Queen Elizabeth* and *Prince of Wales*.

The Medium-sized European Navies

Germany: The German Navy continues with its slow transformation into a blue water fleet whilst struggling with a series of defence cutbacks. The most recent of these was announced at the start of 2004 but the full impact on current fleet structure and future procurement plans has not yet become apparent.

In the meantime, good progress is being made on the new Type 124 *Sachsen* class air defence frigates, with the second class member *Hamburg* now undergoing sea trials and *Hessen*, the third and final vessel, launched in June. *Sachsen* herself will head for the US for weapons trials during 2004 before becoming fully operational. The class will replace Germany's former modified *Charles F Adams* class destroyers, the last of which, *Lutjens*, was decommissioned in December.

Also moving ahead is the Type 212A submarine programme, with first of class *U-31* making her maiden voyage for sea trials on 7 April and *U-32* being launched on 4 December. A total of eight submarines are projected to replace Germany's current 14-strong fleet. Equipped with the world's first fuel-cell AIP system, the design is achieving considerable success on the export market.

Greece: The Greek Navy continues to benefit from the acquisition of surplus equipment from a rapidly downsizing Netherlands fleet, with a seventh *Kortenaer* class frigate (in addition to the two ships originally built to Greek order) transferred towards the end of 2003. As the remaining *Kortenaer* and the two air defence

The Netherlands' frigate Kortenaer, *now* Kountouriotis *in the Greek navy, to where a number of her sister ships have also been transferred.* (Royal Australian Navy)

frigates of the *Jacob van Heemskerck* class are also scheduled for disposal over the next 18-months, Greece may well standardise on Dutch-built units for the core of its surface fleet. This would also permit withdrawal of the two remaining *Kimon* (ex *Charles F Adams*) class destroyers, which are showing their age.

New building programmes are also moving ahead and the second Vosper Thornycroft-designed Super Vita fast attack craft, *Daniolis*, was launched by Elefsis Shipbuilding in July, whilst lead ship *Roussen* had commenced trials by the year-end. Options for two more ships for a total class of five have now been confirmed. Progress on another VT-Elefsis joint venture for a new corvette has been less smooth, with Greece reportedly having second thoughts about the programme because of its high cost. Meanwhile, construction of the first Type 214 AIP equipped submarine is proceeding according to plan at HDW's Kiel shipyard and will be launched early in 2004.

The Netherlands: The continued scaling back of Dutch defence spending is having a particularly severe impact on the Royal Netherlands Navy, with further reductions in fleet strength projected under the 2004-2013 defence plan. In addition to the previously planned withdrawal of the two *Jacob van Heemskerck* frigates, two of the more recent *Karel Doorman* class will also be decommissioned prematurely, leaving a force of just 10 major surface combatants. Other reductions encompass two of the 12 mine-hunters and the entire maritime patrol aircraft force.

On a brighter note, the first two *De Zeven Provincien* air defence frigates are now in service, with the second member of the class, *Tromp*, joining the fleet on 21 March 2003. The lead ship completed weapons trials during the course of the year and will assume command of the joint Belgian/Netherlands Task Group in 2004. *De Ruyter*, the third class member, will commission in 2004, with *Eversten* following a year later.

Turkey: 2003 has been a relatively quiet year for the Turkish fleet, with funding shortages apparently precluding any major developments. An eighth FFG-7 *Perry* class frigate, *Estocin*, was transferred from the USN, taking the name *Gosku*.

Other European Navies

Belgium: The rolling modernisation programme for the *Wielingen* class frigates has continued during the year. In the longer term, there are reports that Belgium might want to acquire the two relatively modern Dutch M class frigates that will soon be decommissioned.

Poland: The ongoing transfer of the five former Norwegian *Kobben* class Type 207 vessels is revitalising the Polish submarine force prior to long term plans for the purchase of new ships. Construction continues at Gdynia on the new Meko 100 corvette programme, whilst the keel of the first *Kormoran* class minehunter was laid during the course of the year.

Portugal: The Portuguese Navy has continued valiant modernisation efforts, with approval of the free transfer of the former US FFG-7 *Perry* class frigate, *Sides*, providing a welcome boost. Portugal would like to acquire further *Perrys* to replace the remaining members of the veteran *Commandante Joao Belo* class but additional transfers may not be forthcoming.

The German Submarine Consortium appears to have won the contact for the replacement of Portugal's submarine force, with a tender to provide two Type 214A vessels proving considerably cheaper than the offer from the rival Franco-Spanish team offering the *Scorpène* design. The proposal encompasses an option for a third submarine if funds become available.

Romania: Work started in August on the rehabilitation of the former RN Type 22 frigate HMS *Coventry*, with delivery to Romania planned in late 2004. The refit of *London* will follow in 2004 for a May 2005 transfer. The refit package, being carried out by Fleet Support Ltd at Portsmouth Dockyard, includes regeneration of existing systems, the installation of the Nautis fire control system and a 76mm gun, as well as new RR turbines.

Scandinavia: The recent trend for Scandinavian navies to move away from a largely anti-invasion focus to a role better adapted for multinational naval operations is accelerating, with most new construction aimed at creating more balanced forces capable of overseas deployment. For example, the new Swedish *Visby* and Norwegian *Skjold* fast attack craft are now being cast in the role of littoral combat ships in a similar fashion to the USN's mooted programme.

In spite of concerns over its cancellation following Norway's withdrawal, work continues on the Viking submarine project that should lead to six submarines being procured for the Swedish (2) and Danish (4) fleets from 2006 onwards. It would appear that the programme is deemed essential for the two countries' industrial bases and is therefore being given a high priority in spite of the availability of competing designs such as the Type 212 and *Scorpène*.

Denmark also continues to renew its surface fleet, with the two large but comparatively lightly armed Stanflex support ships ordered from the Odense Steel Shipyard now close to completion. Vosper Thornycroft has also adopted this design as part of its bid for New Zealand's Project Protector, whilst a smaller but more heavily armed derivative is scheduled to replace the *Niels Juel* class frigates later in the decade.

Norway finally placed an order for series production of the FAC *Skjold* in November. This will see five additional class members join the prototype between 2006 and 2009. Construction is also well underway on the *Nansen* Aegis frigates ordered from Spain's IZAR, with the first scaled down SPY-1F Aegis weapons system handed over to the Norwegian Government at a ceremony at manufacturer Lockheed Martin's New Jersey factory at the start of December. A less positive development was the total destruction of the fibreglass minesweeper *Orkla* after a fire in November 2002, fortunately without fatalities.

Finland terminated the T2000 fast attack hovercraft programme late in 2002 after completion of the prototype, deciding to focus on the modernisation of existing units. However, as with the Viking project, industrial considerations have come into play and a third member of the larger *Hamina* class was ordered in December. A fourth vessel is likely to follow later to maintain continuity of production.

Scandinavia's NATO members have been very active in contributing forces to the ongoing 'war against terrorism'. For example, the departure of four Norwegian missile torpedo boats to protect shipping in the Mediterranean as part of an ongoing commitment to support NATO operations in the area was given particularly wide publicity. However, perhaps even more noteworthy was Denmark's allocation of the frigate *Olfert Fischer* and the submarine *Saelen* to the campaign against Iraq in a show of solidarity with the US commanded alliance.

The Russian Federation

The sharp decline in the fortunes of the Russian Federation Navy that was a marked feature of the post Cold War environment appears to be reaching an end, with the return of several units from lengthy refits and an increase in operational deployment suggesting that some stability might be returning. However, it is clear that the ambitious construction of the Soviet era will remain nothing more than a memory, as future plans call for a focus on smaller ships that are cheaper to construct and maintain. Similarly, the overall size of the fleet will reduce sharply as inoperative vessels previously kept in commission to bolster numbers are consigned to the scrapheap.

As always, maintenance of a credible force of strategic nuclear submarines has been regarded as the top priority and completion of firing trials of the new Bulava strategic missile by the refurbished Project 941 Typhoon class SSBN *Dmitriy Donskoy* (TK208) during the course of the year was therefore a major step forward. The missile, a naval development of the land SS-27 Topol, will also arm the three projected members of the purpose built Project 955 Borey class, of which the prototype *Yuriy Dologorukiy* has been under construction since 1996. In the meantime, the Russian nuclear deterrent has been boosted by the return of the Project 667 BDRM Delta IV class SSBN *Yekaterinburg* (K84) to the fleet after a 5-year long refit and the unexpected re-emergence of the Project 667 BDR Delta III class *Svyatoy Giorgiy Pobedonosets* (K433) after at least 10 years in dockyard hands.

Turning to conventional forces, the prototype Project 677 'Lada' class SKK *St. Petersburg*, will start trials a few months later than planned in

2004. She is somewhat ahead of the prototype Project 885 Yassen class SSGN *Severodvinsk*, laid down as long ago as 1993 and on which much work remains outstanding in spite of reports that additional funding had been advanced to accelerate the vessel's completion. Better progress is being made with the Project 20380 corvette class, with the 2200 ton *Steregushchy* due to enter service in 2005 and a second ship, *Soobrazitelny*, laid down in May. Reports suggest that construction of this class is central to future surface ship procurement, with as many as 20 units planned. Orders for smaller ships also continue, with, for example, two further Project 12322 *Zubr* hovercraft in the pipeline.

Russia's ability to recommence significant naval construction owes much to the success of the export sector, with significant orders from traditional rivals India and China helping to maintain both technical knowledge at the various design bureaux and shipbuilding capacity. The Project 1135.6 *Talwar* frigate programme for India is now virtually complete but construction of Project 956EM destroyers and Project 636 improved 'Kilo' class submarines for China continues. The long delayed conclusion of the deal with India for the sale and modernisation of the Project 1143.4 aircraft carrier *Admiral Gorshkov* will also maintain shipbuilding capacity during its planned five year reconstruction.

The Middle East, Indian Ocean and Africa

A volatile regional environment, as well as the beneficial impact of higher oil prices on many regional budgets, is having a positive effect on naval expenditure in the Middle East and a number of long delayed projects are finally coming to fruition. Spending is also buoyant on the Indian sub-continent, where India's ambitions for regional superpower status are slowly expressing themselves in a considerable naval build-up. The exception to this trend is sub-Saharan Africa, where South Africa remains the only regional nation with aspirations stretching beyond limited local coastal defence.

The Middle Eastern Navies

Egypt: One of the more powerful forces in the region, the Egyptian fleet is bolstering its coastal patrol forces through the acquisition of surplus German fast attack craft. Five Type 148 *Tiger* class vessels have been transferred to date, along with a Type 701 support ship and a Type 760 ammunition transport. Press reports suggest that Egypt is still considering a resumption of the Ambassador III FAC programme but the likely availability of additional German craft as the defence cutbacks there bite may influence the decision.

Israel: In spite of pressures on the overall defence budget, the Israeli Navy is seeking to progress with a major expansion of its blue water capabilities, of which the major element will be a class of three new, Aegis-equipped multi mission corvettes. Financed from the US Foreign Military Sales programme and therefore likely to be built in the United States, the planned ships will displace up to 3,000 tons and include the Mk 41 vertical launch system and a helicopter hangar and flight deck.

Also on Israel's shopping list are an additional two Type 800 *Dolphin* class diesel electric submarines of the type delivered by Germany in the late 1990s. There is some doubt, however, whether the German government will agree to these plans in the light of suggestions that the first three units of the class have secretly been equipped with modified Harpoon-type missiles to provide a nuclear strike capability.

Oman: A decision will be taken early in 2004 on the successful bidder for a new class of three 80m offshore patrol vessels required under Project Khareef. They will represent the first major new construction for Oman since completion of the two Vosper Thornycroft *Qahir* class corvettes in the mid 1990s.

Saudi Arabia: The Type F-3000S *Al Riyadh* frigate programme is drawing towards a conclusion, with the third and final ship, *Al Damman*, due to be delivered by DCN's Lorient shipyard during 2004. Press reports suggest that the NH-90 helicopter may be purchased to operate from the new ships.

United Arab Emirates: Approval of the long-awaited Project Baynunah programme for up to six, 70-metre corvettes was finally announced at the start of 2004. Whilst the local Abu Dhabi Shipbuilding is the prime contractor, the design originates from French company CMN, which will build the first ship at its Cherbourg yard. These heavily armed vessels are intended to function in a multi-role capacity, with the inclusion of a helicopter deck and hangar increasing their flexibility.

Yemen: Very much in the front line of the so-called war against terror, Yemen is embarking on a major expansion of her patrol forces through a contract for ten aluminium 37.5 metre coastal patrol vessels from Australia's Austal Ships. A derivative of the 38 metre 'Bay' class previously constructed for the Australian Customs Service, the new vessels will be delivered from late 2004 onwards.

Indian Ocean Navies

India: Rapidly increasing defence expenditure is starting to have a positive influence on naval force levels, with new construction beginning to enter service and further powerful enhancements planned. In spite of recent tensions with Pakistan, it appears that expansion is aimed largely at balancing the growth of India's other traditional rival, China, which is also undertaking a significant naval build-up.

Focusing firstly on recent additions to the Indian fleet, the most significant development is undoubtedly the arrival of the first two Project 1135.6 *Talwar* class frigates from Russia after delays caused by the need to rectify problems with their Shtil-1 surface to air missile system. Of approximately 3,500 tons full load displacement, these relatively small but heavily armed and stealthy vessels will be joined in India by the third and final class member, *Tabar* early in 2004. A further three, Project 17, frigates of a similar but enlarged design are being constructed in India and the first of these, *Shivalik*, was launched on 18 April, some two years behind schedule. Also running late are the two

Two views of India's new Russian-built stealth frigate Talwar*, seen at Portsmouth on her delivery voyage, July 2003.* (Conrad Waters)

final indigenous Project 16A frigates, *Beas* and *Betwa*, although their commissioning is now imminent. Construction of the Project 15A *Bangalore* class destroyers - a modification of the previous Project 15 *Delhi* - completes the new building line up.

Looking further into the future, the final signature of a deal for the acquisition and reconstruction of the former Soviet-era aircraft carrier *Admiral Gorshkov* at the start of 2004 heralds a significant expansion of India's naval aviation capabilities when she joins the fleet in 2008. Laid-up since she was damaged by fire in the early 1990s, the 45,000 ton *Gorshkov* will be rebuilt from her current hybrid cruiser-carrier configuration and equipped with a ski-jump and arrestor wires to operate MiG-29 fighter bombers, 16 of which are included in the contract. Initially a replacement for India's sole existing carrier, *Viraat*, *Gorshkov* will subsequently operate alongside the proposed 7,500 ton air defence ships, the first of which should be started shortly.

India is also keen to upgrade her submarine arm and negotiations with France's DCN for six locally-built vessels of the *Scorpène* type are reported as being close to a conclusion. In the longer term, India would like to deploy nuclear-powered attack submarines and a secretive development programme should deliver a national prototype by the end of the decade.

Pakistan: Pakistan's fleet remains very much in the shadow of that of her much larger neighbour. In these circumstances, it is not surprising that priority is being given to modernising the submarine force, with the programme for the construction of three *Agosta* 90B class SSKs first agreed with France in 1994 now well advanced. *Saad*, the second class member and the first submarine ever to be completed in Pakistan, was commissioned on 12 December, the event being sufficiently significant to be commemorated by a special series of postage stamps. The final vessel *Hamza* will complete in 2005, with all three submarines being scheduled to receive the MESMA AIP system during build or subsequent refit.

Pakistan also needs to update its

surface fleet, currently built around six former RN Type 21 *Amazon* class frigates and a couple of older *Leanders*. At present, it appears that China is the most likely source of new construction, with discussions for four new frigates currently underway. An additional order for corvette-sized vessels is also under consideration.

African Navies

Nigeria: The only barely operational Nigerian Navy has received a boost through the transfer of two *Balsam* class buoy tenders from the US Coastguard. Additional class members may join the newly renamed *Kyanwa* and *Ologbo* to provide Nigeria with a serviceable local patrol capability.

South Africa: The construction of the Meko A-200 corvettes that form one of the key elements of the South African Navy's ambitious modernisation plan has been delayed by problems with defective cabling that were discovered during sea trials of the first of class, *Amatola*. She was finally delivered around nine months later than planned in September, subsequently arriving in South Africa in November. *Isandlwana*, the second of a total of four ships, set off from Kiel in January 2004, having been handed over to her new owners shortly before Christmas. The vessels still need to be fitted with their South African-built combat systems and other equipment. It will therefore be long into 2005 before they are ready for service. An order for Super Lynx helicopters to operate from the class was confirmed during the year.

In the meantime, old equipment is now being paid off to help finance the new construction, including *Spear*, the first of the *Daphne* class SSKs to decommission, and the remaining four 'Ton' class minesweepers. It was reported that two of the latter, *Walvisbaai* (ex-HMS *Packington*) and *East London* (ex-HMS *Chilton*) have been purchased for further use by a film company. The other two submarines will soon follow *Spear* to the scrapyard, leaving a gap before the new German Type 209 (1400) replacements start to commission from 2005 onwards.

The Indian project 15 destroyer Mumbai, *to be followed by project 15A.* (Vic Jeffery)

Seen here exercising with USS Reuben James, *Pakistan's former RN Amazon class frigates* Shahjahan *and* Tippu Sultan *are now due for replacement.* (US Navy)

Pictured here on exercise in the late 1980s, the last of South Africa's 'Ton' class minesweepers have now been decommissioned. (RSAN)

Australasia and the Far East

Asian maritime defence forces are entering a period of significant expansion. Latent regional instability and mistrust, as well as increasing threats from terrorism and piracy, are combining with improving economic conditions to fuel higher naval expenditure. Whilst Australia, China, Japan and South Korea remain the region's big spenders, most of the major fleets have significant plans for new construction.

Australia: The Royal Australian Navy has had a busy year, commencing with the deployment of the amphibious landing ship *Kanimbla* to the Persian Gulf in January to join the frigates *Anzac* and *Darwin* already serving in the region. Australian forces subsequently played a significant part in naval operations associated with the US-commanded coalition's invasion of Iraq, with *Anzac* providing gun fire support alongside British Royal Navy vessels during the amphibious assault on the Al Faw peninsula. In addition to ongoing operations in the war against terrorism, the RAN has also been helping with the restoration of law and order in the Solomon Islands, a task in which Australia's other landing ship, *Manoora*, and the mine-hunter *Hawkesbury*, participated.

The increasing tempo of RAN operations was reflected in a new Defence Capability Plan for the ten years to 2014, first announced in November 2003. In addition to confirming plans for the construction of three new air defence destroyers to be equipped with an Aegis-based combat system, the review proposed a significant upgrade of the navy's amphibious fleet through the replacement of existing shipping with two large 20,000 ton LPH type vessels and a similar sealift ship from 2010 onwards. However, it was not all good news and *Adelaide* and *Canberra*, the two oldest FFG-7 type ships, will be paid off in 2006 to help fund the new construction. Other plans include placing two of the comparatively recent *Huon* class minesweepers in extended reserve and the replacement of the elderly oil tanker *Westralia* with a converted merchant vessel.

Amongst other developments, a contract was signed for twelve 56m *Armidale* class patrol boats to be constructed by Austal Ships in replacement of the remaining *Fremantles*. The somewhat troubled building programme of the six *Collins* class SSKs was brought to a conclusion with the commissioning of the final class member, *Rankin*, in March.

Brunei: The construction programme for three 2,000-ton *Nakhoda Regam* corvettes that is now drawing to a close at BAe Systems' Yarrow yard in Glasgow hit a snag with the grounding of the first of the class on a sandbank in the River Clyde on 25 November. Fears that the ship might heel over completely resulted in the evacuation of the entire crew but she was eventually safely re-floated on the next high tide.

China: The People's Liberation Army Navy (PLAN) continues its slow but steady evolution from a largely coastal defence force to a true blue water fleet through a balance of foreign and indigenous construction. Overseas contracts have been dominated by the Russian Federation, with eight Project 636 'Kilo' class submarines (for a total of twelve) and two Project 956EM *Sovremenny* class destroyers (for a total of four) are currently on order. The first of the submarines was laid down at the Severodvinsk Shipyard early in 2003 and all eight are due for delivery by the end of 2007.

Local submarine building is largely concentrated on the ongoing production of the locally designed diesel-electric Type 039 *Song* class, although the first member of the Type 093 class SSN has now been launched. Significant effort is also being made in surface ship construction and the first of a pair of two new Type 052B air defence destroyers of around 7,000 tons displacement and armed with the Russian Shtil-1 missile system has now commenced trials. They will be followed by a class of broadly similar Type 052C ships which will, however, incorporate new VLS missiles and a four face phased-array radar system similar to the USN's Aegis. Construction of smaller surface ships is also continuing and the first of a new class of Type 054 frigate was launched during the course of the year. This design may well spearhead efforts to build on China's increasing success in export markets.

Indonesia: A much needed upgrade of Indonesia's ageing naval forces continues to be delayed by lack of cash resources but there are signs of light at the end of the tunnel. For example, Korea's Daewoo Shipbuilding & Marine Engineering has commenced modernisation of the Type 209 (1300) submarine, *Cakra*, and this may herald the transfer of former Korean boats when the new Type 214 vessels now under construction for that country start to commission. There have also been reports of some of the former East German Parchim 1 corvettes rejoining the fleet after a major re-engineering programme designed to resolve ongoing propulsion problems.

The most significant development, however, was the announcement at the start of 2004 of a contract for two new 1,700 ton corvettes from the Dutch Royal Schelde group. The order may be followed by the construction of further ships in Indonesia. However, no sooner was the deal agreed than other shipbuilders attempted to muscle in on the act, with both Italy and China reportedly offering alternative proposals.

Japan: Arguably one of the world's most powerful but lowest profile fleets, the Japanese Maritime Self Defence Force (JMSDF) is slowly coming more into the limelight as Japan itself starts to adopt a more active role on the world stage. For example, JMSDF tankers have been refuelling US and other Allied units on anti-terrorism operations in the Indian Ocean, while the LPD *Osumi* and destroyer *Murusame* set out for Kuwait in February 2004 to support Japanese ground forces stationed in Iraq. There are also active plans for the Aegis equipped *Kongou* class destroyers to provide part of a missile-defence shield against North Korea's nuclear weapons programme.

The most notable new additions to the fleet during 2003 were *Takanami*

The EH-101 helicopter was ordered by Japan during the course of 2003. (GKN)

and *Onami*, the first members of a new class of 5,000-ton general purpose destroyer equipped with the Mk 41 VLS for Sea Sparrow and ASROC missiles. Also entering commission was the third and final 9,000-ton *Osumi* class LPD, *Kunisaki*, which has a similar role and aircraft carrier type profile to the Italian *San Giorgio*. Looking forward, the announcement of plans to obtain a true carrier capability through construction of two 16,000 ton 'through deck' helicopter carriers (given a DDH designation in official Japanese circles) to enter service during 2008-09 provided further evidence of Japan's willingness to develop a force structure suitable for more than limited self defence. According to reports in *Jane's Defence Weekly*, the new vessels will be able to accommodate up to eleven heavy helicopters in a hangar serviced by two lifts but are not intended to operate STOVL designs such as the Harrier or new JSF.

Britain's defence industry scored a rare export success to Japan during the course of the year with the conclusion of a contract for the licence built production of 14 EH-101 Augusta-Westland helicopters powered by Rolls Royce-Turbomeca RTM-322 engines. The new helicopters will be constructed by Kawasaki Heavy Industries and largely used in the mine countermeasures role.

Malaysia: Malaysia is looking to expand her frigate force, with the purchase of up to four modified versions of the *Lekiu* class currently under discussion with BAe Systems.

Meanwhile construction of the Meko 100 corvettes has been making good progress, with the first of an initial class of six shipped to Malaysia by German builder Blohm & Voss for final fitting out by Penang Shipbuilding during April. Fabrication of the first of the two *Scorpène* SSKs being built by France's DCN and Spain's IZAR commenced at the former's Cherbourg shipyard during December.

New Zealand: A decision on the preferred contractor for New Zealand's Project Protector will be taken during 2004. The project calls for the construction of up to three offshore and five coastal patrol vessels, as well as a multi-role support ship.

Singapore: Singapore's first stealth frigate, *Formidable*, was launched on 7 January 2004 at DCN's Lorient yard. The first of a class of six ships derived from France's *La Fayette* to replace elderly fast attack craft, she is scheduled for delivery in 2005. The other vessels will be built in Singapore by Singapore Technologies Marine, with the project scheduled for completion in 2009.

A collision between the 500-ton patrol ship, *Courageous*, and a 52,000 ton cargo vessel in the eastern Singapore Straits on 3 January 2003 resulted in the total demolition of the warship's stern and the deaths of four female crew members. *Courageous* was towed back to port after the incident but the damage may have been so great as not to warrant repair.

South Korea: Another Asian fleet undergoing significant expansion to meet blue water ambitions, the Republic of Korea's navy continued to make headway during 2003. Steady progress was achieved with the local KDX-II destroyer programme, with *Daejoyung*, the third and final class member being launched by Daewoo Shipbuilding & Marine Engineering's Okpo yard on 12 November and lead ship *Yi Soon Shin* being delivered the following month. Of approximately full load 5,000 tons displacement, equipment includes a 32-cell, Mk 41 VLS, Mk 45 5in gun and a hangar and flight deck for Super Lynx helicopters. They will be followed by at least three larger and more capable 7,000 ton KDX-III destroyers equipped with the US Aegis combat system to give a frontline force of nine major surface combatants by 2012.

Korean naval expansion also encompasses amphibious shipping and submarines, with plans for the former focused on completion of two 14,000 ton through deck LHDs capable of carrying 10 helicopters and 700 troops under the LP-X programme. Submarine construction is based on the three Type 214-A submarines designed by the German Submarine Consortium that are currently being built by Hyundai Heavy Industries but development of an indigenous 3,500 ton follow-on is being studied. There have also been rumours, firmly denied by the Government, of plans for a locally constructed nuclear design later in the decade.

Taiwan: Taiwan's fleet continues its relative decline in the face of the rapid expansion in naval power embarked upon by its mainland neighbour and only slow progress is being achieved in replacing current obsolescent tonnage as a result of both economic and political constraints. The contract to acquire the four former *Kidd* class air defence destroyers from the United States has now been concluded and, following re-activation and modernisation in American yards, the ships should be delivered to Taiwan by 2006. Whilst undoubtedly powerful ships, the *Kidds* were first ordered under an Iranian Government contract as far back as 1974 and seem less than a match for the Chinese *Sovremennys*.

Pending delivery of the new destroyers, a policy of make do and mend is being adopted, with the modernised weapons control systems from some of the remaining *Gearing* and *Fletcher* class escorts of Second World War vintage being refitted in the *Chi Yang* (former *Knox* class) frigates. A new class of locally built corvettes is eventually planned as a permanent replacement. Deliberations over the likely origin of the eight diesel-electric submarines that the United States has agreed to help to provide continue, with both price (over US$10 billion) and lack of available designs proving major obstacles to any real progress.

Thailand: Now looking to upgrade its surface fleet after a period of economic austerity, Thailand is another South East Asian country reported to be in the final stages of negotiations to acquire new frigates from BAe Systems. A contract for two ships similar to Malaysia's *Lekius* is proposed, with construction planned to commence during 2004 if the necessary funding can be obtained. China has been Thailand's other recent preferred source of new surface vessel construction and is currently building two 1,500 ton offshore patrol vessels.

The Thai frigate Chao Phraya. *More Chinese-built ships are on the way.* (RAN)

The Americas

In general terms, the outlook for naval funding in the Americas is less positive than in the rest of the world, with most countries focusing on maintaining existing ships or completing tonnage that has already been ordered rather than contemplating new programmes. The notable exception is the United States, where, over the next few years, an uplift in defence spending should reverse the long post Cold War decline in fleet numbers.

Argentina: Severe budgetary problems continue to restrict the modernisation of the Argentinean Navy, with the limited funds available being insufficient to embark upon any major new acquisitions. In spite of this, the fleet remains relatively active and the Meko Type 360 destroyer *Sarandi* joined the USN's *Enterprise* carrier strike group during the summer of 2003, the first time a non-NATO navy had operated in this fashion.

The Brazilian frigate Defensora, *seen at the Battle of the Atlantic Anniversary Review in 1993. Mid-life modernisation of this class is now near completion. (Conrad Waters)*

Brazil: Brazil continues to integrate the aircraft carrier *Sao Paulo* (ex-*Foch*) into her fleet, with the training of pilots for the ship's fixed wing air complement of AF-1 Falcon (A-4 Skyhawk) aircraft taking a high priority. The country's previous carrier, *Minas Gerais* (ex-*Vengeance*) departed to the ship breakers at the start of 2004 after the failure of attempts to preserve her as Britain's last surviving Second World War aircraft carrier.

Modernisation of the surface fleet is centred on the mid-life upgrades of the six *Niteroi* class frigates, a project which should be completed by the end of 2006. New construction plans are focused on completion of the first indigenous *Barroso* class corvette, launched at the end of 2002, and the initial *Tikuna* class submarine, which should now be completed during 2005.

Canada: Although not involved in operations against Iraq, the Canadian Navy has been one of those most committed to the broader 'war against terrorism', with almost all the blue water fleet seeing service in the Middle East since September 2001. Whilst the scale of this commitment is now reducing in the face of growing evidence of overstretch, the *Halifax* class frigate *Toronto* became the 18th Canadian warship to deploy to the region as part of Canada's contribution to the US-led Operation Enduring Freedom when she left her homeport at the start of 2004.

The most important procurement programme remains the acquisition of the former *Upholder* class diesel-electric submarines from the UK, with three of the four class members now in Canadian waters following their initial refit at BAe Systems' Barrow-in-Furness yard. The fourth and final vessel to be transferred, *Chicoutimi* (ex-*Upholder*) will follow in 2004. The project to reactivate these decommissioned submarines has been far more lengthy and problematic than initially envisaged in spite of their relative modernity, although at least one should have reached full operational status by the end of the year.

Looking forward, a decision should be made soon on new helicopters to replace Canada's venerable Sea Kings. However, any longer term renewal of the surface fleet has been made difficult by the final closure of the Saint John Shipbuilding yard responsible for building most of the *Halifax* class after three years without orders.

Chile: Chile's Navy has always been regarded as one of the most professional in South America and the current modernisation programme will also leave it amongst the best equipped. November 2003 saw the christening ceremony of *Bernardo O' Higgins*, first of the two *Scorpène* submarines being constructed by the Franco-Spanish consortium of DCN and IZAR. Delivery is anticipated towards the end of 2004; with sister ship *Carrera* following approximately a year later. At one time it was expected that a follow on order for a further two similar vessels was likely but it appears that a decision has been taken to adopt the cheaper plan of modernising Chile's existing Type 209 (1300) boats.

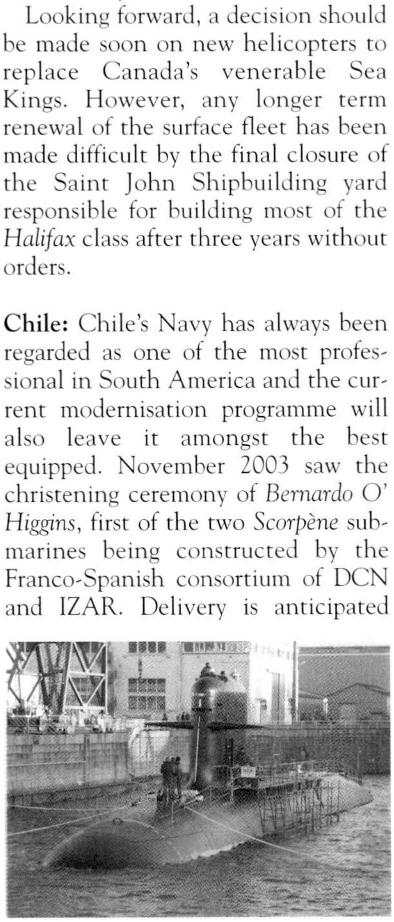

Chile's new submarine O'Higgins. (DCN / IZAR)

The surface fleet, which had shrunk to just three elderly former Royal Navy County class destroyers and three *Leander* class frigates, is also being upgraded. The Type 22 frigate *Sheffield* (now *Almirante Williams*) sailed for Chile from the UK's Devonport Dockyard in December, whilst the former US *Spruance* class destroyer *Fletcher* (DD-963) will follow in 2004. Longer term plans call for a more radical modernisation involving the acquisition of three newly built and three second hand units. However, the glut of fairly modern decommissioned tonnage now entering the market may well prove an irresistible alternative to comparatively expensive new construction.

Peru: It is reported that Peru is discussing the purchase of Italy's four decommissioned *Lupo* class frigates of late 1970s vintage, aiming to combine these with the existing four vessels bought from Italy as new construction to form a standardised squadron of major surface combatants. Completion of this plan would result in the disposal of *Almirante Grau* (ex-HMNLS *De Ruyter*), the last traditional gun-armed cruiser in service anywhere in the world, as well as the former British *Daring* class destroyer, *Ferre*.

United States: The United States Navy is currently at its most active since the end of the Cold War. Operation Iraqi Freedom saw half of the USN's twelve-strong carrier force and an even greater proportion of its amphibious assault ships deployed in support of operations in the Middle East, during which time two of the latter (*Bataan* and *Bonhomme Richard*) operated in their secondary Harrier carrier role. The fleet has also been in demand throughout the rest of the world. For example, the newly operational *Iwo Jima* (LHD 7) was deployed off the coast of Liberia during August in support of local peace keeping efforts, whilst units of the Seventh Fleet have been occupied in maintaining a watching brief on an unpredictable and possibly nuclear-armed North Korea.

These commitments have been met by a fleet that has now shrunk to below 300 frontline ships, the lowest figure reached since the United States' entry into the First World War. In the short term, this reduction in numbers is being counterbalanced by initiatives to increase operational flexibility, including a new Fleet Response Plan aimed at extending ships' availability for deployment through more individually tailored maintenance periods. In addition, the size of the carrier groups is being reduced by the transfer of ships to create more powerful amphibious forces under the Expeditionary Strike Group concept, thereby increasing potential response options in a time of crisis. However, in the longer term, construction will have to increase above the average orders of just over five vessels a year achieved during the 1990s and this is reflected in plans for a progressive ramp up in resources devoted to shipbuilding as the decade progresses.

Clearly, it will take some time for these plans to feed through to fleet composition and numbers are planned to fall as low as 290 during FY 2005 as new commissioning fails to keep pace with ships leaving the fleet. In general terms, the surface fleet is suffering most, with the steady completion of Flight II-A, *Arleigh Burke* class destroyers being insufficient to compensate for the rapid run down of the elderly *Spruances*, which are increasingly expensive to operate. The older, non VLS-equipped *Ticonderogas* will also be retired over the next few years, the first Aegis-equipped vessels to be decommissioned. By way of contrast, the current 12-strong carrier force is considered sacrosanct, with the ninth CVN-68 *Nimitz* class carrier, *Ronald Reagan*, replacing the veteran *Constellation* during the course of 2003. The keel of final class member *George H. W. Bush* was laid at Newport News on 6 September 2003, whilst work continues on the next generation CVN-21, the order for which is scheduled by 2006-7.

The future hopes of the surface fleet rest with the new DD(X) and smaller Littoral Combat Ship (LCS) programmes, the initial orders for which were foreshadowed in the US Administration's recent FY 2005 budget request. The former will be a radical 12,000 ton 'destroyer' with an all-electric integrated power system, a tumblehome hull and 'pill-box' typed superstructure designed to maximise stealth characteristics. Armed with two new 155mm (6in) advanced gun systems and eighty VLS cells in a dispersed configuration, the DDX is primarily intended for land attack missions and could be the prototype for a class of up to 24.

US Ohio *class submarine* Michigan *preparing for her SSGN upgrade.* (USN)

The LCS is intended to be a much smaller, complimentary design capable of high speed combat operations in shallow, coastal waters. Competing teams headed by General Dynamics' Bath Iron Works, Lockheed Martin and Raytheon have been awarded preliminary design contracts for the new vessel, from which one or two prototypes will be constructed during 2006-7. It appears that the three competitors have come up with significantly different responses to the requirement, with single, twin and trimaran hull concepts all featuring. However, all designs will be capable of accepting a variety of different combat modules to meet the initial intended roles of mine countermeasures, anti-submarine warfare and protection against the threat posed by small, swarming boats. Systems deployed will include those that can operate beyond the ship, such as the Remote Minehunting System (RMS) currently under development by Lockheed Martin.

Meanwhile, the future development of the submarine fleet is focused on volume production of the *Virginia* class SSN, the first member of which was christened on 16 August and is scheduled to join the fleet during 2004. A further three boats are under construction, with annual orders projected for another six through to 2008 towards a planned total of around 30 units. The submarine force will also benefit from the commissioning of the third and final *Seawolf* class SSN, *Jimmy Carter*, in 2004, as well as the conversion of four of the *Ohio* class SSBNs into combined tactical cruise missile launchers (SSGNs) and special forces platforms.

Modernisation of amphibious shipping continues, with fabrication work on *Makin Island*, the eight and final *Wasp* class LHD, commencing during 2003. Scheduled for delivery in 2007, she will be different from her sisters in being equipped with gas turbine propulsion. Progress is also being made with the *San Antonio* LPDs and the first of the class was launched on 19 July 2003 for commissioning towards the end of 2004. A total of twelve ships is eventually planned to provide one for each of the amphibious ready groups, with the fifth unit, LPD-21, ordered in November.

WARSHIP NOTES

This section comprises a number of short articles and notes, covering lesser known aspects of naval history and recent developments connected with historic naval vessels.

HMS *WHIMBREL*

Conrad Waters reports on the campaign to save a veteran of the Battle of the Atlantic.

The last remaining example of the famous *Black Swan* class sloops that did so much to win the Battle of the Atlantic, HMS *Whimbrel* is now laid up in an Egyptian dockyard whilst negotiations continue to establish her fate.

The *Black Swans* were designed in the 1930s as powerful escort vessels, with a heavy anti-aircraft armament of three twin 4in mountings and the latest equipment for anti-submarine detection and destruction. Under commanders such as the legendary Captain Johnnie Walker, they earned a reputation second to none as fearsome U-boat hunters during the Second World War: Walker's own ship, HMS *Starling*, sinking the record number of sixteen enemy submarines. The class also served extensively in the post-war Royal Navy, during which time HMS *Amethyst* gained fame in the Yangtse River Incident.

HMS *Whimbrel* herself was completed at Glasgow's Yarrow shipyard, commissioning in January 1943. On completion of work-up at the anti-submarine training school established at Tobermory on Scotland's west coast, she was assigned to Johnnie Walker's Second Escort group, with which she served until June 1943. A busy wartime career also included a tour of duty on the arduous Russian convoys and anti-submarine operations in support of the D-Day landings. Transferred to the Pacific in early 1945 for service with the newly formed British Pacific Fleet, she was

An official photograph of HMS Whimbrel *taken at the time of her commissioning in January 1943.* (Crown Copyright via BAe Systems Plc)

A recent view of HMS Whimbrel *(now ENS* Tariq*) at Alexandria.* (Conrad Waters)

HMS Whimbrel *in dry dock in Alexandria, February 2003.* (Commander Robin Raphael)

employed in escorting tankers of the fleet train until the war's end. Alongside her sister HMS *Crane*, she was one of the warships chosen to represent the Royal Navy at the formal surrender of Japan in Tokyo Bay on 2 September 1945. She is now one of only a few ships that survive from this momentous day that marked the end of six years of conflict.

HMS *Whimbrel* operated for a further year in the Far East before returning to home waters to pay off into reserve. Transferred to the infant Egyptian Navy as *El Malek Farouk* in November 1949, she assumed her current name, *Tariq*, on the overthrow of the Egyptian monarchy. She provided her new owners with nearly 50 years of active service in which she saw action on several occasions, notably surviving an air strike from the French aircraft carrier *Arromanches* during the Suez invasion. Latterly used as an accommodation and stationary training ship alongside another former Royal Navy warship, the former Second World War destroyer, HMS *Zenith*, she has now been replaced in the Egyptian Navy by more modern vessels. Fortunately, the Egyptian Navy has realised the historical significance of the vessels in their possession and have therefore sought offers for their preservation before handing them over to the breakers.

Disappointingly, there has been little official interest in the fate of either warship. More positively, however, a campaign to return HMS *Whimbrel* to her former Liverpool operating berth in the Canning Dock as a memorial to

Two views of the Second World War Z class destroyer HMS Zenith *(now ENS* El Fateh*).* (Conrad Waters)

those who fought in the Battle of the Atlantic is making some progress. An initial examination of the ship was carried out at her current 'berth' in a floating dry dock in the middle of Alexandria Harbour late in 2002, paving the way for a much more comprehensive structural survey in February 2003. Whilst this indicated that there were significant areas of localised corrosion, particularly where there had been an electrolytic action as a result of replacement plates being welded over the original hull below the waterline, *Whimbrel* is certainly in no worse 'starting condition' than many ships that have already been preserved and the considerable efforts made by the Egyptian navy to look after her ensure that stabilisation and refurbishment would certainly be technically feasible. Remarkably, most of her structure is little changed from her wartime days, with original items such as steam gauges and telegraphs manufactured in Nottingham and Liverpool evidencing the complex industrial infrastructure that supported her building. Her original armament has been removed to lighten her sufficiently for the docking period but remains safely in storage on shore.

Preliminary consultation has already taken place with advisory organisations such as the UK's National Historic Ships Committee on *Whimbrel*'s likely heritage status - and hence potential eligibility for lottery and other funding. These have been sufficiently positive to encourage further work on the preservation project. At the moment, protracted negotiations continue with the Egyptian naval authorities to establish an acceptable purchase price for the vessel and the necessary repairs that would be required to ensure a safe passage back to the UK. The conclusion of these discussions will help determine whether an appeal to save HMS *Whimbrel* appears a realistic possibility.

For further information contact:

Conrad Waters,
Public Relations Officer, HMS *Whimbrel*: Battle of the Atlantic Memorial, Two Beeches, Tilford Road, Hindhead, Surrey GU26 6RA
Tel: 44 (0)1428 605634
Email: conrad.waters@btopenworld.com

[STOP PRESS: As *Warship* was going to press the negotiations to purchase *Whimbrel* appeared to be coming to a successful conclusion. We hope to keep readers informed of future developments.]

SLIPPERY SHIPS

David K Brown RCNC examines attempts to reduce frictional drag on hull forms.

During the 1950s numerous laboratory experiments showed that minute amounts of additive in the form of very long molecules (molecular weight of one million or more) could reduce dramatically the frictional drag in flow through pipes. One of the best of these additives was polyethylene oxide (Polyox) but some naturally occurring substances such as guar gum and bluebell juice were also effective.[1] Once the effect was recognised thought turned towards the benefits for ships.

One such test was carried out by Dove at the Admiralty Experiment Works, Haslar in 1965.[2] The resistance of a 16ft frigate model was measured with different concentrations of Polyox 301 injected through four narrow slots at 5, 25, 50 and 75 per cent of the length from the bow. The slots were each fed from a tank holding a solution of Polyox with concentrations of 100, 250, 500 and 1,000 wppm (weight parts per million) in the tanks and the model was tested at speeds corresponding to 15 and 30 knots.

Preliminary tests were run with no flow through the slots and then with tap water flowing. It was found that the best results were obtained with only the 5 and 25 per cent slots in use and with a concentration of Polyox in the boundary layer of 10 wppm; increased concentrations gave little improvement. The frictional resistance was reduced by 21 per cent at 15 knots and by 29 per cent at 30 knots. There was a further 5 per cent reduction in shaft power due to more favourable interaction between the hull and propeller.[3]

There were legitimate doubts over the applicability of these results on a smooth model to the rough surface of a full scale ship. The minesweeper *Highburton* had been carrying out some (unsuccessful) trials of air lubrication and I made out a case for these to be followed by trials of Polyox hoping that much of the gear already installed could be used - it did not work that way.

The *Highburton* was 152ft long and during the trials displaced about 440 tons. Her wooden planked hull was very rough with some planks standing proud and with a poor coating of 'Pocoptic', anti-fouling paint, renewed for the trial. The Polyox was held in a tank, replacing the gun on the forecastle. Faired ducts were fitted port and starboard at 4 and 25 per cent length from the bow with ejection slots 0.07in wide.

Trials were carried out on the Stokes Bay measured mile during September 1968 six days after she came out of dock. There were 13 points along the hull at which samples could be taken to measure the concentration of Polyox in the flow near the hull. There was difficulty in getting anything like a uniform concentration of additive in the flow near the hull with an excess near the keel. Model tests showed that the flow near the bow was quite sharply downwards towards the keel and for the later trials the lower 50 per cent of the ducts were blanked off.

The results were quite similar to those from the frigate model. The best results were obtained with about 10wppm of Polyox and there was little benefit from higher concentrations. The reduction in total resistance at 9 knots was 13 per cent corresponding to about double that figure for frictional resistance alone. The reduction in shaft horsepower was somewhat greater showing that there was again a benefit in hull-propeller interaction.

The trial clearly demonstrated that drag reduction using additives worked and that the benefits showed on models could be reproduced on a real ship in the sea. It was also clear that the temporary installation on *Highburton* could easily be improved. Why then is the use of additives not universal?

The economic balance is bleak. To achieve a reduction in horsepower of 17 per cent at 9 knots required a Polyox flow amounting to 3.7 tons per day which at £840 per ton was valued at £3108. The fuel saving was 0.18 tons per day at £11.5 per ton amounting to £2.07, a balance of 1500 against Polyox on cost. (Costs are quoted at 1970 prices).

This is not the end of the story; the installation could certainly be improved and, made in large quantities, the price of Polyox would fall considerably. There are indications that many of the benefits would be retained if the Polyox flow were intermittent (using less material). The Polyox additive used is not necessarily the best material to be found though by 2003 no one has found anything vastly better. Research has continued in many countries but there is no indication of a breakthrough. The potential has been clearly demonstrated and we await achievement.

Tailpiece

I believe that additives are formally prohibited in the America's Cup yacht racing.

Sources

This article is based almost entirely on a paper:

H J S Canham, J P Catchpole & R F Long. *Boundary layer Additives to Reduce Ship Resistance*, Trans RINA, 1971.

and is used with permission of the Royal Institution of Naval Architects. This paper contains more details of the experimental gear as well as detailed results.

Notes

1 In days gone by, some ship tanks experienced periods in which resistance was abnormally low. It is likely that natural polymers were responsible and modern water purification has prevented occurrence in the last 75 years.

2 H L Dove, *The Effect on Resistance of Polymer Additives Injected into the Boundary layer of a Frigate Model*, (Proc ITTC, Tokyo, 1966).

3 'Thrust deduction' to the uninitiated.

CRESSY, ABOUKIR AND *HOGUE* UNCOVERED

Underwater research at the wrecks of the ill-fated cruisers.

A recent dive has produced remarkable new images of wrecks of the three armoured cruisers, *Cressy*, *Aboukir* and *Hogue*.

The remains of the ships lie 100ft below the surface at a distance of 25 miles off the Dutch coastline. A British diving team spent three days examining the wreck site. Garry Hudson, one of the divers, highlighted the difficulties of the dive: 'It's pretty extreme stuff, beyond what most sports divers can achieve....We had to take down extra tanks and a special mix of gases that would enable us to stay down beyond our limits'.

The three armoured cruisers were patrolling off the Dutch coast in September 1914 when they were torpedoed by the German U-boat *U-9*. All three were oblivious to any possible danger and were lost, along with 1400 lives, in just one hour. Hudson said: 'The story of what happened to these three ships is amazing. One minute you're on patrol, the next all hell breaks loose. It was one of those things that should never have happened and certainly didn't happen again.' The naval expert Professor Eric Grove stated: 'The main criticism after the event was why were they travelling so slowly, why did the other ships stop to pick up survivors and why weren't the water tight doors closed? I would put that down to experience....People were learning on the job what the dynamics of modern naval warfare would be'.

According to members of the dive team all three wrecks are in a pretty poor state. As they sank they capsized, and hence most of the superstructure was crushed against the sea bed under the weight of the hull. Nick Pearce, another member of the dive team, said 'It's a shame to think that in another fifty or sixty years time there won't be much more left to see. It's pretty eerie stuff down there when all you can hear is the sound of your bubbles. A lot of men and boys were on these boats. It's hard to think what they went through so that we can have our freedom today'.

Around 800 men survived the attack, including 15 year-old Kit Wykeham Musgrave who can make the remarkable claim of having been on all three ships as they were torpedoed one after another. Kit's daughter, Pru Bailey-Hamilton, retells the story: 'He went overboard when the *Aboukir* was going down and he swam like mad to get away from the suction. He was then just getting on board the *Hogue* and she was torpedoed. He then went and swam to the *Cressy* and she was also torpedoed. He eventually found a bit of driftwood, became unconscious and was eventually picked up by a Dutch trawler.' Perhaps a case of being the unluckiest and, at the same time, the luckiest man in the Royal Navy.

ADDENDUM AND CORRECTIONS

John Brooks and Pierre Hervieux point out errors in recent editions of Warship.

Warship 2002-3: 'Admiralty Fire Control Tables'

In the 2002-3 edition of *Warship*, two footnotes were omitted from the end of John Brooks' article on Admiralty Fire Control Tables. These were as follows:

105 IWM 10673/2.

106 Vice-Admiral Sir Arthur Hezlet, *The Electron and Sea Power* (London, 1975) pp.244-5. Humble, Chapter 18.

Warship 2002-3: Warship Notes – British Military Powerboat Trust

In reference to this feature, on page 167 of *Warship* 2002-3, 'The ensuing action left 638 American sailors and soldiers dead', Pierre Hervieux writes:

These are old figures and unhappily it is nowadays admitted that the losses were much heavier. In the 1993 book *The Forgotten Dead* by Ken Small, the real figures are 749 American soldiers and 198 American sailors (including one who died in hospital), making the total of 949 men lost. These figures were so high that it seems that the US Authorities decided to amend them to 749!

Warship 2001-2: 'The Royal Romanian Navy at War, 1941-1944'

In Pierre Hervieux's article the reference on page 78 to the sinking of the Soviet submarine *Shch-208* should have read 'between 26 August and 8 September 1942'.

SAVING HMS *STALKER*

Stephen Dent describes efforts to preserve an unusual survivor from the Second World War.

HMS *Stalker* is the last surviving steam powered Landing Ship Tank (LST) and as such she represents a type of vessel that played a major part in the Allied victory in the Second World War. Now the Stalker Trust is being set up, under the auspices of the Maritime Steam Restoration Trust, to save the vessel from being broken up and restore her to working condition. The success of ships such as the *Waverley*, *Balmoral* and *Shieldhall* show that this can be done - that historic vessels don't necessarily have to be simply static exhibits. It is the belief of those working to save *Stalker* that ships in full working order are much more inspiring than those that are just sitting in a dock somewhere, and indeed that this represents the future of historic ship preservation.

The aim of the Trust is for *Stalker* to be brought back to an operational state so that she would be able to provide both individuals and organisations such as the Sea Cadets with sea going training and experience, as well as being able to be used to carry goods. Both of these roles would help pay for her upkeep. Although not a particularly glamourous vessel her unique features compared to more conventional ships mean that she is potentially capable of fulfiling these demanding requirements, while the success of the equally un-glamourous *Shieldhall* suggests that it is indeed possible for such a vessel to be run in an economically viable fashion. She would also serve as a museum and memorial to all the ships that took part in the invasion of Nazi-occupied Europe, and to those of their oft-forgotten crews who paid the ultimate price.

Stalker was a one of about seventy Mark 3LSTs built. Originally *LST(3)3515* (they were possibly the largest class until then known only by a number) she was laid down at Esquimalt Shipyard in Canada in April 1944, and completed and commissioned in June 1945, just too late for active service in the conflict. Renamed HMS *Stalker* in 1947, she instead spent the majority of her

Two views of HMS Stalker *being towed to Cammell Laird's for her hull to be cleaned during the 1950s.* (M. Galt, courtesy of the Stalker Trust)

Stalker *as she now rests, in Pound's yard, Portsmouth, photographed in October 2003.* (Stephen Dent)

Looking aft on the port side, showing the additions on the upper deck. (Stephen Dent)

Interior of the tank deck, looking aft. (Stephen Dent)

Bridge detail. (Stephen Dent)

career as a depot and maintenance ship for submarines, firstly at Loch Foyle in Northern Ireland, and then, after the submarine base closed in 1976, at Rosyth. Many of her sisters had similar harbour based careers, one by one being broken up during the 1960s to 1980s as they became surplus to requirements. *Stalker* was only finally declared surplus in 2001 when submarine repairs at Rosyth ceased, but although offered for scrap on the open market there were no takers. At the end of 2002 she was towed to Pound's Ship Breakers yard in Portsmouth, where she now lies. The yard is due to be redeveloped in the next few years, but it is hoped to be able to rescue *Stalker* before this takes place.

At first glance the vessel appears to be in poor shape, streaked with rust and minus her mast, armament, main derricks, anchors and winches, boats and davits, screws and rudders, main ventilators and many other external fittings and equipment. However, this initial impression is very deceptive, and crucially her hull remains extremely sound. She represents something of a 'time capsule', with her main machinery, two inverted vertical four-cylinder triple expansion engines (the same as were used in the 'Loch' and 'Bay' class frigates) made in Montreal, and auxiliaries; boilers; bow doors and ramps; bridge, funnel and much of her superstructure all still largely intact. Part of her steering gear has been removed but the remainder is still in situ, and, like the boilers and engines, in truly remarkable condition having been barely used throughout the nearly 60 years of her life. Although everything is very dirty and there is some surface rust, apart from the occasional broken or missing part much of the machinery looks as if it would need little more than a good clean before being ready to run again.

Many of *Stalker*'s compartments, stripped of their original fittings and used as stores during her submarine depot ship days, are now full of shelves and filing cabinets, discarded bits of equipment, crumbling linoleum flooring and other debris. Some of her deck houses have been removed, and others added in different locations, while the tank deck is now bisected near the bow by a partition, as well as sporting a couple of small workshops. The main hatch in the upper deck has been covered over and the ramp leading up from the tank deck been welded shut, with a separate access way added in further aft. However, dotted here and there throughout the vessel are examples of her original fittings, and most importantly very little actual damage has been done to her basic structure. The fact that she was towed from Rosyth to Portsmouth without any serious problems attests to her fundamental seaworthiness.

The D-Day Museum in Southsea is one of a number of organisations who have welcomed the project; however, Portsmouth Historic Dockyard already have their hands full with HMS *Victory*, HMS *Warrior*, the *Mary*

The partly dismantled hydraulic/steam stearing gear. (Malcolm Tattersall)

The Stevenson's valve gear of the port main engine. (Malcolm Tattersall)

The tops of the cylinders of the port main engine. (Malcolm Tattersall)

Engine plate detail. (Malcolm Tattersall)

The pump end of the port ballast pump. (Malcolm Tattersall)

Starboard bow view of HMS Stalker. (Malcolm Tattersall)

Stern detail, showing rudders. (Malcolm Tattersall)

Interior view of the bow ramp of HMS Stalker. (Stephen Dent)

Superstructure interior. (Stephen Dent)

Rose and the *M-33* and so feel that they are unlikely to be able to offer *Stalker* a home. For now she is safe at Pound's, where she can easily be seen from the M275 leading into Portsmouth, but one of the Trust's first priorities will be to find her a berth where she can start to receive the attention that she needs.

It is estimated that a total of at least £10 million will be needed to save *Stalker*, of which an initial sum of £50,000, including a deposit of £20,000, is required to purchase her from Pounds. Funding is being sought from the Heritage Lottery Fund and other organisations as well as from private individuals, while additionally from the latter have come many other offers of help and expertise. The Trust is not only looking for help and financial support but also for information, photographs and drawings, and memories of the ship and her career, as well as those of her sister ships.

The Stalker Trust can be contacted via:

Mr M E Tattersall,
39 Fairfield, Hebden Bridge,
Yorkshire. HX7 6JP
web: www.maritimesteamrestoration trust.co.uk

Warship hopes to be able to keep readers informed of the progress of the project to save HMS *Stalker*.

CONFEDERATE IRONCLAD FOUND IN SAVANNAH RIVER, GEORGIA

Port development threatens relic of the American Civil War.

Divers found the remarkably preserved ironclad CSS *Georgia* at the mouth of the Savannah, Georgia, during September 2003. The ship was scuttled by the Rebel forces in December 1864 and now lies in 35 feet of water downstream from the town of Savannah. The problem now is that the ship also lies in the path of a projected multi million dollar expansion and river deepening scheme to open up Savannah Harbor to large modern cargo ships. In response to the plans the Army Corps of Engineers and the Georgia Ports Authority commissioned a $375,000 archaeological study. According to Judy Wood, a US Army Corps of Engineers archaeologist, the *Georgia* is 'still a very nice shipwreck', despite the fact that the surveying team actually found a lot less of the ship than they envisaged.

A salvage operation staged four years after her sinking had actually managed to recover much of the wreck. The surveying team were also hampered by the fact that their high-tech sonar equipment did not work properly and the dive had to resort to probing in and around the wreck in search of artefacts. What has been found so far includes a couple of big pieces of ordnance, fragments of the ship's coal-powered engine and one of her twin 7ft propellers.

The Army Corps of Engineers has already set aside $13 million if it is decided to recover the *Georgia*. According to Scott Smith, Executive Director of the Coastal Heritage Society, more money is needed if the ship is to be preserved in a museum-quality exhibit. The Society hopes to raise the necessary cash from government and also private business. In the long term the Society wishes to see the *Georgia* fully incorporated into Savannah's Battlefield Park complex. Smith thinks that the recent archaeological study 'has been a very positive step' towards this.

It is hoped that the Army Corps of Engineers will release a draft version of a general evaluation report, including an impact statement for public review and comment, towards the end of 2005. In the following year the decision will be made as to whether the river shall be deepened to 48ft, with the necessary money found by 2007.

The very fact that the divers did not find the intact engine they expected to might work in the project's favour, as a recovery effort would probably not need the full $13 million reserved for the project. However, there physically remains enough evidence of the engine to allow historians and archaeologists to approach the question of whether the *Georgia* was underpowered, and hence could not navigate satisfactorily in the river. This led to her being moored as a floating battery. Because of the evidence found in the dive, Wood has confirmed that 'what we're thinking now is that the engine was just too small'.

RUSSIAN SUBMARINE SINKS

Tragic incident sparks painful memories of the Kursk.

In late August 2003 the ageing nuclear powered attack submarine *K-159* sank into the icy waters of the Barents Sea. The incident is a chilling reminder of the *Kursk* tragedy, in which 118 men lost their lives, and remains in the minds of many naval personnel as well as that of President Vladimir Putin. Putin received widespread criticism for not making any public statements when the *Kursk* sank, while the navy reacted slowly and with trepidation, refusing foreign assistance until it was too late.

K-159 was under tow, headed for Polyarny where, as a final part of decommissioning, it was to be stripped down and scrapped and its nuclear fuel removed. The reactors had previously been removed in 1989. Whilst under tow, around 3 miles northwest of Kildin island, the floating pontoons providing buoyancy to the submarine gave way, throwing her onto her side and sending her to the bottom, around 170 metres below.

A total of nine men lost their lives in this, the most recent accident to blight the ageing and under-funded forces of the once proud naval service. *K-159* was built in 1963 to a 1950s design that has recently been causing great alarm amongst environmental agencies. Although Russia has cut its submarine forces by more than half, 126 vessels remain in service. All are suffering from lack of funds and slack safety and security procedures. The 2002 budget for improving nuclear safety throughout the country was $70 million whilst it is estimated that $3.9 billion is needed just to decommission the submarine fleet.

Despite this, Russia's navy chief of staff Viktor Kravchenko believes that this recent incident presents no danger to the environment, going on record as stating 'the radioactive level is normal'.

This time Russian officials acted quicker than in the days after the sinking of the *Kursk*, with Kravchenko and Russian defence minister Sergei Ivanov discussing the accident on Russian television. Putin has also learned his lesson from the *Kursk*, immediately stating 'all reasons for the tragedy will be established'.

The Russian Navy has promised to raise the sub in an effort to recover the bodies of those lost in the accident, whilst a criminal case has been opened. Though the inquiry will almost certainly concern the towing of the sub, Eduard Baltin, a former commander of the Black Sea fleet, pointed to the unseaworthiness of *K-159*, stating she had not been to sea since 1983 and should not have been towed. 'I last sailed to sea with her on research purposes,' Baltin stated 'She sank on me then.'

GUADALCANAL SHIPWRECKS STILL CAUSING DAMAGE

Enviromental concerns at pollution from sunken warships.

According to reports, shipwrecks from the Battle of Guadalcanal fought between August and December 1942 are causing ecological damage in the Solomon Islands.

The 6,800 ton Japanese freighter *Hirokawa Maru* lies just yards off the shore of Bonegi beach. Reports from islanders claim that when the seas are rough, the stench of oil can be detected in the air, while coral reefs and sea life are being harmed.

The Government in the Solomon Islands had asked the US and the Japanese to remove a number of wrecks and tons of munitions, which were dumped on the islands and the surrounding waters during the war. Neither side attempted any clean up during or after the war. The coup that occurred in the Islands during 2000 has further complicated the possibility of finding a solution.

The wrecks, lying off the north coast of Guadalcanal, are a growing ecological danger. Moses Biliki, the Solomon Islands' environmental director in the natural resources ministry, fumed: 'It was someone else's war that just came to our country and we have all this rubbish that has just been forgotten....Something has to be done because over time the iron will corrode further and leakage is more likely'. It remains to be seen whether Washington or Tokyo will answer Mr Biliki's calls for assistance.

RESEARCHING AT THE RUSSIAN NAVAL ARCHIVES

Stephen McLaughlin reports on a recent visit to Russia.

In the summer of 2002 I had an opportunity to visit the Russian State Archives of the Navy (*Rossiiskii gosudarstvennyi arkhiv Voenno-morskogo flota*, RGAVMF) in St. Petersburg for two weeks. Throughout my stay I was guided by Sergei Vinogradov, who has spent a good many years researching the history of Russian dreadnoughts in the archives. He showed me the ropes and also served as translator, since my command of Russian is limited to a reading knowledge (always with dictionary in hand!).

The archives are located near the Hermitage Museum, on Millionaya Street. The entrance to the archives is not obvious, being through a small courtyard. After the inevitable bureaucratic formalities I was issued a pass (*propusk*). I was now, in theory, ready to start work.

Researchers accustomed to the PRO in London or the National Archives Washington will be in for a bit of a surprise at this point. The reading room is small, about two dozen tables in two small rooms. But this is strictly a naval archive, and its size matches its specific focus. Moreover, this archive has material only up to 1940; later materials are held at a separate facility at Gatchina, some distance from St. Petersburg. During the first week of my visit, the archives were well attended, and all the tables were taken. A few latecomers had to find places in corners or widow sills where they could work. The second week was less busy, for reasons that will be described later on.

Most Russian archives use a similar system for organizing materials. The first division is the *fond* (plural *fondy*), which is a group of documents, usually from a single agency – for example, the Naval Technical Committee. Within this broad division there are various registers or lists (*opisi*, singular *opis'*) of documents, not arranged in any particular order. Thus, in looking for files on a given subject (in my case, battleships), you scan through the entire range of activities of a department – submarines, cruisers, destroyers, reports of acceptance trials, technical summaries, memos, etc. It can take a while to locate the file (*delo*, plural *dely*) relevant to your topic. There are some additional finding aids to particular topics – drawings of battleships, for example – but these are usually far from exhaustive. It should also be noted that some lists (especially the older ones) are handwritten, and old Russian script can be difficult to decipher.

The final element of a citation is the individual sheet (*list*, plural *listy*) of paper. A typical citation therefore looks something like this:

f.421, op. 1, d. 1680, l. 28.

Having identified the documents you want, you fill out a request form and turn it in to the archivist; for this purpose you need only to specify down to the file (*delo*) level. Then you wait for the material to appear, not for hours but for days. To speed up the process Sergei had requested some files for me in advance, but due to a recent change in the file organisation, Sergei's citations were no longer valid and nothing useful was retrieved. I therefore spent my first few days in the archives reviewing the finding aids, noting interesting items for future reference.

I started work on Monday and my first documents arrived on Wednesday. These were microfilms, and presented some initial conceptual difficulties. About half of the reader tables were equipped with microfilm readers, somewhat antiquated but familiar enough in principle; what caused me some dismay was the lack of reels. The film comes tightly wound in small containers and there are no take-up reels, so the general practice is to thread the film through the machine and pull it back and forth by hand to view it. Rewinding is a time-consuming and tedious process.

External shot of the Archive. (S McLaughlin)

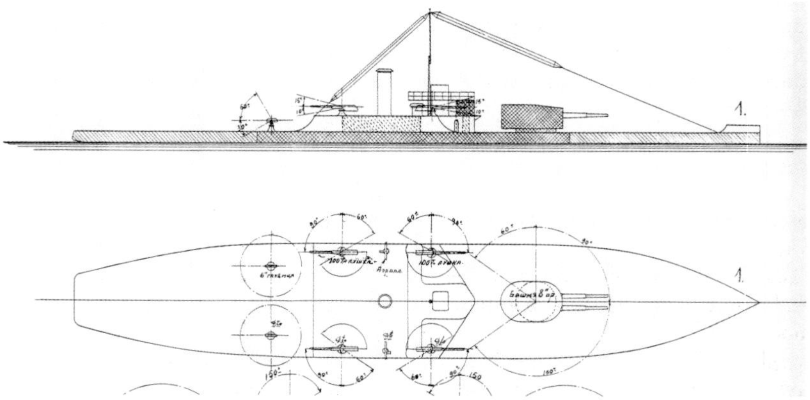

A Russian monitor design dating to March 1915, from the Russian Naval Archives. This design had an armament of two 8in guns in a turret forward, four 4in guns on pedestals amidships, two 6in howitzers on the quarterdeck, and two 40mm AA guns. Displacement was to be 1,900 tons, dimensions 280 x 49 x 6.23ft, with reciprocating engines on two shafts (1,500ihp, speed 11 knots). Armor thicknesses were 3in on the hull amidships and the turret, with 4in on the coning tower, and a 1in deck. (RGAVMF, f. 876, op. 173, d. 268)

As an amateur researcher who has to squeeze archival visits into a limited vacation period, my usual technique is what I call the 'smash and grab' - look briefly at as many things as possible, photocopy anything that looks even mildly interesting, and analyse it all when I get home. This approach is not viable at the Russian archives, since they are not set up for mass photocopying. Photocopying takes a day or two; you fill out a request form and submit it and the material to be copied to the archivist. When your copies are ready, you have a chance to look them over, then you take the bill over to the administrative offices and pay the requisite fee. You get a stamped receipt, which you then take back to the archivist, who in turn gives you the copies. The process can take a bit of time, and should not be left until the end of the day.

The archives cannot make copies from microfilm, nor can it copy blueprints with dark backgrounds. Photocopies of individual pages or of positive (black-on-white) drawings are possible. The largest size paper available is 42 x 30cm, so big drawings take several sheets; one nice feature is that the a full citation for the source of the photocopy is stamped on the back, so you can always cite it properly!

The other method for getting copies of large drawings is to trace them, and several other researchers were engaged in this process while I was there. The well-prepared researcher will want to have tracing paper, pencils, pens, straight-edges and curves handy. Since microfilmed drawings cannot be copied, tracing these as projected by the reader is the only way to walk away with a permanent record. The process is particularly challenging, since your own shadow tends to get in the way, and the image jiggles and shifts as your unsteady hands try to hold the paper in place. Nevertheless, I was able to make some very rough sketches of several very interesting designs. These of course had to be re-drawn later, but it is possible to make quick tracings and notes sufficient to produce finished drawings.

My two-week visit featured both successes and disappointments. I found a lot of material on the early Russian dreadnought design process, and came away with a substantial amount of notes, as well as some rough tracings of microfilmed drawings and photocopies of others. On the other hand, going through the lists to locate the materials I wanted for later Soviet designs proved very time-consuming, and by the time I had identified the items I wanted, it was too late to request them. The archive was due to close the week after I left, and so during my second week no new paging requests were being accepted because there would be insufficient time to extract and re-shelve them. This explained the sudden drop-off in attendance by researchers that last week before closing, and was the major let-down of my visit.

The naval archives house a vast amount of material, and little weeding seems to have been done (perhaps a beneficial side-effect of limited staffing!) I can imagine many topics worthy of research – for example, the intimate relationship between the Naval Ministry and the British firm of Vickers before the First World War. But to make a good job of it, a diligent researcher would need several months of daily work at the archives, since there's no list that says "Vickers Material." Instead, it would be necessary to review all the papers of the departments likely to have had dealings with the firm, following many hunches and false leads. The material is there; only time is lacking.

The pace of research is slower than westerners are accustomed to and I suspect that the volume of material to peruse for any given subject is both more voluminous and more scattered than is usual in the west. Russia, after all, has always been a bureaucratic state, and bureaucracies have a tendency to generate large amounts of paper. This, and the fact that the material on a given ship design is not pulled together in the equivalent of a "ship's cover," probably explains some of the seemingly peculiar aspects of Russian naval writing on ship design – why, for example, authors often give preliminary rather than final weight break-downs, or illustrate articles with early sketches of a design rather than an "as fitted" drawing. In many cases, it is likely that these pieces were the discoverable elements of long and complex design processes, with some papers lost under misleading entries in the registers. Another problem is that fact that drawings have been separated from the related correspondence, presumably for convenience of storage. But this means that in quite a few cases there is little or no identifying information associated with a drawing. Thus while the archive holds a great deal of material, locating it and then making the necessary connections to reconstruct a design process could take years.

Under these circumstances, the achievements of Russian naval writers are all the more impressive. Detailed design histories, soundly based on archival sources, have appeared in book (or booklet) form, as well as in articles in journals such as *Gangut*, *Tsitadel* and the venerable *Sudostroenie*. Nor should the accomplishments of the archivists be overlooked; despite shortages of funds and staffing, they have managed to preserve and make available a vast body of documentary material. It would be wise for the western researcher to bear these facts in mind at those (inevitable) moments when frustration arises over the slow pace of retrieval or the lack of familiar facilities.

A few last details should be noted by anyone looking to conduct research at the naval archives. There are few English-speakers on the staff (how many Russian-speakers are on hand at TNA or NARA?), so unless you have a good command of the language, an interpreter will be necessary. Hours are 10:00 to 17:00 (the usual Russian method of reckoning time) Monday through Thursday, closing an hour earlier on Fridays. Bear in mind that the archives closes for a month or more during the summer (usually from late July to the end of August). There is no cafeteria on the premises, but there are several small cafes and pubs nearby where a quick and inexpensive meal can be obtained. Electrical outlets are available for notebook computers (220V), which are becoming more common in Russia. But, above all, be patient; the process of research can be slow and painful, but it can also be rewarding.

[This note is a modified version of an article that originally appeared in Argonauta: The Newsletter of the Canadian Nautical Research Society *(vol. XIX, no. 4, October 2002). The author is grateful to Bill Schleihauf for permission to republish it.]*

ROYAL NAVY MEMORABILIA!

Michael 'Mike' Crowe, Vice Chairman, Federation of Naval Associations, makes an impassioned plea for links to the past.

As one gets older, there is a very strong urge to look back on life and wish that certain things had gone another way, or to look back and wish certain events could have lasted longer, even though at the time there might have been frustrating and even dangerous things happening to you. Anyone who served in the Royal Navy will look back on the camaraderie and friendships formed at that time, and wonder where their old shipmates are and what they are doing now. These thoughts are often re-kindled when a drawer or box is opened, perhaps turning out mementos and souvenirs. The Bosun's Call, the photos of the runs ashore, the Service Document, a landyard, the station card, the pay book, the medals; artefacts which only see the light of day once in a blue moon or when you move house, and it is at this last occasion, when they may be thrown away. Far more sad, is when the owner dies and sons, daughters and relatives do not realise the inherent historical value of such items.

The past may be the past, but it does not have to be dead and gone forever without the memories of those left behind. It is for this reason that I am appealing for artefacts, that might otherwise be discarded, for a Royal Navy Museum, which will be incorporated into the Isle of Wight Military History Museum. This museum is at present predominantly an Army orientated institution with tanks, guns and other Army vehicles and displays. The Royal Navy Exhibition and Museum will have its own large self-contained building within the museum, representing those who served in the Navy. Rather than a simple display of photographs of Royal Navy ships and Shore Establishments over the years, we are instead concentrating on displays that emphasise the human aspect of the past. Another form of display will be the medals, photos and an accompanying life story of the person who donated the artefacts.

Pride of the exhibits will be a magnificent scale model of the 'Colonial' class cruiser HMS *Fiji*. Over 5ft long, this model has been presented to the museum by the HMS *Fiji* Association for 'safe keeping' and also to remember those who died when *Fiji* was sunk off Crete on 22 May 1941. Moreover, the model also serves as a tribute to the man who painstakingly built her to the same plans that were used when the cruiser was built at John Brown & Co at Clydebank. The model maker was also related to a survivor from the sinking. Another relative of a sailor has offered a tape recording of his father recalling his escape from and survival of the sinking. It is hoped to incorporate a system whereby visitors to the museum can listen to such recordings whilst viewing the model.

A very large part of the exhibition will be concentrate on the HM Ship's Associations, of which there are well over 200 currently very active, with details of their reunions, contact details and an information point containing the HM Ships Association's Newsletter. But it is a sad fact that some are being wound up as there is no continuation of Royal Navy Ships of that name, such as *Fiji*, *Ceylon*, *Gambia* and many more ships named after colonies. A reference section will be housed at the information point where people will be able to procure information regarding ships specification and career histories, so this is also an appeal for any books on the Royal Navy and its ships. The museum will also be able to offer a permanent home for such Associations' artefacts, for instance Standards, Ship's Bells, photos and so on, and if there is a specific day in that Association, such as 22 May in the case of *Fiji*, then a wreath will be placed on the model, some form of remembrance will be observed, and if there are any old shipmates in the vicinity, they will be invited to attend. The Isle of Wight Military History Museum, which is built on the site of an old Army camp, hopes to establish the Camp Church where services may be held such as on Remembrance Sunday.

Artefacts already collected include the White Ensign from a destroyer sunk off Crete at the same time as the sinking of *Fiji*: this is believed to be HMS *Greyhound*. Also assembled are a hammock, an Admiralty issue kit bag, personal lifebelt, Royal Navy Issue Gas Mask, hatbox and uniforms to be displayed on tailors dummies. More hammocks and their stretchers are being looked for to be fixed up to show the very small 'bed space' the sailor had when on board ship. Recorded accounts are required from those who have served in the ships of the Royal Navy with their own accounts of life under 'The White Ensign'.

Although the human aspect is first and foremost at the Museum, other artefacts are required as well. The museum has plenty of outside space for the display of ship's boats, guns, torpedo tubes and so on. There will be room to mount these pieces of equipment with suitably dressed re-enactors to present displays of loading and 'dummy' firing or lowering boats from the davits.

Within many of the group package visitor tours to the Isle of Wight are the reunions for HMShip's Associations, such as those for *Collingwood*, *Coventry* and the 'Castle' class corvettes (Frigates) Association, which have already enjoyed a reunion on the Isle of Wight. A visit to the museum with a buffet in the Tea Room is planned for such associations.

On behalf of the museum, I would be pleased to accept any item or items relating to people who have served in the Royal Navy.

For further details please contact:

Mike Crowe,
Isle of Wight 'Royal Navy' Military History Museum, c/o 7 Heath Road, Lake, Sandown, Isle of Wight
PO36 8PG

GRAF SPEE AS A TOURIST ATTRACTION?

German warship to be raised from the River Plate?

In a bizarre story that could have come straight from Hollywood, reports reached the *Warship* office in January of an ambitious plan to raise the *Graf Spee* and to place her as a tourist attraction in Montevideo, Uruguay.

The story of *Graf Spee's* brief active career and dramatic end is well known. Since then she has lain, broken in two and covered with mud, in the shallow waters of the River Plate, at a depth of 8 metres. But now a German-funded private venture, with the support of the Uruguayan government, is embarking on a three-year salvage plan. The aim is to raise, restore and then site the ship as a major tourist attraction in Montevideo, surrounded as the city is by numerous memorials and graves of those who perished in the Battle of the River Plate, including a huge Anglican church that contains a plaque detailing the 77 British and New Zealand sailors who lost their lives in the battle.

THE WORLD'S WORST WARSHIPS

A year ago *Warship* asked readers to respond to the arguments contained in Antony Preston's book *The World's Worst Warships*. While the title may be described as a little tongue-in-cheek, many readers have taken up the Editor's challenge to comment upon his book. In the cause of stimulating good, informed debate, we here take the opportunity to detail some of the submissions.

The debate is opened by **Rowland Wylde**, *who begins by offering some incisive comments on the general arguments contained in the book, before going on to defend four vessels he believes to have been unfairly accused, and finishing by offering trenchant criticism of three fairly recent British 'duffers'.*

The World's Worst Warships (*WWW*) had a lukewarm notice in the 'Naval Review', the private-circulation journal for officers of the Royal Navy and its associated services. Justifiably in my view, for the salient criticism was that *WWW* neglected the user's viewpoint - yet the final judgement upon a warship design is based upon its utility in service. Antony Preston's list of the factors influencing warship design - Cost, Perceived Threat, Design Competence, Industrial Capacity, Operating Environment, Operational Experience – is all very well but these are not the whole story when it comes to assessing whether a warship design is 'good' or 'bad'. What I felt was lacking from *WWW*'s introduction was a Weberian ideal-type construct of a 'good' warship, because assuming that no sane person deliberately designs a 'bad' warship, let alone a WWW, the measure of 'bad' (or 'worst') can only be the extent to which a particular warship design falls short of 'good'.

The user must largely define the ideal, as warships are designed and built for a purpose, which is ultimately the exercise of Maritime Power by navies. Most major navies can probably cite at least one example of a warship design which seemed to the designers, builders, naval journalists, accountants and so on, to be absolutely marvellous, or at least perfectly acceptable, but which proved indifferent or downright bad in service. This *doesn't* mean that warships should be designed by naval officers; it is not their business, nor do they have the training. But it does mean that Naval Constructors must consult with 'users' (which they do, in my experience), and that the latter should have a clear idea of what they want.

For what it's worth, I believe that given the nature of maritime operations in peace and war, what navies really want of warships[1] is the following (in descending order of priority):

Seaworthiness

The ability to do the required task in the right place, at the right time, in the prevailing sea state without incurring material damage and/or degrading the efficiency of the crew.

Habitability

Not cruise-liner comfort but it is essential to good morale that as much as possible should be done to ensure people are adequately rested and fed, can keep themselves clean, have dry clothing, are working in a comfortable temperature, have an area of private space and so on.

Robust and Reliable Systems

'Systems' meaning everything from the multi-million-dollar Command & Control suite, through the main propulsion machinery, to mundane things like fresh-water and sewage-treatment plants. Anything that can go wrong will, at the worst possible place and time, and the ship with the spares will have been sunk the previous day.

Speed and Endurance

Maritime warfare is essentially about manoeuvre. A good balance between speed and endurance is difficult to define, and the desiderata have changed over the years – e.g. the availability of shipborne aircraft and long-range anti-ship weapons has reduced the requirement for high maximum speed. My personal view is that endurance is a boon under all circumstances, but weather conditions often limit the speed at which a warship can proceed without damaging its hull, equipment, people etc – therefore one should think first of seaworthiness, habitability and endurance and then get the maximum speed possible.

Effective Armament

Another concept difficult to define – but one knows when one has (or hasn't!) got it. Steel warships can very seldom risk a prolonged slugging-match, and should if possible avoid taking hits at all. Victory at sea all too often goes to the side which lands the first damaging blow. Weapon range, rate of fire, accuracy and warhead size are all important, but none can be taken to extremes without degrading the others. One should also remember ammunition supply, always build in as much magazine capacity as possible, and the sensors and control systems necessary to detect/engage the adversary at maximum range.

Resistance to Damage

Notwithstanding the above point about avoiding taking hits, the reality is that warships *will* be hit. It is important that a warship should not be put out of action, or even sunk, by an 'event' which it could have survived without serious effect had it been designed accordingly.[2]

Controllability and Manoeuvrability

Warships do a good deal more accelerating and decelerating, dodging and weaving, and operating in confined waters than the average merchantman. Good control (the ability to hold an ordered course and/or speed) and manoeuvrability (the ability to alter course and/or speed quickly when required) throughout its speed range are important if a warship is to perform effectively, and take evasive action when required.

I would suggest that these qualities have been desirable in warships throughout the age of steam and steel. They are what makes a 'good' warship, and the art of the naval constructor lies in getting the balance right in a particular design, bearing in mind the additional consideration that the service life of his creation will be 20-30 years; so allowance must be made for ease of maintenance/upkeep, and a margin allowed for installation of additional equipment and so on.

I doubt that there has ever been a 'perfect' warship. (My own favourites would be the eight RN *Southampton* class of the 1933-35 Programmes, but that is beside the point.) I doubt that there could even be a definitive list of 'good' designs; because every design is a compromise, different navies have different requirements, and every naval professional, enthusiast will have a different view influenced by their own knowledge and experience. A *definitive* list of 'bad' designs would be even harder to put together, because all practical designs will fall short of the ideal. Where does the division lie between 'good' and 'adequate', or 'adequate' and 'bad'?

If there is to be a list of 'World's Worst' that reflects more than the views of one individual I suggest there should be an agreed criterion, with a number of qualifying conditions. The criterion for WWW status, I believe, should be that a warship is/was *manifestly* unfit for its purpose at the time it entered service - i.e so deficient that the design should have been revised or rejected by naval professionals[3] before the ship was launched.

As for the qualifying conditions, imposed in the interests of fairness and good sense, I would propose:

- Some eccentricity/weakness in an otherwise acceptable design doesn't necessarily qualify the warship for WWW status, especially if it can be remedied or compensated for.
- 'One-off' ships should be viewed sympathetically. Warship design is very much an art, and it is sometimes necessary to build a full-size vessel to test new equipment or concepts. Some design changes will almost always be necessary before subsequent vessels of the same type are built, that is the purpose of building a prototype.
- Defects must be obvious at (or before) the ship's entry into service. The fact that a ship may subsequently be rendered obsolescent and/or subjected to an unwise conversion doesn't mean the original design was bad.
- The ship must actually enter service in the role for which it was designed (thereby proving that the naval professionals responsible were truly unrepentant/oblivious of their errors).
- There must be a lower size limit. In the Frigate/Destroyer/Cruiser field I believe this should be 1000 tons standard displacement (based upon the *Grimsby* class sloops of the 1931-34 Programmes). Below a certain size, ultimately determined by the operating environment, it is not possible to build a warship without significant shortcomings.
- Consideration should be given to the consultation/design process itself, because in reality WWW are symptomatic of gross errors by the relevant naval professionals. When warship designers have to work under pressure, and/or in undue haste, errors may be made which in retrospect seem almost incredible (e.g. the Type 1 'Hunt' class escort, a new design drawn up very quickly, had to have one of three gun mountings removed and permanent ballast installed in order to confer acceptable stability). It will also be the case that under autocratic or totalitarian regimes errors are far more likely because consultation among naval professionals is often constrained or forbidden, a definitive list of WWW would have to include a fair number from Nazi Germany and the USSR, but that is indicative more of political attitudes than of the competence or otherwise of their warship designers.

That is really the contribution I wished to make to the debate, which as I said earlier I believe (as, I'm sure, does Antony Preston) is actually about what defines a *good* warship. However, I'm not going to miss the chance to plead on behalf of three defendants I consider unjustly accused; and nominate three personal *bêtes noires* to take their place in the dustbin of history.

Unjustly Accused:

Powerful and *Terrible*

Good seaboats, good endurance, about as fast as reciprocating machinery allowed, capable of maintaining high speed for long periods, the guns and their crews better protected than in previous 'protected' cruisers – what must a ship do to stay off that WWW list? These ships certainly received a lot of criticism when new, but most of it was ill-informed. The design concepts cannot have been that bad because five years later the *Drake* class were laid down with in dimensions, armament and complement almost identical to the *Powerfuls* and having the much-reviled Belleville boilers. The most significant difference was provision of an armoured belt; and it can be argued that the latter was a mixed blessing because navies were tempted to use armoured cruisers as fast battleships – with eventual disastrous consequences at the Battle of Jutland.

The large protected cruiser definitely had a place in the late-Victorian Royal Navy. The *Powerfuls* had a comparatively short active life not because they were unsuitable for their intended roles, but because the strategic situation and the Royal Navy's operational concepts changed between the beginning of the Boer War and the end of the Russo-Japanese War. That period saw growing mutual suspicion between Britain and Germany[4], and consequent realisation that the principal theatre of operations in a future naval war would be our Home Waters. An additional (but related) consideration is that Fisher, who became First Sea Lord in 1904, had little time for Protected Cruisers.[5]

One final criticism to be refuted is that the *Powerfuls* were 'the most extreme manifestation of the folly of building cruisers to match specific opponents', which is allegedly foolish because 'in practice the intended opponents never meet'. This doesn't stand up. Firstly because the pair weren't 'extreme', but a well-balanced design whose dimensions were determined largely by the requirements for seaworthiness, speed, endurance and effective armament. Secondly, because intended opponents may meet if some thought is given to cruiser deployment – the battles of the Falklands (1914) and the River Plate (1939) being examples.

'Broad beamed' Leander *class firgate* HMS Hermione*: a controversial nomination as a WWW.* (CPL)

HMS *Swift*

Definitely a candidate for the Prototype Defence. Fisher's requirement was for a destroyer capable of 36 knots in operational service, and it was necessary to build *Swift* to demonstrate that with current technology the requirement was unrealistic.

The original concept of a 36-knot version of the 'River' class hull was ruled out at an early stage. Designers and builders had learned from the *Cobra* debacle (now *there* was a WWW!) and insisted upon a hull large and strong enough to carry the necessary machinery and proceed at the required speed, the result was that even when only capable of about 34 knots in service the ship was too large and expensive to be procured in quantity. But that didn't make *Swift* a bad warship, let alone a WWW. She was a sound vessel, capable of 30 knots or more in a seaway and (as completed) well-armed. *Swift*'s only intractable faults were vulnerability of the extensive steam plant to action damage (she was only a 'demonstrator' – had more been built this could have been remedied) and poor endurance (a fault shared with the 'Tribals' – high-power direct-drive steam turbine machinery was extremely inefficient).

Swift was very active throughout the Great War. Initially with the Grand Fleet, but she was allegedly unable to cope with North Sea weather conditions – I suspect the real reason was poor endurance, but with Fisher back in the First Sea Lord's chair nobody liked to say so.[6] Then in Dover Command, where together with the similarly fast but 'short-legged' 'Tribals' she was employed in combat service for the duration. Hardly the mark of a genuine WWW!

HMS *Hood*

Having avoided the trap of comparing *Hood* with other Royal Navy battlecruisers, the ship was designed from the start as a fast battleship, armoured on the scale of the contemporary *Queen Elizabeth* class, Antony Preston's criterion for listing *Hood* is that she was built before all the Great War lessons had been identified and digested.

Had the ship been designed in the early 1920s she might indeed have been armoured on the 'all or nothing' principle (actually a pre-1914 idea, and there is not much *operational experience* to prove that it was sounder than the principles upon which the *Queen Elizabeths* were protected); and might indeed have been more like *Nelson* and *Rodney* (not exactly the RN's most successful battleships). But as things were *Hood* was intended for service during the Great War. Had it continued into 1919, as most political and military leaders expected, *Hood* would probably have joined the Fleet before the fighting ceased despite the design having been modified to incorporate certain lessons from Jutland.

That *Hood*'s protection against 'plunging' fire wasn't to the standard that would have been specified at a later date, and she was never modernised on the scale of the *Queen Elizabeths*, hardly makes her a WWW. It was of course acknowledged in the 1930s that *Hood* should be modernised, but due to pressure of circumstances and other work, that was never done. Even so it has never been *proved* that inadequate horizontal protection was the cause of *Hood*'s loss. Sometimes, in the heat of battle, terrible things happen.

Finally, concerning *Hood*, Antony Preston didn't mention what I consider the most serious design weakness. After the loss of *Audacious* in 1914 (Footnote 2) it would have been wise of the designers to carry to upper deck right aft to the stern, as in the *Nelsons*, *KGVs* and *Vanguard*. As things were *Hood* had little more freeboard at the quarterdeck than pre-war capital ships, and throughout her career 'wetness' aft was a considerable inconvenience.

To be replaced in the dustbin by...

Some duffers built for the Royal Navy between the Second World War and the Falklands Conflict, in descending order of awfulness:

***Leander* Class Frigates**

A controversial choice, perhaps, but I don't subscribe to the view that the *Leanders* were the finest post-war escort built for the RN or anyone else. The Type 12 (*Whitby* and *Rothesay* classes) was adequate as an ASW frigate for the 1950s, and a great improvement over wartime designs, but not sparkling. When the requirement arose for a general-purpose escort, to enter service in the early 1960s and have a service life of at least 20 years, we should have plumped for something somewhat larger than a Type 12 (on grounds of seakeeping, habitability, endurance, and being able to make significant upgrades without having virtually to rebuild the ships). But the RN got *Leander*, in her salient characteristics just a tidied-up version of *Rothesay* with a perfunctory nod toward acknowledging the air threat, and in the era of the anti-ship missile and nuclear submarines inadequate and obsolescent when she entered service. Subsequent (considerable) expenditure of imagination, effort and money could never redress those fundamental shortcomings of the design.

Type 42 Destroyers

In a moment of post-Imperial angst MOD(N) was conned by the Treasury into accepting that worthwhile savings could be made by putting expensive and complex equipment within a hull whose weight (steel is cheap) and enclosed volume (air is even cheaper) had been reduced to a minimum.

The result was indeed ships with impaired seaworthiness, cramped accommodation and working space, poor endurance, and limited scope for subsequent enhancement.[7] More seriously, and these are crucial reasons why the design should never have been accepted in the first place, the Type 42s were 'topweight-critical' from the start,[8] and in other respects unduly vulnerable to action damage[9].

A good many remedial steps have been taken since the Type 42 entered RN service – and especially since 1982 – but that doesn't affect the argument that *as designed and completed* the Type 42 had unacceptable weaknesses.

Type 14 Frigates

As a design exercise (the minimum-size ASW ship that can effectively hunt a fast submarine in average North Atlantic conditions, disregarding any other threats) the Type 14 would have been valuable. If one could plead the Prototype Defence they might just escape. But building a class of twelve proves somebody was really serious.

At the time of the Korean War, with memories of the Second World War still fresh, the RN planned and ordered frigates with no effective defence against air or surface-vessel attack – in fact without any weapon having a maximum effective range greater than 2000yds. Reversion to the traditional destroyer 'iron-deck aft of the bridge' layout was a mistake, considering that it had already been proven that it was better to carry the forecastle-deck back to the ASW-weapon area. They fared so badly in conditions which can be encountered in the North Atlantic that at least one was nearly lost through stress of weather on fishery patrol off Iceland; and for most of their lives they were employed in second-line or ASW-training roles. Widely mocked as 'futility' frigates, there was never any question of significant upgrading to meet developments in the perceived threat. How can these pathetic little ships have escaped the *WWW* List yet the Type 21s were included?

Type 42 destroyer HMS Gloucester*, a design 'that should never have been accepted'?* (CPL)

***Andreas Lüdke** from Germany takes up the baton, also arguing for a number of ships to be let off the hook, taking issue with some of Antony Preston's comments while endorsing others, and finally clearing up a little matter of semantics.*

Monitor was the right ship in the right place at the right time. She did founder in bad weather (in a place where she shouldn't have been – not her fault!), but this, cynical though it may sound, was no unusual fate in the 1860s. It is agreed that the USN, misinterpreted facts and learned the wrong lessons; but blaming her for having been too successful at Hampton Roads is quite unfair.

Although the points speaking against the *Borodino*'s design features are certainly convincing, one cannot hold the ships' performance at Tsushima against them. After the ordeal the Russian ships had been through and the condition they were in they should no longer be regarded as a fleet, but as a 'T' asking to be crossed. I doubt that British-designed vessels would have fared significantly better under the given circumstances.

The four-stacker DD's deserve better, too, though with reservations. Their crime was to come too late in the First World War to make their numbers bear, followed by a bout of block obsolescence for the rest of their lives.

Frontline units will always clamour for more and the situation in 1917 being what it was, those responsible simply had to freeze an existing design in order to just get anything done at all. With the benefit of hindsight one might come to different conclusions, but latter day historians are not faced with making decisions which might lose a war. My suggestion would be to exclude all four-stackers completed up to 1919, but retain the remainder. (By the way, why was there no large-scale cancellation like after the Second World War? Was there some small print in the building contracts?)

If, however, block obsolescence constitutes such a crime we should in all fairness include Type VII and IX U-boats as well as *Essex* class CV's, the former for getting their crews killed after 1943, the latter for all the expenses required to keep them going after 1945.

Antony Preston provides good arguments in his attempt to exonerate K-class subs, but please consider this: an operational requirement that necessitates the inclusion of large openings in a submarine while at the same time exposing it to conditions which positively invite collisions, ramming, and friendly fire is bordering on the criminal. The K-class are in the right book, steam or no steam.

While discussing criminal ideas I might as well turn to HTP-powered submarines. The very idea of using a propellant that 'reacts strongly' when coming into contact with seawater, and subjecting this stuff to rough handling by dockyard mateys and depth charge explosions is somewhat ludicrous at best and makes these craft worthy companions of the K's. Still I think they should not be included in *WWW*, because they weren't proper warships, but extensive feasibility studies. Most of them weren't even armed. As to ideas that look good on paper but fail to transform into successful warships, we should perhaps include all those hydrofoils and hovercraft of the past decades.

The *Yamatos*' main fault was their lack of air cover. Yet I can't blame her builders of not anticipating Midway and the rapid progress of radar. When they were conceived everybody else was planning new battleships too, so one cannot really blame the Japanese for going for the best. Sure, they were a doubtful expenditure of the taxpayer's money, but would the construction of half a dozen CV's in their stead have made a difference? As the Japanese couldn't even successfully hide their battleship construction one can safely assume that USN planners would have learned very early about CV building in the opponent's shipyards. They would have responded in kind, thus nullifying the element of surprise the Japanese were so eager to secure. As it is relatively easy to assess the size of a carrier's air group by simply looking at the ship, another element of surprise would have been lost.

On the other hand, the 18in gun was kept a secret until the end of the war. The Japanese loved having nasty surprises up their sleeve, and considering the performance of Zero fighters and Long Lance torpedoes, the 18in guns might have given good account of themselves under different circumstances.

So in the end they got steamrollered into obsolescence, but to include them in a 'worst'-list seems too unfair to me: 'White elephants they may have been, but magnificent white elephants all the same...'

Talking of white elephants I think there are some even whiter examples of this species. The French *Jean Bart*, a ship pressed upon a navy that never even wanted her in the first place and got rid of her ASAP. Or the German large cruiser SMS *Blücher*: she was built with 9in guns, because the navy staff were duped into expecting a similar calibre on the new British battlecruisers. Instead of including her in their own battlecruiser squadron the German High Command should have cut their losses and put the blame on the usual wily scheming of 'Perfidious Albion'. *Blücher*, however, could have been turned into the mother of all Imperial yachts.

The chapters on *Bismarck* and *Hood* came to me as a bit of a disappointment, if only because of just another (too) lengthy telling of the tale. The conclusion part is almost a bit of an add-on. *WWW* is, after all, aimed at a readership that has (hopefully) outgrown the reliance on bits of potted history that come with model kit assembly instructions. What justification is there for a list of countries visited in a book of technical analysis? As to *Bismarck*: her main fault seems to have been the inability to live up to the propagandistic exaggerations of both friend and foe. This hardly merits the inclusion in a list of 'lemons'.

True, her weak stern will rightfully keep her out of a list of really great designs, but the other points mentioned against her don't carry that much weight. Arming her with 6in secondary guns instead of a homogeneous HA/LA battery did make sense in the 1930s. While RN and USN battleships were only meant to beat off destroyer and aircraft attacks (apart from their other duties, of course), German battleships had the additional mission of commerce raiding. In an encounter with escorting cruisers, bent for a torpedo attack, something with more stopping power than a 5in and a higher rate of fire

The doomed Bismarck, *one of the few ships that all seem to agree is a WWW.* (CPL)

The Soviet Sverdlov *class cruiser* Aleksander Suvorov, *undeniably impressive to look at, but 'outdated while still on the drawing board'?* (CPL)

than a 15in would have been useful.

Furthermore, I perceive a certain inconsistency in the author's line of argument. Apparently the Admiralty had full knowledge of the particulars of *Bismarck*'s armour layout. They also had the construction plans of *Baden* and the opportunity of scrutinizing her after the First World War. Why then, one wonders, was *Tirpitz* held in such awe? Following Antony Preston's line, their Lordships should have said 'Come on, she's nothing but a repeat *Baden* with rakish lines - nothing to worry about, really!'

So, if *Bismarck* was so outdated a design (*Bayern* entered service in 1916!), pitting the equally elderly *Hood* against her cannot - even in retrospect - be seen as unsound thinking.

Reducing *Bismarck* to size is a good and perhaps long overdue idea. Unfortunately, the author is making an about-turn and inflates her all over again. By quoting contemporary British claims that she was some twenty years ahead of *Hood* he falls into the pit of painting a larger-than-life picture of the opponent's abilities he so aptly described in the foreword.

So, who else is to join the list? *Casco* class monitors, of course. Denny-class steam gunboats for not living up to expectations. *Sverdlov* class cruisers for being outdated while still on the drawing board. And German 6in gun destroyers, because their gun crews could not manhandle the heavy rounds in anything but calm weather.

When assessing warships one should also take a look at the workforce. Hence I'd like to include *Gorgon* and *Glatton* with their heat-retarding insulation of crumpled newspapers, and German Type XXI U-boats: any quality problems encountered in their construction were predictable, because one cannot expect slave labourers to take pride in a job well done.

Finally, let me add that *WWW* was a most enjoyable read indeed. I'd like to mention for the next (of, let's hope, many) reprints that 'Popovkas' is not a 'mutation'. In Russian 'Popovka', being a term of endearment, changes to 'Popovki' when used in the plural. Using an English plural in this context is quite legitimate.

From across the Atlantic **Philip Sims** *offers up an intriguing defence for the US 'flush-decker' destroyers, while arguing for the inclusion of the 'pathetic' battleships* Idaho *and* Mississippi *of 1906, as a politically driven waste of designers' time and taxpayers' money.*

The short lived monitor Glatton*, scuttled in Dover harbour after her 'insulation' caught fire.* (CPL)

Rating the 'Flush-Decker' Destroyers

While most of Anthony Preston's targets richly deserve to be on a 'World's Worst Warships' list, the inclusion of the 'Flush-Decker' Destroyers' is an anomaly. (I will leave it for others to challenge his inclusion of 'Civil War Monitors' – at least the first generation – but do note that, without them, my return address would be Arlington, VA, CSA!)

It is hard to think of any other class of ships that successfully served with nine contented users: the US Navy, the US Coast Guard, the Royal Navy, the Royal Canadian Navy, the Royal Norwegian Navy, the Russian Navy, the Imperial Japanese Navy, the Standard Fruit Company, and the United States Army. The USCG had six ships for prohibition patrols during the intra-war period. The Japanese ship was the captured DD 224 and three ships, sold into commercial service and modified to become high-speed banana carriers (DDs 287, 290, 295), were taken over by the Army for use as high-speed transports for carrying vital supplies to forward outposts.

Antony Preston's book mentions the conversions from fast torpedo attack ships (DD) to APD (high speed transports), DMS (high speed minesweeper), DM (light minelayer), and AVD (light seaplane tender). It is suggested that the use of conversions were forced into being due to the overhanging inventory of old destroyer hulls preventing new ships for those missions from being built. It is very difficult to convince navies to spend money on new ships for new missions until the value of that mission is first proven by fleet experience. Conversion of existing older hulls often provides that experience at low cost. There were additional odd modifications such a the DD 163 and DD 259 being converted to water barges YW-57 and YW-56 with three other ships being assigned as 'Light Targets'. The DD 259 was converted to CIC training ship IX-98. The record of successful role changes for the flush deck destroyers is unmatched by any other class of warships. The reason for so many useful mission changes was, in modern terms, the 'modular' nature of the original weapons layout. When the two large triple torpedo tubes on each side were unbolted and removed, the ships then had deck space, load carrying capacity and ability to accept vertical moment for a new mission. The new items could be located amidships and aft in a region of modest freeboard; this allowed fitting of boat davits or seaplane cranes or mine rails or sweeping gear or additional K guns for depth charges. A standard destroyer's configuration, with centreline torpedo tubes, was not nearly as adaptable.

The ships also had flexible, 'modular' machinery such that the USN and RN could remove various boilers and stacks for conversions. The RN replaced two forward boilers, sacrificing some top speed but still leaving them among the fastest convoy escorts during the Second World War, with fuel tanks and stores to make the ships suitable to serve as long range escorts.

A feature that is important in a warship, but rarely mentioned, is a tolerance for being laid up and then readily activated. The flush deckers were very storage tolerant and, being straightforward machines, the crews for them could be rapidly trained. Their simple, but still lethal, weapons did not become technologic orphans during a long period of layup (unlike modem electronics).

Antony Preston's thesis that 'the resources devoted to the *Wickes* and *Clemson* classes might have been better directed toward production of that 'austere' design so many people argued for' ignores the fact that the US tried both accelerating the existing DD production lines and starting a massive building program of the radically austere *Eagle* boats. The attempt to factory produce small-and-simple *Eagle* boats resulted in no new escorts in service before the Armistice. However, the Armistice was a surprise to most war planners who expected the war to last well into 1919 when the 'Scheer Program' would have resulted in the deployment of a large number of long-range U-boats. The large number of flush deck destroyers would have been needed as convoy escorts if the war reached into 1919.

The fact that flush deckers were seen as numerous peas-in-a-pod and as First World War leftovers was invaluable to Franklin Roosevelt as he presented reasons for the destroyers-for-bases deal: the 'over-age destroyers' are 'the same type of ship which we have been from time to time striking from the naval list and selling for scrap for, I think, $4,000 or

$5,000 per destroyer. On that basis, the cost of the right to lease seven naval and air bases is an extremely low one from the point of view of the United States Government i.e. about $2,500,000!'[10] If the ships had been perceived as newer and more valuable, it would have been even more difficult getting the swap past the isolationists. Of course, the ships given to the UK were not from the scrap line but those in-service which the USN filled with ammunition, spares and supplies. From the other side of the Atlantic, the view of the value of the flush deckers was a bit different. Admiral of the Fleet James Somerville's opinion was 'had there been no American 'four stacker' destroyers available and they not gone into service escorting trade convoy's when they did, the outcome of the struggle against the U-boat and the subsequent outcome of the European War itself might have been vastly different'.[11]

During WWII, the flush deck destroyers were awarded numerous Presidential Unit Citations (PUC). Thirteen ships received one PUC, one ship received two and the *Osman Ingram* and the *George E. Badger* each received three for being part of the USS *Bogue*'s hunter/killer team.[12] The definition of the award is 'The Navy Presidential Unit Citation is for extraordinary heroism in action against an armed enemy. The unit must have accomplished its mission under such extremely difficult and hazardous conditions to set it apart from and above other units participating in the same campaign. The degree of heroism required is the same as that which would be required for award of a Navy Cross to an individual.'[13] The key words for evaluating a ship's value are 'accomplished its mission'.

The Navy Unit Citation (NUC) is a lesser award than a PUC but is for 'any ship...which, subsequent to December 6, 1941, distinguished itself by outstanding heroism in action against the enemy'.[14] The NUC was awarded to 17 different flush deckers with one ship (USS *Kitty*, APD 15) getting 19 total, the last one being awarded for action on 7 May 1945.[15] The spring of 1945 is well after the US Navy's Second World War building program had produced large numbers of new ships of all types. The obvious question is 'what was a 'worst warship' doing in heavy combat that far forward, if many better ships are available?' The answer is that they still met the military need.

The flush deck destroyers were numerous, tolerant to mothballing, highly adaptable, and useful to nine different owners. They saved England and fought in the Pacific from first to last. The flush deck destroyers actually belong on the short list of the 'World's Best Warships'.

The Runts of the Litter: *Idaho* and *Mississippi* of 1903

USN battleships had grown in size and combat power over decade in since the Spanish-American War, resulting in the 16,000 ton *Connecticut* class. The perceived huge size of the new ships caused worries in Congress on their expense and, within the navy, on being able to afford sufficient numbers to cover the needed stations. Theoreticians like Captain A T Mahan also thought that more numerous smaller battleships gave a better return on investment. The 1903 budget called for three more *Connecticuts* and two limited-displacement ships of 13,000 tons. Several design options were studied but 'Line officers uniformly expressed their disappointment at what could be obtained on 13,000 tons'.[16] The chosen ship design severely squeezed every other feature of the ship in order to carry almost as much armament as the 16,000 ton ships. The result was the *Mississippi* class, of 13,000 tons. These ships show what a naval architect will do in order to reduce displacement while maintaining armament. First of all, the designer cut the hull length resulting in a crowded topside, then cut the freeboard aft resulting in a wetter ship. A shorter hull length and less freeboard made the ship more vulnerable to underwater damage. The armour belt was thinned. Propulsion power and fuel load were reduced which resulted in a slower, shorter-ranged ship. A lighter and shorter ship inevitably has worse seakeeping; the ships were also reported to be bad rollers.

One history of the First World War era battleships summarises the results: 'They were 3000 tons smaller than the preceding *Connecticuts*, and had only two thirds of their power, yet attempted to carry nearly as heavy an armament. Not surprisingly the *Idaho* and *Mississippi* proved unsatisfactory in service'.[17]

The Navy didn't know what to do with them, because if they operated with the big ships of the main fleet, their tactical limitations on speed, range, seakeeping and vulnerability would set the battleline's limitations. They were, what is called in modem terms, a 'force de-multiplier' - their addition to the battle group decreased the performance of all the ships operating together. The First World War semi-battlecruiser *Blücher* was such a ship and was deservedly left behind at Dogger Bank.

The *Mississippi* (BB-23), delivered in 1909, actually participated in some useful activities, notably in May of 1912 transporting a detachment from the 2d Marine Regiment to El Cuero, Cuba to protect American interests. In 1912 the *Mississippi* was assigned to the Atlantic Fleet Reserve and then assigned, in December 1913, duty as 'aeronautic station ship' to support forces ashore rebuilding the naval air station at Pensacola, Fla. A service career of only fours years between being commissioned as a new battleship and assigned to duty as a berthing barge has to be a record. With the outbreak of fighting in Mexico, *Mississippi* deployed to Vera Cruz to serve as a base for seaplanes. The ship supported nine reconnaissance flights over an 18 day period. On 21 July 1914, the *Mississippi* was turned over to the Royal Hellenic Navy at Newport News Virginia to become the *Lemnos*.[18]

The *Idaho*'s USN career was even less eventful. She participated in various training exercises but her last trip was to Villefranche, France to decommission on 30 July 1914 for hand over to the Greek Navy to become their *Kilkis*.

The Greeks needed the ships because of an on-going arms race with their Turkish rivals, which the Turks had started in 1912 by allowing public speculation of an imminent order from Britain of three modern battleships each armed with ten 13.5in guns. The Royal Hellenic Navy responded in 1913 with an order for eight 14in gun battlecruisers from Germany and there was later speculation about an order of a *Lorraine* type battleship. The Turks jumped the gun by acquiring an already under-construction Brazilian battleship, in addition to one already under order for themselves. The Greeks felt they needed interim ships to counter the imminent arrival of the Turkish battleship. For operations in the Aegean Sea, the small ship disadvantages of the *Mississippi* class's reduced speed, range and freeboard did not matter as much and the US Navy was willing to sell them immediately at a low price.

The pro-German attitude of the King of Greece led to a major show of naval force by the neutral nations near Salamis in September 1916 and, in October, the seizure of the Greek fleet. The *Lemnos* and the *Kilkis* were demilitarised. After Greece joined the Allies in July 1917, the two ships were used by the Greek Navy as depot and training ships, and so, sat out the rest of the war.

In 1919, the *Lemnos* was allowed to at least to pretend to be part of the victory and show the flag at Constantinople.

The fate of the class in Greek service after 1918 can be traced in *Jane's Fighting Ships* from the era. In 1919 the ships 'can make only 12 kts now'. In 1920, it was stated that 'they will probably go on the Sale List in 1921'. In 1924, the word was 'It is understood that proposals for reconstruction of the two ships are under consideration'. The 1925 edition reported 'These two ships are now being reboilered at Piraeus'. *Jane's* 1926 reported progress: '*Kilkis* was recently re-boilered at Piraeus; *Lemnos* is now in hand'. The works completion was recorded in 1927. In 1929, the *Kilkis* was listed as a Gunnery and Navigation School Ship but, in the 1930 edition, both ships had disappeared from the Greek Navy section. The 9,500 ton armoured cruiser *Averoff* became the largest ship in the Greek Navy. The two battleships remained permanently in harbour (*Lemnos* disarmed and used as accommodation ship, *Kilkis* remaining armed as a training ship) in the 1930s. They were both sunk in harbour during April 1941 by German and Italian bombers and scrapped in place after the war.

The *Mississippi* class of 1908 deserve to be included on any list of the World's Worst Warships. They were unwanted by the Navy that built them (due to inadequate performance), purchased by a desperate smaller navy and were interned to uselessly sit out the First World War. After the war, the Greek Navy found them to have unreliable boilers and quietly hulked them when they were only 22 years old. One last set of indignities was reserved for the poor ships when Second World War losses were listed in the 1946 edition of *Jane's*. The *Lemnos* did not rate being mentioned at all. The *Kilkis*, sunk by dive bombers, was listed as an 'Anti-Aircraft Port Defense Ship', total failure in her last mission.

Next, Warship *designer* ***Stephen Dent*** *throws his hat into the ring.*

I found this an engrossing book – wide ranging, thoughtful, and thought-provoking on several levels. It has many strengths, not least the fact that since the author is very much an establishment figure, when he attacks the establishment (for example – particularly relevant at the moment – incorrect or selective use of intelligence material) his criticisms really carry genuine weight.

But, since part of the book's intention (inferred more than stated) is to encourage debate, I'm happy to join in and disagree with some of Antony Preston's choices as 'bad' warships.

To begin with, when just about every French battleship up until the *Dunkerque* and *Strasbourg* in the 1930s was, frankly, rather poor (and even they were far from perfect, as John Jordan lucidly pointed out in *Warship 1999-2000*), it does seem a bit harsh to lambast the *Normandies*, which weren't even completed, and the *Borodinos*, which were not even French. Naval historians could deliver a pretty devastating broadside of criticism against just about any French battleship from *Redoutable* onwards (though, to be fair they were just about the bizarre looking collection of vessels ever built).

While Antony Preston lists some of the various factors that can *contribute to* a ship being bad he leaves it a bit more open as to exactly what actually *defines* a WWW. Taking it as read that by definition a warship is meant to be dangerous to her enemies and potential enemies, I'd suggest that one criteria for a WWW has to be whether she is also dangerous to her own crew, possibly even more so than to her foes. HMS *Captain* seems to fulfil this particularly well, being pretty much a disaster waiting to happen.

All of which leads neatly into the controversial subject of the battlecruiser. There is no doubt that *Courageous*, *Glorious* and *Furious* (in their original guises) merit inclusion, as being the absolute extreme of this whole debatable concept. I believe that one factor (albeit a minor one) in the loss of HMS *Campania* in 1918 was that when she dragged her anchor and collided with *Glorious*, the officers on the latter had grave difficulty in getting a prompt response from a jaded, fed up crew. While months of incredibly tedious inaction must have been one cause of this, I can't help but wonder whether serving on a ship, which after Jutland must have been clear to everybody was a potential death trap, may have been another. Knowing that the chances of surviving any serious action were pretty low cannot have done a lot for morale. Hence an indolent, surly bunch of seamen.

But should *Courageous*, *Glorious* and *Furious* really be in there, and likewise *Hood* (regardless of whether or not she was really a 'fast battleship' – I'm not aware of too many people referring to her as that at the time), or would a more deserving candidate as a 'worst warship' be the originator of the whole battlecruiser idea, the *Invincible*? Recently there have been a number of 'revisionist' studies suggesting that the battlecruiser wasn't such a bad concept after all, and blaming the catastrophic loss of three of them at Jutland on explosion of unstable and improperly stored propellant. While clearly this was the case, it does rather ignore the fact that the explosions had to occur as a result of enemy shellfire penetrating to where the propellant was stored, and this cuts right to the root of the whole concept of 'eggshells armed with hammers'.

I'm delighted that Antony Preston didn't include the much derided *Blücher* in his book, for it has always seemed to me that she represented far closer to what the battlecruiser – or 'Dreadnought cruiser', to perhaps be more accurate – should have been – i.e. taking the basic 'Dreadnought' concept of uniform main armament, and applying it to the armoured cruisers of the day. Designers don't deliberately set out to produce bad ships, and those who came up with *Blücher* can't have been total imbeciles – they must have been working on what seemed to be the logical progression of the armoured cruiser concept in the light of what else was going on in naval construction at the time. Her detractors can point to her loss in the first major engagement in which she took part, when she was up against British battlecruisers with far greater gun power, but is this really the fault of her design, or of the fact that the emergence of the 'classic' battlecruiser had resulted in the creation of a completely false tactical doctrine, of these heavily armed but lightly armoured ships slugging it out with each other, with predictably catastrophic results?

Prior to Dogger Bank the British battle cruisers had scored two notable successes at Heligoland Bight and the Falklands, but both of these were against much weaker foes (and indeed at the latter battle the *Scharnhorst* and *Gneisenau* had shown notable ruggedness despite taking terrible punishment), creating a false sense of security which the spectacular photographs of the *Blücher's* demise only served to reinforce.

Suppose, instead of battlecruisers armed with the guns of battleships but still with the protection of cruisers, development had carried on along the lines of 'all-big-gun' armoured cruisers (and indeed, as D K Brown has pointed out in *The Grand Fleet*, during 1907-8 the RN did look at the idea of 15,000 ton armoured cruisers, with eight 9.2in guns[19]), then surely tactics would have evolved in a different and far less potentially cataclysmic direction, with such ships operating in a more traditional cruiser fashion, and getting out of the way when the big guns of the battle fleets came into play. If they had found themselves engaged in battle with their opposite numbers, it would have been against ships that they were far better able to stand up to. I suppose it would have meant a more cautious approach to battle tactics, and I suppose *Scharnhorst* and *Gneisenau* might have taken even longer to succumb, but I can't imagine that such considerations would have unduly bothered the unfortunate crews of *Indefatigable*, *Invincible* and *Queen Mary*. (Granted, when the *Queen Elizabeth* class came along they'd have rendered such cruisers obsolete overnight, but then they effectively did that to the battlecruiser anyway.) I've long thought that it was a strange idea from Fisher (to balance, to be fair, his many good ones), and one which should have been seen through much earlier than it was. So I would nominate the *Invincible* and her two sisters as 'worst warships', for being the progenitors of the whole fatally flawed line.

However, there are other candidates for this dubious honour. How about the two Japanese 'battleship/carriers' *Ise* and *Hyuga*? I have to admit rather mixed feelings about suggesting these two since, from the moment I first saw a picture of *Ise*, they have always been just about my favourite ships, for the simple reason that they were so utterly bizarre looking. But, really, what on earth were the IJN thinking of when they decided to convert them? They effectively ruined two perfectly acceptable battleships, but in no way gained anything like two even half usable carriers. I know this was partly because of problems with the production of the aircraft intended to operate from them, but even if they had got this right, what were they actually intending to do with the ships? The conversion of the *Mogami* makes rather more sense, in the light of the obvious success of the *Tone* and *Chikuma* as aircraft carrying cruisers, but they had the advantage of decent speed, which the battleships certainly did not. *Hyuga* had lost a turret in an accident, but this is hardly the most compelling reason for the total conversion of her and her sister. If operating aircraft was meant to become their primary role, then there was no way they could have a place in the traditional battle line, so their main armament became effectively redundant. If they were supposed to remain viable as battleships then the air conversion just pointlessly diminished their fighting power, and made them much more vulnerable to damage or even sinking.

Perversely I suppose the one thing that can be said for *Ise* and *Hyuga* was that by their conversion they may well have been spared being part of the force that met its end in the Surigao Strait in 1944. So, assuming that most of their crews got off when they were sunk/semi-sunk in the sum-

The German 'semi-battlecruiser' Blücher, *unfairly derided and 'the mother of all Imperial yachts'.* (CPL)

mer of 1945, I guess they served some purpose, albeit indirectly, in saving the lives of a lot of young men who were then able to play their part in rebuilding their country after it had reached a devastated nadir. I'm sure that not too many of them will have seen it like that at the time, and I'm certain that was not the intention of whoever decided on the conversion in the first place. Whatever, they just produced two badly designed ships. But I am rather glad that they did.

What about the British submarine *X-1*? Apparently she was the only RN vessel to be built after the First World War and scrapped before the Second. As unenviable records go, that takes some beating. Regardless of the problems with her propulsion plant, she was surely again a totally flawed concept, right from the start. Why did no one see through it more quickly?

Finally, sticking my neck out a very long way indeed, how about the *Dreadnought* herself? My argument is that presumably one of the aims of a successful warship is to be sufficiently powerful and intimidating that any potential enemy takes one look and decides that perhaps annoying the owner of that particular warship wouldn't really be a terribly good idea. In other words, the basic concept of deterrence. It can be argued that *Dreadnought*, far from achieving this, actually fanned the flames of Anglo-German rivalry, by giving fresh impetus to the naval arms race that was one of the underlying causes of the First World War. (The counter argument is that something of her ilk was imminent anyway, and that by building first Britain managed to acquire a lead which she was able to hold on to until the High Seas Fleet was safely shut up in Scapa Flow a decade and a half later.) As a deterrent, she really wasn't very successful; a pertinent and slightly alarming comment on the overall concept. However, I am rather moving out of the narrow field of naval architecture, and into broader ones of politics, philosophy and mass psychology, which really are beyond the realms of this debate. So I think I'll stick with HMS *Invincible* as my nomination for 'Worst Warship'.

It seems only appropriate, since **Eur Ing David K Brown, RCNC** *has contributed to every edition of* Warship *since the very first, for him to round off the discussion (at least until next year…).*

Antony Preston lists six factors that have a major influence on ship design:

Cost
Perceived threat
Industrial capacity
Design competence (including, I hope, experience, so lacking today)
The operating environment
Incorrect post-battle analysis

I would agree with all these but add 'available weapon systems'.

He then reminds readers that a ship is the largest mobile structure on the planet (and warships are, today the most expensive single artefact in the defence budget). This leads to the view that warship design is a highly professional business and there is no place for the amateur, instanced by the capsize of the *Captain* and the claims made for the 'short, fat frigate'. I cannot resist quoting from the response by the Italian designer Brin to an amateur design by the German Kaiser: 'The ship which your Majesty has designed would be the mightiest, most terrible, and also the loveliest battleship ever seen….This wonderful vessel has only one fault; if she were ever put into the water she would sink like a lump of lead'!

The score for 'worsts', by nationality is USN 6, RN 10, Russia 4, Austria 1, France 3, Sweden 1, Germany 3, Italy 1, Japan 3. This suggests that the number of errors is roughly proportional to the number of designs. Included in the catalogue of errors are a number of popular favourites, notably *Bismarck*. There is a general tendency to overestimate the capability of the potential enemy and Antony Preston frequently criticises 'Intelligence services'. I think he is a little unfair as intelligence, if it is to be of value, must usually present a 'worst case' scenario. It is then up to the Staff to add a pinch of salt.

Opinions will differ. One or two ships in the book are close to my own list of 'best' designs, but it is to be hoped that the book will provoke serious debate. It is, perhaps, even more difficult to select a similar number of best designs but this, too, is important. In the euphoria of success it is all too easy to miss the lessons and sometimes the margin between success and disaster is very fine. (Perhaps the K-class submarines are an example of this fine margin)

I will attempt to summarise Antony's views on the problems of his 10 RN ships (with occasional dissenting views).

Captain's failure was design incompetence by Lairds following Coles' unsound concept. One may see

HMS Indomitable: *with her sister ships* Invincible *and* Inflexible *a not unexpected nomination. (CPL)*

Powerful, *Swift* and, possibly *Courageous* as follies of grandeur. It is no coincidence that the latter two derived from Fisher concepts: bigger and faster regardless of the cost.

My studies of *Polyphemus* suggest that she was primarily an armoured torpedo boat and that the ram was a minor afterthought (though Froude's model tests on the shape of the ram may be seen as the origin of the bulbous bow). In almost all successful torpedo attacks in the nineteenth century the victim was stationary making the slow speed of her torpedoes less important. (I believe that she was intended as part of the RN plan to attack the French fleet in Cherbourg harbour).

Hood and, to a lesser extent, *Implacable* suffered from major, last minute design changes and it would have been 'better' to start afresh. However, both were built in the middle of a war and it may have been justifiable to press on rather that wait another two years for a better design. *Implacable*'s low upper hangar could only hold Seafires. These were never very good FAA aircraft though the Pacific fleet overcame some of their problems.

The K-class submarines suffered from problems over their role and also from technical faults. The need for a fast fleet submarine was perceived into the 1930s and cannot be dismissed as nonsense. The technical problems such as low freeboard forward, water entering the boiler room on the surface down air intakes and even funnels were largely solved in the last, *K-26*. (Scotts deserve some credit for their *Swordfish*, an earlier steam submarine, whose retractable funnel was adapted for the Ks). If one or two prototypes had been built these problems would have been ironed out. HTP submarines could probably have been made to work safely but the effort was not worthwhile once nuclear power was proven.

As for the Type 21, Whitehall thought they were getting a very cheap *Leander* equivalent (I am assured that Vospers never quoted £3.5 million), perhaps they transgressed the rule that one does not design second rate ships. They were old fashioned in armament as built but were well liked, perhaps because of their fine accommodation for both officers and men. Their speed increased by 1.5 knots once I arranged for a transom flap to be fitted to *Avenger*. The problem with the aluminium structure was primarily fatigue. A major failure in the aluminium could throw an unacceptable load on the steel hull.

Many major advances are made as a result of studies into what went wrong and for this reason the book is of great value (and very readable). Lessons from success tend to be more difficult and problems arise in the design of a batch II when the reasons for the success of the batch I are forgotten. This book is essential reading for young Staff officers and Constructors. It should provoke heated argument in the mess.

Notes:

1 This pertains primarily to frigates, destroyers, cruisers etc. Submariners, Naval Aviators, Mine Warfare specialists etc might see things differently.

2 Consider the losses of the 'Super-Dreadnought' HMS *Audacious* (mined, 1914) and the aircraft carrier HMS *Ark Royal* (torpedoed, 1941). In each case the ship was hit just once, in the machinery spaces, and the weather was fairly benign. Both sank after remaining afloat several hours, in each case due to comparatively slow flooding which nonetheless couldn't be pumped out. It had been a lesson from the 1914-18 War that ships should have some petrol/diesel generators, in order to provide electrical power for pumps etc., should the steam supply to turbo-generators fail as a result of action damage: *Ark Royal* had been designed with two diesel generators for that very reason, but unfortunately it was later decided to replace them with higher-capacity turbo-generators.

3 Among 'naval professionals' I would include naval officers and naval constructors, and also commercial designers and builder of warships.

4 See A Marder's *British Naval Policy 1880-1905*, pp.544-5.

5 *Ibid.*, p.490.

6 Bear in mind that it had been stipulated for the 'M' class destroyers (1913-14 Programmes), admittedly not by Fisher, but very much in line with his thinking, that speed was more important than endurance. Wartime operational experience soon disproved that.

7 See Antony Preston's comments in the UK section of *Conway's All The World's Fighting Ships 1947-1995*.

8 'Topweight-critical' does not mean the ship has inadequate stability in its normal operating condition, but that a comparatively small reduction of Metacentric Height will unacceptably impair stability.

9 *Sheffield* was knocked out during the Falklands Conflict by a single Exocet missile, a weapon which the RN itself had procured before *Sheffield* was completed, but against which she was virtually defenceless. This was not a 'lucky' hit. The missile hit more or less exactly where one would expect an Exocet to strike, and despite the fact that the warhead didn't explode caused a major fire and severed the fire main and the main electrical power cables.

10 Philip Goodhart *Fifty Ships that Saved the World*, (Doubleday & Company, Inc., Garden city, New York, 1965) pp.179, 183.

11 John D Alden, *Flush Decks and Four Pipes*, (United States Naval Institute, Annapolis, 1965), p.23.

12 *Ibid.*, p.97.

13 "Grunt" Web page at http://www.gruntsmilitary.com/npresunit.shtml. 'Navy Unit Citation' at http://members.aol.com/dischargecert/nuc.htm#isr

14 *Ibid.*

15 Alden, pp.97-99.

16 Norman Friedman, *U.S. Battleships; An Illustrated Design History*, (Naval Institute Press, Annapolis), pp.45-46.

17 Anthony Preston, *Battleships of World War I*, (Galahad Books, New York City), p.165.

18 Details of both ships USN service from 'The Dictionary of American Naval Fighting Ships', http://www.hazegray.org/danfs/

19 David K Brown RCNC, *The Grand Fleet: Warship Design and Development 1906-1922*, (Chatham Publishing, London, 1999).

NAVAL BOOKS OF THE YEAR

Robert Budd & Phillip Gummet (eds.)
Cold War, Hot Science: Applied Research in Britain's Defence Laboratories 1945-1990
Science Museum, 2002
445 pages, 54 illustrations
PB Price £34.95
ISBN 1 90074 747 2

Warship readers will probably turn to the chapter covering naval R & D by Tom Wright, who chooses to concentrate on aircraft carriers and nuclear submarines. There is a list of 'ship' orientated R & D establishments, which reminds me of a meeting called by the first DG Ships of the heads of his research laboratories. There was one too many for the seats as the Admiralty Distilling laboratory had been forgotten, as has Wright. (It was on Portland breakwater and distilled fresh water.) His point is valid; in the early post war years there were too many small establishments.

The section on submarines concentrates on noise reduction and is basically correct though propeller noise was mainly due to pressure fluctuations at blade rate rather than cavitation. His account implies happy co-operation between ARL, AEW (Wright interprets AEW as Admiralty Experimental Works quoting his PhD thesis in support of his error. Since I was his examiner, I can assure you that he got it right (Experiment) in his thesis) and AUWE which, regrettably, was only true in the later years.

He is correct in emphasising the shock in 1957 when the USS *Nautilus* participated in the RN exercise Rum Tub. Even those who had read reports of nuclear submarine performance were staggered by the reality. Machinery silencing is covered adequately. While accepting that one cannot cover everything I feel that some mention should have been made of other work. There is little mention of AEW's work on surface ship propellers which gave the RN a 10 year lead in quiet propellers over other navies which included Connolly's work on propeller strength. Then submarine control (Booth) and seakeeping (Lloyd) deserve mention and, above all, Kendrick's work on pressure hull strength was vital to US designs as well as British.

There is another 'naval' chapter by Eric Grove on Command and Control in which the British contribution was notable though, perhaps, swamped by USN efforts in later years.

However, there is much of interest in the non-naval chapters. I started to list those I found particularly interesting but that would be unkind to the others. The first two chapters deal respectively with fixed wing and rotary wing aircraft work. One is left with the impression that the former, almost entirely 'in house' at RAE went very well while industry performed less well on the latter. Ground to air defence is followed by AFV when from a poor wartime base, the UK led the world in tank design (including weapons) for many years.

The next two chapters cover infra red and radar. There are chapters on lasers and on chemical and biological warfare. The chapter on physiological research refers to the Talbot committee on life saving which estimate that of 30,000 fatal casualties in the RN, two thirds got into the water and died there for lack of sound life saving gear.

Finally, there is a chapter on organisation. This reviewer has strong views on the subject having spent much of his career in this sort of work and, since retirement been a consultant to the Trinity House R & D committee and much of this book confirms his views (Prejudices). Initially, there were too many small laboratories, often quarrelling. Some rationalisation was needed but centralisation went too far. Too often one was faced with the argument that electronic warfare was more important than seakeeping and the latter should be dropped. 'Priority' is a word which confuses, it can mean urgency or importance and they are not the same. Finally, several chapters support the view that a successful team should have some ability to freelance (in the mid-1970s 10 per cent was seen as a guide line for unplanned work).

This is an expensive book but those involved in the initiation or direction of research should read and ponder on every word. Many others will just enjoy it.

Eur Ing David K Brown, RCNC

Joel C E Blamey DSC DSM
A Submariner's Story: The Memoirs of a Submarine Engineer in Peace and War
Periscope Publishing, 2002
278 pages
14 photographs
PB Price £17.99
ISBN 1 90438 102 2

Originally written as a private manuscript for the benefit of his family, this fascinating book is an account of Joel Blamey's 28-year career as a submarine engineer in the Royal Navy. Commencing when he was first conscripted into the branch from general service in 1926, the narrative follows the author's duties in various roles as he progressed from Engine Room

Artificer (ERA) through to Engineering Officer. During this extended period he witnessed the development of the submarine from relative infancy until its assumption of the status of the new capital ship, retiring not long before the advent of nuclear propulsion. For this reason alone, his story is an invaluable record of the evolution of the Royal Navy's submarine arm.

In fact, *A Submariner's Story* is far more than this, with the author's stated intention of keeping his chronicle as non-technical as possible being reflected by an engaging writing style that makes it difficult to put down. Given his length of service, Joel Blamey came into contact with many famous submariners in the course of his career and it is especially interesting to read his impressions of them. At the same time, his professional occupation as an engineer ensures that the text is not totally devoid of references to submarine technology, with the practical difficulties of maintaining often complex and temperamental equipment in cramped, environmentally hostile conditions coming in for particular note.

Whilst the author's initial peacetime service between the wars was not without incident, it is inevitably his wartime years, spent largely at sea, that makes for the most compelling reading. During this time he saw active service against all three of the major Axis powers, including three and a half years in the mine laying submarine *Porpoise*. Converted to carry fuel and ammunition to the besieged island of Malta, *Porpoise* was involved in many hazardous operations, being particularly fortunate to survive a depth charge attack that damaged her main batteries and left her unable to dive whilst operating far into enemy waters. A subsequent, last minute transfer to the submarine *Strongbow* to replace its sick Engineering Officer resulted in a move to the Eastern Fleet and another close escape from death following a severe attack from a particularly aggressive Japanese escort group off the coast of Sumatra. The conclusion of the War did not bring an end to the dangers faced by the submariner. For example, a collision with an underwater pinnacle during exercises in *Sidon* off the west coast of Scotland demonstrates that such mishaps are not only the prerogative of the modern Navy.

A Submariner's Story presents a unique inside view of life in the Royal Navy's submarine service from an engineer's perspective. It is an essential acquisition for anybody with a specific interest in submarine operations and an entertaining read for the more general enthusiast.

Conrad Waters

Richard Hough
Admirals in Collision
First published 1959
Reprinted 2003
174 pages, illustrated
PB Price £14.99
ISBN 1 90438 113 8

Dreadnought: A History of the Modern Battleship
Introduction by C S Forester
First published 1965
Reprinted 2003
268 pages, illustrated
PB Price £22.99
ISBN 1 90438 111 1

The Big Battleship
First published 1966
Reprinted 2003
167 pages, illustrated
PB Price £14.99
ISBN 1 90438 114 6

Falklands 1914: the pursuit of Admiral von Spee
First published 1969
Reprinted 2003
173 pages, illustrated
PB Price £14.99
ISBN 1 90438 112 X

All published by Periscope Publishing, 33 Barwis Terrace, Penzance, Cornwall. TR18 2AW www.periscopepublishing.com

With the untimely death of Richard Hough in 1999 Britain lost one of her most popular, readable and prolific naval historians. He had written over a hundred books (admittedly not all on naval subjects), and while many of his better-known works remain available, others have been out of print for some time. Now Periscope Publishing, who have hitherto largely concentrated on books and videos relating to diving, have commendably taken the plunge and reprinted four that have been hard to get for far too long.

While the basic facts of the story of the protracted birth of the great ship that was to become HMS *Agincourt* are well known, in *The Big Battleship* Hough goes into it in real depth, uncovering a labyrinthine tale which amongst other things proves that controversy over arms sales, far from being a relatively recent phenomenon afflicting governments who go about proclaiming an 'ethical foreign policy' and then getting pilloried for their frequent departures from this stance, happened even back in the sure, certain days of Empire. (The difference being that the disputes were more often based on matters like payment than on moral questions.) It is quite extraordinary stuff, full of evocative descriptions of pre-First World War Tyneside, a collection of decidedly colourful characters, and some serious and unexpectedly widespread political wrangling. The ship's brief and not really terribly active career is relegated to little more than an afterthought to the epic tale of her conception and creation, with its dramatic culmination of her being seized at gun point from her owners.

Hough's ability to bring to life characters and events from the past in vivid manner is equally well demonstrated in *Admirals in Collision*, the rather better known story of the collision between the Mediterranean Fleet battleships *Victoria* and *Camperdown* in 1893, and the subsequent court martial and enquiry. Also apparent here is his rare talent in making the most arcane of naval matters, in this case the complexities of manoeuvring on exercise, totally comprehensible to the lay reader. Doubtless in the fullness of time someone will write an account of HMS *Nottingham*'s recent embarrassing (though, fortunately, not fatal for either the ship or any of her crew) collision with a rock in the south Pacific, but it will be quite a book if it is as good a read as this. It should be noted with all three of these titles that they were written a good few years back, so Hough didn't have the benefit of much recent research. Balancing that, however, he did have the immense advantage of still being able to interview people who had been present at the events described.

'The Pursuit of von Spee' was originally the title of what is here presented as *Falklands 1914*, a name which has a good deal more contemporary resonance. It is debatable whether this change of title was really necessary, but if not, it is a minor quibble, for this is again a fine piece of historical writing. The German East Asiatic Squadron's brief, action packed wartime career and its violent demise are recounted in lucid, often harrowing, fashion. As with all his naval history, Hough never loses sight of the fact that these vessels were crewed by people just as real as their opponents in the Royal Navy. As such, the account of the final action off the Falklands makes particularly grim reading, and the fact that the few surviving German officers then had to sit down to dinner with their vanquishers seems today more than just a little sickening.

However, there are criticisms of all three volumes. The printing of the covers is rather gloomy, and certainly won't help to sell the books, while the back cover of *Admirals in Collision* features the inexcusable error of spelling Admiral Tryon as 'Tyron'. (It should be added that this is not the first instance that this mistake has been made, and doubtless it won't be the last either.) But by and large the slightly 'budget' production values work fine, for although the reproduction of the illustrations could perhaps have been a bit better, they are only a minor element of these books. (Though it is a pity is that the captions in *Admirals in Collision* tend to disappear down the gutter.) Where this whole approach does have a more widespread negative impact is in *Dreadnought*, where, it being a large format, illustrated history, the photographs (a fine, diverse selection) are of much greater importance, and sadly too many of them have lost quality in reproduction. *Dreadnought* is a straightforward, non-technical (Hough was a narrative, not a technical, historian) history of the twentieth century battleship, and seldom deviates from the conventionally accepted line on subjects like how good the *Panzerschiff*, *Bismarck* or *Tegetthof* actually were, or whether *Tiger* was inspired by *Kongo*. He does equivocate on whether or not the basic battlecruiser concept was sound, and makes the unusual but engaging observation that Fisher would have absolutely loved the American *Alaskas*. The whole thing is immensely readable, and as an introduction to its subject *Dreadnought* remains hard to beat.

It is very sad that Richard Hough died at such an early age, for had he lived longer then doubtless he would have produced more books as good as these, and with history as popular a subject as it is at the moment they would have sold well too. As it is, it does seem odd that a more mainstream publisher hadn't snapped these titles up some time ago. Still, that is their loss, and indisputably Periscope's (and our) gain.

Stephen Dent

Ross Watton
Anatomy of the Ship: The Cruiser *Belfast*
Conway Maritime Press, 2003
120 pages, heavily illustrated
HB Price £25.00
ISBN 0 85177 956 5

The cruiser HMS *Belfast*, completed in August 1939, was mined that November and broke her back. She could have been a CTL but a 26-month reconstruction at Devonport put her back into service in time to join in the sinking of the German battlecruiser *Scharnhorst* on Boxing Day 1943. After service off in Normandy in 1944 *Belfast* joined the British Pacific Fleet. She spent her remaining career mainly in the Far East and provided NGS during the Korean War. After a major refit at Devonport 1956-59 when she received an enclosed bridge, she returned to the Far East as flagship until June 1962. She finally paid off in 1970, the last Second World War cruiser in commission since when she has been preserved (not 'museum

ship', please) in London. This latest re-issued 'Anatomy of the Ship' title provides full technical data on the ship, 22 pages of photographs and 90 pages of perspective and 3-view drawings of the hull, machinery, weapons systems and equipment, right down to the admiral's bunk covered with one those ubiquitous Pusser's blue-grey covers bearing the big Admiralty anchor which had got very thin by the 1970s and never kept you warm. This work will gladden the heart of the dedicated rivet counter and devoted model-maker.

Lawrence Phillips

Peter Beisheim (ed.)
Building Model Warships of the Iron and Steel Era
Chatham Publishing, 2002
144 pages, heavily illustrated
HB Price £20.00
ISBN 1 86176 129 5

Warships have always been popular subjects for a model. Today, with the considerably increased availability of authentic and official plans (albeit at quite a cost from some sources) of iron and steel warships, their popularity has increased even more. Concurrent with this has been a marked advance in the quality and standard of workmanship found on these models. Modern materials and continuing improvements in power plants and radio control equipment have all played their part, with the result that there is little difference nowadays between the standard and quality of detail on a static showcase scale model and a scale working model.

To demonstrate this, Peter Beisheim, himself a first class model-maker, has brought together nine expert builders of warship models, to describe their particular approach to the type of model which they build, and to touch on their methods (lack of space precludes more details).

The range of historic types covered goes from miniatures to large scale working models. The latter are always eye-catching but for perfection in miniature Philip Baggaley's 1/1250 scale waterline model of Second World War warships are amazing examples of the miniaturist's art. At the opposite end of the scale is William Mowll's large 1/48 scale, working model of HMS *Warrior* (1860). In his chapter on building large scale working models he describes the techniques of constructing hulls in glass fibre, and discusses many other aspects of making and detailing the many parts and fittings for such ships, and the selection and installation of power plants.

Still on the subject of large models, Brian King's aircraft carrier HMS *Glorious* is a superb example of a rarely chosen subject for a model. Admiralty 'as fitted' drawings are essential when considering such a model. In his notes on the building of this model he includes some helpful advice on dealing with the somewhat complex hull shapes often encountered on capital ships. Apart from the many fittings and structures in the ship, builders of aircraft carriers also have to be ready to construct a variety of aircraft, as photographs of this model show. Brian King has long been an advocate for the use of photo-etched parts on a model, and this is covered, as is his use of clear perspex for many fittings.

Wood and metal have long been the principal materials for ship modellers, so Peter Beisheim's methods of building a model of HMS *Hood* in plasticard are of particular interest as this material is now becoming widely used.

In 'Miniature Warships of the Second World War' Philip Baggaley describes the way he builds well-detailed 1:1250 scale waterline models, and offers advice on tools, materials, cases and forming seas. The accompanying photographs reveal the amount of fine detail which is included.

Another interesting chapter is that by Eric Dyke, in which he shows how the use of laminated balsa wood can be used to construct hull and superstructure for waterline models of good size, taking as an example his model of HMS *Ocean* of 1900.

Smaller warships have always been popular with modelmakers, particularly those widely referred to as MTBs. With, in most cases, a hull of hard chine design, and with few fittings, they make excellent working models. David Jack has long been an expert in this field, and here he has chosen to describe the construction of the Sub-chaser *SC1055* at 1in24 scale. The power plant and radio control gear are all-important, and the selection of suitable equipment and its installation, are well covered.

The inclusion of plastic kits of warships may seem slightly unusual, but great strides have been made in this form of model. Production methods may impose limitations, but Loren Perry explains how basic kits can be modified, and further improved even more by the addition of photo-etched and specially made commercial fittings.

Submarines, for long an almost disregarded as a subject for a model, have made a remarkable breakthrough in recent years, with great strides being made in the techniques of building fully working and submersing models. David Merriman III provides a good and useful insight into the construction and operation of such craft, using his model of the USS *Skipjack* as the role model.

Finally, there is the static display model, in this case a large-scale static model of the aircraft carrier USS *Enterprise*, 1975. This excellent 12ft long model is somewhat reminiscent of the large models once to be seen in the windows of shipping company offices, and now in museums. Stephen Henninger presents a fascinating account of what is involved in the construction of such a very large undertaking.

This is an interesting book in that it provides the reader with an overview of the different approaches to, methods of, and wide range of materials used, in building warship models. Peter Beisheim was faced with a very difficult task in electing not only the methods of construction to be described, but the type of warship to be portrayed. At least two more chapters would have provided scope for the inclusion of examples of the smaller types of warship popular with modelmakers.

The book is well illustrated with many photographs and diagrams, including a colour section of 25 images, which illustrate the amount and quality of detail on the models.

John Bowen

George Franklin
Britain's Anti-Submarine Capability 1919-1939
Frank Cass, 2003
224 pages, 24 illustrations
HB Price £39.50
ISBN 0 71465 318 7

It has been generally believed that the Royal Navy neglected the protection of merchant shipping between the two world wars and, in particular, 'not one exercise in the protection of a slow mercantile convoy against submarine or air attack took place between 1919 and 1939' (Roskill). The author of this new work seeks to change this view and, by and large, succeeds. He is unusually well qualified as a seaman officer with an engineering degree and an MPhil in modern history.

The main body of the book is arranged topic by topic, starting with Strategy. The reader is reminded that until about 1936 the principal maritime threat came from Japan. Even when Germany re-started a submarine building programme the first class of boats was small and were thought only suitable for operations in the Baltic. In particular, with France as an ally the English Channel could be blocked and U-boats would have to transit round to the north of Scotland, much reducing their time on station. The following chapter, Organisation, is in many ways the most fascinating. The key Directorates of the Naval Staff were traditionally in the hands of the gunnery branch (Plans) and the torpedo branch (Tactics) and they were stepping stones to the higher posts. The new Anti-Submarine Branch had to fight hard for its corner and may have over stated the success of ASDIC led operations. Success in ASW was welcome to the gunnery officers who felt free to concentrate on the battleship duel.

The chapter on Sensors, with a clear annex on ASDIC, follows Hackman's classic book. The weapon was predominantly the depth charge of the First World War. The 'dead time' between loss of ASDIC contact and dropping the charge from the stern was recognised. Trials had been carried out with ahead throwing weapons but without success since the ASDIC of the day could not locate the target with sufficient accuracy for a lethal charge. The technology of the day was not up to it, a recurring theme. The RAF's irrational love of the flying boat and the failure to develop an air dropped depth charge were more serious.

The Admiralty thought that older destroyers, sloops and, in coastal waters, trawlers would suffice in the opening phases of a war on trade. By and large, the progress of the war prior to the fall of France justified their view. Protection of coastal convoys was seen as important and an 'Admiralty design' trawler was produced. Two prototypes were built and formed the basis for a large building programme. Prototype conversions of commercial style trawlers were also carried out. ASDIC sets were stock piled. The requirement for a speed of 20 knots together with a heavy AA armament for ocean escorts proved incompatible with the desire for low cost. The 'Flower' class corvettes were originally procured as superior trawlers for coastal work.

The author lists a number of convoy escort exercises; roughly one per year and infers that there were considerably more. Previous writers claiming that there were no such exercises were clearly wrong, possibly confused by the use of battleships and carriers to simulate slow merchant ships. (It is not cheap to hire merchant ships for an exercise). Exercises were carried out involving submarines attacking on the surface at night. (In fact, peace time exercise rules forbade submarines to operate submerged at night). The difficulty of seeing a surfaced submarine at night, possibly in low buoyancy trim, was fully appreciated but there was no solution until radar was developed. There is brief mention of anti-submarine patrols during the Spanish civil war but I suggest that more could have been made of the effect of density layers.

Most pre-war doctrine proved valid in the opening months of the war. Up to May 1940 only 14 merchant ships were sunk in convoy and several U-boats were sunk. But, there was a degree of over confidence in ASDIC leading to the idea of hunting groups and even exposing the few fleet carriers in anti-submarine pursuit. *Courageous* was sunk and *Ark Roycl* near missed in such operations. The sea is large and hunting groups had little value until Ultra told them where to look.

The author rightly concludes with a tribute to the Tactical Division of the Staff and to the men at Portland. This is a very important book both in the lead up to the Battle of the Atlantic and in the more general case of incorporating new tactics and equipment into an existing staff organisation.

Eur Ing David K Brown, RCNC

Hans Mehl

Naval Guns: 500 Years of Ship and Coastal Artillery

Chatham Publishing, 2002

215 pages, 400 photos

HB Price £40.00

ISBN 1 86176 201 1

This is a picture book; the author tells us so '...by providing a wealth of pictorial material'. On each page (with a few exceptions) there are two photographs of guns preserved in museums or on board the original ship. Each photo is accompanied by a short text passage. There are also two colour sections of 34 illustrations and a few line drawings. The earliest picture is of a fourteenth century Danish gun and there are numerous examples from the great days of the eighteenth and nineteenth centuries. There are plenty of more modern guns including coastal defence artillery. The photographs are of high quality and clearly reproduced. They come from a very wide range of countries and sites and, among the smaller navies, there are 'export' versions of guns from major naval powers. Inevitably, the brief texts leave much unsaid and sadly some half truths have crept in. The author recommends his readers to buy books by Campbell, Padfield and others if they wish to find out more about technical data, a rather expensive operation. If you only require a series of good photos of guns, this book is recommended.

Eur Ing David K Brown, RCNC

A D Baker III (ed.)

The Naval Institute Guide to Combat Fleets of the World 2002-2003: Their Ships, Aircraft and Systems

Naval Institute Press, 2003

1,030 pages

HB Price £155.00

ISBN 1 55750 242 0

The combat capabilities of warships in days of old could be determined by looking up their displacement, speed, the size and number of their guns and the thickness of their armour in *Jane's Fighting Ships*, Weyer's *Flottentaschenbuch* or *Flottes de Combat*. But as seaborne systems get ever more complex warships fit less clearly into reference book format. Arthur Baker, retiring Editor of the US Naval Institute Press *Combat Fleets* found that increasingly sophisticated command and control outfits, surveillance systems, communications capacity, sensors, data transfer systems and high tech weaponry now packed into warships are too complex for their capabilities to be reduced to tabular form. His readers have depended on the Editor's 'remarks' under each warship class to find a path through the electronic maze. The past few decades have seen new ships of vastly greater capabilities than the vessels they replaced but built in fewer numbers. The high cost of major naval systems, however, often require existing programmes to be stretched or delayed. The calibre of naval personnel and the demands made on them has increased but Baker believes that the centralising of command functions ashore, made possible by improved communications and data handling, has diminished traditional command responsibility and decision making at sea. The quality of military leadership is declining, he believes, and he questions the need for expensive command facilities afloat if operational decisions are made ashore. In 1129 pages *Combat Fleets* covers almost 200 navies. The 50 pages on Great Britain give a positive picture of the Royal Navy; the projected two new fleet carriers, the new *Astute* class SSNs (*Astute*, *Ambush* and *Artful* have been named), the new Type 45 air defence destroyers (the first – and perhaps only – six will be *Daring*, *Dauntless*, *Diamond*, *Dragon*, *Defender* and *Duncan*) displacing 7,350 tons with a complement of 190, the 16th Duke-class frigate, HMS *St. Albans*, recently commissioned, HMS *Ocean* already doing the business and to be followed by the assault landing ships HMS *Albion* and HMS *Bulwark* and by the four Bay class dock landing ships. *Combat Fleets* began life as an English-language version of the famous French *Flottes de Combat*. It is curious that the United States did not produce their own home-grown warship reference work and chose to translate *Flottes de Combat* rather than adapt *Jane's Fighting Ships*. However, *Combat Fleets* is well under half the price of *Jane's* whose £380 price sadly limits its availability.

Lawrence Phillips

George Moore
Building for Victory
World Ship Society, 2003
196 pages, 52 photographs, 21 drawings,
Price £27.00 + £5.00 p&p UK (£18.00 to Society Members)
ISBN 0 95433 101 X

Can be obtained direct from the Society at The Gables, School Lane, Elton, Peterborough, PE8 6RS (Cheques to World Ship Society)

Students of the naval aspects of the Second World War have always found difficulty in reconciling the planned UK building programme with what actually emerged. This carefully researched book by a regular *Warship* contributor provides a mass of tabulated data together with a text which clarifies the conflicting influences which governed the programmes. Foremost of these conflicts was the Admiralty's efforts to ensure that there was a balanced fleet when the war ended opposed by the Treasury view (largely supported by the Prime Minister) that only ships which could complete during the war should be ordered.

There were internal conflicts too. The First Sea Lord for much of the war, Dudley Pound, was a strong advocate of the battleship, opposed by many, including the DNC Stanley Goodall, who realised its day had passed. There was great debate on the need for carriers and over their configuration. Once a design was approved further problems appeared. There were genuine shortages of material and labour, as many young men had been called up leaving labour and management in the hands of older men. The increased complexity of warships altered the balance within shipyards; lack of electrical fitters was a particular problem. These real problems were exacerbated by union intransigence and lack luster management. Bombing and the blackout compounded the difficulties.

Despite all these problems, the author brings out the magnitude of the triumph of the shipbuilding and supporting industries. Despite heavy losses, the navy of 1945 was far bigger and individually more capable than that of 1939.

The Appendices are a vital, and fascinating, part of the book. Appendix 1, which runs to 26 pages, lists all the major warships ordered from 1936 onwards with important dates. The Admiralty Job numbers and the builders' number are given which are essential to the understanding of contemporary documents. Appendix 2 sets out the programme and expenditure approved each year by the Cabinet. Appendix 3 defines shipyard capability in terms of number and size of building slips. Appendix 4 lists the estimated completion dates and the slip from time to time. Appendices 5 and 6 summarie the merchant shipbuilding effort which, inevitably, clashed with naval work. Appendix 7 provides a graphical presentation of the way in which effort was allocated while 9 compares naval output with that of tanks and aircraft.

The author's text and figures are supported by an exceptionally long bibliography and list of sources, including some four pages of Public Record Office (now The National Archive) documents alone.

Many of the 52 photographs are of ships under construction and have not been reproduced before. A particularly poignant photo from 1948 shows three aircraft carriers completing at Harland and Wolff; we are never likely to see three carriers completing together, nor a ship of any sort from Harland and Wolff. The 21 line drawings of designs which were never built are of great interest.

This is a splendid book which I have no hesitation in recommending though I must confess to bias having commented on the author's drafts!

Eur Ing David K Brown RCNC

D R Messimer
Verschollen: World War I U-Boat Losses
Chatham Publishing, 2003
351 pages, 14 photographs, HB Price £25.00
ISBN 1 86176 213 5

During the First World War the German Navy commissioned 435 submarines, of which 203 were lost from all causes. Post war analysis explained 113 as lost due to enemy action, 33 to 'non-enemy action' leaving 57 as 'verschollen' or lost without trace. The author points out that the evidence is weak in at least 32 other sinkings.

The 14 page Introduction provides an excellent short summary of the operational aspects of the U-boat war and also outlines technical developments on both sides. The bulk of the book gives individual accounts of all 203 losses: 67 main stream U boats, 74 small UB boats and 62 small minelayers, the UC. Because most sinkings were on the surface or in shallow water there were often survivors whose exciting narratives give life to the book. By the end of 1917 sinkings of U boats were frequent but there was no sign of any general loss of morale though

I have argued (*Warship* 2003) that there was a loss of competence, particularly amongst commanding officers.

The value of a book like this depends on its accuracy; impossible to verify fully without re-doing the author's extensive research. (He was a lecturer in military history in the USA). However, a few spot checks supported the author in every case. He disagrees with official sources in a few cases and his reasons for so doing seem valid. The author refers to poor workmanship and inferior materials as the cause of many problems, perhaps accounting for some of the unknown losses.

It would have been useful to include some analysis of cause of loss, locality and so on but this is available elsewhere. Anyone researching into the history of submarine warfare during the First World War will find this book invaluable.

Eur Ing David K Brown, RCNC

Gordon Williamson
U-boat Bases and Bunkers, 1941-45
Osprey Publishing, 2003
64 pages, illustrated
PB Price £10.99
ISBN 1 84176 556 2

Gordon L Rottman
Japanese Pacific Island Defenses, 1941-45
Osprey Publishing, 2003
64 pages, illustrated
PB Price £10.99
ISBN 1 84176 428 0

These slim, medium format paperbacks form part of the first batch of 'Fortress', a new series from well known military publisher Osprey. While it will doubtless be of considerable interest to military history enthusiasts and fortress buffs, at first glance the books would seem to be of only passing appeal to naval historians. However, it must be borne in mind that many of the world's major fortresses were built to guard against attack from the sea, that ships and fortifications have frequently engaged one another, and that when they haven't been doing so a vociferous 'ships versus forts' debate has raged on. Add to that the fact that one of the first titles is concerned with the Nazis' massive U-boat bunkers, and the relevance to *Warship* readers becomes clear.

Gordon Williamson's book covers the design and construction, defensive principals, careers and eventual fates of all the U-boat bunkers. Touching on the human side of the story, mention is made of such things as the appaling conditions of the forced labour used to construct the bunkers, and the less than perfect behaviour (though understandable in the circumstances) of the U-boat crews when in port. There is a description of the Brest bunker, on the basis that this was a fairly typical example; and very useful sections on the status of the bunkers today, including directions to all those in France (helpfully noting that in a number of cases the bunkers are still in use by the *Marine Nationale* with consequent security restrictions on access and photography), and on further reading and research. This latter is effectively an acknowledgement that the book is basically just an introduction to a considerable and fascinating subject.

The author concludes that the bunkers were 'a defensive triumph', for while some U-boats were damaged by masonry dislodged by bombing, none were destroyed while in the bunkers. Their defeat was at sea, not in port. The photographs are interesting, making it all the more of a pity that many of them are poorly reproduced. Some of the present day shots are particularly bad.

Simultaneously with the construction of the bunkers Germany's ally Japan was building a very different set of fortifications to defend her vast and rapidly acquired empire in the Far East. Due to the terrain, the distances involved, and Japan's relative poverty of resources and technology, the defenses built across the Pacific were predominantly field works, simple structures making maximum use of local terrain and materials. These are the subject of Gordon Rottman's book. Given the nature of the defences that were built, the ferocious fighting that took place during their capture, and the effects of half a century of a particularly unforgiving climate, it is not surprising that comparatively few survive in any sort of condition. One point that is emphasised is the relative ineffectiveness of preliminary bombardment against these targets. For all the sound and fury, the only sure way of eliminating these positions was by slow and bloody hand to hand combat.

Rottman correctly points out that the very lack of standardisation in what the Japanese built makes it hard to give comprehensive descriptions. There seems to be a lot of 'or's, 'alternatively's and so on, tending to cover most options. A more obvious weak point is that no indication is given as to the source of the rather mixed bag of illustrations, though presumably they came from a US Army manual.

The less said about the colour artworks in both books the better. They have the kind of slick, lifeless, quasi-realistic air about them that is so common with computer generated art and which, while it would look fine on a computer game, really adds nothing here. While they may serve to attract younger readers, they achieve little else apart from taking up space that could have been better used in other ways, and increasing production costs. The one on p.6 of the U-boat book is a notable shocker.

While neither book can be described as essential, further volumes in the series will be worth keeping an eye out for, especially since forthcoming subjects include the defences of Corregidor and Manila, Oahu and Pearl Harbour, and American Civil War era coastal defences.

Stephen Dent

Marc Milner
Battle of the Atlantic
Tempus, 2003
256 pages, 78 illustrations, 26 maps
HB Price £25.00
ISBN 0 75242 853 5

The Battle of the Atlantic was the longest single campaign of the Second World War, commencing only a few hours into the conflict with *U-30*'s sinking of the passenger liner *Athenia* in the evening of 3 September 1939. The next 12 months were christened the 'Happy time' by U-boat crews as pickings at sea were plentiful and right up until the spring of 1941, the Germans could feasibly have won the campaign. That they did not was due to a combination of factors, 'Ultra', airpower, logistical infrastructure and superior resources, including trained manpower. To these Milner has picked out three which he believes were vital: the allies implementation of widespread use of radar, hard fighting at sea and the contribution of the Royal Canadian Navy. As Milner is Professor of History at the University of New Brunswick, the appearance of the RCN is not surprising, and it is a refreshing change that his interpretation of the conflict comes from a mid-Atlantic stance, rather than an Anglo-centric viewpoint.

But however commendable this may be the work is let down on several points. Basically, for a book heralded on the jacket flap as 'based on mastery of the latest research' the result is somewhat disappointing. What we have in fact is another narrative of events with a little analysis thrown in here and there. There is no examination of the key characters and many of the passages are lifeless. Key events, such as the two pages detailing the sinking of the *Bismarck*, are covered at an alarming rate, with little wider appreciation of grand strategy. Milner is on safer ground when explaining the tactical details of the convoy battles, which he does with clarity, and the technical and technological side of the story, accompanied by excellent maps and diagrams.

Yet all this is let down by the fact there are no references in the text, and the bibliography is dreadfully sparse, listing just eighteen sources, of which only one is a primary published source. The fact the work is part of a series entitled 'Battles & Campaigns' and is clearly aimed at readers new or relatively new to the period, would have led one to expect at the very least a guide to further reading, or more preferably a substantial review of the literature, showing exactly where this work fits in with the wider scholarship. The excellent illustrations and maps might help to justify a price of £25, but the concept does not. This is not to criticise an author too much on this point, as there is a clear series style to be adhered to. This book will be of limited appeal to those who actually work in and produce new research in the period, unless they have a deep interest in the activities of the RCN. For those with a passing interest or new to the subject, there are plenty of less expensive alternatives on offer.

Martin Robson

Robert M Grant
U-Boats Destroyed: The Effect of Anti-Submarine Warfare 1914-18
Periscope Publishing, Reprinted 2002
172 pages, 61 photos, 7 maps
Price £14.99
ISBN 1 90438 100 6

U-Boat Intelligence: Admiralty Intelligence Division and the Defeat of the U-boats 1914-1918
Periscope Publishing, Reprinted 2002
195 pages, 12 photos, 11 maps and diagrams
Price £14.99
ISBN 1 90438 101 4

U-Boat Hunters: Code Breakers, Divers and the Defeat of the U-Boats, 1914-1918
Periscope Publishing, 2003
178 pages, 20 photos, 3 diagrams
Price £14.99
ISBN 1 90438 115 4

Written by a Professor at the Divinity School of the University of Chicago, this trilogy represents the results of a lifelong study into the means by which German submarines were destroyed during the First World War. The first two books were initially published in the 1960s but have been long out of print, whilst the concluding volume has recently been made available to the public for the first time. Considering the amount of time taken in its creation, it is not surprising that the series draws on a huge range of authorities. Official records from German, British, French and American sources have been supplemented by a wide variety of published accounts, whilst the concluding book even makes use of reports of present day divers posted to the internet. As such, the books probably represent the most comprehensive survey of this subject that has yet been produced.

The opening volume adopts a broadly chronological approach to its principal purpose of analysing German submarine losses. In the early years, a large proportion of destruction was the result of traditional methods such as gunfire and ramming, with the use of ruses such as decoy or Q-ships also having a marked impact until their secret was discovered and the use of convoys made them of less relevance. Later on, the impact of new technology made itself much more apparent, with the depth charge in particular assuming importance as 'the weapon with the greatest future'. However, as Grant explains, the most destructive anti-submarine weapon of the First World War was undoubtedly the mine. Used offensively to hinder access to the U-Boat bases and close transit routes such as the Straits of Dover, much of their success was due to the poor geographical position of the ports then available to Germany.

The author's second book, *U-Boat Intelligence*, has a different emphasis, looking more at the use and practical effect of intelligence operations in prosecuting the U-Boat War. Although strenuous efforts were made to obscure the extent to which the British Admiralty were able to read German naval codes in the immediate aftermath of the Great War, Grant makes it apparent that interception and decoding of signals had an increasingly marked impact on the anti-submarine campaign as the conflict progressed. Interception was particularly effective in directing the offensive minelaying campaign that aimed to destroy U-Boats on passage to and from operations and which was largely responsible for the progressive decline in the usefulness of the submarine flotillas based in Flanders. However, deception was only one of a range of methods used to gain information, with radio direction finding, the inspection of wrecks by divers and sophisticated interrogation methods all having their place. It is interesting to note how even trivial personal details gleaned from questioning were used to give an impression of omnipotence when interviewing future prisoners, thereby gaining more valuable revelations.

The trilogy's final instalment brings the story up to date by incorporating information that has become available to Mr Grant during the three decades since the first two books were written. As such, it is a much less discrete volume than the other works, with much of the emphasis being on elaborating the circumstances behind U-Boat losses that have already been described in the previous books, as well as the efforts that went into salvaging information from them. There are also some particularly interesting chapters on the large cruiser submarines, whose long-range and lengthy operations were especially vulnerable to radio interception. These voyages extended as far as the North American coast but yielded little in the way of tangible results in return for the effort expended.

As a general observation, it should be noted that the author is quite focused in his area of study, concentrating on the destruction of submarines to the general exclusion of wider considerations regarding the conduct of the anti-submarine war. For example, whilst passing reference is made to the successful use of intelligence to divert shipping from areas of danger, this key defensive tactic falls largely outside the series' scope. Perhaps a more significant detraction relates to the limitations resulting from the books' preparation and publication over an extended period, which inevitably results in a degree of duplication. In some instances Grant's original findings have been modified by his subsequent research: it seems unlikely, for instance, that his initial conclusion that 'not very many U-boats seem to have been sunk simply in consequence of intelligence discoveries' has remained unchanged by the additional information he unearthed concerning on this area.

Notwithstanding these comments, Grant's trilogy is required reading for anybody interested in First World War submarine operations and Periscope Publishing deserve a hearty commendation for making it available to the public. From a broader perspective, perhaps its greatest interest is the clear evidence it provides that effective intelligence, particularly the breaking of enemy codes, was equally as decisive in the conduct of anti-submarine warfare in the Great War as the successful conquest of the Enigma machine was to prove in the Battle of the Atlantic some twenty years later. There is surely still something to be learned from this in the current age of network centric warfare, in which timely transmission and management of information is considered to be of paramount importance.

Conrad Waters

David Westwood
Anatomy of the Ship: The Type VII U-Boat
Conway Maritime Press, 2003 (Revised Edition)
95 pages, 25 photos, 100 line drawings
HB Price £25.00
ISBN 0 85177 933 6

First published in 1984 in Conway's 'Anatomy of the Ship' series this new edition conforms to the series style with a brief text (4 pages) followed by tabular details, a photographic section and then a very large number of line diagrams of the ship and its equipment.

The Type VII U-boat was a major player in the Battle of the Atlantic with 704 boats built, mainly of the VIIc variant. It was designed by Schürer in 1928 based on the Spanish E1 from the illegal German front organisation IvS in the Hague. It is surprising how little submarine technology improved between the wars as the design was derived from the First World War's UBIII design, though somewhat bigger.

The original Type VII had an operational diving depth of 100m based on a factor of safety of two on the estimated collapse depth. The Type VIIc/41 with a stronger steel could dive somewhat deeper (20 per cent). There are many wild stories of extreme diving by U-boats and it would have been welcome if the author had explored this topic more thoroughly and included at least one structural section. (It is believed that Germany developed a more accurate calculation for frame strength enabling them to be lighter with the saving put into thicker plating.)

The photos are very well selected, both of exterior and interiors. The drawings are well done both of the boats and equipment such as torpedoes. The dramatic increase in AA armament is well illustrated. Grohner's book on German Warships draws attention to the individual variations between boats, mainly in flooding holes in the casing and something on those lines would have been welcome. A large scale profile and deck plan is reproduced on the reverse of the dust jacket. This book is a worthy record of an important class of ship and will be welcome, particularly to model makers.

Eur Ing David K Brown, RCNC

Norman Friedman
U.S. Amphibious Ships and Craft: All Illustrated Design History
Naval Institute Press, distributed in Europe by Greenhill Books
2002, 659 pages
HB Price £57.00
ISBN 1 55750 250 1

The American Pacific campaign of the Second World War, mounted on such a colossal scale, gave the US Navy and US Marine Corps almost unmatched experience and authority in amphibious warfare through the second half of the twentieth century. This latest of Norman Friedman's highly regarded US warship design histories for the Naval Institute Press covers in detail the development of amphibious ships in the US Navy from the 1920s, through the extraordinary expansion of AW forces in the Japanese war, its evolution during the Cold War to the huge AW capability in the US Navy today which includes eight new *Wasp* class helicopter carriers and twelve *San Antonio* class dock landing ships building or on order; all much larger than Britain's HMS *Ocean*, *Bulwark* and *Albion*. However, only three important opposed amphibious landings have been mounted by the western nations since World War Two: one by the US forces at Inchon in Korea in 1950, and two by the British, at Suez in 1956 and in the Falkland Islands in 1982. Others planned to take the North Korean port of Wonsan in 1951 and the intended amphibious landing in Kuwait in 1991, 'both came a cropper due to mines'.

Despite fifty years of 'nonuse' the US Navy's AW capability has been effectively deployed in regional, ethnic and religious confrontations ('chaos in the littoral') that have multiplied in the world disorder following the Soviet collapse. However, the military need for such massive full war AW capability is being questioned in the US. 'It is difficult to imagine where the United States might want to conduct a major opposed amphibious assault within the next twenty years or so', writes former Director of Central Intelligence, Admiral Stansfield Turner, in the latest issue of the *US Naval War College Review*. He suggest that China might be a possibility 'but one had to wonder if the United States would ever risk placing a major force ashore in a country so vast as China and one with over a billion people, some three million of whom are under arms'. He believes that future funding for major AW construction will be closely scrutinised and suggests that 'the capability to put troops ashore in remote areas reasonably quickly, either by helicopter assault or assault across a beach, in modest numbers and against modest opposition' will be more attractive future budgetary option.

This work of commanding authority and depth, by a world-class strategist, is an essential reference for all involved in amphibious and expeditionary warfare.

Lawrence Phillips

Ian Hawkins (ed.)
Destroyer
Conway Maritime Press, 2003
416 pages, 46 photographs
HB Price £19.99
ISBN 0 85177 947 6

Compiled by the son of Lieutenant Commander F W Hawkins, who lost his life when the destroyer HMS *Boadicea* was sunk by a German HS 293 missile whilst supporting the Normandy landings, this book is an anthology of accounts of the war at sea during 1939-1945. Using a chronological approach and adopting a largely British perspective, the anthologist has assembled a unique collection of material in the hope of providing a vivid image of what the war at sea was really like for the small ship sailor.

Whilst predominantly a compendium of first hand accounts, Mr Hawkins has adopted quite a broad approach in his choice of sources. As such, newspaper cuttings, extracts from published histories of the naval war and even the odd fictional narrative supplement the diary entries, personal reminiscences and official reports that comprise the vast bulk of the book's constituent parts. Some liberty has also been taken in ensuring a strict match between these sources and the title *Destroyer*, as accounts of service in other small vessels such as sloops and submarines also feature. These observations should not be taken as a criticism, however, as the overall balance of the final compilation works very well in engaging the reader's attention. For example, the precise, impersonal tone of the more official reports provides a strong and interesting contrast with the more vivid prose of the powerful personal recollections.

In view of the editor's strong association with *Boadicea*, it is not surprising that much material relates to 'B' class destroyers. The book therefore provides particularly strong coverage of that class of ship. Although every reader will have his particular favourite, the various accounts of HMS *Beagle*'s heroic rescue of the crews of destroyed US landing craft from the middle of a minefield whilst under the command of Lieutenant Commander N R Murch make for particularly memorable reading. The wide range of the sources used in compiling the book inevitably means that a word of caution is appropriate regarding the accuracy of some firsthand material. Equally, however, it also succeeds in throwing a fresh light on some famous actions.

All in all, therefore, *Destroyer* is a thoroughly researched and well produced book that achieves its dramatic aim of recording for posterity the real life experiences of a generation of wartime sailors.

Conrad Waters

Roger Chesneau
Hood: The Life and Death of a Battlecruiser
Cassell, 2002, 192 pages
HB Price £25.00
ISBN 0 30435 980 7

The nineteenth and last battle cruiser built for the Royal Navy, HMS *Hood*, lies at the bottom of the Denmark Strait with 1,418 of her men. The loss in action with the German battleship *Bismarck* and cruiser *Prinz Eugen* in 1941 of the biggest and the most famous and ships in the British Fleet was a catastrophe that shook the nation. The recent discovery and filming of the wreck of HMS *Hood* has stimulated many books of varying quality, all exploring reasons for her spectacular loss. This one, by an established naval technical historian, is well ahead of the field. Britain's battle cruisers, all laid down between 1906 and 1916, had an unhappy history. Conceived by Fisher as super-fast armoured cruisers, they developed into a hybrid without a clear role. Their battleship armament was carried at far greater speed but at the cost of protection. Predicted gunnery ranges of 10,000 yards, with low shell trajectories, required vertical armour on warships' sides. Early engagements in the Great War showed that gunnery exchanges at 20,000 yards were feasible and that plunging fire onto warships' decks rather than their sides necessitated heavier horizontal armour. The open question is whether *Hood* was lost because her armour was penetrated, her torpedoes exploded or because there were residual defects in the ammunition handling chain to the main turrets. Chesneau traces the concept of the battle cruiser, the design of the *Hood*, suspension of her building at John Brown's while the lessons learned from the magazine explosions in three British battle cruisers at Jutland were examined and which resulted in additional armour being worked into the ship, her interwar employment and her final action. A major rebuild, delayed while older capital ships like HMS *Warspite* and the other *Queen Elizabeths* were modernised, was scheduled to begin in 1938. War came before this could be done and an old First World War battle cruiser was sent into action with a modern armoured battleship. A first class book on a tragic tale that began on 31 May 1916 and ended, almost 25 years to the day later, on 24 May 1941.

Lawrence Phillips

The Royal Navy Handbook: The Definitive MoD Guide

Conway Maritime Press, 2003
208 pages, fully illustrated in colour
HB Price £14.99
ISBN 0 85177 952 2

Billed as a new departure for the MoD, a new way of providing information in greater detail than before,

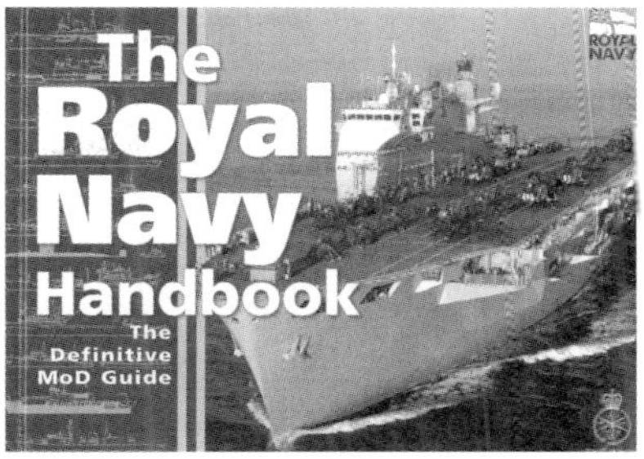

this little book is packed with information on all things Navy. Indeed, the book contains details not only of the Royal Navy's order of battle, but also of those forces now to be found at sea on a regular basis. This has allowed the inclusion of such weapons systems as the Apache AH 1 and the Nimrod MR 2. It also contains authoritative information on a lot of new projects intended to maintain and improve Britain's maritime capabilities over the next several years. Amongst the most detailed are projects such as the Navy's *Astute* class submarines, T45 destroyers and the Future Surface Combatant, and the RAF's Nimrod MRA 4.

The authority of the book is underlined by the inclusion of a foreword by the Secretary of State for Defence and an introduction by the First Sea Lord, both setting out their shared vision for the future of the service.

As far as can be told, the equipment details are accurate and the illustrations are well chosen, although the inclusion of many new projects meant a total reliance on computer generated images in these sections. Addresses of relevant web sites have also been included, leading this reviewer to discover yet more excellent photographs, in this case of HMS *Leeds Castle* off South Georgia.

And it is on this subject that I have one of my only two slight quibbles with the information. The 'Castle' class was not a private venture, as stated on p.54, but the result of some very detailed studies carried out under the leadership of D K Brown, both at Bath and at Haslar. It was only their construction that was started as a leap of faith by Hall Russell, prior to orders being placed.

The second quibble relates to the caption of the photograph of HMNB Portsmouth, on p.193, which refers to the 'recently restored' HMS *Warrior*. I suspect this caption has been left unchanged for some time, as the *Warrior* has been in Portsmouth for several years now.

These minor quibbles aside, this book represents good value for money, not only for the information it contains, but for the insight it gives on the MoD's future plans for the Navy.

W B Davies RCNC

Fritz Kohl and Eberhard Rossler

Anatomy of the Ship: The Type XXI U-Boat

Conway Maritime Press, 2002
Revised edition, 128 pages
HB Price £25.00
ISBN 0 85177 922 0

The German Type VIIC U-Boat that bore the brunt of the Battle of the Atlantic had severe operational limitations in low underwater speed and short submerged endurance. Most of its time was on the surface where it was more vulnerable to detection and attack. Allied technical advances, particularly centimetric radar, and improved convoy escort group ensured that maritime air cooperation was winning the battle by mid-1943. The Germans, however, made a quantum leap in submarine design that year with their projected Type XXI U-Boat. With electric motor main power (from huge batteries), long underwater endurance at high speed and schnorkel gear to allow the diesels to recharge the batteries at periscope depth it promised far wider cruising range and greater tactical mobility. Shortages of labour and materials delayed the programme and the first operational Type XXI did not deploy until March 1945. It had been a close call. Had the Type XXI been deployed in numbers against north Atlantic convoys just a year earlier the history of the twentieth century could have turned out very differently. Many Type XXI boats fell into Allied hands and were exploited in early Cold War submarine design. The Soviet 'Whisky' class boats were essentially German Type XXIs with 16 knots submerged speed and range and endurance for blue water operations and, later, schnorkel capability. The technological response was better airborne radar, improved active sonar for surface escorts, passive sensors like SOSUS and more effective anti-submarine weapons and the development of SSK, the Patrol submarine, as an anti-submarine weapon. This revised title in Conway's 'Anatomy of the Ship' series comprises 43 pages of superb photographs, 65 pages of detailed technical drawings and a large scale fold out plan on the reverse of the jacket.

Lawrence Phillips

JJ Colledge; new edition revised and updated by Lt Cdr Ben Warlow RN
Ships of the Royal Navy: The Complete Record of all Fighting Ships of the Royal Navy from the Fifteenth Century to the Present
Greenhill Books, 2003
367 pages
HB Price £25.00
ISBN 1 85367 566 0

The publisher's 'blurb' describes this book as 'comprehensive', 'astonishing' and 'authoritative', and rightly so. This is a welcome re-appearance of Colledge's original, two volume labour of love, revised into a single volume in 1987 and now, fully updated and revised by Ben Warlow, who will probably already be known to many readers for his many other works on the Royal Navy's warships. In fact Lt Cdr Warlow writes in his Preface that, used alongside his own book on the Royal Navy's shore establishments, it should now be a straightforward matter to find out the details of any particular ship of the Royal Navy, of any era since the fifteenth century.

A major question to be asked of any reference work published now, is with alternative sources of information freely available through the Internet is such a book necessary? With regard to Colledge the answer is definitely yes, and I can certainly see a place for this work on many people's bookshelves complementing, rather than being replaced by, information from the web.

The book itself is arranged alphabetically, as a dictionary. Each page is laid out in a two-column format, with the ships name or number printed in bold type, and therefore easy to find, followed by some brief details. To take a typical example, my late father's ship, I can find, on page 193, the following entry;

> ***Liverpool.*** Cruiser. 9,400 tons, 591.5 (oa) x 62.3ft, 12-6in, 8-4in. Fairfield 24.3.1937. Arr. 2.7.1958 McLellan,Bo'ness, for BU

From this I know exactly what the ship displaced, her dimensions, armament, builder, where and when she was laid down and when and where she was broken up. I can also see that she was one of eight ships to bear the name *Liverpool*, starting with a 5th Rate in 1741 up to the Type 42 still in service with the Royal Navy today. Each vessel named, (and there are 60 classes of ships represented, up to, and including warships of the modern Royal Navy), is given the same treatment, only trawlers, tugs and auxiliaries being excluded.

On first looking at this book I did wonder whether or not it should have been illustrated. But it struck me that it would be impossible to choose which ships to include and which to leave out, without making the book unwieldy and incredibly expensive. There are, after all, other books on the market if you want photographs and plans.

It is also, most definitely, a book for the naval enthusiast, naval historian, naval modeller or naval wargamer. And, as the late David Brown, former Head of the Naval Historical Branch said in his Preface to the 1987 edition, this book should be at the elbow of the Ships' Names Committee 'as an invaluable source'. I wonder if they had a copy to hand when they were choosing the names for the Royal Navy's proposed, new aircraft carriers?

I heartily recommend buying this book and I feel certain that there are many readers who will do just that.

Andy Field

Geoffrey Till
Seapower: A Guide for the Twenty-First Century
Frank Cass, 2003, 430 pages
HB Price £55.00
ISBN 0 7146 554 2

Naval power in the coming century will be of huge importance to nations that can deploy it, believes Geoffrey Till, Dean of Academic Studies at the Joint Services Command and Staff College, and he has produced a big book to explain why. This wide-ranging study of maritime power, past, present and future, shows that there is more to it than just grey-painted ships with numbers on their sides. It explores the development of naval theory, covers the constituents of seapower, navies and their technologies, securing and exploiting command of the sea, naval diplomacy, merchant shipping and expeditionary warfare. Corbett never tired of reminding the Navy that the real point of seapower is not so much what happens at sea but how that influences the outcome of events on land; this principle underpins the shift in naval attention over the past few years from power *at* sea to power *from* the sea. In discussing joint operations, the author considers that the distinctions between sea, land and air power are becoming so blurred that that inter-service disputes over who should own what platform are steadily more futile. Although there is room for creative tension between the services, the strategic imperative is to cooperate. Professor Till carries lightly his considerable scholarship. His book is a *tour de force*, a milestone work, and is essential professional reading.

Lawrence Phillips

WARSHIP GALLERY

In this section, we publish photographs of warships which are unusual, remarkable as images, mysterious or otherwise of special interest to readers. The section is not intended for standard ship portraits, but for out-of-the-ordinary pictures which illuminate aspects of warships not evident in the usual views. Recent editions have included photographs relating to specific events such as the US Landings at Casablanca in 1942 and British naval involvement in the Russian Civil War during 1919-20, but this year we are instead featuring images from a variety of sources. We would very much like to hear from readers with any unusual pictures which might appear in future issues.

One of a number of photographs that have recently come to light, this is captioned on the back simply as 'after the war'. We would be interested to hear from readers who can tell us any more about this unusual scene.

A dramatic photograph of the *French aircraft carrier* Charles de Gaulle *in March 1998. She is scheduled to visit Portsmouth in June 2004 as part of celebrations to mark the centenary of the Entente Cordiale.* (P Creteau)

The torpedo gunboat HMS Speedy moored at Portsmouth, visible behind her are visible Baker's covered slip roofs and the chimneys of Greene's Foundry, both parts of the mid-nineteenth century development of the dockyard. The story of this is one of the subjects covered in the forthcoming Conway Maritime Press book Building the Steam Navy. (CPL)

The handsome and long-lived Swedish cruiser Fylgia, *photographed early in her career.* (Daniel G Harris)

The battlecruiser HMAS Australia, the then flagship of the Royal Australian Navy, passing through the Suez Canal in 1919. (RAN)

In sad contrast to the photograph on the facing page, this is Australia, *stripped of many of her fittings and with her second funnel lying on her deck amidships, ready to be towed out to be scuttled off Sydney, on 12 April 1924.* (RAN)

INDEX

Page references in *italics* refer to illustrations.